Toronto Observed

FRONTISPIECE. *The overlapping layers of Toronto's history. The 1845 porticoes of Osgoode Hall are on the left; on the right is the clock tower of the Old City Hall against the backdrop of the Cadillac-Fairview Building at the corner of Queen and James Streets.*

Toronto Observed
Its Architecture, Patrons, and History

William Dendy & William Kilbourn

Photographs by Bruce Litteljohn & William Dendy

Toronto
Oxford University Press
1986

This book was produced with the support of
THE CITY OF TORONTO THROUGH THE TORONTO ARTS COUNCIL
and
THE CANADA STUDIES FOUNDATION

CANADIAN CATALOGUING IN PUBLICATION DATA
Dendy, William, 1948–
Toronto observed
Includes index.
ISBN 0-19-540508-0
1. Historic buildings—Ontario—Toronto.
2. Toronto (Ont.)—Buildings, structures, etc.—
History. 3. Architects and patrons—Ontario—
Toronto—History. 4. Architecture—Ontario—
Toronto—History. I. Kilbourn, William, 1926–
II. Litteljohn, Bruce M., 1935– .III. Title.
FC3097.7.D46 1986   971.3′541   C86-094147-7
F1059.5.T688A22 1986

CONTENTS

PREFACE

*'All the material and intellectual forces of society
converge towards the same point; architecture . . .
[is] humanity's grand writing and principal form of
expression in its diverse states of development!*
—Victor Hugo, Notre Dame de Paris

'We shape our buildings and they shape our lives.'
—Attributed to Winston Churchill

Toronto has grown so quickly and changed so radically in recent years that
it seems scarcely possible there should be anything substantial left of the
familiar wood and brick and stone of its earlier architecture. A distant
glimpse of that space pod and needle towering in the clouds, a swift arrival
on the world's widest expressway, a first glance at the glittering downtown
skyline—readily evoke fantasies of the ephemeral, the ultra new, the post-
modern. This first impression is accurate enough. In their enthusiasm for
progress the rich and powerful of Toronto, the private and public patrons
who have shaped this place over the past two centuries have let go many of
our best buildings and streetscapes. Time and again a lust for the grandest,
the latest, or the most fashionable has led to casual neglect or cavalier
destruction of our urban heritage.

But there is other news as well. Against the oblivion that grinds inexorably down upon all our hopes and monuments, an urban identity stubbornly
roots itself deeper and blooms on. Spells of inertia, economic depression,
and sheer good luck, flashes of architectural vision, enlightened patronage, and the resistance of stubborn citizens with minds of their own about
arranging the shapes and spaces around them have composed for us a complex urban music, derived from every generation of the city's past, in whose
harmonies and dissonance we can still recognize ourselves and know who
we are.

William Dendy's *Lost Toronto* was an elegy for architectural treasures
that have been lost. *Toronto Observed* identifies a number of those that are
still with us, to be learned from and celebrated. Here, for information and
entertainment, are accounts of seventy-seven buildings and architectural
groupings, along with stories of their patrons, their architects, their users,
and their social context. They are arranged in order of time, from 1813 to
the 1980s. Each historical period is introduced by an evocation of the forces
and the leaders that have figured most prominently in Toronto's history—

from the military outpost of the Simcoes to the miniature government village of President Peter Russell; the Little York of John Strachan and the Family Compact; the rising British colonial town of free traders and railway builders; the expansive, exuberant High Victorian provincial capital, proud of its vast Dominion and Empire; the Edwardian city of financiers and philanthropists; the expanding community struggling through two world wars and their aftermaths; and the exploding multicultural metropolis of the later twentieth century.

This book is not an architectural history of Toronto nor a systematic account of taste and patronage over the past two centuries. But as an essay or primer in both subjects, *Toronto Observed* is meant to be readable literature in its own right, to act as a useful guide to the direct experience of the buildings themselves, and to offer both comfort and weaponry to those who wish to preserve or enhance elements of the city's past.

Our criteria for choosing particular buildings for this book and omitting others, have been first, that they were extant in the year of the book's publication; second, that in some way they were architecturally or historically significant, either for their own sake or for their context; third, that whether the simple journeyman work of a builder or the sophisticated masterpiece of a major architect, the buildings were beautiful; and fourth, that they were at the time of their construction located in or related to the town of York or the city of Toronto. (Some of the most interesting buildings in Metropolitan Toronto today, such as Gibson House in North York, St John's Church, York Mills, Todmorden Mills in East York, and Montgomery's Tavern in Etobicoke, were part of the Upper Canadian countryside when they were put up.)

Even within these limits, constraints of time and space have obliged us to leave out many fine buildings. Several of these are mentioned in the main text, though not in separate articles; many others, regretfully, not at all. Toronto is still a city of churches, and among the interesting ones we have had to ignore are: Little Trinity, King Street East; St Michael's Cathedral; St Andrew's Presbyterian; Maurice Cody Hall (formerly St Paul's, Yorkville); St John's, Norway; St Stephen's-in-the-Field; St Andrews-by-the-Lake; Metropolitan United; Our Lady of Lourdes; St Paul's, Power Street; Jarvis Street and Walmer Road Baptist Churches; the former Cathedral of St Alban the Martyr; St Thomas, Huron Street; and a few churches, chapels, and synagogues constructed since 1945.

Among the secular buildings we should like to have included are the Enoch Turner Schoolhouse; 'Oaklands' (now De La Salle College); a number of the houses on Wellesley Street East and in Don Vale; 'Spadina'; the commercial buildings on Queen Street West between Soho and Spadina;

Victoria College; the Royal Conservatory of Music (formerly McMaster University); the Massey Factory; the College Wing of the Toronto General Hospital; the National Club; E.J. Lennox's Postal Station at 758 Queen Street East; the Island clubhouse of the Royal Canadian Yacht Club; the Loew's and Wintergarden Theatres; Walker Court in the Art Gallery of Ontario; the Princes' Gates and other CNE buildings; College Park (formerly Eaton's College Street store); the Eglinton Theatre; several 1950s and 1960s head offices in Don Mills, including Ortho Pharmaceutical, the IBM Building, and Oxford University Press; Scarborough College; the Colonnade; the Ontario Medical Association and the College of Physicians and Surgeons buildings; Tranby Court by Klein and Sears; 90 Shuter Street by Trow and Pollard; the Sun Life complex; and a great range of houses, built from 1840 to the present, throughout the city.

In a definitive history of Toronto architecture all these buildings—in addition to those that have been destroyed—would be given their due. Other elements too would figure in such a work more prominently than they do here: building materials and methods, for example, labour history and the changing world of trades and crafts, the contribution of Toronto's non-Anglo-Celtic communities, and above all the role of women as patrons and users. Over the past two centuries the shape and character of Toronto have been profoundly affected by a number of outstanding women, from Elizabeth Simcoe to Jane Jacobs, Phyllis Lambert, and several leading municipal politicians, as well as thousands of other women whose influence perforce was exercised indirectly through the actions of men or else by their writing and commenting or by their anonymous choices as consumers. As for female architects, planners, and chief executive officers, they have yet to take their rightful place as co-creators of the human environment in our city.

Having said this, we make no apology for concentrating on the buildings featured in this book. It is above all the account of a formidable, varied, and fascinating urban heritage. The scope and character of the buildings we have chosen to discuss range from the simple good taste of early Toronto's best remaining houses, banks, churches, and public buildings to the brilliance and grandeur of Osgoode Hall, University College, St James' Cathedral, Old City Hall, Union Station, New City Hall, Eaton Centre, Roy Thomson Hall, Ontario Place, and the great bank towers. We discuss residential areas, from the Annex and Wychwood Park to the contemporary St Lawrence Neighbourhood, and seven decades of differing styles in apartment buildings, from Riverdale Court to Sherbourne Lanes. We include a fort, a castle, a jail, a theatre, two libraries, two synagogues, two clubs, three cemeteries, a hotel, a bathing pavilion, several university buildings, a subway station, and such mixed-use complexes as Harbourfront and the Terminal Warehouse Building. Business is represented by the Front Street warehouses, the Gooderham & Worts industrial complex, Simpson's store, the Bay Street Canyon, the former Toronto Stock Exchange building, York Square, and the A.E. LePage building. The architectural styles we discuss range from Georgian to Classical, Gothic, and Romanesque Revivals, to Beaux Arts, Art Deco, International Modern, and Post-Modern Expressionist.

A few words on the genesis of this book and its method of preparation. In 1983 the Toronto Club asked me if I would be interested in writing a history to celebrate its sesquicentennial as the second-oldest gentlemen's club in North America. Eventually the Club agreed to sponsor research for a book—to be written in collaboration with the architectural historian William Dendy—on patronage and architecture in Toronto, in the context of the various historical forces and ideas that had affected them. It was understood that an acceptable publisher would have to be found at the outset and that the book would be written and distributed in the normal manner of a Canadian trade book. We then approached the Editorial Director of Oxford University Press Canada, William Toye, who agreed to work with us on the project.

I proposed that it consist of general introductory essays on half-a-dozen periods of Toronto's history, with individual pieces on each of the buildings and groups of buildings we decided to feature. Mr Dendy and I then drew up lists of the architecture to be included, which we found on comparison were remarkably similar—and much too long! After pruning, the master list was reduced to seventy-seven entries. The photographer Bruce Littel-john joined us and he and Mr Dendy are responsible for almost all the modern photographs in the book.

As to the method of writing, the introductory essays were written by myself. The essays on individual buildings were mostly written by Mr Dendy—with changes being suggested by the Oxford editors, Mr Toye and Patricia Sillers, and by myself. In several cases I wrote the first draft, and in a few other cases (in the last section) my contribution was written separately and then integrated with Mr Dendy's. He and I are of course jointly responsible for the book's judgements on buildings and their patrons and architects, as well as for the selection and accuracy of the facts presented.

As for sources, the chief primary materials are the buildings themselves, upon which these words and pictures are a direct commentary. Questions about other source material may be directed to me care of the publisher. The most useful general lists of both primary and secondary material can be found in the footnotes and guides to further research and reading contained in two fine recent books, *Toronto to 1918* by J.M.S. Careless and *Toronto Since 1918* by James Lemon. Their authors kindly provided me with galleys to read at an early stage in this book's preparation. Elizabeth Kilbourn, former arts critic with the *Toronto Star*, the CBC, and *Canadian Art* magazine, provided invaluable comment on both our writing and our architectural judgement throughout. We are also grateful to the architects, planners, historians, archivists, librarians, and private possessors of documents and pictures who have helped. For advice on most of the pre-1965 entries, we would like to thank William Greer of the Toronto Historical Board; for reading the first four introductory essays, Christopher Armstrong of York University; for advice in their fields of expertise, Charles Stacey, John McGinnis, Stephen Otto, Mary Allodi, Edith Firth, Margaret Baily, Brian Tapping, and Sis Bunting Weld; and for photo research and other assistance, Brenna Brown. Lastly we wish to thank the Toronto Club for its generous financial assistance, and in particular its Sesquicentennial Project Committee for their support and understanding over the past two-and-a-half years.

Victoria Day 1986   WILLIAM KILBOURN

This book is an unabashedly enthusiastic portrait of a city that means a great deal to me. The process of choosing the buildings to write about and the preparation of the text has been both gratifying and frustrating. Gratifying because the value of architecture and architectural patronage to a growing city like Toronto was amply demonstrated by the results of my research and it was a pleasure to convey this. Frustrating because there was neither the space nor the opportunity to write about all of the buildings that made up our first list of subjects. The frustration is all the greater as the work comes to an end because in the Toronto of the 1980s not even the relatively small number of buildings described are safe from destructive alteration or demolition. The laws that support architectural and historical preservation in Ontario are woefully lax and ambiguous, leaving far too much to the good graces of politicians and often unsympathetic owners. Large and small brutalities and indignities are inflicted on Toronto's architecture every day, making nonsense of original designs and the care that earlier owners—as well as countless Torontonians of today— put into maintaining their architectural heritage. Something must be done to strengthen official legislation and to encourage both government and building owners (especially those who are concealed behind faceless corporate identities) to recognize the value of both fine architecture and human streetscapes in the city.

My research drew on many sources and I indicated some of them in the body of the text. Much of the information I have used has been gathered over the last ten years and I am grateful for the liberal and ungrudging assistance I have received from the staff of Toronto's several public and private archives and libraries, and especially from the staff of the Baldwin Room of the Metropolitan Toronto Reference Library. The essays on Toronto's first and fourth City Halls owe a special debt to the 1985-6 exhibition—'Meeting Places: Toronto's City Halls'—at the Market Gallery, curated by Stephen A. Otto and Douglas Richardson.

My greatest debt of gratitude is owed to my parents who have always encouraged me to look at architecture and to enjoy the experience. To Professor R.M.H. Shepherd and Norma Bliss I owe my first chance to come to Toronto and to experience the community as well as the architecture of University College and Hart House. For their editorial assistance my thanks go to William Toye and Patricia Sillers, of Oxford University Press, who helped me give form to ideas that were often diffuse. Finally I would like to thank my friends Olga Williams and Deborah St George Butterfield, as well as Howard Moran, J. Gregory Fraser, Richard Meen, and Larry Richards for their encouragement during the writing. Without this, the work might never have been completed.

WILLIAM DENDY

PHOTOGRAPH CREDITS

BRUCE LITTELJOHN—Frontispiece, Plates 1, 2, 3, 4, 5, 6, 8, 9, 19, 20, 28, 29, 30, 31, 32, 36, 39, 40, 43, 45, 49, 66, 67, 83, 88, 101, 102, 107, 110, 111, 119, 123, 124, 142, 145, 146, 148, 149, 154, 160, 161, 173, 179. Mr Litteljohn acknowledges the generosity of Pentax Canada for lending the special equipment for his Pentax 6-7 camera.

Unless otherwise specified all other modern photographs are by William Dendy.

CANADIAN PACIFIC CORPORATE ARCHIVES: Plate 104.

CITY HALL, TORONTO, RECORDS & ARCHIVES: Plate 143 (1983-130-12A, P. Goodwin).

CITY OF TORONTO ARCHIVES, James Collection: Plate XX (SC478-14); XXV (265); XXVI (226); XXVIII (495); XXIX (1116); XXX (2021); XXXI (219A); XXXVII (983-70-2); XXXVIII (SC128-192); 144 (986-13-13).

METROPOLITAN TORONTO LIBRARY BOARD: Plate I (T30592); VII (T10339); VIII; IX (840); X (826); XI (T31037); XIV (T10348); XVII (*Canadian Illustrated News*, 2 April 1870); XVIII (*Canadian Illustrated News*, 3 January 1863); XIX (T10279); XXI (T13684); XXIII (E1-39a): XXIV (968-12-658); 5; 11; 37.

ONTARIO ARCHIVES: Plate II (S1072); IV (S2015); V (2624-9); XVI (S4308).

PUBLIC ARCHIVES CANADA: Plate VI (C99558); XV (PA119996); XXII (PA96488); XXXV (7690); 53 (PA73567); 59 (RD440); 61 (RD292); 69 (C53924, National Map Collection); 71 (C87228); 72 (RD380); 87 (RD455).

ROYAL ONTARIO MUSEUM, TORONTO: Plate XII (946.15.254); XIII (955.175).

SUN LIFE OF CANADA: Plate XL.

TORONTO TRANSIT COMMISSION: Plate XXXIV (13897).

UNIVERSITY OF MICHIGAN, WILLIAM L. CLEMENTS LIBRARY: Plate III.

UNIVERSITY OF TORONTO LIBRARY: Plate 90.

Special thanks are due to Tim Belch, Media/Public Relations Manager, Ontario Place, for the aerial view of Ontario Place (Plate 155); to John Lindsay for the photographs of the Wintergarden Theatre (Plate XXVII) and the Eglinton Theatre (Plate XXXIII), which appear in his book *Turn Out the Stars Before Leaving*, published by the Boston Mills Press; to Ed Mirvish for the interiors of the Royal Alexandra Theatre (Plates 81 and 82); to Raymond Moriyama, Moriyama & Teshima Architects, for the photographs of the Metropolitan Toronto Reference Library (Plates 156 and 157); to Barton Myers Associates for the photographs by Ian Samson of Barton Myers' house (Plate XXXIX) and Sherbourne Lanes (Plates 163, 164, and 165); to Douglas C. Rowland for the Public Archives Canada photograph of the Ortho Pharmaceutical Building (Plate XXXV); and to M.S. Yolles & Partners Limited for the photograph of Benvenuto (Plate XXXVI).

Prologue

THE PLANTING OF SIMCOE'S CAPITAL

Toronto began in the summer of 1793—the morning of Tuesday, July thirtieth to be exact. That was the day John Graves Simcoe—who had been appointed first Lieutenant-Governor of the newly created Upper Canada in 1791—his wife Elizabeth, and their three youngest children set up house beside Garrison Creek between the edge of Toronto Bay and the forest. The evening before, Simcoe and his wife had dined with Chief Justice Osgoode in the village capital of Newark (Niagara-on-the-Lake), waiting for a favourable wind to carry them across the water. In the late summer twilight the Governor's party boarded ship to the music of the Queen's Rangers band, and the sails of HMS *Mississaga* were unfurled in the freshening breeze. She headed out of the Niagara River into Lake Ontario, sailing north through the night to drop anchor near shore at the first crack of dawn. There the ship's master waited for the resident Canadian fur trader, St Jean Rousseau, to pilot them past a peninsula (now Toronto Island) to safe harbour in the bay. An advance party of soldiers had begun clearing a campground at the water's edge, near the spot that was to become the site of Fort York (see pp. 19–21). A large tent, purchased in London from the effects of the late Pacific explorer, Captain Cook, served the Simcoes for council chamber, bedroom, living-room, and nursery.

That afternoon the Simcoes travelled eastward by boat to the mouth of the principal river and there walked in a splendid grove of oaks chosen for the site of the new town. The Governor and his surveyors made plans to erect the town's first row of buildings near the river, along the little cliff that rose above the waters of the bay; to fortify Gibraltar Point at the tip of the peninsula protecting the harbour; and to cut two trails—named after British cabinet members Sir George Yonge and Sir Henry Dundas—north and west into the wilderness. In the meantime Elizabeth Simcoe recorded her explorations and discoveries in diary and on drawing pad. She noted that her favourite white cat quietly sat sentinel at the door of the tent 'amid the beat of drums and the crash of falling trees'. The river, she remarked, was to be called the Don, and those bold white cliffs to the east 'appeared so well we talked of building a summer residence there and calling it Scarborough'. She praised the low wooded peninsula that 'breaks the horizon of the lake, which greatly improves the view', and she delighted in the water of the Bay for being so beautifully clear and transparent.

1. *John Graves Simcoe, 1791. Oil portrait by Jean-Laurent Mosnier.*

Simcoe had chosen his town-site not for pastoral tranquillity, however, but because he expected war. The Thirteen Colonies had been irretrievably lost to republicanism. Simcoe had fought the Americans during the Revolution and he expected it would be only a matter of time until Britain would have to fight them again. Simcoe made Toronto his capital because its natural harbour and protected bay could be fortified against attack by water, and because it afforded a naval base from which to control Lake Ontario. Though isolated from civilization and supplies, the surrounding region could be farmed to grow most necessities; the great pines of the Don Valley would provide splendid masts and ships' timber. Toronto's unique advantage, however, was the long arm of the peninsula: a sandbar that had been piling up over some 7,000 years as the current of the Niagara River cut into the highlands of Scarborough and arced back to form an unusually well protected harbour.

There was another connection between this site and the Great Lakes. For centuries there had been occasional Indian encampments in the Toronto region—notably on the east bank of the Humber River, the southernmost point of the portage that led north through the Holland River and Lake Toronto (re-named Lake Simcoe in honour of his father) into Georgian

II. *Elizabeth Simcoe in Welsh dress, before she came to Canada*

Bay, thus forming a shortcut to the Northwest. It was down the Toronto portage that Champlain, on his way past Lake Couchiching in 1615, dispatched a party of Hurons led by his young interpreter Étienne Brulé. In September of that year Brulé became the first European to visit the site of Toronto. Later in the seventeenth century Toronto was visited by a number of explorers from Québec travelling to the interior of the continent. The brown-robed Franciscan, Father Hennepin, the first man to record the wonders of Niagara Falls, arrived by brigantine from Fort Frontenac and stayed among the longhouses of the Iroquois village of Teiaigon, on the Humber, for three weeks in the late fall of 1678, until he could venture south across the lake. The Sieur de la Salle reached Teiaigon on 15 August 1680 with the shipwrights he had brought to build a vessel for sailing down the Mississippi. He waited there until his supplies could be transported over the 'mountains' above the Toronto Carrying Place, before he began portaging north and west to the top of Lake Michigan.

Both French and English traders vied for the furs brought to the Toronto Carrying Place by various tribes of Indians. No permanent French post was established, however, until 1720, when a small fort was constructed near the mouth of the Humber; it was in use for about a decade. A larger log fort, 180 feet square, was constructed in 1751 on what is now the CNE grounds (at the foot of Dufferin Street). It was named Rouillé for the French colonial minister, and its garrison varied in size from eight to fifteen soldiers, supplemented by labourers who grew supplies nearby and tended the boats, the garden, the bakery, and the blacksmith shop. (Fort Rouillé's last officer, Commandant Douville, was related by marriage both to the French officer who captured Captain George Washington in a frontier battle in 1753, and to the heroine of Montreal, Madeleine de Verchères.) French Toronto was never more than a satellite of Forts Frontenac and Niagara, however, and the other important posts to the west. It played only a minor role in the long struggle between the French and English for control of the fur trade and the interior of the continent. As the defences of New France began to crumble in 1759, the Toronto garrison carried out instructions to burn everything at their post and return to Montreal. The following year the American adventurer, Major Rogers and his Rangers, took possession in the name of George III. Still, the fleur-de-lis that flew over Fort Rouillé testified that this land had been part of the French regime in North America for the better part of two centuries. Toronto's longest-reigning sovereign was not Queen Victoria of England, but the Sun King, Louis XIV, who ruled France from 1643 to 1714.

Though Toronto came under British rule by the Treaty of Paris in 1763, nothing was done with it until after the American Revolution split the empire of the St Lawrence and the Great Lakes in two. Because the British wished to protect their Indian allies, they believed that the land they inhabited should be acquired only by treaty. They therefore negotiated with the Indians for the river lands on either side of Kingston and Newark, which they could then offer to prospective new settlers. Aware of Toronto's potential value as a link in the transportation network of the Great Lakes, the Governor-in-Chief at Quebec, Lord Dorchester, negotiated the purchase of the Toronto region from the Mississaugas, who occupied land along the north shore of Lake Ontario. He then sent his surveyors to draw up plans for a possible town-site. In August 1788 HMS *Seneca* arrived in Toronto Bay with 149 barrels of goods and a small amount of cash, valued at £1,700 in all. Toronto was acquired at the cost of 2,000 gun flints, 24 brass kettles, 10 dozen looking-glasses, 2 dozen laced hats, a bale of flowered flannel, and 96 gallons of rum (among other things). But for another half-decade the bay remained empty save for the rare canoe of a travelling Indian or one of St Jean Rousseau's colleagues in the fur trade.

It was Simcoe's arrival in Upper Canada that changed the course of Toronto's history. Disagreeing with his superior, Lord Dorchester, about the acceptability of Kingston as a defensible naval base, and with the leading citizens of Newark, who thought the search for a capital should stop with them, Simcoe planted both base and capital in the wilderness at Toronto. There he would do battle with the two influences he most disliked in North America: those of revolutionary democracy and aboriginal 'savagery'. Four weeks after his arrival at Toronto, in a single gesture against both, he ordered a cannonade salute in celebration of the Duke of York's victory against the armies of the French revolution, and renamed his temporary capital York, to replace the Indian name. He intended his permanent capital to be located on the River Thames—even further into the western wilderness—and called London; from there he could provide the focus for a prosperous British colony in the future. But the first Loyalist settlers of the province were horrified. York was preposterous enough, but London (commented Richard Cartwright, the leading merchant of Kingston) could be decently visited only by Montgolfier's newly invented contraption, the hot-air balloon.

Simcoe decided that his temporary capital must have not only a British name but elegant waterfront buildings. As his officials followed him to York over the next three years, they built their houses at the edge of the bay on what is now Front Street. They were to be compensated for their pains by *douceurs*—the reward of 100-acre parklots stretching north from the town limits at what was called Lot (now Queen) Street. By the possession of these and other parcels further north, they would become part of a landed aristocracy. Simcoe could create his capital with the officials he chose. His founding aristocracy in York were mostly men who had served as members of his personal staff or in the British army in America—or both: for example Peter Russell, his Receiver-General, who had been assistant to the British Commander-in-Chief in the revolutionary war; William Jarvis, Simcoe's civil secretary; John Scadding, his estate manager from back home in Devon; Dr James Macaulay, Simcoe's regimental surgeon, whose lands eventually became Toronto's first working-class suburb and the site of the first Anglican church built for the poor, Holy Trinity (Plate 15); and Major John Small, first clerk of the Executive Council, whose Berkeley House, at the corner of King and Berkeley, was enlarged by stages from a log cabin, in which the Council often met, into an elegant thirteen-room mansion (demolished in 1925). It was Small who killed Attorney-General White in York's first duel in 1800.

Simcoe's other vital asset for town building was the Saxon entrepreneur and architect, William Berczy, who immigrated to York in 1794 with five dozen German families in tow, after an unsuccessful colonization scheme south of the border. Berczy and his Germans built several of the first houses and roads in York and were rewarded with attractive land in Markham

Township that became the first important farm settlement; they were the prime suppliers of farm produce and labour to the capital. Berczy himself built a substantial house and company store in town; but in 1805, when he felt insufficiently rewarded for his efforts, he left for the more civilized society of Montreal, there to establish himself as one of Canada's premier portrait painters.

Choosing to ignore Lord Dorchester's opposition to a naval base at York and his refusal to furnish it with substantial armaments, Simcoe constructed a stockade and barracks for the garrison* and storehouses on Gibraltar Point, thus covering both sides of the entrance to the bay. A government wharf was built and two wings of a brick building were planned to hold legislature, courts, and Government House. The Simcoes received visitors—aristocratic refugees from revolutionary France among others—beneath the simple wooden pillars and portico of 'Castle Frank', the province's first summer retreat, set high above the Don Valley.

In July 1796, three years after his arrival at York, Simcoe departed from Upper Canada on a temporary leave that proved to be permanent when he was reassigned to military command in the West Indies. His capital had taken root, however. Two dozen substantial dwellings graced King Street and the waterfront. The last of the officials who had helped Simcoe set up the government of Upper Canada at Newark were now reluctantly committed to removing themselves to their new properties at York and were not prepared to move again. Simcoe's senior executive councillor, the Honourable Peter Russell, was put in charge. He and his colleagues, their families, and the friends they invited to join them constituted the first society of this village outpost of the British Empire. They made a lasting mark on the character of Toronto.

---

*These were located immediately above the east bank of Garrison Creek, which ran into the bay close to what is now the corner of Bathurst Street and Lakeshore Boulevard. The present Fort York was built in 1813 above the west bank of the Creek. The Valley cut by Garrison Creek has been filled in.

III. *The town of York in the autumn of 1803 as depicted by Surgeon Edward Walsh, 49th Regiment, showing (l. to r.) the houses of Duncan Cameron, Dr W.W. Baldwin, William Allan, Peter Russell and just to the left of the town blockhouse (with flag), near the corner of what is now Berkeley and The Esplanade, the capital's first government buildings, which were burned by American invaders in 1813.*

I

MILITARY POST AND COLONIAL TOWN
1797–1841

The elderly Irish bachelor Peter Russell,* president of the Executive Council of Upper Canada and administrator of the province, played a crucial role in shaping and building its capital. Formerly civilian secretary to the British Commander-in-Chief in revolutionary America and later Governor Simcoe's assistant in Upper Canada, Russell had been a competent number-two man who did not, however, lack the initiative and imagination required of a leader. 'I have extended this Town Westward towards the Garrison,' he wrote to Simcoe in 1797 from the new house overlooking

---

*An eighteenth-century gentleman (1733–1808) whose gambling debts had forced him to leave Cambridge University before he could prepare himself for a career in the church, he bought a commission in the army instead, which he eventually sold to provide for his father and sister.

IV. *Peter Russell*
by William Berczy

the bay that had been built by William Berczy for Russell and his half-sister Elizabeth. At a stroke of the pen Russell thus added to his town what has become the financial core and downtown centre of the city. In between these new town lots west of modern Yonge Street and Governor Simcoe's original town-site, Russell reserved land for such future public institutions as a court-house, a church, and a market—all soon to be built there and maintained in one form or another in that area ever since. He fitted out a blockhouse for 70 soldiers at the garrison and topped it with a lighthouse to guide ships into the harbour. 'I flatter myself that Your Excellency will not be displeased with what I have done,' he concluded.

Russell busied himself with everything: from fitting suitable occupants into the new town lots as quickly and fairly as possible and improving the trails that connected York with the rest of the province, to ordering adequate supplies of brick and lumber for future public construction and providing a suitable grazing ground for His Majesty's oxen. One of his most important acts was to let a contract to one Asa Danforth for a road extending eastward to connect with the Loyalist settlements on the Bay of Quinte.

The tract of forest chosen by Russell as his due for being Executive Councillor stretched north from about Queen and Peter Streets to the present Eglinton Avenue and included what is now Russell Hill Road. (To keep his

v. *Elizabeth Russell*
by William Berczy

table supplied, he brought in an English miller, brewer, and agriculturist named John Denison to farm part of it. Denison himself later became a successful farmer on a tract granted to him by Russell, and the founder of a prominent Toronto family.) After retiring in 1800 Russell spent the last eight years of his life in York, adding to his vast acreage in and around the Toronto region by judicious purchase. He also arranged for his debt-ridden cousin William Willcocks, the Mayor of Cork, to make his way in Upper Canada by settling his large family on Duke Street, where he became a merchant, a magistrate, and postmaster of York. Willcocks in turn persuaded the Baldwins, another Irish family in straitened circumstances, to immigrate to Upper Canada.

The young scion of this house, Dr William Warren Baldwin, married Phoebe Willcocks, and when his medical practice, and the grammar school he kept in his father-in-law's house, were not sufficient to occupy him, he responded to the dire shortage of lawyers in the province by having himself examined before the Chief Justice, after which he was duly licensed by the legislature to practise law. On one occasion Dr Baldwin reputedly excused himself from court in the middle of his argument in order to deliver a baby, and then returned in time to sum up his client's case. He derived his fortune not from either practice, however, but from his wife's

VI. *'Fort at York, 1821' by John Elliott Woolford*

inheritance of the vast Russell estates. Here he was to build Spadina House, three miles from York on the brow of the escarpment, and the grand avenue leading north from the bay by which it was reached. An amateur architect, Baldwin designed not only 'Spadina' and his own impressive brick town house at Front and Bay, but was involved with the construction of several other buildings in York, of which the Bank of Upper Canada (Plate 6) is the only one to survive. Later in life Baldwin sat in the Legislative Assembly as a Reform member critical of the governing clique. He eventually conceived the form of responsible government that made possible the transition from imperial rule to British Commonwealth. But the best image of Dr Baldwin in Peter Russell's York is that of a young *philosophe* of the Enlightenment—assisting the old Receiver-General with amateur experiments in chemistry, playing the flute by the grate fire of Russell Abbey (a name derived from Woburn Abbey, the seat of the Duke of Bedford, his English Russell relative), or listening to the old man as he read aloud from favourite writers such as Dean Jonathan Swift or from Russell's own history of the American Revolutionary War, which Edward Gibbon is supposed to have read with favour.

These Anglo-Irishmen of early York were connected by family ties but did not really form the basis for the group that was eventually known as the Family Compact. Russell died in 1808 at the age of seventy-five. Willcocks

VII. *York from the Island, 1828, drawn by J. Gray (aquatint by J. Gleadah)*

was never entirely successful at anything. And the Baldwins—by virtue of their wealth, culture, and liberal political inclinations—held themselves aloof from those of His Majesty's leading subjects in York who in fact formed the establishment of the town until their political power was undermined by the 1837 Rebellion.

The town-site laid out by Simcoe and Russell blossomed in the first decade of the eighteenth-century into a row of one- and one-and-a-half-storey Georgian frame houses, strung along the waterfront from the Parliament Buildings near the Don River, through to the fortifications and barracks of the garrison at the foot of modern Bathurst Street. A church, a school, a market-place, a customs house and post office, a court-house and jail—plain wooden structures on King Street—were added to York's stock of public buildings. Retail merchants, innkeepers, and small manufacturers—a distiller, a brewer, a baker, a tanner, a potash maker, and a printer—did their work on premises in or attached to their homes. In addition to these town dwellers there were the saw and grist millers who had established themselves further up the Don River beside a good source of water power. Servants and apprentices lived in for the most part. Other labourers, usually in very short supply, occupied cabins back from the waterfront, on the edge of the forest.

More refugees arrived in town to repair their fortunes. For example, in

1809 the Loyalist soldier Stephen Jarvis joined his cousin William Jarvis, the provincial secretary, and was given a government post and a militia command. Both men's sons eventually married into the family of William Dummer Powell, the only early Chief Justice who stayed long enough in York to become a major social and political power there. The French Royalist officer Laurent Quetton de St George became a leading merchant, at first moving in from the settlement of French aristocratic refugees north of the town to set up shop in a room of Willcocks' house, and then quickly turning enough profit to build York's first brick residence at King and Frederick (1807; demolished).

The government village increased in population from under 300 souls in 1799, the last year of Russell's administration, to 700 at the outbreak of the War of 1812. But there emerged in this decade no single resident leader in the style of Russell. His successor as provincial administrator was largely absent because of his duties in Québec as Commander-in-Chief of British forces in Canada. And the next Lieutenant-Governor, Francis Gore, spent the most critical years of his term, from 1811 to 1815, on leave in England. It was during Gore's time (1806–17) that a handful of resident office-holders in York—including members of four families, the Powells, Ridouts, Jarvises, and Boultons—became accustomed more or less to governing the province and its capital themselves. Most lacking was an obvious and resolute leader; but this changed on the morning of 27 April 1813. The British military commander had made a strategic withdrawal of his troops from Fort York in the face of an overwhelming force of invading Americans. The chief negotiator with the American commander was the newly arrived rector of St James Church, the Rev. John Strachan, whose ferocious defence of the property and persons of the captured town during his shipboard interview with the American commander, General Dearborn, brought a quick stop to the looting and firing of York begun by the American troops. Strachan threatened Dearborn with the future wrath not so much of God Almighty as of the British Navy. It was said later that it was difficult to tell from the interview which of the two men was the conquered and which the conqueror.

Strachan had not been brought up a gentleman. The penniless son of a Scottish stonemason who had managed to acquire a university education, he came out as household tutor to the Cartwright family of Kingston in 1799. In short order, however, he had got himself ordained in the Church of England, had married a rich Montreal widow,* Ann McGill (whose brother-in-law later founded a university at Strachan's urging), and until

---

*Strachan had wanted to marry Ann Wood himself but had no money. When the elderly bachelor Andrew McGill proposed to her, Strachan is reported to have told her: 'Tak' him, I can afford to wait.' Andrew's early death left her an income that enabled Strachan to build his handsome home in York after he and Ann married and moved there.

VIII. *John Strachan, about 1827, when he was forty-nine*

he was made rector of York in 1812 ran the best school in Upper Canada, at Cornwall, to which leading families of York sent their sons to be educated. Many of these young men distinguished themselves in the militia during the war and by 1815 were ready, under Strachan's guidance, to run the city and the province. Strachan was particularly close to the most brilliant of them, John Beverley Robinson, who had lost his father at an early age. Robinson became acting Attorney-General at twenty-one, and was later the leader of the government party in the Assembly until in 1829 he was appointed Chief Justice, Speaker of the Legislative Council, and President of the Executive Council—all this while he was still in his thirties. Strachan himself was a member of both these latter bodies and, given his moral and intellectual authority, he became in effect the Governor's first minister, the most influential politician in the province during the 1820s. His avowed goal was to 'preach civilization' as well as the gospel. By that he meant the spread of British civilization in the frontier post to which he had been called. Among the many institutions Strachan founded were King's College, the ancestor of the University of Toronto, and the Toronto General Hospital. He planted his elegant two-storey brick residence on Front

IX. *King Street, 1835, showing the jail with the stocks in front, the Fireman's Hall (designed by John Howard) facing Church Street, the Court House, and St James' Church. Watercolour by John Howard.*

Street West ('The Palace', 1818; demolished), with its shade trees, carriage sweep, and liveried footmen, to set an example to his fellow townsmen.* His former pupil D'Arcy Boulton Jr busied himself with a similar project by constructing The Grange (Plate 4).

In 1821 Strachan was a founding director of the Bank of Upper Canada whose president, William Allan, was York's foremost capitalist. Allan had begun as a merchant in Peter Russell's time, taken over the postmastership of York from William Willcocks, become collector of customs, and built his own private wharf. He not only served as a major of militia at Queenston under General Brock during the War of 1812, but managed between campaigns to attend to his wholesale business in such a manner that he profited enormously from supplying the British Army. Allan went on to head the town's first insurance company and, in due course, to become both a legislative and executive councillor of Upper Canada.

Under successive lieutenant-governors, York's Family Compact continued to dominate both town and province. But a flood of British immigration, which increased the population of York five-fold in the late 1820s and early 1830s, required the creation of an adequate administrative and taxing structure to cope with the expansion. The City of Toronto was incorporated in 1834 with a population of 9,000. Under Lt-Governors Colborne and Head, Strachan and his associates continued to exercise great

*His brother James, visiting from Scotland, asked him in amazement if he had come by it all honestly.

x. *The Parliament Buildings, Front Street, between Simcoe and John Streets. Watercolour by John Howard.*

political influence, even assembling in the drawing-room of his 'Palace' on Front Street to plan the final assault that defeated William Lyon Mackenzie's rebels in 1837. But the practices of oligarchic government could not stand the scrutiny of Governor-General Durham, who had been sent out to find a remedy for a society that the Family Compact and successive British governors were no longer capable of ruling. Durham recommended Dr Baldwin's solution of responsible government, along with union of Upper and Lower Canada as the Province of Canada. After various administrative experiments, Governor-General Elgin in 1848 brought in responsible government by summoning as his chief advisers the Reform leaders Robert Baldwin and Louis Lafontaine, who could command a majority in the elected House. By this time the direct political control of the province by the Family Compact had crumbled.

The pre-eminence of Toronto's traditional leaders, however, and their common interest in the affairs of the city by no means disappeared. The continuity of an informal élite in the history of Toronto can hardly be better illustrated than by the founding of the Upper Canada Club in rented premises early in 1837, and its later development as the Toronto Club (see pages 126–8). Descendants of the first generation of York's leaders were heavily represented on the club's membership rolls. So too were the rising business and professional men—many of whom also held senior government posts—who had settled in Toronto more recently.

XI. *William Warren Baldwin, c. 1830. By Théophile Hamel.*

Two members of the Toronto Club who contributed significantly to the shaping of the city may be singled out as representing the two original sources of leadership in York. One, William Botsford Jarvis, was a scion of the Family Compact; the other, Robert Baldwin Sullivan, owed the start of his career to Governor Simcoe's most senior official. President Peter Russell's assistance to the Baldwin family of Cork in the 1790s eventually led Dr Baldwin's sister and her merchant husband to move their family business to York in 1819. Their son Robert Baldwin Sullivan became a law student in his Uncle William's office, and was librarian to the House of Assembly until he was called to the bar in 1828. The most effective counsel for Reformers in need of legal assistance, young Sullivan was unanimously chosen second mayor of Toronto by City Council in 1835, succeeding the radical Mackenzie. Though a Reformer himself, he was a temperate one and was sufficiently respected that the Lieutenant-Governor appointed him president of his executive council and commissioner of Crown lands the following year. As mayor, Sullivan brought effective leadership to Council. He made the city's Hook and Ladder Company a useful fire-fighting outfit (in contrast to the old volunteer bucket brigade) and attacked the menace to public health of raw waste dumped in the streets by having the

XII. *Joseph Bloor's brewery, Rosedale ravine, built in the early 1830s, and the blockhouse at Bloor and Sherbourne. Watercolour sketch by Paul Kane (n.d.).*

city's first sewer built. In 1840, as a member of the Legislative Council of the United Province of the Canadas, and president of its Executive Council, he was a major figure in the provincial administration. But as the leading exponent in print of his uncle's doctrine of self-government, he assisted the Reform party leader, his cousin Robert Baldwin, by resigning with him in 1844 and returning to power only when their common aim of responsible government was acceded to in 1848. Sullivan was also a director of the Bank of Upper Canada (Plate 6), president of the St Patrick's Society, and a promoter of the Mechanics' Institute, predecessor of the public-library system. He spent his last years on the bench as a judge of the Court of Common Pleas.

One of Toronto's professional and intellectual leaders for nearly forty years, Sullivan had held high office both before and after the watershed of the 1837 rebellion. His fellow club member, Sheriff William Botsford Jarvis, though on the other side of the political spectrum, also figured in Toronto's history during both periods. The Sheriff's great moment of glory came in December 1837 when, rightly apprehensive of an uprising that others in authority ignored, he and a small platoon of riflemen ambushed and turned back Mackenzie's rebel army at Mrs Sharpe's farm (at the corner of College and Yonge), as it headed down Yonge Street to attack the otherwise undefended city. Sheriff Jarvis's other claim to fame was the building of his mansion 'Rosedale' in 1827. On the large grant of land surrounding it, the city's oldest surviving residential suburb later grew when Jarvis began to sell off bits of his property to support his family. By then Toronto was an expanding and prosperous city, a very different place from the little world of the Family Compact into which he had been born. In 1861, three years before he died, Jarvis created a last great nostalgic moment when he held a garden party at 'Rosedale' for the veterans of the War of 1812, in which older members of the Jarvis family had served with distinction—a lifetime ago, in the years of Toronto's infancy.

1. *Fort York. Soldiers' barracks, built in 1813–14 after the original fort was destroyed in the American invasion of 27 April 1813; in the distance (looking east) is Toronto's 1985 skyline.*

FORT YORK

1813–15, Garrison Road at Fleet Street West

1841, Exhibition Park

As you stand in the grassy meadow of Fort York—lightly shielded by earthworks, trees, and sky from the roar of railways to the north-east and roadways to the south—you have an ideal prospect on Toronto's past and present. Immediately around you is a grouping of weathered log and red-brick soldiers' quarters. In the distance, high on the eastern horizon, you can see a cluster of bold towers that represent the present power centre of the city, planted within the town-site of 1797. Washed by the several lights and weathers that change them momentarily, these towers seem more ephemeral than the solid grounded remnants in front of you of the vanished red-coated, fife-and-drum imperial world. But, old and new, both are real enough; both are significant in the story of our city—past, present, and future; and for nearly two centuries there has been a historic link between them.

Fort York is not only one of the oldest continuously maintained military establishments in Canada, but its eight remaining structures are the oldest group of buildings in Toronto.* (Look at the keystone over the entrance to the powder magazine, dated the 54th year of the reign of His Britannic Majesty George III.) They were put up shortly after their predecessors were destroyed during the American occupation of April 1813. On the day of the battle, 27 April, the defenders took a grim toll of the enemy, by blowing up the magazine's several hundred barrels of gunpowder into a deadly rain of logs and stone. The Americans' burning of government buildings on this site and elsewhere was avenged several months later by the British raid on Washington and the firing of the White House.

The Fort's triangular location was chosen because it was protected by the lake (all the lands now to the south of it are fill), by the once-deep valley of Garrison Creek to the northeast (which reached the lake near the foot of Bathurst Street and is now railway land), and by a dry moat and earthwork revetments to the west put in by General Isaac Brock in 1812. It stood above the only entrance to Toronto Bay and was complemented by fortifications on Gibraltar Point, the long sandy peninsula opposite. Ironically the Fort, whose site was chosen because it was the best place from which to defend harbour and town, was starved of funds by the British government and was never properly equipped with batteries and other defences, let alone enough British soldiers, before the War of 1812. The rebuilding program that began in 1813, when the American forces left, was serious: not only did Napoleon dominate Europe from Madrid to Moscow, but the Amer-

ican navy on both the lakes and the Atlantic Ocean was putting up a strong challenge to His Majesty's ships. By 1816 the Royal Engineers had designed and supervised the construction by local labour of eighteen buildings capable of housing 1,000 men. One was a large and well-appointed commandant's headquarters, which burned down in 1826. The handsomest of the present buildings is the one-storey ten-room quarters for senior officers. With its thick red-brick walls, white wood trim, panelled windows, heavy iron latches, splendid brick fireplaces and hearths, and its main door embellished with a delicate fanlight transom and side lights, it is typical of Georgian buildings in North America at the time. Its basement of cut stone includes a kitchen, a wine-cellar, and a double-vaulted treasury for military and political documents. In 1834 a kitchen and drawing-room were added on the ground floor.

The economic and social effect of the Fort on the little town was enormous. Local brickworks and bricklayers put 160,000 bricks into the senior officers' quarters alone. Along with these workmen, a swarm of sawmill operators, carpenters, stonemasons, and others were paid in scarce hard currency (sterling), as were the carters who lugged materials not manufactured locally down from Kingston and the St Lawrence by sled in the winter of 1814. The population of the Fort in its early years was greater than that of the town. The quantity of flour, pork, oats, peas and other food brought over from the market at York was considerable: one order alone, for 24 January 1815, totalled £678. The profits of York importers like William Allan and Quetton de St George—on wine and plate and crystal and other things for the officers' mess—made them the richest men in town. The soldiers provided business for the local grog shops that was literally staggering. Some visitors said Toronto seemed to have almost as many taverns as houses—until the later nineteenth century, when the British army left and the temperance movement took root. York's social and cultural life depended greatly on the balls and feasts, concerts and entertainments, provided at the officers' mess. In turn, the wives and daughters of the leading citizens welcomed the officers to their homes.

Late in 1837 the barracks was emptied when the authorities sent the troops eastward to deal with the Papineau Rebellion in Lower Canada. The rising led by Mackenzie in Upper Canada had to be put down by the gentlemen of the province acting in their capacity as local militia. One aftermath of 1837, and of the undeclared border war of 1838–9 with the Ameri-

---

*The stone lighthouse of 1808, now standing between Centre Island and Hanlan's Point, is probably the oldest single building in the city, though it is possible the Scadding Cabin, which was moved to the Exhibition grounds, is older. There are a few eighteenth-century buildings in outlying areas, such as Todmorden Mills on the Don.

2. *Detail of the doorway in Plate 3*

3. Senior officers' quarters (1814–15)

cans, was the decision to build a new and more modern fort. It was placed on the nearby headlands to the southwest and designed as a star-shaped fortress according to the principles of the French military engineer Vauban—though it was half a star, because of the lake on the southern boundary.*

Old Fort York was not simply abandoned and replaced by the new fort (re-named Stanley Barracks in 1893 after the Governor-General), but instead remained in use for both storage and some residential purposes. During the American war scare of 1861 it was equipped with a battery of seven guns and more earthworks, since its 'replacement' had never been developed into anything more than a barracks. But from its completion in 1841 until it was ceded to the Dominion of Canada in 1871, the new fort housed the British garrison in Toronto. Later the local Canadian militia—in particular its oldest regular permanent regiment, the Royal Canadian Dragoons—made it their headquarters. Here troops mustered for the Northwest Rebellion in 1885, for the Boer War in 1899, and for two world wars. In 1953 all its buildings were torn down, except for the handsome two-storey building that housed the officers' quarters; this was turned over to the city for renovation to become the offices of the Toronto Historical Board and the site of its Marine Museum of Upper Canada. Built of finely edged blocks of Queenston and Kingston limestone, with an exposed full basement, thick walls, recessed casement windows, and beautifully fitted stone staircases that seem to fly on half arches, it is an excellent example of the Royal Engineers' superb workmanship: there is nothing else like it in Toronto. The only other remnant of the new fort, its gates, was saved by Spencer Clark for his collection of architectural remains at the Guild Inn in Scarborough. The parade

square that once held the drills and musical rides of the Royal Dragoons is now a Canadian National Exhibition parking lot.

The Old Fort was restored and renovated in 1932–3 in preparation for Toronto's centennial in 1934. At that time it ceased to be a residential facility and became a place for regular historic re-enactments of military history, a museum, and a space where a great variety of festivals, celebrations, and outdoor rallies could be held. Perhaps the Old Fort's greatest contribution to Toronto has been that it provided a focus for public interest in restoration and preservation. The longest battle of Fort York, as it turned out, took place between 1905 and 1909, when city politicians and transportation officials did their best to ruin it with a streetcar line. They were defeated by a militant group of citizens and journalists led by members of the Ontario Historical Society. C.W. Jefferys drew a cartoon for the Toronto *Star* that showed the ghosts of the Fort York garrison with bayonets fixed ready to fend off the shadowy form of a giant streetcar moving inexorably towards them. The caption read 'The spirit of 1812—"Halt!"'

Fort York was the focus of the more recent conservation movement in Toronto that began in the late 1950s, when Metro Chairman Frederick Gardiner, on behalf of a group of developers who coveted the land, tried to have the Fort totally relocated on filled land near the water. The pretext was that it stood in the path of the construction of the Gardiner Expressway. It was one of the few battles that Chairman Gardiner ever lost. He later said that he would 'rather fight 24 members of Metropolitan Council any day than 24 historically minded women [of the Toronto Women's Historical Society]'. Under the supervision of Brigadier John McGinnis, then managing director of the Toronto Historical Board and himself designated by Mayor and Council as the city's first Historic Person, the buildings of the Old Fort were restored in the 1960s to resemble closely their original state.

---

*Old Fort York was one of the last in North America to be designed to fit the character and contour of its terrain.

21

THE GRANGE

Grange Park, at the north end of John Street
1817–18; with additions c.1843 and c.1885

There is probably no house in Toronto whose form and restored interior better suit modern ideas of the elegance of Little York than The Grange. A symbol of the aristocratic society that Governor Simcoe and the early colonial establishment of Upper Canada hoped to perpetuate, it provides the late twentieth century with a supremely romantic image of colonial Toronto. A paragon of Late Georgian simplicity, built symmetrically in red brick, with a pediment on the skyline and a columned portico, it was once the centrepiece of a suburban estate that now lies buried within the heart of the city behind the Art Gallery of Ontario—though its spacious lawn and oval carriage drive survive.

When the Town of York was founded in 1793 the first settlers were given land grants in and around the new town-site according to a very specific plan. Land was virtually the only thing the colonial government had to give its settlers; and though its real worth was untested, it attracted many people from Britain who had an almost mystical respect for land and the status it conferred. There were large lots within the town itself intended for shops and houses; a row of 100-acre park lots, numbered westward from the Don River, and fronting on Queen Street East and West (then called Lot Street); and, north of Bloor Street, 200-acre farm lots. Virtually any of the early settlers were eligible for town lots or farm lots. But the most important men in the colonial establishment were granted park lots, which were intended to be suburban estates —an appropriate setting for the colonial gentry. From the 1820s on, the park lots were subdivided by their owners and profitably sold in building lots to create a series of new districts for the town.

D'Arcy Boulton Sr (1759–1834), a member of a land-owning family in Lincolnshire, was a second son and did not inherit the family estates. After training in the law, and an unsuccessful business career, he immigrated to the United States and in 1801–2 settled in Upper Canada. His rise within the colonial establishment began with an official appointment as an attorney in 1805, followed by his appointment as Solicitor-General in 1807 and as Attorney-General in 1815. Both of Boulton's eldest sons benefited from their father's connections; but D'Arcy Boulton Jr (1785–1846), although trained as a lawyer, had little taste for either politics or law. He held minor government positions (providing a small but fairly certain income), and turned instead to business, opening a dry-goods and grocery store on the southwest corner of King and Frederick Streets. In January 1808 he married Sarah Anne Robinson and on 30 March of the same year purchased the 100 acres of Park Lot Thirteen that had been originally granted to Robert Gray, his father's predecessor in office.

Park Lot Thirteen, supplemented by the purchase of about twenty additional acres, became The Grange estate, which originally extended from Queen to Bloor. From the beginning Boulton planned to make the lot the site of a gentleman's suburban home with house, gardens, pleasure grounds, and only enough active farming to support the horses and cows the family itself needed. A house was planned in 1808, to be constructed in brick (a material both unusual and very expensive in York at the time). But it was not until 1817–18, during the reconstruction that followed the War of 1812, that Boulton was able to carry out his building project. No architect or builder is recorded for The Grange; the mason in charge of the bricklaying very likely produced the design in consultation with his patron. The centre-hall plan, and symmetrical five-bay elevation with a pedimented centre standing slightly forward of the main block of the house, follows a pattern common throughout eighteenth-century Britain for small country houses and suburban villas. The permanence of its finely laid red brick, the formality of the façade, the elegant proportions of the windows (slightly shorter in height on the less-important second floor), and the fine detail of the main cornice and of the panelled door under its semi-circular fanlight, all represented the grace and permanence of the life Boulton wished to live in Upper Canada and bequeath to his children.

The interior plan and treatment were equally straightforward. The centre hall, wider than a corridor or vestibule, was large enough to be used as a ballroom. Each of the main rooms opens from this hall, which extends past the main stair to a north door. The drawing-room on the east side faces south, with the morning-room behind. (Between the two there was originally a narrow passage that led to a conservatory attached to the east side of the house, since demolished.) On the west side was the dining-room, and behind it were two small rooms, now used as service spaces; in the corridor between them stairs led down to the kitchens and service rooms in the basement and up to the several bedrooms of the second floor.

Around 1843 D'Arcy Boulton had several changes made to The Grange that gave it an up-to-date stylish character. The west service wing was added; inside, the corridor between drawing-room and morning-room was taken out to expand the drawing-room. Upstairs, the bedrooms on the east side of the hall were combined to create a large music-room that could be used for important entertainments. Externally the new work continued the old style of the house; but inside everything—plasterwork, door mouldings, new mantels—was in the Greek Revival style fashionable in Toronto and in most of North America at the time.

After D'Arcy Boulton's death the house passed to his widow and then to his son William Henry, and finally to William

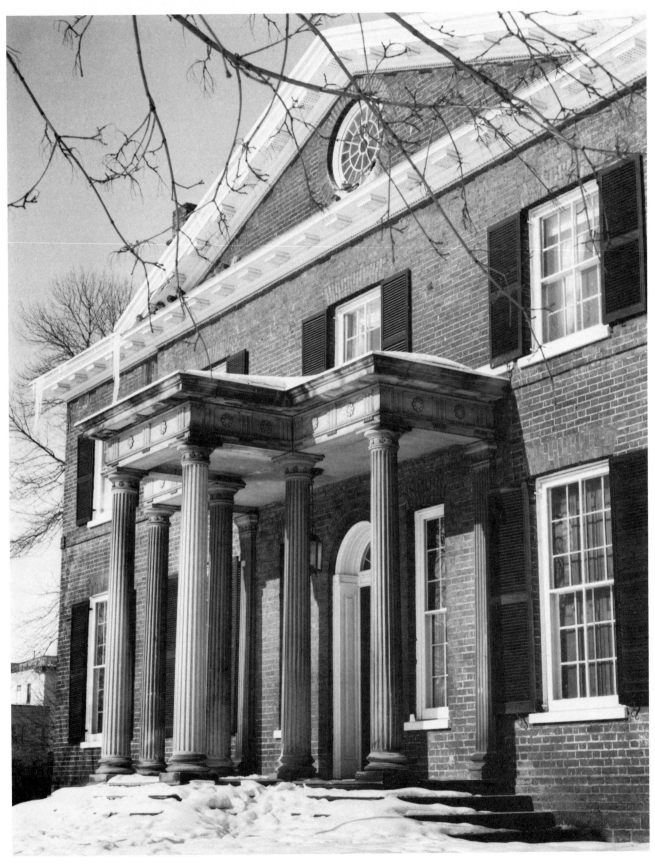

4

Henry's widow. In 1875 she married Goldwin Smith, the famous English historian who became Toronto's leading intellectual and the most acerbic political commentator of the later Victorian era. In the last quarter of the century The Grange became an even more potent symbol of Toronto's history and society than D'Arcy Boulton could have imagined. Goldwin Smith and his wife made several changes in the house, working with architect William Strickland. The original staircase was removed in 1885 and replaced with one in heavy Victorian oak, and the furnishings of the interior gave it a well-stuffed Victorian look. Goldwin Smith also extended the 1843 west wing, adding a new study hung with fine Morris wallpaper. Most important, Smith rebuilt the original wooden portico with Doric columns and entablature in stone. The design may not have duplicated the original porch, but it expressed the spirit of the original with a sensitivity and lack of meddling with detail that are rare in the Victorian period.

A visitor to The Grange today sees the house restored (in 1971 under the leadership of Mary Alice Stuart, in celebration of Canada's Centennial in 1967) as a 'gentleman's house' of the 1840s. The most dramatic part of this work was the removal of Goldwin Smith's oak staircase and the building of an elegant free-standing spiral stair. There was no definite evidence to be found of the original form of the staircase, but with the restored rooms (which include some of the original Boulton furniture), it creates exactly the air of cosmopolitan and stylish sophistication that D'Arcy Boulton sought when he built The Grange in 1817–18 and had it redecorated in the 1840s.

Boulton intended his purchase of land to be an astute investment in property that could later be profitably subdivided, and the sales began shortly after The Grange was completed.

The fifty-one acres north of what later became College Street were purchased by the newly founded King's College in 1828 to form the western part of the university campus. Boulton's heirs continued to sell land and the estate became smaller, but the house itself was uncompromised and its continued preservation remained an important civic concern. In 1902, on the suggestion of Sir Edmund Walker, who guided the foundation of the Art Museum of Toronto (now the Art Gallery of Ontario), Mrs Goldwin Smith ensured the preservation of the house by providing that, after Goldwin Smith's death, the house and remaining grounds would be deeded to the Gallery. She died in 1909, her husband in 1910, and the property was formally transferred in 1911. Until 1918, when the first part of Darling & Pearson's new buildings for the Gallery was opened, The Grange was used as exhibition space. Thereafter it was used for offices and teaching rooms. The Classicism of the first gallery buildings was generally sympathetic to The Grange; and the first building of the Ontario College of Art, erected next door in 1926 to designs by G.A. Reid, was even more sympathetic. In 1967, when plans were made to expand the Gallery (designs by the Parkin Partnership, completed in stages in 1974 and 1977), the early schemes called for wings to extend south on either side of The Grange, which would have held it in a pincer-like grip. However, the original deed of gift, which designated as public park the land south of a line drawn in front of the house façade, reigned. Unfortunately the scale, massing, materials, and colour of the new building are unsympathetic to the house. But one can be thankful that the enthusiasm for Canadian history that flowered in 1967 led to a lovingly executed restoration of The Grange.

5. *The Bank of Upper Canada, c. 1872,*
shortly after the wing to the right was added for De La Salle College

6. *The Bank of Upper Canada and restored adjacent buildings. The Fourth Post Office is on the far right.*

THE BANK OF UPPER CANADA

252 Adelaide Street East at George Street (NE)

1825–7 by Dr William Warren Baldwin; portico added 1843–4 by John G. Howard; additions in
1850–1 by F.W. Cumberland and Thomas Ridout, in 1871 and 1876 by Henry Langley; restored 1980–2

One of the key elements in the creation of important architecture is patronage. Simply paying for a building does not amount to patronage. It requires active participation in the design process that determines the character of the building, its significant details and materials, and often its interior fittings. When the Bank of Upper Canada was built, William Warren Baldwin was not only a director involved in the planning for the new building and thus one of its patrons; he extended his influence to the drawing board and, working with the builders, became its designer.* The self-confident quality of his building makes it a fitting introduction to bank architecture, which holds a central position in the history of Canadian architecture and architectural patronage.

In the eighteenth and early nineteenth centuries a gentle-man's interest in, and knowledge of, architecture was taken for granted. In many cases landowners, prosperous farmers, professional men, and clerics made up for the dearth of professional architects in the period by stepping in to design houses and farm buildings for themselves and their friends, as well as occasional churches and such public buildings as courthouses. Using one of the many large and small architectural pattern books published during the period as sources for the basic patterns, decorative motifs, and other details, they relied on skilled local craftsmen for execution. This approach was well established in Britain, where the results in numerous houses and small public buildings are virtually indistinguishable from the work of more highly trained professional architects of the period.

---

*Recent research has confirmed the importance to the amateur architect of the builders and local craftsmen who could carry out his ideas. The contractors for the Bank were Hall, Kennedy & Co. It has been suggested that Francis Hall—who had worked in England with Thomas Telford, the leading engineer of bridges and canals—designed it; but there is no firm evidence that would cause us to reject the explicit statement in 1850 that Baldwin was the designer.

7. *Portico, added by John Howard*

The tradition of the amateur architect was introduced in Canada by the gentlemen soldiers and officials who were stationed or lived in the colonies. In the Town of York John Strachan of 'The Palace', D'Arcy Boulton Jr of The Grange, and other members of the Establishment were all interested in architecture. However, the work of the amateur architect is very hard to trace in Toronto except in the work of Dr William Warren Baldwin (1775–1844). Born in Ireland into the minor landed gentry and educated in Edinburgh as a doctor, he practised both medicine and law in Upper Canada. By his marriage to Peter Russell's niece he eventually became one of the largest landowners in York. He designed two houses for his country estate at 'Spadina' and the Courthouse and Jail of 1823–4 on King Street East. Of the buildings he designed only the Bank of Upper Canada, the oldest bank building in Canada, still stands.

Most of the leaders of the Family Compact were associated with the Bank of Upper Canada: John Strachan, as the leader of the group that first sought the charter; William Allan, as its first president (until 1835); and as directors, D'Arcy Boulton Jr, Henry John Boulton, and Dr Baldwin. For eleven years the Bank held a monopoly in Upper Canada, issuing paper currency, handling the credit accounts that allowed merchants in York to prosper, and mortgaging the lands that represented the wealth of the Family Compact. If its relations with government were at times rather too intimate, they nevertheless gave the corporation a semi-public dignity, which its directors strove to express in the Bank's architecture. Its first office, at the southeast corner of King and Frederick Streets, had little distinction. The Bank's new building, on semi-residential Duke Street (next to the gardens of Chief Justice Sir William Campbell's house), was implicitly different from normal commercial architecture: inspired by the free-standing townhouses and villas of fashionable Regency England, it was elegant, gentlemanly, and residential. (Most banks in Britain were family companies and many pre-1850 banking 'houses' were established in large former houses, where office functions fitted easily into former living-rooms.) Solid and block-like in outline and mass, the building was approached by a high flight of stone steps (possibly the present ones) and sheltered by a porch or portico. The main entrance is double-doored, over-arched with a semi-circular fanlight and flanked by two narrow hall windows (all of which, for security reasons, could be covered by heavy pine inner doors that still survive.) The handsome door, and the porch—which allowed the building to step confidently out into the streetscape—were the strongest parts of the design. A cornice and a parapet above it concealed the roof and its dormers with short rows of balusters set over each of the windows. The parapet was later removed, probably because it interfered with drainage from the roof. Gone too are shutters—to be closed during storms, summer heat, and winter cold—that hung on either side of each window and softened the rather dour quality of the greystone walls.

In January 1843 (when Baldwin was suffering his last illness) John Howard began work on the present stone portico of paired Roman Doric columns, matched with pilasters flanking the door. He completed it in 1846 with a fine wrought-iron railing above the cornice in the fashionable Greek Revival style. It seems likely that Howard's portico* repeated at least the outline of one that had earlier been conceived by Baldwin because its overall form, its place in the design, and the straightforward pattern-book detailing of the Doric order are very similar to such features of the portico that Baldwin provided for his house on Front Street in 1835. However, whether conceived by Baldwin or Howard, the portico is emphatic in its effect: it gives banking and the Bank itself a semi-public and non-commercial status. The whole building is a triumph of patronage as a formative influence in Toronto architecture.

In 1850–1 Frederick Cumberland (an architect who was as much a part of the Establishment as Baldwin), with his first partner Thomas Ridout, added a three-storey brick wing facing George Street, to provide offices and a residence for the Cashier of the Bank, T.G. Ridout (Dr Baldwin's nephew by marriage and the father of Cumberland's partner). In 1861 the Bank of Upper Canada moved most of its operations to a new office at Yonge and Colborne Streets to be closer to the city's financial district; but in 1866 the company collapsed because of ill-advised mortgages on unsaleable land. The Duke Street building was purchased by the Christian Brothers in 1870 to be used as De La Salle College, for which Henry Langley in 1871 added a large mansarded wing to the east, followed in 1876 by the addition to Baldwin's building of a mansard roof, which changed its precise cubic character. Langley, also in 1876, linked the College to the Fourth Post Office. In later years the building was owned by the United Co-operatives of Ontario and they added (c. 1940–1) a small block to the north end of Cumberland's wing. (Much was made of the fact that the United Farmers of Ontario, a radical political party, was sheltered in a former bastion of the Establishment.) The casual neglect and deterioration of the building during the late 1960s and 1970s—when it was used as an egg-grading station—came to a climax in a fire on 30 June 1978. Seemingly destined for demolition—although it had been designated under the Ontario Heritage Act in 1975 and declared a National Historic Site in 1979—it was finally rescued and largely rebuilt (1980–1) under the aegis of Sheldon Godfrey—a property developer in the best sense. This transformation is probably the best example in Toronto both of what determined restoration can do, and of the problems it faces. Today the Bank is leased for offices, Henry Langley's addition provides classroom space for George Brown College, and Toronto's Fourth Post Office is now not only a museum but a post office once again.

---

*The portico was clearly thought to be so effective as a symbol of banking that Howard repeated it, with little change, to ornament the entrance of his 1845 building for the Bank of British North America at Yonge and Wellington (demolished; replaced by the building in Plate 42).

8

CAMPBELL HOUSE

160 Queen Street West at University Avenue (NW)
(Originally at Duke and Frederick Streets; moved 1974)
1822

The symbolic quality of Late Georgian architecture in the Town of York is also evident in the house of Sir William Campbell (1758–1834), which was built a few years after The Grange (Plate 4). Though smaller than The Grange and not far from the centre of town on a large urban lot, its stately pedimented symmetry declared its owner's position in government and society. Campbell was a lawyer, born in Caithness, Scotland, who fought in the American Revolutionary War and settled first in Nova Scotia. He moved to York and in 1811 became judge of the Court of King's Bench. The position brought with it a comfortable salary, as well as a social position equal to that of more established families, like the Boultons and the Robinsons.

Campbell's building plans were undoubtedly delayed by the War of 1812. When the house was finished in 1822 his family was grown and it had to accommodate only himself and his wife—and their entertainments, which must have increased in scale and frequency while he served as chief justice between 1825 and 1829. Campbell chose as its site the north side of Duke Street, which lay just outside the original plan of the town and had a quiet residential character. He purchased considerable land and placed the house at the top of Frederick Street. The view south to the lake was obviously important to him. So too was the way in which the Town of York saw his house: its pediment was clearly visible from King and Front Streets, a symbol of Campbell's position and of the majesty of the legal system he represented. When, in 1825, the Bank of Upper Canada purchased from Campbell the lot at the corner of Duke and George Streets as the site for its new bank (Plate 6), they built with a similar eye to effect—and Campbell received the ideal neighbour.

When the Campbell House was built the red-brick pedimented image that had defined The Grange remained basic for important houses in York. But the later date of the Campbell House is clearly evident in the proportions and form. The symmetrical façade is narrower, the five windows across the front taller and closer together, giving it a greater verticality. Details, such as the elliptical window in the pediment, are more elongated and elegant, and—like the main door, with its side lights and semi-elliptical transom—more elaborate in design. Even the decorative mouldings and the glazing bars in the windows are thinner, and more sharply linear.

These new refinements and variations of detail developed from older forms under the influence of the American Federal style.* The result was an up-to-date house that still satisfied the need for a traditional image.

Duke Street prospered as a comfortable residential street until the middle of the century, when the expansion of the city offered newer, more fashionable places to live. Campbell's gardens were taken over by industry, but the several later owners of the house—including an elevator company and a manufacturer of horseshoe nails—respected its character. Its interior was gutted; but the façade, and the Greek Revival Doric porch (added in the 1850s), remained unchanged. Even a 1902 addition for the Fensom Elevator Company was designed (by J.W. Siddall) in the Georgian style.

In the 1960s, when Duke Street was unfortunately renamed to make it a convenient part of Adelaide Street East, Toronto began to discover its history and its architectural heritage. Both the Campbell House and the Bank of Upper Canada became symbols of what the Town of York had once been, and the possible nucleus for a revitalization that would be sensitive to the city's layers of history. In 1971, just as many independent owners of shops on King Street and other properties in the area were renovating their buildings and the rebirth of the area seemed certain, the owners of the house decided that a parking lot on the site was an absolute necessity (along with the tax savings and redevelopment potential that are characteristic of an empty site in the heart of Toronto). The City of Toronto lacked the strength to force preservation of its fifth-oldest building where it had been meant to stand. Instead the Advocates Society, with admirable civic spirit, stepped in and moved the house, of some 300 tons, to the northwest corner of University Avenue, on the Queen Street property of Canada Life. The forced relocation of the Campbell House is a great pity: its present site falsifies both its history and the history of Toronto. And its subsequent restoration—with the main floor and basement a museum and the upper floor a lawyers' dining-room—arouses mixed feelings. But to have lost the house would have broken one more of the few links Toronto has to its early history.

---

*The columned front porch and curving staircase inside, added during the restoration of 1972, are complementary.

'DRUMSNAB', THE FRANCIS CAYLEY HOUSE

5 Drumsnab Road (E)

1834; second floor added 1856 by William Thomas

'Drumsnab' is one of the very few Regency villas to survive the growth of Toronto. Built in 1834, it was a testament to the love of nature that middle-class English settlers cultivated even under difficult pioneering conditions.

The founders of York brought with them a refined urban culture. Both the ten square blocks of the original Town of York and the small city that gradually developed from them, were re-creations of an English provincial capital. But the small porpertied class that was dominant in York loved the beauties of the natural landscape, and the country house; whether a villa or part of a full working farm, it denoted a cultured gentleman of position. Castle Frank—a rustic Roman 'temple', built of logs, perched above the Don River—was built as a summer retreat for Governor Simcoe and his family while they were still using a tent-house on the lakeshore during the winter.

The rooms in the first Late Georgian houses in York—like The Grange (Plate 4) or Strachan's 'Palace' on Front Street—were formal spaces that did not cummunicate easily with the surrounding gardens and landscape. But a little over a decade later, in the 1830s, house design began to change and plans became less formal, with rooms that opened wide to the gardens and landscape through bay windows and French doors. They were completed with balconies and broad verandas that blurred the distinction between inside and outside. This style, which was often accompanied by fanciful or exotic (often Oriental) details, is usually described as Regency, and echoed fashions established in England as early as the 1790s.

Relatively few sites in and around Toronto were sufficiently picturesque for a Regency house. Villas were built along Front Street west of Bay, to take advantage of the view across Toronto Bay. John Howard built Colborne Lodge (Plate 10) among the low hills at the mouth of the Humber River. The best sites were east of Yonge Street, where the Don River and several of its small tributaries had sliced deep ravines through the height of land marking the shore of the prehistoric lake that had once included Lake Ontario. It was in this area, south and east of the intersection of Parliament and Bloor Streets, that Simcoe had built 'Castle Frank' in 1796. In the same year a 200-acre farm lot north of Bloor Street East was granted to Captain George Playter, who built a small log house at the top of Parliament Street. The western part of the estate later became 'Rosedale', the home of William Botsford Jarvis—a simple, four-square house that John Howard transformed into a verandaed villa in 1835. The eastern 119 acres, including the Playter house, were sold in 1834 to Francis Cayley and renamed 'Drumsnab' (a Scottish word for a conical sugar-loaf, first applied to a hill in the Don Valley visible from the site). A new house with this name was built further east overlooking the Don Valley, a little to the north of the site of Castle Frank.

It is likely that Cayley designed Drumsnab himself. A classic example of a simple Regency villa, it was oriented to the south and dedicated to a view of the Don Valley landscape. It was originally one storey high with a low peaked roof, built with thick fieldstone walls that were covered with stucco for a smooth effect. A contemporary watercolour shows the house surrounded by a wide veranda very like the present one, onto which the various rooms of the main floor opened for panoramic views. As at The Grange, the kitchen and service rooms were located in the basement; on the main floor, with its twelve-foot ceilings, were both the reception rooms and bedrooms. The accommodation was not elaborate, but Cayley—an amateur artist with a Victorian taste for whimsy and drama—painted frescoes to decorate the wide central hall and the adjacent drawing-room, the latter with scenes from *Faust*. Cayley never married, and the house was essentially a bachelor's domain until 1850, when his brother John married Clara Boulton, daughter of Henry John Boulton of Holland House (Wellington Street West, demolished). In 1856 William Thomas was called in to enlarge the house for John Cayley. He added a full second storey and attic in stuccoed brick, with restrained Italianate frames around the new windows. Except for the addition of a massive oak staircase at the north end of the hall, the ground floor was left unchanged with the original arrangement of veranda and French doors. The second floor included a new drawing-room with French doors giving access to a balcony over the veranda, and three new bedrooms. During the next twenty years the Cayleys made other additions to the house, including a bathroom with hot-and-cold running water on the second floor, and terraced gardens and orchards.

John Cayley inherited the house on his brother's death in 1874, but in 1877 he decided to sell it. By then almost eighty acres of the original Drumsnab estate had been subdivided to create what is now east Rosedale. Eight acres remained around the house (including several outbuildings), with a further twenty-six acres in the valley. The house was purchased by Maunsell B. Jackson and remained with his descendants until 1965, when it was sold again to M.F. (Bud) Feheley, who with the assistance of Eric Arthur restored it as a showcase for a fine collection of Canadian furniture and Inuit art. While the Jacksons owned the house most of the remaining gardens were subdivided. The construction of the Prince Edward viaduct between 1915 and 1918, and of the Bloor Street approaches to the Don Valley Parkway in 1961, further altered the surroundings of the house. But with all these changes to both house and landscape, Drumsnab today—particularly with its stucco painted an airy pink—remains a perfect example of a Regency villa.

COLBORNE LODGE

Colborne Lodge Drive, High Park
1836–7 (and later) by John Howard

No Toronto architect contributed more to the re-creation of the world of Regency architecture than John Howard (1803–90). His training in England was primarily in the business of speculative housing; but before coming to Canada in 1832 he had carefully observed many of the most fashionable and up-to-date buildings in southern England. Once in York he mined this store of images to create buildings—public and religious, commercial and residential—that helped to satisfy the growing taste for architecture that combined historical style with invention. Howard was largely responsible for the popularity in and around Toronto of the Regency house, with its verandas, informal planning, and attractive placement within a landscape. The best, and the best-preserved, of these villas is Colborne Lodge, the country house Howard built for himself, at the southern edge of the estate he called High Park, overlooking Lake Ontario and the mouth of the Humber River.

Howard's career developed quickly in Upper Canada. Appointments as drawing master at Upper Canada College (in 1833) and as Surveyor to the new City of Toronto (in 1834) assured him a basic income, to which architectural commissions added considerably. As early as 1833 he began to consider buying a country estate and farm, which could be run by hired staff and provide a retreat from the city. But his ambition was not fulfilled until the spring of 1836, when he purchased for £324 the approximately 160 acres that form the core of present-day High Park, from James Cull, publisher of the *Albion of Upper Canada*. A long-term lease added another 47 acres.

The first designs for the house were made in 1836 and Howard proudly circulated a model among several friends, calling the project Howard's Folly. Work was completed in 1837 and the new house was named after Sir John Colborne, Lieutenant-Governor of Upper Canada from 1828 to 1836 and Howard's first patron. Howard and his wife moved in on 23 December, and thereafter Howard divided his time between a house in town and Colborne Lodge, sometimes making long, difficult winter trips daily in order to enjoy its seclusion.

The form of Colborne Lodge has much in common with that of 'Drumsnab' (Plate 9), particularly in the extensive use of verandas and French doors to open the house to the surrounding garden and view. But while Drumsnab is quite formal in its centre-hall plan, Colborne Lodge brought the visitor up the entrance drive from the lakeshore road to an apparently insignificant door on the west front and inside to a small square entrance hall. The plan was dominated by the living-room, with a three-sided south-facing bay window (common in Regency houses) that was so wide it almost encompassed the entire room. Outside, a veranda follows this three-sided bay on the south façade.* The interior is centred on a massive chimney, with three tall stacks rising above the roof. It was the functioning core of the house, serving the fireplaces of the livingroom, the kitchen behind (later to become the dining-room), and a small bedroom to the east. When first built, the house was one storey high, and the long slope of the roof and its beams must have made it look like a multi-sided tent. Later Howard added a new kitchen- and bathroom-wing to the north, with a bedroom on the second floor, and a master-bedroom in the attic-storey above the former kitchen. The new bedroom was a 'penthouse' above the main roof, backed against the main chimney (which was probably raised at this time); it became a tower-like centre for the composition.

Howard intended his land purchases to lead not only to the pleasures of country living, but to profit through development. As early as 1836 he considered dividing part of the estate into villa lots; but it was not until 1855, when he was planning his retirement, that he advertised the land for sale, having laid out lots of three to twenty-five acres connected by carriage drives—'with the view of forming a suburban retreat for professional and business men in the city'. Little came of the plan. In 1857 he advertised to sell High Park (which was now to be called 'Ontario Park') in 5-acre or larger lots, with restrictions on both the use and cost of the buildings to be erected there. This plan was also unsuccessful. Sixteen years later, in 1873, in the midst of a general agitation for parkland in Toronto, Howard offered High Park to the city as a western park, in return for an annual salary until his death.

Howard's wife died in 1877 and was buried in the private plot west of the house, her grave marked by a cairn of Howard's design and surrounded by discarded cast-iron fencing from London's St Paul's Cathedral. Howard was also buried there. After his death the city made several changes in the park and purchased land to bring it up to an area of approximately 400 acres. Colborne Lodge was left to moulder away until 1925, when the Women's Canadian Historical Society, with city funding, undertook its restoration. In the 1960s the restoration was improved and corrected by the Toronto Historical Board, which now administers Colborne Lodge as a furnished museum for the city.

---

*A visitor might assume that this plan is completed behind and that the house is octagonal, when in fact the back of the house is squared.

10

XIII. *King Street, looking west, 1844/5. The Market on the extreme left is on the site of the present St Lawrence Hall. St James' Church is in the background. Oil on canvas by John Gillespie.*

II

THE RISING CITY

1841–1867

In 1841 Toronto lost both its original reasons for existence. It ceased to be the capital of a province, which disappeared into the legislative union of the two Canadas; and its importance as a military post all but vanished: the post-rebellion era of undeclared border warfare against a variety of American 'liberators' ended in 1842 when Lord Ashburton and Daniel Webster negotiated what proved to be a lasting peace between the British Empire and the United States.

The colonial town of 1841 would have been recognizable to Simcoe or Russell. Though much filled in back to King Street and further north, it was still mainly a settlement strung out along the bay. The boundaries were marked on the west by the new military barracks near Fort York (which now houses the Toronto Historical Board in the Exhibition Grounds) and by the Gooderham and Worts flour mill and distillery near the mouth of the Don River. Along the waterfront between the two stood the simple Georgian homes of the original élite, and behind them the more commercial and institutional buildings of King Street. The two most extensive of these were the Legislative Buildings and Upper Canada College.

In 1841 it was not yet clear that the economic depression that had helped precipitate the 1837 armed uprising against the Family Compact was over. But hard times soon gave way to the first great burst of progress and prosperity the city had ever experienced. This boom, followed by an even greater one in the 1850s, brought radical and permanent change. By the 1860s Toronto's waterfront was a different world, with its complex of wharves, grain elevators, and warehouses, and the tracks and terminals of three railway lines. Further north were three- and four-storey factories and hotels and hospitals—even a crystal palace of glass and steel inspired by the one that housed London's great industrial exhibition of 1851.* Incoming ships' captains could see a dozen or more tall church spires silhouetted against the horizon.

For the underlying forces shaping this transformation one must look to the changing patterns of world and local trade, powerfully reinforced by the arrival of the railway age. But Toronto's original Establishment also played a significant role. Though the seat of the Governor-General and the meeting-place of the brief annual sessions of the legislature removed to Kingston (1841–4) and Montreal (1845–9), Toronto's leading citizens felt no need to follow: it took more than a single political fiat to kill strong roots or to overcome the power of social inertia. The law courts of Upper Canada remained where they were; so did aspects of the provincial administration. Toronto was also the location of the long-planned provincial university, which finally opened its doors in 1843.

One remarkable thing the Family Compact did during the generation after the Rebellion was to get a strong grip on local government. The first three mayors of Toronto had been well-known Reformers. But from 1837 on, the city council was dominated by Tories who chose one of themselves for mayor. John Powell—grandson of William Dummer Powell, an early Chief Justice—was mayor for three years. He had little to recommend him except that he was a hero of the Rebellion: while reconnoitering up Yonge Street he had shot and killed the rebel military leader Captain Anthony Anderson, after giving his word of honour to rebel ex-mayor Mackenzie, his captor, that he was unarmed. Two other mayors—lawyer Henry Sherwood, a former pupil of John Strachan, and William Henry Boulton, son of D'Arcy Boulton Jr of The Grange—each gave competent leadership in their respective three years in office. So did George Gurnett. He was elected mayor four times, even though he had started his career as a vitriolic journalist and fomentor of riots, and his attacks on the Establishment's enemies more than once embarrassed even his allies. Thanks in no small part

---

*The smaller version in Toronto was actually copied from a crystal palace in Dublin.

XIV. *View from Helliwell's wharf, looking towards the rear of the Second City Hall, 1849. Pencil drawing by F.H. Granger.*

to these last three mayors, Toronto in the 1840s acquired better roads, a big stone jail, a new City Hall (the building that now houses the City art gallery in the South St Lawrence Market), its first waterworks, and gas-lit streets. In the 1850s John Beverley Robinson Jr and William Allan's son each served a single term as mayor, in the tradition of *noblesse oblige*. But by then the mayoralty tended to go to a variety of railway promoters, merchants, and other businessmen who could obtain support from Tory power brokers and the Orange order.

The men who contributed most to the rapid growth of Toronto between 1841 and 1867—and chiefly benefited from it—were relative newcomers to the city. Unlike members of the Compact families during this period, whose income still chiefly derived from holding public office and from the sale of their lands, the new men were self-made merchants, builders, and industrialists. John Macdonald came out from Scotland as a boy and stayed on to clerk in a dry-goods shop when his father's regiment was called home. Instead of pursuing a call to enter the Methodist ministry, in 1849 he opened a little shop at Yonge & Richmond Streets, far from York's only, and expensive, shopping district on King Street East. With his flair for communicating the gospel, he produced clever advertising that lured customers in droves. He contributed his share to Toronto's new prosperity by acquiring a net-

XV. *The south front of 'Oaklands', c. 1895, as it was in John Macdonald's lifetime, before additions were carried out after 1900 for later owners. The main entrance is at the base of the tower. The house is now occupied by De La Salle College.*

work of European purchasing agents and building a grand wholesale department store on Wellington Street East whose façade suggested a Venetian palazzo. To crown his success he built 'Oaklands' (1860), which still stands at the top of the Avenue Road hill—a floridly Gothic mansion with gables and gingerbread, turrets and towers—and turned to philanthropy, giving financial support to Methodist churches, the Salvation Army, the General Hospital, Victoria University, and the causes of temperance and the Lord's Day observance.

Another leading citizen who began his career as a drygoods merchant was William McMaster, whose wealth enabled him to bequeath to Toronto a Baptist university.* In 1867, after the old Bank of Upper Canada had sunk in a sea of debt, he could afford to create the Canadian Bank of Commerce. His associates in this venture included Macdonald of 'Oaklands'; another mercantile family named Howland, whose offspring were to be prominent in public life from that day to this; and James Austin, new owner of Dr William Warren Baldwin's property and builder of the present 'Spadina' (northeast of Casa Loma on Spadina Road), who left McMaster's bank in 1869 to start up his own, the Dominion.

*Another McMaster legacy was a street, Rathnelly, named after his summer home in the area.

Toronto's biggest industrial complex of the period, Gooderham and Worts, spreading out from the windmill and distillery that had been planted near the Don in the 1830s, had already provided capital in 1856 for founding the Bank of Toronto. The Gooderham and Worts families were both pillars of Little Trinity, constructed in 1843 on King Street East just north of their business establishment (and now Toronto's oldest surviving church). Besides Gooderham and Worts, a whole range of manufacturers contributed to Toronto's mid-Victorian prosperity. William Christie began baking biscuits; Theodore Heintzman began manufacturing pianos; Hunter, Rose started publishing. Jacques and Hay eventually employed 400 hands in their saw-mills and furniture factory. The Hayes brothers' foundry built the first Toronto steamship to cross the Atlantic.

The many talented architects who began practising in Toronto around the mid-century built splendid homes for their bourgeois clientèle. As members of the same class themselves, they also lavished their talents on their own homes, while seeing to it that the city's various public institutions were provided with magnificent new structures. William Thomas, for example, whose house still stands on Church Street (Plate 18), designed St Michael's Cathedral nearby, and, after the great Toronto fire of 1849 destroyed the original town market, St Lawrence Hall (Plate 16). The fire gave F.W. Cumberland the opportunity to replace the charred ruins of the little Anglican parish church with the grandeur of the present St James' Cathedral (Plate 19). Cumberland—whose firm also built University College (Plate 24), the Mechanics' Institute (predecessor of the Toronto Public Libraries), Egerton Ryerson's Normal School, the Seventh Post Office (Plate 23) on Toronto Street (now housing the Argus Corporation), the central portion of Osgoode Hall (Plate 28), and his own magnificent house, 'Pendarvis', still standing on St George above College—was arguably the best of Toronto's early architects. He was certainly the most affluent, for thanks to his primary profession of engineering he was a full participant in Toronto's first feverish age of railway building.

Cumberland was outshone in this field only by the great Polish engineer Casimir Gzowski, who made his fortune in the construction of the Grand Trunk Railway, connecting Toronto with Montreal and with the upper-lakes port of Sarnia. Gzowksi, and his partner David Macpherson, built Toronto's first great rolling mills to supply themselves with tracks, spikes, bridge-work, and other necessities. (The railways called into being other businesses, such as the locomotive works owned by James Beaty, a newspaper publisher, and James Good's foundry at Queen and Yonge.) Gzowski's catholic tastes ranged from the furnishing of his magnificent mansion, 'The Hall',*

---

*Demolished 1904; now the site of Alexandra Park.

XVI. *Casimir Gzowski and his family at 'The Hall', about 1855*

designed by Cumberland, to a breathtaking variety of sporting, cultural, military, business, and professional activities in Toronto. He helped organize Canada's civil engineers, the Toronto Stock Exchange, the Toronto Philharmonic Society, the Toronto Rifle Association; as president of the Ontario Jockey Club he obtained from Her Majesty, whom he later served as honorary aide-de-camp, the Queen's Plate for Toronto. But Gzowski is best remembered as the man who covered the waterfront with railways at the beginning of Toronto's first railway age. By 1856 Toronto was connected by rail with Georgian Bay to the north, with Hamilton and hence New York City and Detroit to the west and south, and with Montreal to the east.

The railways did not make Toronto a metropolitan centre, but rather reinforced heavily a pattern already established by geography and canals and government regulation. The two great pathways through the barrier of

XVII. *The Great Western Railway Station (demolished), Yonge Street at The Esplanade (SE), 1870*

the Pre-Cambrian shield and the Appalachian Mountains to the interior of North America are the St Lawrence/Great Lakes System and the Hudson and Mohawk River Valleys. These pathways converge at the western end of Lake Ontario. Having already overwhelmed Hamilton in size and commercial power, Toronto and its merchants, assisted by the city's early status as a capital, could take full advantage of these two converging routes. Once the first canals were completed between 1825 and 1845, it was all the easier for Toronto to play off the route from New York City against the route from Montreal in order to get the best prices and transit charges for its imports and exports. The coming of imperial free trade in 1846 hurt Montreal's protected status in shipping Canadian staples to Britain. That same year the United States acted to help its eastern seaports by eliminating the levies on goods in transit to and from Canada. Both moves helped Toronto greatly in getting out from under the metropolitan shadow of Montreal. The Reciprocity Treaty, concluded with the United States in 1854, was a further step towards improving Toronto's position. Among the many new trading patterns brought by the railway age and free trade was the shipping of grain to the U.S. from the new farm belt of the American midwest through the upper lakes by rail via Collingwood and Toronto, and

XVIII. *Torchlight procession given in honour of George Brown by the citizens of Toronto, 1862*

thence across Lake Ontario to the American ports that fed into the Erie Canal and the Hudson. One lake captain who benefited from this traffic in the 1850s and 1860s became the patriarch of a prominent twentieth-century Toronto family named Jackman.

In spite of being interrupted by spells of economic depression, the trend of Toronto's commercial and industrial growth moved relentlessly upwards in the quarter-century before Confederation. The city's population, which in 1841 was 14,000, reached nearly 50,000 by 1867. Though formal political democracy had replaced government by a restricted élite, Toronto's newly acquired wealth accentuated the distance between rich and poor. In 1867 the largest single ethnic group, after the English, in Toronto's population—and the only major exception to its overwhelmingly Protestant and British character—were the Irish Catholics who had immigrated here mainly around 1850 as a result of the potato famine. About 10,000 in number, they contributed heavily to the nearly 3,000 household servants and the over 2,000 unskilled labourers who made up the city's two largest and lowest-paid occupational categories. Many could not secure even menial occupations and were destitute. While there was a certain sympathy and some minimal provision for the 'deserving poor', as they were called,—such as the Roman Catholic House of Providence on Power Street, one of Toronto's largest new buildings*—the city's business leaders tended to view the condition of the working classes, who put in a 12-hour working day, as something that could not, perhaps even should not, be altered.

The chief spokesman for this viewpoint, and a wealthy businessman in his own right, was George Brown, publisher of the *Globe*. He fiercely opposed the printers' unions of the 1870s and anything that interfered with the free play of the labour market. In other matters, too, Brown was the archetypical Toronto leader of the mid-Victorian period. He had arrived from Scotland via New York in 1843 at the age of twenty-six, and with his father began publishing a Presbyterian weekly, the *Banner*. The next year he founded the *Globe*, which eventually became a political daily, and in 1849 entered provincial politics as a Reformer. When the new network of railways enabled the *Globe* to be rushed to the farms and towns of Toronto's hinterland, George Brown became the most influential man in Canada West. Not only a powerful writer of editorials but also a great orator, he won the hearts and minds of the delegates who came into Toronto on these same railways to the first big 'Clear Grit' party conventions. As leader of the party he reshaped it, under the banner of Liberalism, to stand for the business interests of Toronto as well as the farmers of the province. Though the city itself was almost the only significant area of Canada West that he could not quite carry against the Conservatives, he did convert its Board of Trade to his own conviction that a new and greater Canada should open up and exploit the vast Hudson's Bay Company territory of the Northwest before American commercial interests moved in. He also gave voice to Protestant resentment at being yoked to the more conservative and smaller population of Catholic-dominated Canada East. He persuaded his readers and followers that a federation of all the British North American provinces was the answer to their various aspirations. The Confederation of 1867 could not have happened without his leadership. George Brown widened Toronto's horizons to the dimensions of the second-largest nation on earth. 1867 began a new chapter in the city's history.

---

*It was demolished in the 1950s to make way for the Richmond Street exit from the Don Valley Parkway.

11. *The Second City Hall*, c. 1872, *looking west to the intersection of Front and Wellington where the Coffin Block stands on the site later occupied by the Gooderham Building* (Plate 66)

THE SECOND CITY HALL

91 Front Street East at Jarvis Street (SW)

1844–5 by Henry Bowyer Lane; rebuilt 1850–1 by
William Thomas and renovated 1876 by
Stewart & Strickland

For the first ten years of its existence, after its incorporation in 1834, the City of Toronto had no proper City Hall. In a time of rebellion and strained economic conditions, City Council prudently curbed any architectural ambitions it may have had and was satisfied to occupy the second-floor assembly room of the Market Building (constructed in 1830–1) at Jarvis and King. There was no compelling incentive to build a new City Hall until 1843, the year that Kingston—which had been created capital of the United Canadas, over Toronto's objection, in 1841—opened a palatial City Hall of its own. A site was acquired on the south side of Front Street sloping down to the lakeshore, and City Council advertised a competition to design a new administrative home of which it could be proud.

Eight projects were submitted and the competition was won by Henry Bowyer Lane, a British-trained architect in his late twenties who had immigrated to Toronto in early 1842. Because his aunt had married into the Boulton family, Lane could count on sponsorship among Toronto's élite. But like most aspiring architects of his period, he entered competitions in order to publicize his talents and reach a wider circle of prospective clients. Most of the designs submitted were

43

12. *The South St Lawrence Market (originally the Second City Hall)*

Classical in style; but Lane hedged his stylistic bet on the taste of City Council by sending in both a medieval English design and a classic design in the Italian taste. In a decision characteristic of many nineteenth-century competitions, the Building Committee chose the medieval design, in the Elizabethan Gothic style, which had definite historic associations and was newly fashionable in Canada for houses and churches; but the entire City Council had in mind a rather more conservative image of City Hall and reversed the decision. They chose the Italian design, which Lane had estimated would cost an economical £7,000.

The new City Hall, completed in 1844–5 can best be described as Palladian, following the same basic eighteenth-century pattern as most Late Georgian public buildings in Canada, including the old Market Building. The central block had pediments facing north and south and a lower ornamented tower, with a clock-face on each side and topped by a diminutive domed cupola. Inside there were city offices on the first floor, a galleried council chamber on the second, and the main police station in the basement. Wings to either side along Front Street housed shops on the ground floor and offices

above. Behind there were two parallel rows of galleried shops on the east and west sides of a market court at the level of the waterfront, several feet below Front Street. Lane's budget permitted very little in the way of architectural grandeur. Stone was used prominently to face the ground floor of the centre block, to frame the upper-floor windows, and for a two-columned portico that sheltered the entrance to the Council Chamber and the City offices. But elsewhere in the building Lane worked with brick, exploiting the contrast of 'white' brick against red brick walls to approximate the effect of Classical pilasters, string courses, and cornice.

Within five years of its completion numerous structural faults were apparent in Lane's building; and in 1850–1 William Thomas was commissioned to redesign completely the shops along Front Street. There were more alterations in the early 1870s by Henry Langley and in 1876 by Stewart & Strickland. But in real terms Lane had provided exactly what City Council hoped for when the competition was organized in 1843: a very visible symbol on Front Street of Toronto's own sense of its continuing importance—particularly in relation to Kingston. To the many people entering

13. *The South St Lawrence Market: renovated interior, showing the windows of the Council Chamber of the Second City Hall (now the Market Gallery)*

the harbour by ship (roads were still little more than rough trails), the City Hall was a prominent landmark. (See Plate XIV.) With its pediment and clock tower (the clock providing a notable convenience before the advent of wrist-watches) and its three arched Council Chamber windows outlined in white brick against red brick walls, the City Hall rose above the streetscape as a readily identifiable symbol of city government, and of the enduring traditions of British urban culture transferred to North America.

In Late Victorian Toronto, however, with its taste for grandiose, picturesque buildings, the small size and unpretentious brick of Lane's City Hall satisfied none of the popular ideas about architecture; it was also too small for the needs of a fast-growing city. In 1886 Toronto began construction on the Third City Hall on Queen Street West (Plate 77). Since the old City Hall was in the centre of Toronto's wholesale produce district, the council decided in 1898 to rebuild it as a much larger market. Once again a competition was held. It was won by John Wilson Siddall with a design for a great market shed, whose iron and glass roof overarching the old

building was perfectly in keeping with the Baroque taste of Edwardian Toronto. When completed the shed extended all the way from the Esplanade to the rear of St Lawrence Hall (Plate 16), covering the width of Front Street. Finished in 1901, the project resulted in the demolition of the side wings of the Second City Hall, the pediments, the clock tower, and the stalls behind. But in one of those crazy romantic gestures that sometimes occur in Toronto architecture, the centre block and most of the Council Chamber were preserved and became the centre-piece of the new market façade. This was an early instance of architectural preservation in the City, in a period that usually made very little of the immediate past.

In the 1960s this bit of Early Victorian Toronto came into its own again when a new generation of Torontonians discovered the South St Lawrence Market, with its stalls of fresh food and produce. In 1975–7 the market, and the central block of the Second City Hall, were renovated. The old Council Chamber became the Market Gallery, home to the City's collection of art about Toronto, and to travelling exhibitions on art, architecture, and urban planning.

THE COMMERCIAL BANK OF THE MIDLAND DISTRICT

13–15 Wellington Street West (S)

1843–5 by William Thomas

Banking was, and remains, both an intensely political activity and a necessary element in the commercial growth of Toronto. From the beginning the importance of Toronto banks was expressed in their architectural form. For example, the 1825–7 Bank of Upper Canada on Adelaide Street East (Plate 6) was built splendidly in the tradition of a large English townhouse. After the political and economic turmoil of the late 1830s, Toronto experienced a measure of political stability and unparalleled population and economic growth. The union of Upper and Lower Canada was of particular importance because it permitted banks chartered in one province to do business with the other. As banks became more numerous and more prosperous, they expressed their new prominence in more imposing architecture.

The Commercial Bank of the Midland District was founded in 1832, in direct competition with the Bank of Upper Canada. As the name implies, it was directly involved with the importers, manufacturers, wholesalers, and retailers who were supplying the new farming settlements and towns in southern Ontario. In 1843 the Commercial Bank purchased a large site on the south side of Wellington, at the foot of Jordan Street. Visible from King Street, as well as from Yonge, the new bank would be at the heart of commerce in Toronto.

The commission was given to William Thomas. He had been trained in the eclectic and Classical traditions of Regency England, and his English career was quite successful until ill-advised ventures in speculative housing led him to Toronto in early 1843. Thomas designed a three-storey façade of grey Queenston stone (only the façade was of stone because of the expense), and to underline the Bank's importance he set the building back from the street behind a cast-iron fence with stone piers. Steps, originally lit by tall cast-iron gas lamps, lead up to the two doors from the sidewalk; and the façade is projected at each end to frame the doors. The west door leads to the main ground-floor counting room; the east up to the offices and manager's apartment on the second and third floors. The stone facing of the ground floor is cut with deep horizontal channels between each course. The contrast between the light on the surface of the wall and the deep shadow filling the channels cut in its stone facing was designed to give the building a visually strong base. For the two storeys above, Thomas designed a smooth, visually lighter wall ornamented by a pair of unfluted pilasters over each entrance, and by the frames of the windows. The central windows of the second floor are pedimented for extra ornamentation, and above the cornice Thomas raised a parapet bearing carved allegorical details and a globe of the world. In front of the second-floor windows elaborate cast-iron 'balcony' railings cast a filigree of shadow, contrasting with the rectilinear simplicity of the design.* The detail of the façade, particularly the frequent use of the palm-leaf motif, is in the 'modern Greek' style, inspired by Greek architecture of 500 to 250 BC.

Thomas and his colleagues used style to call up specific associations, as well as to separate their buildings from the eighteenth century, its traditions, and its generally Roman architecture. Because Greece was a 'recent' rediscovery for them, while Rome and its architecture were well known if not old-fashioned, the Greek forms seemed highly appropriate for the architecture of banks, warehouses, railway stations, and shops—the new monuments of nineteenth-century commerce.

Elsewhere in Toronto's banking district, which was developing along Wellington and Yonge Streets, stylistic eclecticism was equally apparent. John Howard, who in 1843 had submitted a design for the Commercial Bank, designated in 1845 a new head office for the Bank of British North America within sight of Thomas's building, on the northeast corner of Yonge and Wellington. It too could be classed as 'modern Greek', but Howard also borrowed details from the Bank of England as rebuilt by Sir John Soane to give his Toronto patrons added cachet. (High on the cornice of his building he placed a large sculpted cockle-shell flanked by rosettes, the symbol long associated with the Bank of England and its power.) Down Yonge, at the northwest corner of Front, Kivas Tully designed in 1845 a new building in a Renaissance Revival style for the Bank of Montreal. It was still Classical, but it recalled Florentine palaces associated with the Medici and others, who provided Italy with bankers as well as princes and popes. Next door to Thomas's Commercial Bank on Wellington, Cumberland & Storm designed in 1858 a Venetian Gothic office block for the Edinburgh Life Assurance Co. that also evoked Venetian palaces. In many commercial buildings the stylistic associations are obscure; and some companies simply opted for architectural splendour to display their wealth and position in the city—Charles Moore & Company, for example, whose warehouse of 1857 still stands at 5–7 Wellington West. (Its façade is appropriate for a firm that imported food, wine and liquor—a smorgasbord of mainly Classical detail.) Thanks to the wide choice of historical styles available for commercial and banking architecture in the nineteenth century, these buildings made distinctive and impressive additions to the streetscape. While the interest shown by businessmen and their architects in ornate architecture may

---

*In the late 1860s the façade was extended to the east and Thomas's design was continued.

14

have stemmed from preoccupation with creating a grandiose corporate image, their buildings were objects of admiration for citizen and visitor alike.

Fortunately Thomas's Commercial Bank has survived in the face of dramatic changes in style and architectural criteria. The accounting firm of Clarkson Gordon renovated—in fact, virtually rebuilt—the building behind its façade for its own office use. In the 1960s, when the Canadian Imperial Bank of Commerce planned the development of Commerce Court, the line of Jordan Street was maintained through the new complex to provide a continuing place in the streetscape of Toronto for Thomas's façade. In the mid-1980s the building's future is less secure: the same Bank of Commerce is using it as a bargaining piece in downtown land development.

THE CHURCH OF THE HOLY TRINITY

Trinity Square
1845–6 by Henry Bowyer Lane

Holy Trinity was the fourth Anglican church to be founded in Toronto, but the first to be created with a dominating sense of the church's mission to the poor and to the working classes of the city. In a period when churches of all denominations sold or 'rented' their pews* to support new construction and pay the incumbent's salary—banishing the poor to gallery seats far from the heart of the service—Holy Trinity put no restrictions on seating. Rich and poor alike were accorded an equal place.

The great expansion in the number of Anglican parishes in mid-century Toronto was made possible by patronage from the city's bureaucratic and growing commercial aristocracy: the Boultons gave land for St George the Martyr on John Street in the west end of the city; the Gooderhams supported Little Trinity on King Street East; and the Allans, Jarvises, and Cawthras, St Paul's on Bloor Street East. But the patronage of Holy Trinity was concerned not simply with buildings and facilities but with social purposes. The attitudes that guided the foundation of Holy Trinity had their origin in the English response to the drastic social change that accompanied the Industrial Revolution. To many of the newly prosperous members of the upper middle classes, the Church of England seemed increasingly detached from the needs of society, and especially from the needs of the burgeoning urban poor. As a result, many new parish churches were founded and supported by private patrons to restore the Church of England to its traditional role of protector and guardian of the less fortunate. It was in this spirit that Mrs Mary Lambert Swale of Settle in Yorkshire, daughter of a wealthy businessman and wife of a socially concerned cleric, left in her will of 1844 a bequest of £5,000 to Bishop Strachan for 'the erection of a Church in the diocese of Toronto to be called the Church of Holy Trinity; the seats of which were to be free and unappropriated forever.' The gift, which had a buying power of well over a million dollars in today's currency, provided for the building of the new church, the endowment of an income for the rector, and offerings in aid of the poor. With such munificent backing, Strachan was able to attract further support from Torontonians. Most important was the donation of a large property by the Hon. John Simcoe Macaulay. It had been the site of his father's estate and was in the heart of the working-class suburb called Macaulaytown that had developed just north and west of Queen and Yonge Streets.

Henry Bowyer Lane received the commission to design the new church because of the success of his work at St George's and at Little Trinity. Strachan had a general idea that the new building should be 'a substantial church of brick with a good stone foundation in the good old English style [the Gothic style of the fifteenth and sixteenth centuries, which he saw as emblematic of the glorious history and national virtues of Britain], and fitted up with neat benches, and without pews.' The Rev. Mr Swale, who administered his wife's will, was more exact in his wish for a Gothic church, calling for one 'in the form of a long cross and that the reading desk and pulpit should not be placed in front of the Communion Table so as to obstruct the view of it'. Lane's design followed the ideas of both men. The Tudor Gothic detailing of Holy Trinity is very like that found in his earlier work at St George's and Little Trinity: broad, flattened tudor arches for the windows and doors, decorated with stone mouldings, and drip moulds that appear to be applied to the smooth surface of the walls as extra detail rather than growing organically out of the wall.* It is without the high tower usual in parish churches of the period and stands in the centre of Trinity Square, created by Strachan from the gardens of the Macaulay house. (Such a placement was very unusual in Canada, where most churches are sited on street corners.) Money that might have been spent on a tower to announce the church above the city skyline went instead to provide a very large auditorium-like nave, with walls high enough to raise the church well above surrounding houses. Below the edge of the roof on all sides of the façade, painted plaques of carved Tudor roses, kings' heads, masonic symbols, and medallions ornament the main cornice. The main façade faces west with an over-scaled door flanked by two tall, thin stair turrets joined by a parapet of open-work Gothic arches. Above this door, and at the east end of the church above the main altar, are wide traceried windows. It was the main door and these windows that attracted the visitor approaching Trinity Square through the crowded streets of Macaulaytown—particularly when the door was wide open before service, or at night when the church was lit for evening service and the windows poured colour into the square through their stained glass.

From the 1840s on, High Church leaders emphasized the social program of the Anglican Church and at the same time worked to restore the rich texture and emotional impact of the liturgy and sacraments, and to provide appropriate settings for them. Eighteenth-century English churches, and those built later in Canada, usually gave central prominence to the pulpit—often concealing the altar in the process. By

---

*In eighteenth- and early nineteenth-century churches, pews were 'box pews' completely enclosed and entered through small doors. Pew 'renters' provided their own prayer books and cushions, and often foot-warmers for their comfort. Only St James' Cathedral retains its enclosed pews. The open pews found in most churches today were called 'benches'.

---

*The inspiration was Sir Charles Barry's cruciform church of 1826, St John's, Cloudsley Square, in the middle-class London suburb of Islington.

15. *West front, looking from the terraces of the Bell Canada Building*

contrast, Holy Trinity has a large undivided nave with a west gallery, north and south transepts, and a chancel at the east end, with the pulpit on one side and the reading desk on the other, allowing the raised altar to be clearly visible.

Bishop Strachan and Holy Trinity's first Rector, Dr Henry Scadding, were only moderate High Churchmen; but the congregation, and especially its middle-class members who supported the ministry to the poor, embraced the Anglo-Catholic movement wholeheartedly. Guided by William Stewart Darling (assistant to Scadding after 1853, and then second Rector after 1875), Holy Trinity was the first Anglican church in Canada to embrace the revival of Catholic ritual. The interior of the church as Lane completed it was bare and simple, but gradually it was redecorated as a setting for the liturgy.* As well as sponsoring the architectural elaboration of the church, Darling restored the important place of music in the Anglican service. For his choir of men and boys he introduced in 1857, for the first time in Canada, plainsong and Gregorian chant, and in 1868 he vested the choir in white surplices.

Each innovation, which critics thought smacked of Rome and Popery, caused a scandal in Protestant Toronto. When, on 3 June 1855, Darling led a chanting of the Creed, the *Globe* reported that half the congregation walked out. Over the next thirty years the *Globe* continued to report and editorialize with great relish on every controversy at Holy Trinity. Finally, in 1881, an anti-Darling faction in the congregation succeeded in driving the Rector out. Ill in health, Darling retreated to Europe and died in Italy five years later.

Even with a growing public-school system, many working-class children received their best chance for an education in Sunday School. In 1856–7 a Sunday School was built at Holy Trinity, in the angle between the chancel and the south transept. The design—provided free by William Hay, who was a member of the congregation—is very different from Lane's work, being both simpler and more striking, with high gables facing east and south flanking a low cloister-like porch of brick arches. In 1861 Hay provided designs for a rectory (occupied first by Darling, as he had a family, unlike Scadding). The L-shaped house has in its high gables and chimneys a medieval style that complements the school. In 1857 Hay had also designed a house for the first Rector, Henry Scadding, and five years later added a third floor and balcony, creating the tall, narrow effect of a London townhouse. From the balcony Scadding could enjoy a panoramic view over Toronto to the lake. The house has been restored and now contains the offices of the Inner City Angels, who are carrying on a part of the church's work by providing cultural programs for children.

In the 1980s few downtown churches remain as close to their roots and to the social reasons for their existence as Holy Trinity. Like most Toronto churches, it saw the expansion of the city gradually drain away much of its congregation—a change that accelerated for Holy Trinity as Macaulaytown disappeared with commercial redevelopment. After the turn of the century Trinity Square was systematically enveloped by high-rise T. Eaton Company warehouses. In the 1960s Eaton's planned a redevelopment that required the removal of the Old City Hall (Plate 77) and the church. Holy Trinity seemed doomed to disappear in the march of progress. But the parish refused to give up its building and its mission to the downtown area. After years of complex bargaining, the church was left intact at the heart of the Eaton Centre (Plate 158).

Holy Trinity was severely damaged by fire in 1977, but restoration is in 1986 almost complete. In particular the interior is being returned to its High Victorian character, but with such new elements as four richly symbolic and dramatic stained-glass windows, by Stephen Taylor, dominating the south wall. In the broader context of downtown Toronto the church, and the square and park around it, provide a refreshing historical counterpoint to the modernity and commercialism of the Eaton Centre. In 1985 the City completed a comprehensive replanning of Trinity Square, to designs by architect Ron Thom and landscape architect Stephen Morehouse. This creates a simple, yet elegantly varied, urban park on several levels around the church, linking it to Bay Street and solving many of the problems of scale and architectural detail caused by the building of the Eaton Centre.

*In 1858 James Henderson—a great admirer of Darling's work (though he worshipped at St Paul's, Bloor Street)—presented stained glass for the east window depicting the Four Evangelists; designed by William Hay, it was made by Ballantyne of Edinburgh. In 1867–8 the chancel was raised and extended into the nave to provide space for a choir, communion rail, and seats for the clergy. This work, designed by Gundry & Langley, included coloured decoration of the nave with stencilled patterns and a deep blue chancel ceiling sprinkled with gold stars. In 1883 the architect Frank Darling, son of the Rector, moved the organ into the new chancel, redesigning its case and adding a wooden reredos in the Gothic Style.

16

ST LAWRENCE HALL
151 King Street East at Jarvis (SW)
1849–50 by William Thomas

In the early nineteenth century balls and assemblies were as important in Toronto as they were in the setting of Jane Austen's novels—an essential part of middle- and upper-class life. Equally important, especially in a capital city, were the frequent political, religious, and educational public meetings that were both a form of entertainment and a part of the political life at the time. To provide accommodation for such activities the magistrate who served as York's municipal government chose a site on the southwest corner of King and Jarvis Streets—which since 1803 had been designated the Market Block—and in 1831 ordered construction of a Market

Building.* A handsome but simple Palladian design by James Cooper, it had a market courtyard and shops, and over the front entrance was an assembly hall that was also used as a council chamber until the Second City Hall (Plate 11), with adjoining market facilities facing the waterfront, was opened in 1845 on the south side of Front Street. By then the simple brick Market Building was not considered elegant enough for society entertainments, and a competition was organized

---

*The heavy debt this incurred was one reason for the incorporation of the city of Toronto three years later.

for the design of a new façade. It was won by William Thomas; but nothing more was done, probably because of cost.

The situation changed dramatically on 9 April 1849 when fire destroyed much of the King Street commercial area, including St James' Cathedral (see page 19). The City seized the chance to replace the Market Building (though its north block had been only slightly damaged) with a grander public building that would become a proper monument to the importance of Toronto and its dominion over the St Lawrence, as well as an appropriate centre for the city's social and public life. William Thomas received the commission, carried out his 1845 plan with only a few changes, and produced his masterpiece: a Palladian design for a grand and richly ornamented structure in white brick and honey-coloured stone that would not have been out of place in any of the great European capitals.* Its size and finish reshaped the streetscape of King Street, and its height overtopped the cupola of the new City Hall, making it the chief landmark of the city.

With its triple-arched entrance, the majestic Corinthian columns of its portico, its elegant classical windows, its mansard roof and dormers, and its domed cupola, St Lawrence Hall is grandly eclectic, bridging Toronto's Late Georgian heritage and the Victorian character that would define so much of its nineteenth-century architecture. Fifteen bays wide and three storeys high, the façade is arranged in two wings, on either side of a central block, with shops on the ground floor. Its wide central arch originally led back to the market arcade, with smaller arched entrances on either side, one of which led to a ballroom upstairs.** The centre of the façade is dominated by a four-column Corinthian portico whose pediment, enriched by the city's arms, stands against a high attic storey that shelters the coved ceiling of the ballroom. The attic storey supports a circular 'temple' whose twelve Corinthian columns in white-painted wood rise to a domed roof with clock faces. (The cupola originally contained the city's fire bells.) On either side of the portico unfluted pilasters, supported on the cornice of the shop-windows below, march across both wings between the windows and provide the classical regularity and handsome relief that establish the stately dominance of St Lawrence Hall in the streetscape. The Classical outlines of Thomas's design are richly decorated. Sometimes elaborate details were included almost for their own sake, as in the stone balustrade of the central portico, the delicate wrought-iron railing across the side wings, and especially in the panelled balustrade and the pinnacles that rise against the sky atop the attic storey. But in other places sculptural decorations embody local themes. Keystone heads over the main arches depicting the guardian deity of the St Lawrence, flanked by the deities of Niagara and Lake Ontario; garlands of Canadian fruits and flowers; and various allegorical insignia—all

proclaim civic and patriotic pride, a heritage of Nature's bounty, and high aspirations to culture, wealth, and power. In its full effect St Lawrence Hall is a superb amalgam of formal Classicism and Victorian embellishment.

On the second floor of the central block were City committee and reception rooms, and on the third floor were supper rooms and the grand ballroom—St Lawrence Hall itself—which boasted a highly decorated ceiling and a magnificent chandelier. According to *A Handbook of Toronto* (1858), 'It is admirably adapted for concerts, being easily filled by the voice, and having no echo to mar the performance, and is in fact the only place in the city for lectures and fashionable concerts.'

St Lawrence Hall was inaugurated in a whirl of activities. In January 1851 a regimental ball was led by His Excellency the Governor-General and Lady Elgin, with 500 guests. The wine flowed, the crystal glittered, and the band played until 5 a.m. On 1 April an anti-slavery lecture was given by the British M.P. George Thompson, and the next day the American abolitionist Frederick Douglass gave another lecture on slavery. Over the next twenty years there were soirées, balls, art exhibitions, political meetings, concerts, and theatrical events that drew just about everyone in the city at one time or another. Torontonians crowded in for performances by the celebrated divas Jenny Lind (1851) and Adelina Patti (1860); and for General Tom Thumb (1862) and Jem Mace (1871), the world boxing champion, whose demonstration of the manly art was followed by a concert. Fathers of Confederation D'Arcy McGee, John A. Macdonald, and George Brown all spoke in St Lawrence Hall, and the Canada First movement launched its campaign there for an expedition to avenge the execution of the Toronto Orangeman Thomas Scott by Louis Riel. After at least one political meeting, unruly crowds on King Street had the riot act read to them, and the troops were summoned.

By the mid-1870s more elaborate facilities to the north—the Grand Opera House of 1873–4 on Adelaide Street West (demolished) and Massey Hall of 1894 (Plate 70)—usurped St Lawrence Hall's most important uses, though many of its rooms continued to be occupied by meetings and other activities. In the 1890s it was disfigured by new shopfronts and obtrusive signs, and the rooms on the second and third floors were largely forgotten, though the market and shops continued to prosper. The building, however, was respected. When the north and south markets were rebuilt in 1899–1901 St Lawrence Hall was preserved, though it was more-or-less unused for the next half-century.

In 1952 the second floor became the home of the National Ballet of Canada, whose persistent desire to stay there became a major factor in the Hall's preservation—especially in 1960, when it was threatened by a project for an office building on the site. This proposal solidified public opinion in favour of preservation, and restoration was taken on by the City of Toronto as a centennial project. Work began on 16 August 1966. Surmounting grave financial difficulties, and the disas-

---

*Its specific inspiration came from Chatsworth, the country house in Derbyshire of the Duke of Devonshire.

**In the restoration of 1967 the central arch became the main entrance to the upper floor's ballroom.

17

trous collapse of the outside half of the east wing, construction companies, unions, architects, preservation groups, and historical societies—all under the leadership of Professor Eric Arthur, and City commissioners Harry Rogers and George Bell—worked on until the building rose from its state of dilapidation. Magnificently restored, St Lawrence Hall reopened on 28 December 1967 with a song recital in the ballroom by Elizabeth Benson Guy that recreated one given there by Jenny Lind in 1851.

The elaborate design of St Lawrence Hall marked the beginning of the Victorian age in Toronto architecture. Its restoration, in turn, marked the beginning of the renaissance of the 'Town of York' area of downtown Toronto, and stands as the most notable early success of preservation in the city. The building still fits elegantly into the larger streetscape. With Toronto's renewed interest in its past, and with the continuing use of St Lawrence Hall, the most active years of our original meeting-place and market are probably with us now—and will, one hopes, be prolonged far into the future.

OAKHAM HOUSE

322 Church Street at Gould (SW)

1848 by William Thomas for himself

Architects have always enjoyed building their own houses. From John Howard's Colborne Lodge (Plate 10) to Barton Myers' house on Berryman Street, such residences not only symbolize success but provide opportunities for working out favourite ideas or styles, with few controls but cost and with only the architect himself and his family to cater for. William Thomas arrived in Canada in 1843, fleeing the economic slump in England that had led to his bankruptcy in 1840, and bringing few assets other than his considerable knowledge of English architectural style. By 1848, the year he began 'Oakham House', he was firmly established as one of the leading architects in Canada. For himself, and his wife and eight children, he built a large house, with a drawing office attached, to succeed a rented house at 5 York Street (in a neighbourhood quickly becoming too commercial for comfort) and an office at 55 King Street East. The chosen site, on land purchased from the McGill Estate, was at the heart of Toronto's newly fashionable northern suburb. The house faced east onto Church Street, the office faced north onto Gould, and not far to the east was the recently opened Jarvis Street.

During his five years in Canada Thomas had demonstrated his skills in many styles, both classical and medieval, and had built houses and villas in all of them. For himself he built a large but relatively simple symmetrical house of white brick with stone trim in the wide-windowed Elizabethan style of the sixteenth century. Like most of the houses of the period in Toronto, it was planned as much for convenience as for effect, with spacious rooms opening into a central stairhall. (The interior has been almost totally changed over the years.) What gave the house distinction was its late-medieval style, which contains many Gothic elements. It was not a surprising choice, given the fact that the house was within sight of St Michael's Cathedral (on Bond Street), Thomas's most important commission to date, and was built with the fees from that commission. But the main features of the design— the sharp gables of the Church Street front with their open-work pinnacles and heraldic beasts, the pointed arch of the front porch with its colonnettes and carved heads of a king and queen, and the lively detail of the tracery and frames of the triple front windows—recalled the Elizabethan and early Gothic Revival architecture of Thomas's native Gloucestershire and Warwickshire. Thomas inscribed the name of the house above the front door, completing the design in a whimsical mood with carved figures of a unicorn and a dragon to top the front gables (they were removed in 1952).

Thomas lived at Oakham House until his death from diabetes on 26 December 1860. In August of the previous year, with many of his children already on their own, he had tried to take advantage of the government's return to Toronto by offering the house for rent; but with no success. After his death it was purchased by John McGee, an iron founder with a successful shop on Yonge Street. The McGee family sold the house in 1898 to the City, which in 1900 added a large wing to the west side and transformed it into the Working Boys' Home. The addition by D.B. Dick, though much larger than the original house and conspicuously taller, remained generally true to Thomas's style—except in its use of a liver-coloured brick. Until the 1970s the entire building was painted a creamy colour that concealed the difference. The paint has since been removed by methods that have damaged some of the original stonework. In 1958 the building was purchased to serve as the student union of the newly established Ryerson Polytechnical Institute. The latest restoration, executed by George Kneider Architects, added a glass-and-wood wing to the south and reorganized the interior. The new work has the angularity of the 'ski-chalet modern' style popular in the mid-1970s.

Although much of its stonework is badly weathered, the exterior of Oakham House retains much of the whimsy and nostalgic fancy that was characteristic of early Gothic Revival design.

18

ST JAMES' CATHEDRAL

106 King Street East at Church Street (NE)

1850–3 by Cumberland & Ridout; spire, porches and exterior details
1872–3 by Henry Langley, basically following Cumberland's designs.

While the fire of 9 April 1849 gave the City an opportunity to rebuild the Market on a far grander scale as St Lawrence Hall (Plate 16), the destruction at the same time of the Cathedral Church of St James, seat of the Anglican Bishop of Toronto, was a disaster for its congregation. The rebuilding of the church took much longer, was ultimately much more expensive than the building of St Lawrence Hall, and was complicated by controversy.

The site of St James', on the north side of King Street, was set aside by Peter Russell in his 1797 plan for the expansion of York, while he was laying out the Court House Square to the west and the Market Square on the south side of King. The first church, built of wood, was begun in 1803; it was opened in 1807 and was expanded in 1818. It was rebuilt in stone in 1830 and again, after a fire, in 1839 as an unpretentious Georgian church that was nevertheless one of the most important buildings in Toronto. Its wooden spire, which contained the city's public clock, dominated the mostly two- and three-storey buildings of the surrounding streets.

When rebuilding was discussed after the fire of 1849, there were those in the congregation who wanted a new church of a size and processional plan appropriate to a cathedral, and those who wanted a much less expensive parish church. There was also discussion about the propriety of re-orienting the church to move the main door from the south to a more proper west end* of a new building, and then leasing the King Street frontage of the churchyard for commercial building. Indeed, commercial leases were approved by both the Legislature and the Vestry. But in the first real involvement of the Toronto public in what now would be described as planning and aesthetic issues, there was vehement protest from Toronto's citizens. Finally on 1 July 1850 the Vestry reversed its position on the leases and then chose to locate the new church at the very centre of the six-acre churchyard, to ensure that none of the land would ever be alienated. The building committee decided to give it a north-south orientation.

Before all the controversies were settled, the Vestry advertised in June 1849 an open competition for designs for the new church. It was to be built in white brick with stone dressings, and it was to be Gothic. Ten years earlier the classical image of the eighteenth-century church had held unquestioned sway, but in the intervening decade the Church's idea of itself had become identified with the Gothic style. Eleven architects from the United States and Canada submitted designs, including Kivas Tully, William Thomas, and F.W. Cumber-

land of Toronto. Cumberland won the competition. On 21 December 1849—at the same Vestry meeting that decided the new church should be a cathedral and not a parish church—Cumberland was confirmed in the commission. On 1 January 1850 Cumberland formed a partnership with Thomas Ridout Jr (whose stepmother was Cumberland's sister-in-law), and shortly after he brought into the office William G. Storm, the son of a Toronto builder. Before the first stage of the new St James' was completed, Storm had replaced Ridout as Cumberland's full partner.

Cumberland was now asked to prepare a new design that would fit the foundations of the old church. The design was accepted, but the site was moved to the centre of the churchyard, despite Cumberland's efforts to accommodate the plans to the old foundation. However, no further changes were made and the first masonry was laid in early September 1850.

The basic design was traditional enough to satisfy the most conservative members of the congregation. It duplicated the wide nave, aisles, and south tower of the old building, allowing most of the pew holders the same place in the new building as they had had in the old. The single-towered form of the church, and the projected spire, were commonly associated with large or important English churches, whether Classical or Gothic, as well as with many medieval cathedrals.* Cumberland included a narthex and vestibule across the entrance front, transepts to the aisles (kept small and low-ceilinged because of cost), and a five-sided chancel as a setting for the altar. Simply framed and untraceried pointed lancet windows—in triplets against plain wall surfaces—characterize the Early English style of the twelfth century and call to mind Salisbury Cathedral, the best-loved and most easily recognized example in the nineteenth century of what an Anglican cathedral should be. The most decorative details of Cumberland's design—the polygonal chancel with its traceried windows, the pinnacles, the entrance porches, and the buttressed tower**—were derived from the fourteenth-century Decorated style, which was revived in the mid-nineteenth century because it was considered emblematic of the highest achievement of Gothic architecture.

Though the high cost of stone severely restricted its use for both structural and decorative detail, Cumberland used it in the piers of the nave arcade, where it gives the clustered shafts an obvious strength that enhances the solid sheltering

---

*Christian churches in Europe are traditionally sited to face east—towards Jerusalem.

*Cumberland's design was partly inspired by Richard Upjohn's Trinity Church (1840–6) at the west end of Wall Street in New York—the most lavish and best-publicized church in North America at the time.

**These features were not completed until the 1870s because of cost.

19. *St James' Cathedral from the northeast*

character of the interior. Stone was also used for the mouldings and the window tracery because it allowed a sensuous richness of pattern that was impossible in other materials. Most of the building was worked in brick, however, and Cumberland used it—especially in the buttresses—in broad geometrical forms.

The dimensions of the interior—especially the distance from the front steps into the nave—are not large. But Cumberland was able to dramatize the path a visitor followed towards the chancel by elaborate framing of the entrance, and by varying ceiling height in the vestibule and narthex. The heavily timbered wooden roof (originally dark coloured, now painted white) is the most striking feature of the nave; with its wide cornice, it gives the nave a dramatic sense of enclosed space. The moulded beams have medieval sources, but their massive thickness and obvious structural power are Victorian. The chancel Cumberland designed was larger than that of the old St James', and architecturally much more interesting because of its polygonal shape. Under its curved vaults the space seems to swirl—an effect that is matched by the painted decoration of entwined gilt foliage.

St James' was opened for services on 19 June 1853, complete in most of the essentials of Cumberland's design. In 1866 the tower was completed by Henry Langley to the base of the spire, to accommodate a peal of bells and a new city clock, and in 1872–3 were added the Ohio cutstone pinnacles and porches, and the spire itself in wood and copper. The Cathedral was then, briefly, one of the tallest buildings in the world, and of course a prominent Toronto landmark.

While the exterior was being completed, alterations were made to the interior of the church, notably in 1870 when the chancel was redecorated as a memorial to Bishop Strachan.

The most important new interior work, however, was carried out under the supervision of Frank Darling in 1888, when the galleries were removed from the side aisles, making the interior space more open, as Cumberland had intended. At the same time splendid organ cases were installed. Thoroughly Queen Anne in style, with jolly well-fed angels trumpeting the Glory of God, they bring a note of 'Sweetness and Light' into the severity of Cumberland's interior. The most interesting window, dedicated to the memory of the Hon. William Jarvis, is at the north end of the east aisle. It was made in the Tiffany Studios in New York and has an unusual depth of luminous colour. The modelling of drapery and background is done by layering the folded coloured glass; paint, used only for the detail of faces and hands, has an impressionistic quality.*

St James', like St Lawrence Hall, was one of the few nineteenth-century buildings in Toronto that were thought worthy of attention in the 1960s. The City gradually cleared out the commercial buildings to the east, as far as Jarvis Street, to create a park. The idea was not new. In 1849, when this portion of the block had been burnt over, it had been proposed for redesign as St James Square. The 1960s project was similar. Although the present St James Park has a bandshell, some sculpture, and a Victorian herb and flower garden, it still lacks clear definition and a lively relationship with its neighbourhood.

---

*Modern windows, installed between 1940 and 1970, include those in St George's Chapel by Peter Haworth, lunettes inside the front porch by Yvonne Williams and Stephen Taylor, and windows off the west aisle by Rosemary Kilbourn (then with Yvonne Williams' studio), depicting, among other things, the first St James' Church and the present Cathedral.

20. *Main entrance and porch*

21

THE YORK COUNTY COURTHOUSE

(Now THE ADELAIDE COURT THEATRES)
57 Adelaide Street East (S)
1851–3 by Cumberland & Ridout

In the 1850s the face of Toronto changed dramatically. The first new public buildings in this period—St Lawrence Hall (Plate 16) and St James' Cathedral (Plate 19)—were a direct response to the devastation caused by the fire of 1849. But the next ten years saw the erection of new buildings for government, for the University of Toronto, for charitable institutions, for suburban parishes, and for private clients. They changed the look of the city, giving it new landmarks and a more monumental sense of itself. Among the architects responsible for this change, who worked to express the character and role of each building they designed, as well as the taste of their clients, none was more important than Frederick William Cumberland, working first with Thomas Ridout and then with William G. Storm. The first of Cumberland's

buildings was the York County Courthouse, a Greek Revival monument to the traditions and tempered severity of the Law.

York's first courthouse was housed in one wing of the 1796 Legislative Buildings at the foot of Parliament Street. In 1797 Peter Russell, the administrator of Upper Canada, made a more suitable provision for the courts by setting aside a block on King Street East, between Toronto and Church Streets, as a site for a proper courthouse. But it was not until 1823–4 that a new courthouse with a matching jail, designed by John Ewart, was actually built. Both buildings were set back from King Street and defined between them a rather shapeless open space extending north to Adelaide, known as Courthouse Square, which was never properly developed or landscaped. By 1851 shops had been built across the King Street frontage of the Square, blocking Ewart's courthouse from view. When Cumberland's new courthouse was built, facing north across Adelaide, the Square was left as a small open space in the centre of the block.

Like many courthouse architects, Cumberland adopted the Greek Doric order, with its weighty proportions and aggressively plain surfaces, to express the court's unimpeachable authority. An applied portico, with four wide squared piers set against the façade, supports a heavy and unadorned cornice across the front of the building. The piers seem to crowd the windows and the main door, clipping off the ends of the pediment over the door and overlapping the Corinthian door jambs, as if such elegant details as the doorframe and its pediment were too frivolous for a courthouse.

To accommodate the Courts and the County Council in the same building, Cumberland designed a long building with a central block and two side wings linked by stairhalls. Visitors entered through a columned vestibule to find the council chamber directly in front on the main floor, with the principal county offices to the right and the court offices to the left. Stairs on each side of the vestibule led to the Assize Court in the centre block and, in the side wings, to the Recorder's Court and the Division Court. The third floor contained offices and opened into the court galleries; in the basement were holding cells, more offices, and an apartment for the caretaker. Along the south side, overlooking what remained of Courthouse Square, were offices for the County Council executive and, on the second floor, chambers for the Justices and their staff, reached by separate entrances from the Square and a graceful spiral staircase. Grey-gold Ohio stone was used for the central block, but Cumberland's budget did not extend to stone facing for the side wings. Accordingly he worked out strong forms in brick—broad flat surfaces and panels framing the windows—and reserved the expensive stone for window surrounds, sill courses, and the cornice. At the rear of the building, facing Courthouse Square, Cumberland left behind the power of Neo-Classicism for a surprising evocation of the Regency Georgian style used in houses thirty years earlier: a two-storey five-bay pedimented façade in plain brick that echoes the design of The Grange (Plate 4) and Campbell House (Plate 8), both of which had been

22

built for an earlier generation of Justices. The domestic style of this building was considered appropriate, in the terms of High Victorian architecture, to its use by the judges, who had nothing to fear from the law.

Cumberland's work here did not receive the popular acclaim given to St James' Cathedral, and his other public buildings. But most of the criticism was levied at the County Council for restricting the use of stone, and for placing so important a building on a site that allowed no distant view of it and condemned the façade to stand in gloomy shade for the greater part of the year. The Courthouse continued in use until 1898–9 and the completion of the Third City Hall (Plate 76), which contained far more spacious court facilities. In succeeding years York County, and then Metro Toronto, treated the building with slight regard. In 1903 the wings were unceremoniously severed from the centre, the west wing to be remodelled by F.H. Herbert as showroom and office space for the Con-

sumers' Gas Company. In the 1950s and 1960s the Courthouse was maligned as dark, dirty, and ugly—like many other buildings that Toronto had prized a century before.

In 1977–8, however, the centre block was renovated by Lett-Smith Architects, with generous government support, as the Adelaide Court Theatres and Restaurant. Much was altered to suit the new uses, but a good deal—particularly Cumberland's Doric exterior—still survives. Unfortunately Courthouse Square has been a publicly owned parking lot for many years, bordered by the parking garage that blights the length of King Street between Church and Toronto Streets. The valuable King Street frontage is obviously a prime development site, and what happens there will determine the future of Courthouse Square. The space could disappear entirely or—like Trinity Square (see page 50)—in the hands of a sensitive patron it could finally become the city square that Peter Russell intended.

23

THE SEVENTH POST OFFICE

(Now THE ARGUS CORPORATION)

10 Toronto Street (W)

1851–3 by Cumberland & Ridout, later Cumberland & Storm; altered 1874 by Henry Langley; renovated 1959

No government institution in the nineteenth century was more important than the post office. Any reading of diaries, correspondence, or newspapers from the period shows clearly the dependence of Canadians on the mails, for basic information as well as for personal and official business. Before April 1851 the mails were the direct responsibility of the Colonial Secretary and the Post Office Department in London, independent of both the colonial administrations in British North America and the elected provincial assemblies. Complaints about the service were many: postage was expensive and a constant drain on the local economy, particularly for the many newspapers that could be circulated only by mail; and local postmasters were appointed by a Deputy Postmaster General who, though resident in Quebec, reported only to London. Even though postal service was central to the life of Canada, the Post Office Department had absolutely no interest in architecture. It was left to the local postmaster to buy, rent or build—from the profits of postage and service charges—a suitable office where the mail could be sorted and held until delivery.*

The postal service was one of the many aspects of colonial government that Lord Durham was asked to investigate after the Rebellions of 1837–8 in Upper and Lower Canada. Changes took several years, but finally in April 1851 the legislature of the United Canadas (Canada East and Canada West) was given control. This was a period of general economic prosperity, and new post offices in Toronto and Montreal (1851–2), Hamilton (1853), and Kingston and Quebec City (1855) were among the many elaborate public buildings commissioned by the legislature to give physical presence to its political authority.

Frederick William Cumberland's design for the Seventh Post Office was in the Greek Revival style—which, according to enlightened architectural taste of the 1850s, gave the appearance of newness and 'modernity'. The front is defined by a two-storey portico of four Ionic columns set between plain corner piers supporting a bold cornice of wide sharp-edged mouldings (and, against the skyline, by a grouping of the Royal Arms). For this façade Cumberland reproduced without change the side portico of the Erectheum temple on the Acropolis in Athens, built in the late fifth century B.C. The elegant spareness of its linear detail symbolized for nineteenth-century architects the 'chaste' artistic and cultural glories of ancient Greece. The four Ionic columns set off the building by day, and the light from four monumental cast-iron lamps set it off by night.

Cumberland provided two entrances (one reserved for women) that opened into a stone-paved public hall. The west wall of this room was divided by two Doric columns containing mail boxes, and by three wickets for service. The rest of the wall was glazed with large sheets of plate glass, in polished brass frames, through which the rented post-office 'boxes' (pigeon-holes) could be seen. Behind this glass wall were the Postmaster's office and the sorting room, and upstairs were the offices of the Post Office Inspector and his assistants, reached by a stair from a door on the south side.

The Seventh Post Office marked the beginning of the architectural distinction of Toronto Street: over the next fifty years it was followed by neighbouring buildings that were among the finest in Victorian Toronto. Alterations were made by Henry Langley in 1874 to house the Department of Inland Revenue; he rearranged the interior and replaced the two front doors with one in the centre. In the late 1930s the building was taken over by the Bank of Canada. In 1959—when the Government of Canada knew virtually nothing about the fine buildings it owned and had no interest in them as monuments—demolition seemed inevitable, until it was purchased by the Argus Corporation for use as their head office.

The renovation of 10 Toronto Street was carried out at a time when fashion in both government and private architecture had led to the neglect of much of Victorian Toronto and, on Toronto Street itself, to the piecemeal destruction and replacement of many of its monuments by the most banal modern office buildings. Like the contemporary renovation of the Commercial Bank (Plate 14), the preservation of the Seventh Post Office building was a crucial act of patronage. It was a model for the active appreciation, and further preservation, of Toronto's Victorian architecture, both as monuments and as working buildings—to the benefit not only of private enterprise but of the city as a whole.

---

*Only York's second Postmaster, James S. Howard, tried to provide more than minimal accommodation for the post office. In 1833 he built a large double-entranced townhouse next to the Bank of Upper Canada (Plate 6) on Adelaide Street East, the ground floor of which housed the post office; during his tenure his family lived on the upper floors. When this house, known to historians as the Fourth Post Office, was acquired by De La Salle College and renovated after 1873, a mansard roof was added, the doors were bricked up, and the windows altered. After the façade was painted, the existence of the original building was in time completely forgotten. Its form was discovered in 1980–1 during the restoration of the Bank of Upper Canada, and the house was reconstructed by Sheldon Godfrey as an office building and a functioning post office and museum.

24

UNIVERSITY COLLEGE

King's College Circle, University of Toronto

1856–9 by Cumberland & Storm; restored 1890–1 by D.B. Dick

University College is not only the crowning glory of architecture in Toronto, it is perhaps the finest building in Canada. Romanesque in the manner of the twelfth century; High Victorian in style, material, craftsmanship, and picturesque composition—it is the best and most complex of the many buildings designed by Cumberland & Storm. Many other buildings in nineteenth- and twentieth-century Toronto approach it in excellence of design. But in very few does the use of a full range of European, English, and North American architectural precedents and the talents of designer, builder, and craftsman result in a building that is a work of architectural genius. In company with the Parliament Buildings in Ottawa (commissioned by the same government, finished seven years later, in 1865, and involving many of the same guiding patrons and craftsmen), it represents a synthesis of national purposes and internationally recognized architectural standards and taste. It was also a truly 'modern' building. Seeking to express the functions and purposes Victorians attributed to a university, while using historical sources in new and inventive ways, the architects created a building that was completely attuned to its own period and location.

University College is the oldest teaching college in the University of Toronto, which traces its history to the founding of King's College, Toronto, in 1827. King's was modelled on Oxford and Cambridge colleges, which at the time required that the teaching staff accept Anglicanism. The basic principle of linking religion with education bothered few in the colony, but the Government endowment of King's—alone among the several colleges in the colony—caused endless political wrangles. Finally in 1849 King's College was refounded as the University of Toronto, which was to have no troublesome religious affiliation. In 1853 an additional act of the legislature founded University College as the residential teaching college within the University, leaving the larger body to conduct examinations and grant degrees.

King's College began its career with the purchase of 168 acres of land as a University Park. The college building was to be located where the present Legislative Buildings now stand (Plate 67), and both University Avenue and College Street were laid out as grand entrance drives from Queen and Yonge Streets respectively. Several plans were produced for an appropriate building, but it was not until 1842 that work on a palatial Greek Revival complex, designed by Thomas Young, actually began. Only the east wing was completed, in 1845, when the building fund ran out. Even then, most of the College's facilities were located in temporary quarters in the Parliament Buildings on Front Street West (unused by the provincial government, which had moved to Montreal and then Quebec). When the government returned to Toronto in 1850 the refounded University of Toronto was forced to relocate in the Young building and a small brick building named Moss Hall, built in the same year. The neglect and indifference of the government that plagued these years reached a climax when the government expropriated the central 64 acres of the Park (the present site of the Legislative Buildings and Queen's Park) as well as the Young building, which became the University Lunatic Asylum. University College first opened in 1853 in the again-unused Parliament Buildings, but was once more forced to move in 1855 when the government returned to Toronto.

In the midst of this political chaos enrolment in the University was dropping dramatically. In 1852, by which time many of its Anglican students had transferred to Trinity College (founded in 1850 by John Strachan), there was only one graduate; in 1855 there were only four. Had a decision not been made to build a new home for the University and University College, both might have disappeared completely. But in February 1856 the Governor-General of British North America, Sir Edmund Head, acting by Order-in-Council, authorized the Senate of the University to construct a new building to house its teaching and administration, as well as the university residence. An expenditure of £75,000 from its endowment was authorized, to which the government added a special grant of £20,000 to establish a Library and Provincial Museum that would be open to the public. The Governor-General had the greatest influence over the form of the final Cumberland & Storm design—the influence of a patron working directly with his architects to incorporate his personal preferences and vision into the design. Edmund Head (1805–68) was the model Victorian civil servant. Descended from the titled country gentry and related through his wife to the upper levels of the aristocracy, he was both a respected classical scholar, who in his youth taught at Oxford, and a politician of conservative tastes, liberal intent, and philosophic turn of mind. His early work in the civil service had drawn him into large-scale public architecture, an interest that was coupled with a devotion to European painting. (He edited writings on Western European art by the German scholar F.T. Kugler. Among Head's other publications, the title of his short book *'Shall' and 'Will'; or Two Chapters on Future Auxiliary Verbs* (1856) reveals a pedantic side to his intellect.) Head was also deeply interested in university curriculum and reform. When he first came to Canada as Lt-Governor of New Brunswick, he was instrumental in reshaping the curriculum at King's College, Fredericton, to include the natural sciences, medicine, and the law as well as the more traditional classical subjects. His appointment as Governor-General in late 1854 brought him into an official association with the University of Toronto just when it was beginning to develop a similar modern curriculum. During the seven years of his tenure in Canada his interests ranged widely, but architecture was in the forefront and he was involved in choosing the designs of government buildings for Ottawa. He did not arrive in Toronto until late 1855, but he immediately interested himself in the University and its building work—partly

because of the immense budget: of all the buildings in Canada and the U.S. up till then, only the Capitol in Washington was larger and had cost more.

Cumberland & Storm received the commission to design University College in the spring of 1856; shortly afterwards Cumberland left on a tour of Ireland and England to examine other university buildings. The possible sources of inspiration were many. Cumberland's specific choice was the Oxford University Museum, designed by Deane & Woodward, which was already under construction and widely published. The museum was one of the quintessential monuments of High Victorian design, celebrating craftsmanship as well as the period's interest in patterns of colour and texture to make permanent decoration. Also, its design and construction involved John Ruskin, whose writings were the backbone of Victorian artistic theory. Even before its completion, the new building was undoubtedly known to Head. To him, as to many in Oxford, its scientific functions and modern facilities symbolized a new vision of an up-to-date university. For his first designs Cumberland borrowed the polychrome High Victorian Gothic Revival style of the Museum. Head—in one of the most celebrated exchanges between patron and architect recorded in Canada—accepted the plan but rejected the style, probably as being too 'churchy'. The discussion and the changes were recorded by John Langton in a letter to his brother in England.

> . . . Cumberland drew a first sketch of a Gothic building, but the Gov. would not hear of Gothic and recommended Italian, shewing us an example of the style, a palazzo at Sienna which, if he were not Gov. Gen. and had written a book on art, I should have called one of the ugliest buildings I ever saw. However after a week's absence the Gov. came back with a new idea, it was to be Byzantine; and between them they concocted a most hideous elevation . . . the Gov. was absent on a tour for several weeks during which we polished away almost all traces of Byzantium and got a hybrid with some features of Norman, of early English etc. with faint traces of Byzantium and the Italian palazzo, but altogether a not unsightly building and on his return His Excellency approved.

Instead of Gothic, Cumberland turned to the Romanesque Revival style of twelfth-century England and used it with an authenticity, in detail and overall effect, that had never before been seen in North America. The architect left no comments on his choice of style. Langton, though not certain that he liked it at first, compared it with a coalition government, describing it as a synthesis of several influences that could be seen as specifically Canadian:

> When our Government were taunted in the House for their want of policy and unnatural alliance of parties and they were asked whether they called themselves a conservative or a reform or a coalition Ministry, one of them replied that they call themselves the Government of Canada. So we, if asked,

25. *Main entrance*

26. *Gates and colonnettes flanking the main entrance*

may call it the Canadian style; and to an uncritical eye it is a very respectable and rather imposing structure.*

The many forms Cumberland used to enrich the exterior of University College—towers, long roofs, gables, and chimneys—are splendidly picturesque. Viewed from the east when it is silhouetted against the setting sun—across Queen's Park, from Bay or even Yonge Street—the building and its main tower are romantic and painterly in the tradition of English landscape art.** Every element, however, is used with a precise (almost Classical) intent. For example, the many towers mark the principal entrances to the building, and the variations in their mass, height, and form indicate the relative importance of these entrances, and of the interior spaces to which they lead.

The building was arranged around a quadrangle of about 200 square feet, left open on the north for future expansion. The principal front faces south, and at its centre the ceremonial main entrance is set off by a 100-foot high tower that is capped by an asymmetrical stair-turret.

At the east end of the façade an almost invisible entrance leads to the offices and classrooms that take up most of the ground floor in the south wing (and two floors in the east wing). Around the corner, on the east front, an octagonal stair-tower marks another door leading to classrooms and offices; the north end of the east wing was originally occupied by the university's Convocation Hall (rebuilt in 1890–1 as two floors of classrooms and offices), which had its own square entrance tower. The west wing was devoted to student and staff residences, and to the kitchen and dining-hall. On the quadrangle side an extended cloister porch, heavily beamed and columned in wood, shelters entrances to several staircases. On the south front a short stone-built 'cloister' and a tall, thin tower mark the entrance to both the west wing and the circular 'Chemistry School' (now the Croft Chapter House). Another tower rises above the entrance to the dining-hall (now the Junior Common room), beside which Cumberland raised the kitchen roof into a tall glazed monitor for ventilation. Anyone strolling round the Croft Chapter House, into what is now the quadrangle of the Sir Daniel Wilson Residence (1953, by Mathers & Haldenby), can see the west wing stepping down from the windows of the dining-hall to form a low cottage roof over the Dean's Residence. This is one of several purposeful variations that included richly carved round-arched windows for the Library and Museum and small dormers for the residence wing; changes in roof profile; and changes of material, from the golden-grey stone of the south front to the mix of wood and brick (with very little stone) on those parts of the residence wing the public was never expected to see.

Though Cumberland's basic design was indebted to the Oxford Museum, his use of Romanesque was much richer in effect and more elaborate. The carved ornament—outside in golden-grey stone and inside in stone and wood—is the great glory of the building. Colonnettes, arches, multi-patterned capitals, and a range of rounded, toothy, or zig-zag mouldings (such detailing seems to have come from the pens of William Storm and John Morris, the Clerk of the Works) are created with far more imagination than in previous English and North American works in the style, and with a more obvious intent to exploit the skills of the sculptors and carvers.* The decorative interest extends to virtually every exterior wall surface, in which golden-grey Ohio stone and dark-grey rock-faced Georgetown stone are juxtaposed.

The focus of the decorative detail is the main entrance. With roofed and panelled piers flanking the central gabled arch, it relates both to a Roman triumphal arch and to eleventh- and twelfth-century church portals. The thickness of the wall is cut back in six successively smaller arches, each set off by a different pattern of moulding; the three most elaborate arches are supported on colonnettes and the three lesser arches on piers. The depth and multiplication of the mouldings emphasize the wall's thickness and strength. All the mouldings and carved patterns have historical precedents, but they are massed and varied with a clear enjoyment in the forms, and in the effect of light and shadow across curved surfaces or caught by deep undercutting. The gable that frames the portal is carved with a 'fishnet' pattern of entwined cords. The details, which were carved in situ, display the superb craftsmanship that was lavished on them. One slip of the chisel in the undercutting of the patterns and whole blocks of stone would have had to be replaced. In counterpoint to the patterns of the carving, the wrought-iron gates in front cast shadows across the carved surface, and the sinuous lines of their hinges spread with a plant-like vitality across the heavy wooden doors.

The visitor enters the building through a low, rather dark vestibule and proceeds up three steps to a stairhall and through a richly carved arcade into the two-storey Atrium, which is evenly lighted by stained-glass windows. Out of this high space corridors run east and west and a side door leads out into the quadrangle. The stairs on each side of the hall are enclosed within plain brick walls; but light from the upper hall, and through an open arcade on the first landing that overlooks the corridor, attracts and directs the visitor. The Atrium itself is the unifying space in the plan, accommodating day-to-day traffic on the ground floor between the east and west halves of the College, while traffic on the second floor between the East Hall (formerly the Library) and West Hall (formerly the Museum) can be seen above. At each of the other entrances variations in level, ceiling height, and quality of light are worked into the design—delighting the eye

*Early Days in Upper Canada: Letters of John Langton (1926) edited by W.A. Langton, p. 292.

**About 1860 Sir Edmund Head painted an evocative watercolour of the College, looking west through the trees of Queen's Park, that is now in the University College collection.

*These were German craftsmen specially assembled for the work. When the College was completed many of them went on to Ottawa to work on the Parliament Buildings.

27. *Cloister on the west side of the quadrangle*

and confirming the sense of event proclaimed by the exterior. At the same time the interior has a monumental severity—a still, religious, almost ponderous seriousness. It is as if Cumberland had sought a timeless building that would evoke the past and yet assume a place in the unbroken continuum of cultural history to which the university was dedicated.

The arcade and upper wall separating the stairhall and the Atrium, and most of the decorative details, were executed in Caen stone, imported from the same French quarries that had supplied twelfth-century builders. The carvings fully exploit both the medieval tradition of naturalistic foliage patterns and human figures, and the Romanesque tradition of grotesque devils and monsters. Above the arcade the carv-

ing spreads across the entire wall surface up to the moulded parapet of the balcony, which is topped by a balustrade of branching wrought iron. The Atrium design includes a floor of English encaustic tiles in a complex geometric pattern of earthy reds, yellows, and browns, highlighted by black and a crystalline blue—all colours that were part of the basic clay, not a glaze that could be worn away. Much of the decorative effect throughout the building comes from the richly carved woodwork and ceilings in red pine. The wood was left unpainted, its natural red-gold colour being enhanced by stain. (In the restoration of the 1970s the wood was cleaned to expose its original red-gold tones.)

The completion of University College—which marks a

coming-of-age of architecture in Canada—inspired great public interest. As the various sections were finished the *Globe* published a series of long descriptions and assessments of the work, proferring criticism that was for the first time equal to the subject, and praising the building's naturalism, craftsmanship, and didactic use of historical allusions.

The landscaping in the orignal plans included a botanical garden on fifty acres north of the College (never actually developed), as well as the creation of what is now Queen's Park east of the College. Completed in 1859–60 and named in honour of Queen Victoria, the park was opened by Edward, Prince of Wales, in the summer of 1860. Its centrepiece was McCaul Pond,* in which the towers of the College were reflected. The plan for Queen's Park was the work of Edwin Taylor, an English nurseryman-designer who had trained with Sir Joseph Paxton and was influenced by Paxton's work at Birkenhead Park, near Liverpool. To provide the University with some continuing income from its land-holdings, Taylor laid out 51 large residential lots on the north side of College Street overlooking Queen's Park, which the University planned to rent out on long-term leases for the creation of an exclusive 'garden suburb' close to the heart of the city. As part of the development Cumberland built one faculty house, as well as his own house, 'Pendarvis', in 1859–60, at what is now 33 St George Street. For many years, under the name 'Baldwin House', it was headquarters for the history department; it is now the International Student Centre. The new suburb never rivalled either Rosedale or Jarvis Street as a fashionable area, and the lots were taken up very slowly. One of the finest houses, Sir Joseph Flavelle's 'Holwood' (Plate 89), was not built until 1901. Holwood and the other former residences on Queen's Park Crescent now house various university functions.

Over the last 130 years University College has been the centrepiece of the developing campus and the example to which later university architects reacted positively or negatively. Until 1890 the building survived with few changes. However, on the evening of 14 February 1890 a college servant named Pride, carrying a tray of lighted oil lamps to a meeting of the College Literary Society, slipped and fell. The resulting fire spread quickly, gutting the main tower and all the building to the east. Fortunately little of the stonework was damaged and the restoration carried through over the next two years by D.B. Dick largely followed the original plans in spirit and in many of the details. The University also commissioned Dick to design a separate Library on the east side of the Front campus; accordingly the University College Library was restored in a much simpler form. The Museum became West Hall, the College's principal assembly room; and in anticipation of a new Convocation Hall for the whole University the north end of the east wing was redesigned as two floors of classrooms and offices. Dick made no changes in the Atrium. The woodwork he designed—particularly the Gargoyle Staircase in the east wing, with its spectacular dragon newel post—continued the magnificent tradition of craft and detail that Cumberland & Storm had begun. In 1899 the College residence was closed and the west wing was converted to faculty offices.

The Laidlaw Library, designed by Mathers & Haldenby, was built in 1963, closing the north side of the quadrangle. The three-storey façade of pale limestone was an inspired modern addition to the established character of the College, with a ground-floor arcade to provide a Classical backdrop to the stage-like terrace that runs across the north side of the quad. The terrace continues around the west and south sides and a row of maples transforms the space into a leafy island of peace in the middle of the crowded campus. Finally in the 1970s a campaign led by the alumni of the College made possible the restoration of the interior of the building. Also, changes were made to the foyer and to East Hall (where a large balcony was installed). Some of the modernization compromised the effects that Cumberland & Storm had carefully designed; but the project did bring the services up to modern standards, particularly in the area of fire prevention.

Everywhere in University College the spirit of the designer and the skill of the craftsman speak to the visitor and the day-to-day user as they discover and savour the variety of detail and range of effect. The power to induce this experience is what makes a building live—for its original users as well as for generations thereafter—and is one of the essential keys to greatness in architecture.

---

*The pond was replaced in the 1890s by a bandstand, and then in 1969 by an equestrian statue of Edward VII, originally made for New Delhi and presented to the City of Toronto by Henry Jackman.

28

OSGOODE HALL

130 Queen Street West at University Avenue (NE)

East wing, 1831–2 by John Ewart; remodelled and the west wing built 1844–5 by Henry Bowyer Lane; the centre block rebuilt 1856–60 by Cumberland & Storm; with later additions by G.W. Storm (1880–90), Burke & Horwood (1896–9), Vaux & Bryan Chadwick (1927); restored and extended to the north 1972–3 by Page & Steele

Osgoode Hall is the home of the Law Society of Upper Canada, which was founded on 17 July 1797 in Niagara-on-the-Lake as the regulatory body for the legal profession in the province, as well as the teaching and examining body for prospective lawyers. The formation of the Society and its governors, the Benchers, was confirmed by the Legislature in 1797, and its powers were extended by later legislation. The Act of 1822 made it possible for the Society to own land, and in 1828 part of John Beverley Robinson's park lot was purchased as a site for a building large enough to contain the many functions of the Society.* The building was to be named

after William Osgoode, the first Chief Justice of Upper Canada. Planning began in 1829 when the Society retained as architect John Ewart, who was then working on buildings for Upper Canada College on King Street West, and for the Legislature on Front Street West. In 1823 Ewart had designed the York County Courthouse and Jail on King Street East, to which the first scheme for Osgoode was closely related. The design was for a U-shaped two-storey building facing Queen Street, with a centre block ornamented by a wide pediment on panelled pilasters. To either side, house-like blocks with separate entrances were connected to the centre by long wings.

*The site chosen was important in itself. In 1827 Robinson had sold the north half of his lot to King's College, the predecessor of the University of Toronto, to form part of University Park. A large building was planned where the present Ontario Legislative Buildings (Plate 67) now stand in Queen's Park. Only one wing of the scheme was completed, in 1842–5; but the College had purchased in 1827 a long strip of land running north to

the site from Lot Street (later Queen Street), which it laid out in 1829 as a formal carriage-drive entrance to its campus (later to become University Avenue). The location of Osgoode Hall, beside the gates to the drive, took advantage of the grand scale of the College's plans in order to underline its own public importance and its association with education.

By the time construction began in 1831 the project had been cut back to only one three-storey pavilion built of red brick.

To accommodate future expansion the new building was placed at the east side of the site, where it faced south down York Street for maximum visibility in the developing town. As completed in 1832, at a cost of just over £2,200, Ewart's building was similar to a large aristocratic house, with a centre-hall plan: a kitchen, service rooms, and students' dining-room in the basement; on the main floor the Benchers' dining-room on the west side, and a library and administration office across the hall; on the second floor the Convocation room, above the dining-room and offices; and more offices on the third floor. In 1833 the building was extended to the northwest with a three-storey wing of offices and student rooms. Designed by William Warren Baldwin, who intended that it should conform to Ewart's masterplan, it was awkwardly arranged, difficult to heat, and never really satisfactory.

In the aftermath of the Rebellion of 1837 the buildings were taken over by the government for use as a military barracks. The army did not vacate Osgoode Hall until 1843, and when the Society commissioned John Howard to make a survey of needed repairs, he found enough 'bruises', 'bayonet holes', and 'bugs' to make a major rebuilding necessary. In February 1844 the government reluctantly granted only £500 to pay for the repairs. But a supplementary agreement to lease space for the superior courts of Chancery and Queen's Bench made repairs and expansion possible. A Building Committee— which included Henry Bowyer Lane's patron, William Henry Boulton—was formed, and several architects were asked for proposals for repairs and additions. Apparently only Lane replied, sending two alternate plans. His design in the Palladian style was chosen in early August. Tenders were called at the end of the month and the work was finished in 1845.

Lane's additions to Osgoode Hall were his finest work. Retaining the basic materials of both the Ewart and Baldwin buildings and the layout proposed in Ewart's masterplan, Lane added to the front of the Ewart building a monumental portico of Ohio stone—inspired by the Palladian traditions of eighteenth-century English architecture—with two-storey fluted Ionic columns supporting a pediment, raised on an arcaded ground floor of channelled masonry. Across the front were fluted pilasters between the central windows, unfluted ones at the corners of the block, stone window-frames, and a full Ionic cornice and parapet extending around the block. The entire scheme was repeated in a new building attached to the west end of the Baldwin building that was designed to house the new superior courts.* Porticoes such as Lane

designed—raised high on arcaded 'basements'—were originally used as the dominant features of large country houses for the British landed aristocracy, and these associations with established power led them to be adapted for English court-houses; in Canada in the 1830s and 1840s they were instantly recognized symbols of the Law, and of the court-houses in which it was administered. Artistically, however, the renovations to the Baldwin building were less successful. Lane rebuilt the second and third floors of the interior to house a two-storey library, above which he raised an octagonal dome ringed by round-arched windows. Across the ground floor he constructed an arcade fronted with half-columns finished in stucco. Although this part of the design was awkward and unclassical, the domed building gave Osgoode a skyline that was identifiable from a distance, and the two porticoes supplied the air of public grandeur the Benchers desired.

By the mid-1850s the three courtrooms Lane had provided in the west wing were inadequate for the expanding needs of Toronto's superior courts. The growth of the Osgoode Hall Law School must also have taxed the facilities. In late 1856 the government granted £10,000 to defray the costs of expansion (the legislation for this was vehemently opposed by William Lyon Mackenzie), on the understanding that the Benchers would include significantly more courtroom space. This they did. Cumberland & Storm, who had just begun construction of University College (Plate 24), were awarded the commission.

To give the Law Society and Osgoode Hall a grander image, Cumberland & Storm proposed replacing the Baldwin wing with a new centre block. The accepted design, sent out for tender in May 1857, provided offices, storage space for records on the ground floor, and facilities for the Courts of Common Pleas and Queen's Bench, and a library on the second. The new centre block, which ultimately cost five times the original government grant, was officially opened on 6 February 1860 and was greeted with high praise.

> The legal fraternity are now magnificently lodged; in no other city upon the continent has such splendid provision been made for its accommodation. . . . It now remains for the gentlemen of the long robe themselves to give Osgoode Hall a more than architectural fame, to make it in fact the Westminster Hall of British North America; . . . to hasten the advent of the time when the traveller from other lands, the gray-haired British judge; the defender of constitutional rights; the world-renowned orator shall look upon Osgoode Hall lovingly and reverently as the place wherein a Bacon, a Brougham or a Curran won enduring fame. That time may come, and though the building may be dimmed by the dust of years, the associations which will then crowd around it will invest it with a grandeur mere architectural beauty, however glorious, cannot itself supply. (*The Globe*, 7 February 1860.)

The design of the central façade is closely related to Lane's Classical pattern for the side wings, but the architects enriched the details and elaborated the surfaces. The predomi-

*The Palladian symmetry of Lane's design required that the west wing be the same width as the east, but it was made half again as deep to accommodate the Chancery Court on the ground floor, with its associated offices, and the Court of Queen's Bench and a small practice court on the second. To match the stone, and to cover the unfashionable red colour of the brick walls, the block was painted a cream colour. The paint was later removed.

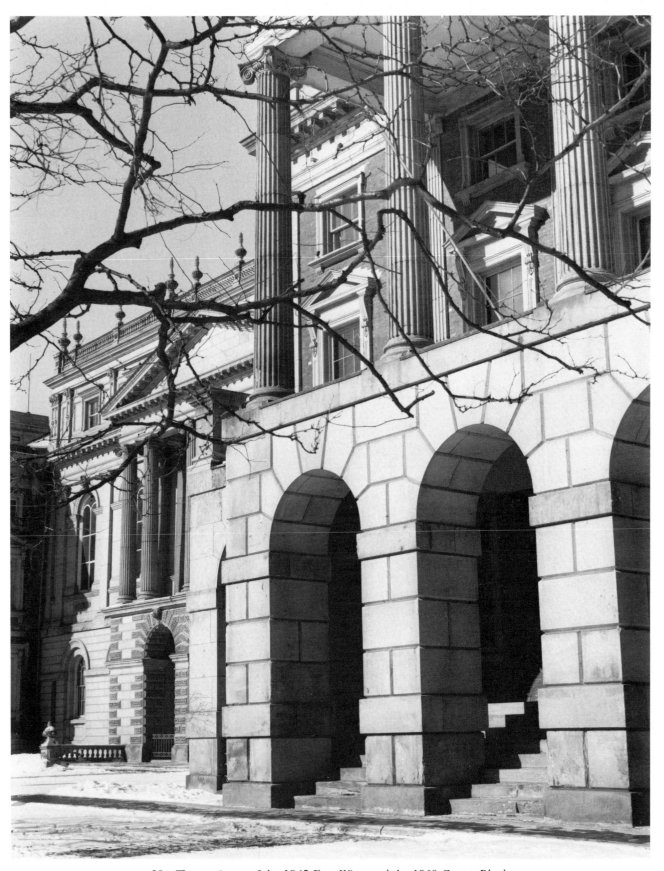

29. *The porticoes of the 1845 East Wing and the 1860 Centre Block*

30. *Second-floor hall surrounding the Atrium*

31. *The Library*

32. *Second-floor colonnade and the stained-glass ceiling of the Atrium*

nate horizontals of Lane's side wings—established by the top level of the arcades on which the porticoes stand, and by the extended cornice around the roof of the blocks—are continued across the new façade. But Cumberland made his second-storey façade (behind which is the library) as high as the second and third floors of the side wings, and above the level of the cornice he raised an attic storey to give the centre block primacy in the long, symmetrically arranged façade, and to announce the majestic scale of the new interior. Marking the principal entrance at the centre is a portico, visibly related to Lane's design in height and positioned over an arcaded base, but made wider, with six columns instead of four. A comparison of the two Lane porticoes and the new one clearly establishes the difference between Early Victorian and High Victorian taste as it developed between 1845 and 1860. Lane's

portico is straightforward, regularly spaced, and textbook-correct in detail. Cumberland turned to seventeenth-century French precedents and paired the outer columns of the portico, giving it a stronger outline and a more interesting shadow pattern against the wall of the façade. The stone surfaces are alive with detail, particularly in the lower arches and piers, where the edges are elaborately moulded and the flat surfaces are heavily vermiculated to catch light and hold shadows in constantly changing effects. The same sense of ornamented design extends to the wall surface of the block, which is entirely faced with Ohio stone. Whereas Lane's wall surface is a neutral plane on which his window- and door-frames float, much as if they were drawn on paper, the round-arched windows on the ground floor of the new building—which repeat the rhythmn of the arcades—are set deep within a wall faced in layered stone. At the second-storey level unfluted Ionic pilasters, spaced between the round-arched library windows, continue the pattern of the portico across the width of the façade. The attic storey is even more elaborate, with short panelled Corinthian pilasters and deeply moulded panels set between square windows in moulded and corniced frames. Across the attic, tying the composition together, is a balustrade inset with pedestals supporting covered urns, placed to repeat the spacing of the columns and pilasters of the second and third storeys.

Lane's work was inspired by eighteenth-century English country houses; Cumberland's was guided by the garden front of the Palace of Versailles. His details are richer, though in some places slackly related, but the result has the grandeur of the original, particularly when seen through the trees of the front garden. The change in inspiration is significant. In the 1840s architectural taste in Canada placed high value on fine materials, scenic effects, and fine workmanship; but in matters of style it was conservative and limited. Lane's work at Osgoode had been, despite its virtues, very old-fashioned. Cumberland drew on wide-ranging sources, particularly the current admiration for all things French—and he could expect many Torontonians to understand the references to Versailles and European architecture, and to appreciate the magnificence and dignity they conferred on the Law Society and Courts.

The Classical grandeur and meticulous detail of the exterior are reflected in the richly ornamented interior, though the plan is simple. A visitor enters under the main portico and proceeds through a columned vestibule into a narrow cross-hall leading to the east and west wings, then into the stairhall and the two-storey north hall, around which are court offices (and, on the north side, a practice court). Most visitors climb the stairs to an upper hall. On the south side is the Library and on the north the entrance to the upper arcades around the north hall, which lead to the Court of Queen's Bench on the west side and to the Court of Common Pleas on the east. The plan is spacious and convenient, but what makes it outstanding is its succession of spaces, dramatically varied in height, colour, and lighting, with virtually every wall space articulated in Classical forms—in such details as arches, pilasters, and cornice mouldings.

The main entrance leads from the bright light of the forecourt into a low, windowless vestibule. The cross-hall and stairhall are higher and more spacious, and the brighter light visible in the north hall beyond—coming through domed skylights of tinted glass over the stairs—clearly directs visitors towards their destinations. The north hall (described as an atrium at the time because of its skylight roof) provides the generous waiting-room area traditional in court buildings. Cumberland's atrium is grandly Venetian: lower-level arches on heavy panelled piers echo the portico arcades and support a balustraded arcade of paired Ionic columns on pedestals. The inner space is roughly a cube, enclosed by a deep cornice, over which rises the coved and beamed skylighted ceiling whose centre dome is glazed with patterns of lead and stained glass. The atrium was considered magnificent in 1860 (as, since its restoration in 1973, it is today):

> An open vestibule runs around it; the pure white Caen stone pillars supporting which, form a beautiful contrast to the deep though brilliant colours of the tesselated pavement beneath. This is made more striking by the light from the window roof directly above. We know not if in this arrangement the architects have purposely taken nature as their guide, but certainly the combination would suggest that idea. The dark floor below; the colourless stone around, and the blue and gold tinted windows above are all copies of what we see when the landscape looks most charming. It is astonishing what an amount of taste it is possible to throw into the most commonplace things when one is so gifted. The window of which we speak is almost a marvel in its way. The iron frame which supports the glass is wrought into an ornament, instead of being a blemish, and a light airy graceful character is given to the whole. (*The Globe*, 7 February 1860)

The atrium's grandeur is matched by complex vaulting over the stairs and by the panelled and heavily corniced ceilings of the courtrooms. But the climax of the design is the palatial Great Library—112 feet long by 40 feet wide, with a ceiling 40 feet high—which occupies the entire south front of the central block. It has the most elaborate plaster ceiling created in nineteenth-century Canada—beamed, coved, and domed over the centre of the room.* At the east and west ends are shallow coffered vaults supported on Corinthian columns that are raised high on pedestals to frame two levels of oak bookcases. There was probably never enough space here for all the Society's books, but in designing Osgoode Hall and its Library, Cumberland & Storm were expressing the Society's sense of its importance as much as providing functional space. The Great Library follows the tradition of Oxford and Cambridge libraries—like the Codrington at All Souls, Oxford—and of aristocratic libraries like the Duke of Marlborough's at Blenheim. It was, and is, a working space; but it could just as easily become a banquet room or ballroom if the occasion demanded. There is no grander room in Canada.

Over the next hundred years several additions were made to Osgoode to house the expanding Law School and the needs of Ontario's superior courts. Those along the west side—by Kivas Tully in 1883 and Burke & Horwood in 1896–9—are probably the best, for they respected the classicism that Lane and Cumberland had established, while also expressing the vigorous character of their respective Late Victorian and Edwardian periods. Fortunately through most of the twentieth century Osgoode was little touched by modernization, and the restorations of the early 1970s (which included the building of new courtrooms to the north) have maintained the grandeur that was first unveiled when the Cumberland & Storm central block was opened in 1860.

---

*This parallels the effect of the domed ceiling of the library that Lane built in 1844–5.

33

THE DON JAIL

Gerrard Street East (N)

1857–64 by William Thomas & Sons

Among the kinds of public buildings that evoked the most concern and rhetoric in the nineteenth century were prisons. Unlike the institutions patrons usually chose to support—mental asylums, hospitals, and orphanages—prisons were not obviously humanitarian. There was a strong belief that law-breakers should be punished; sentences and conditions were harsh by anyone's standards. But as the century progressed, the ideas that influenced both the management and design of prisons became less overtly brutal and more scientific. Offenders were segregated according to sex, often according to age and crime, and put in individual or double cells. New buildings were located in healthier districts; prison farms became common. Buildings were more carefully designed for supervision, and for ventilation and warmth. Architects tried to find new, scientifically correct ways to build efficient buildings, while at the same time exploring historical styles and detail for exterior forms that would convey both the punishment that motivated the administration of the law and the hoped-for penitence. This is particularly true of William Thomas's Don Jail, where the late Italian Renaissance details are massive, often overbearing, and occasionally deliberately ugly.

Toronto's previous jail had been built, to designs by John Howard, in 1840 on the south side of Front, between Berkeley and Parliament on land that had formerly been occupied by the legislative assembly. It was built of stone and brick and had a central block from which three cell-wings radiated. The plan type, called a panopticon, had been developed in the late eighteenth century to allow guards standing at the centre of the building to oversee activity in the cell-block wings. Howard's jail was designed to accommodate 40 prisoners. By 1855 the premises had deteriorated (probably from lack of maintenance) and were so overcrowded that grand juries complained of the conditions. In 1857 the jail population had risen to 180 and the Sheriff threatened to close it. In March of that year William Thomas was asked to prepare plans for a new building, basing his design on the most advanced English and American examples. Accordingly he, like Howard, used the panopticon plan. His model was Pentonville Prison in London (1841–2) by Sir Charles Barry, probably the most famous prison of the period. Like Barry, Thomas relied on architectural style to set the ominous atmosphere of the new building. There was to be a tall central administration building, behind which a central rotunda would give access to two front

78

34. *The main entrance*

wings and two radiating rear wings that together made an ideal panopticon plan. Council decided, in November 1857, to build the two rear wings first, at a cost of £30,000. But shortly after, Mayor William Henry Boulton instructed Thomas to prepare a new design that would include all the necessary accommodation in the administration block and front wings only. Thomas was given a £500 fee to do the new work.

The building history of the Don Jail was confused by the wrangles of Toronto politics. The first contractors, who were favoured by Boulton, proved incompetent. To protect themselves they tried to have the commission taken away from Thomas and given to a local firm of engineers, Lindsay & Milks. Thomas was eventually confirmed in his position, new contractors were engaged, and the cornerstone was finally laid on 29 October 1859 for a building consisting, as Boulton had wanted, of a central administration block and two side-wings. Thomas died of diabetes on 26 December 1860, but work continued in the hands of his sons. The building was almost complete in 1862 when a fire seriously damaged the interior, but it was finally occupied in January 1864. Throughout the jail project two things emerge clearly: the humanitarian ideals that motivated it, and the strong sense of architecture that defined the building's form and image. Behind the project was, in the words of a correspondent to the *Globe* in 1859, a desire to have 'the satisfaction of a prison suitable to accomplish the ends of justice and humanity instead of herding people together as so many animals.' The site chosen, on Gerrard Street East, on the city's Industrial Farm above the still sweet-running Don, was praised for its panoramic views, and throughout his work Thomas was frequently complimented for his design, and for adding to the beauty of the city.

In execution the simplicity of Thomas's panopticon design was compromised by placing a double row of cells back-to-back down the centre of each floor of the wings, with corridors running along the outside walls. The change made comprehensive supervision impossible. What remained intact was the architectural quality of the building that stressed both its public character and its function as a prison. The jail's central block, which houses administration and service spaces, rises four tall storeys from the crest of the hill on which the building stands. Its south façade is faced in pale golden stone and the side walls in 'white' brick of a matching colour, with stone trim. The smooth stone of the first two floors is framed in rusticated corner piers to form a base for the more ornate upper floors, where side piers, and a pediment supported on rusticated Doric columns and piers, give the jail an uncanny but symbolically appropriate resemblance to Osgoode Hall (Plate 28) and the air of a courthouse.

The vermiculated rustication of the columns and piers of the portico makes these major elements of the design—those that should be the most finished and refined—seem the roughest and least complete. The columns are 'bound' in straps of primitive rough stone—much as the inmates were confined by the stone walls. Such details were borrowed from Italian Mannerist architects of the late sixteenth century and are summed up on the front entrance, where rusticated columns are set against an arched door frame worked in fully vermiculated stones. The scale is intentionally huge to dwarf the incoming prisoner or visitor; and above the heavy wooden door the rusticated stones and the central keystone, with its bearded head that might personify Time, all seem on the verge of dropping down to close the door and seal it forever behind the condemned prisoner. In contrast to the centre, the side wings are drab white brick with repeated rows of tiny stone-framed windows, as if to embody the endless monotony of time for the imprisoned. Thomas's architectural program was psychological in its emphasis, and the adamant dislike and fear it has inspired over the last 100 years give proof of the power of manipulative architecture.

The original building has been much added to and is today mostly unused. But years of overcrowding (caused by the system, not by the building) have made the Don a byword for all that is bad in the penal system. John Howard's Asylum on Queen Street West (1844–50) evoked the same negative feelings, where the building became a symbol of the faults of the mental-health-care system and was demolished in a largely symbolic gesture of change in that system. Though the Don could be adapted to modern practices in penology, its days as a jail may be numbered. Several efforts have been made to find a new use for it. One proposal, that it be used as the new headquarters of the Toronto Humane Society, was rejected mostly because of the building's associations. The success of Thomas's symbolic 'representational' architecture (*architecture parlante*) may ultimately be its undoing. Unless public appreciation can be aroused for the stimulating art behind the forms, and for the creative strength of the architect, the Don will go the way of the Asylum, much to the detriment of Toronto's composite architectural character.

35. *The Austin Tomb, St James Cemetery*

THE CHURCH OF ST JAMES THE LESS AND ST JAMES CEMETERY

635 Parliament Street (E)

1857–61 by Cumberland & Storm;
cemetery laid out in 1842 by John G. Howard

Death was a constant companion in nineteenth-century Toronto. Fever, the complications of childbirth, and the vagaries of medical science and non-science all mocked the permanence of comfortable houses, monumental banks, and grand public buildings. The twentieth century can hide the terrors of death behind hospital walls, but the nineteenth century could not. Instead it sought to soothe the pain and sustain the memory of short lives with carefully orchestrated observances of sorrow in plaques, stained glass, and the design of cemeteries and their monuments.

Toronto's first cemeteries were the military burial grounds established by the colonial garrisons. Victoria Square, at the west end of Wellington Street, commemorates the principal burial ground laid out on the Ordnance Reserve. (Last used in 1862, it was here that John Graves Simcoe buried his infant third daughter, Katherine, in 1794.) There were at least two other military cemeteries, several plots connected with private houses outside the town, and a number of denominational cemeteries. But the first planned cemetery—and long the principal one—was included in the two-acre churchyard laid aside in 1797 by Peter Russell for St James' Church on King Street. By the 1820s, as the town advanced around St James' and the cemetery was being filled to capacity, William Lyon Mackenzie, among others, pressed for its closure and for the establishment of new cemeteries well beyond the town limits. (Such agitation for burial grounds hygienically removed from the centre of town was one aspect of the civic-improvement movements in early-nineteenth-century England and America.) In 1826 Mackenzie and his supporters were able to establish a new six-acre cemetery at the north-west corner of Yonge and Bloor Streets in Yorkville. Known somewhat misleadingly as Potter's Field Cemetery, it served as a non-denominational burial ground until the Necropolis on Winchester Street (Plate 43) was opened in 1856.

The Church of England was slow to react to the need for a new rural cemetery. But in the wake of cholera epidemics in the early 1830s—which the popular press blamed in part on the notoriously swampy condition of the crowded St James churchyard*—and the rapid expansion of the city's population, plans were begun for a new rural cemetery. J.G. Chewett's 1834 map of the city shows a cemetery laid out in a regular pattern on land north of Shuter Street and east of Parliament. However, the project was not carried out; and it was not until 1842 that John Howard was commissioned by the Parish of St James to create a park-like cemetery of the type that had become fashionable in England and the U.S. in the 1830s. The 65-acre property rises gently from Parliament Street and then falls away abruptly to the Rosedale ravine, with a view towards the site of Simcoe's 'Castle Frank'. Howard laid out a series of carriage drives—each originally named after a different saint—that followed the contours of the property, and sites for family plots were planned to take advantage of the rise and fall of the land. Over the next sixty years some of Toronto's most important families erected private mausoleums in the grounds. (The most interesting are the Austin Tomb, completed in 1865, a miniature Italianate house with a stone and cast-iron fence surrounding the plot; and the Gzowski Tomb of 1861, designed by Cumberland & Storm in the Egyptian Revival style associated in the nineteenth century with an assured afterlife, and set into the terrace overlooking the ravine to face the rising sun.) From the beginning it was assumed by cemetery designers and trustees that the carefully planted and groomed environment, even when scattered with tombs and monuments, would be enjoyed almost as a public park or botanical garden; and, unlike most churchyards in the period, arrangements were made from the beginning to admit the public on foot and in carriages at certain hours. Until the 1880s, when Toronto developed more conventional parks, St James Cemetery, and Toronto's other cemeteries, were favourite places for summer outings.

When Howard laid out the cemetery he reserved for the mortuary chapel one of the finest sites in Toronto. A temporary 'dead house' was built before work began on a perma-

nent chapel, which was delayed because of the need to rebuild St James' Cathedral after the 1849 fire. Finally, in 1857, Frederick William Cumberland & William G. Storm were commissioned to design a small cemetery chapel, with a basement that could be used as a dead house and service area (and is now used as a crematorium). Because of the social importance of the cemetery and the ceremonies held there, the budget was unusually large. The freedom of design this allowed resulted in the finest of Toronto's nineteenth-century churches.

St James the Less is placed on the crest of a hill, where it can be seen from Parliament Street and the main entrance to the cemetery. With its monumentally heavy bell tower and its broach spire, it forms a pyramidal composition that is a carefully worked completion of the gently rising knoll. The tower is gracefully tall, to the tip of its needle-like spire, and yet its base is finished with rough random-coursed masonry and a hugely spread buttress at the outer corner that makes it appear massive enough to be a modelled outcrop of living rock. The tower balances the broad gable of the nave roof and shelters the open timbered porch, giving the entire chapel a serene monumentality that is perfectly attuned to the picturesque cemetery and its emotional associations.

The wooden porch, with its heavy champfered timbers, is deeply shadowed by a roof folded down to below shoulder height, but light floods in through the open framework of the sides. Inside, the chapel is walled with plain yellow brick and enclosed with a heavy cross-beamed roof that calls to mind the interior of an overturned boat. The thickness of the masonry walls is emphasized by trefoils of deep-set stained glass. As the architects showed in their presentation drawings, shafts of light angle through these windows and through the triangular dormers set into the timbering of the roof. At the east end, light from the triple-lancet chancel window draws the visitor's attention towards the lower-ceilinged, wood-panelled chancel—the climax of the interior—which is framed by a wide stone arch supported on pairs of colonnettes. Additional electric light—usually so destructive of the character of Victorian interiors—plays up the original values of the design, illuminating the arch and making it an even more dramatic proscenium for the chancel.

Few religious interiors in Canada show such architectural control. In St James the Less, Cumberland & Storm eliminated all but the most expressive forms and effects, superbly manipulating light and shadow and a variety of materials. Standing in the centre of the carefully tended cemetery landscape, it is one of the few religious buildings in Canada with the power to express not only the nineteenth century's fearful respect for death, but also its confidence in the pattern of life and in the afterlife beyond death.

---

*'It is well known that when a hot summer's sun acts upon such low wet soil, it will crack and open to a considerable depth, and who can say but pestilence and death may be exhaled from such chinks.'—*The Canadian Freeman*, York, May 2, 1833.

36. *The Church of St James the Less*

37. Mackenzie House, c. 1890

MACKENZIE HOUSE

82 Bond Street (W)

1858

Among the houses that survive in Toronto from the period before Confederation, few represent the type of house likely to have been owned or rented by the city's middle classes. Appropriately—given William Lyon Mackenzie's role in the history and politics of Toronto—the best existing house of this kind is the one in which Toronto's former rebel and first mayor lived from 1859 until his death in 1861. Thanks to a careful restoration, it survives in roughly the same condition Mackenzie knew.

82 Bond Street is the only remaining unit of a short row of three houses built, in Toronto's ubiquitous white brick, for speculative sale or rental in 1858. No architect is known for the house, and in the world of contemporary builders it is unlikely that an architect was involved or needed, since it conformed to standard house patterns of the time. Raised on an 'English basement' that allowed the basement rooms to be well lit, it is three windows wide, with two floors and a dormered attic storey. It can best be described as Late Georgian and is of a general type that was once common in almost

all eastern North American cities and (in both brick and wood) crowded Toronto's streets south of College between the Don River and Bathurst Street. There are few details to set it apart in the streetscape. The fine quality of the front brickwork, the flared stone lintels over the door and windows, and the narrow fretwork frieze in wood set below the eaves all have a neutral decorative character. Only the grandly tall main entrance, with a wide-panelled door set under a high transom, is noticeably unusual. In the Mackenzie house, as in most houses with 'English basements', the main rooms on the parlour floor are a few feet above street level. In Toronto houses of this type it was normal to have an outside front stoop with steps leading up to the main entrance. Here, however, the steps are located within the vestibule, as they were in cities like Québec, where the winter climate made outside stairs treacherous.

Though the house has none of the flamboyance, monumentality, or elaborately fine materials found in larger buildings of the period, it represents the most common type built in mid-nineteenth-century Toronto. Few such survive, but they are important today because they recall the human scale of the nineteenth-century city and a vanished way of life. The balanced proportions of the height and width of the house front, of the windows and doors, and even of the panes of glass in the windows, give it a simple elegance that reflects a long Classical tradition. Plans of Toronto repeatedly proposed the development of squares and grand urban open spaces in a consciously European manner, to be bordered or framed by similar houses. Bond Street itself is part of the McGill Estate, subdivided between 1840 and 1842, and developed in the 1850s. It included McGill Square to the south—between Bond and Church, and open to Queen Street—where Metropolitan (United) Church now stands; and St James Square to the north of Gerrard—between Victoria and Church, where Cumberland and Storm's Normal School of 1851–2 once stood on land now swamped by buildings of the Ryerson Polytechnical Institute. Neither of these two squares, nor any of the other similar spaces proposed in Toronto, were completed as planned—usually because of cost. But many houses like Mackenzie's provided a handsome complement in the streetscape to the more consciously urbane and stylish buildings of the city.

Before the Upper Canada Rebellion of 1837, in which Mackenzie played a leading part, he lived in several rented houses in Toronto, the last a brick house (demolished) with a spacious garden on the west side of York Street, between Queen and Richmond. Mackenzie fled Toronto on 3 December 1837 with a price on his head. His family followed soon after and he remained in exile in the United States until an amnesty allowed his return to the city in early May 1850. Mackenzie was elected MLA for the riding of Haldimand (defeating *Globe* editor George Brown) in 1851, and he held it until 1858. He also edited another newspaper. Though his economic situation and his health became more and more unstable, he had the backing of Torontonians who revered him both as a folk hero and as a martyr to the Establishment. In 1856 a pamphlet was widely circulated calling for his relief and the purchase of a 'Mackenzie Homestead', and a fund-raising committee was formed. Its secretary-treasurer was James Lesslie, one of Mackenzie's long-time friends who had served as alderman in 1834 and was later a successful banker and newspaperman. Over the next two years more than £1,200 was raised in public and private donations, with another £1,000 pledged (but uncollected). On 20 October 1858—with the Mackenzie family in increasing need of a proper house after Mackenzie retired from the legislature—Lesslie advertised in the *Globe* and elsewhere for the payment of overdue subscriptions in aid of the purchase of a 'Good house and lot, with Garden, Orchard, and Pasturage for a Cow and Horse, in the City or its immediate vicinity', where Mackenzie and his family could be secure. In the spring of 1859 the house on Bond Street was purchased for £900 (about $3,600 at the time). Because of the Depression that plagued the city between 1857 and 1860, the Committee had been able to buy a larger house than they might have expected.

Mackenzie, who viewed this homestead as his just and over-due reward for a lifetime of service, was distressed by the long delay in obtaining it. On 17 October 1859, however, the *Globe* published a letter from him, thanking his supporters for the gift and praising the house for being situated 'in a delightful part of Toronto, where my family reside in a more comfortable dwelling of their own than they or I ever before occupied.' Characteristically he could not restrain himself from also stating that the homestead

> now affords the clearest evidence that although the people of Upper Canada are not allowed to control those non-political offices and that state patronage which in other countries affords an obvious means of rewarding or at least upholding ancient public servants, they eminently possess the disposition to be just and even generous toward all such.

As restored by the Toronto Historical Board (with the addition behind of a re-creation of Mackenzie's pre-Rebellion print shop), and as operated by them as a museum, Mackenzie House, as it is now called, presents a conjectural vision of middle-class life in Toronto in the late 1850s, constructed from written evidence, from research into the materials used, and completed with furnishing and equipment of the approximate period. The restoration is enlivened by costumed guides cooking in the basement kitchen and serving baked goods to visitors in the adjoining dining-room (which the family would have used as an everyday living-room). The main floor—with its vestibule, stairhall, and double drawing-room—seems crowded and overstuffed, and is significantly different from the spacious elegance of the larger restored Toronto houses, such as The Grange (Plate 4), that belonged to members of a more prosperous class. Nevertheless the rooms are high and well-proportioned, and the furniture and objects that fill them indicate the effort the Victorian middle class of this period put into endowing their houses with sentimental and personal associations. Mackenzie House, with its elegant Late Georgian façade, represents the taste of the mid-Victorian period for enjoying homey comfort behind a formal and urbane exterior.

The walled garden to the north now contains relief sculptures in Queenston limestone by Emmanuel Hahn and his associate Louis Temporale—after drawings by C.W. Jefferys—of William Lyon Mackenzie making a speech, and of two portraits of his colleagues Samuel Lount and Peter Matthews, who were caught and hanged after the 1837 rebellion. Originally done for the Niagara Parks Commission, these sculptures were later stored away and neglected for many years until they were donated to the City of Toronto in the 1970s, restored by Louis Temporale, and erected in the Mackenzie House garden.

38. *Mackenzie House today*

39. *Pure Spirits Building*

40. *Distillery Building*

THE GOODERHAM AND WORTS COMPLEX

Trinity and Mill Streets

1859 by David Roberts, Sr; rebuilt and extended in
1869 and later by David Roberts Jr

From the late 1850s on, Toronto was a manufacturing and industrial city. The wealth produced in its factories made possible the elaborately designed banks, fire houses, public buildings, and churches to which Victorian Toronto pointed with pride. These factories, built with little of the Classical or medieval detail prominent in other Victorian buildings, were nevertheless designed by the same architects who created many of the city's most impressive public and domestic buildings, and who brought to their industrial projects the same appreciation of materials, workmanship, and technique.

No Canadian industrial complex of the nineteenth century is more completely preserved than that of Gooderham and Worts. The company was established by two Yorkshiremen, James Worts and his brother-in-law William Gooderham. Worts arrived in York first, and in 1831–2 built a windmill at the eastern edge of the harbour to power a gristmill. William Gooderham arrived in 1832, bringing capital and a contingent of relatives, many of whom worked for the milling company. Their joint enterprise was a success; it was made more efficient when the windmill was replaced by a steam engine in 1835. In 1837–8 the company expanded into distilling and malting, using surplus grain, and became one of Toronto's most profitable businesses.

The oldest building in the Gooderham and Worts complex is the five-storey block on the west side of Trinity Street next to the railway lines that form the southern limits of the site. Its rectangular form, 300 feet long, is carefully proportioned and deceptively simple. At the foundation level the walls of rock-faced Kingston limestone, weathered to a silver-grey, are three-and-a-half feet thick. Their height is interrupted only by slightly raised sill courses that wrap around the building and by the regular repetition of unframed windows and doors cut through the thickness. The building represents the severe and practical simplicity of early Victorian industrial design at its best. It housed several functions: an elevator on the south side raised grain from the cars of the Grand Trunk Railway to storage on the upper floors; on the lower level, at the eastern end, a 100-horsepower steam engine powered by six low-pressure boilers (with an adjacent 100-foot chimney) ran eight sets of grindstones; the western end of the building contained the distillery apparatus. With David Roberts Sr superintending construction, four-to-five-hundred men worked on the project, with four lake schooners moving stone from the Kingston quarries. Begun in April 1859, the building was finished in early 1860 at a cost of more than $25,000. It was one of the most expensive building projects in Toronto in the period.

The distillery replaced the windmill (demolished in 1856) as the landmark of the eastern harbour. The desire for such visibility—and corporate pride—had been among the reasons for building it so expensively in Kingston stone. The other reason, the invulnerability to fire damage of the stone walls, was proved on the night of 26 October 1869 when a keg of benzine kept in the basement broke open and caused a fire that spread quickly up the elevator shafts, through the entire building, and destroyed the wooden structure of the inner floors; but the outer walls were left standing. Shortly after the fire the interior was rebuilt by David Roberts Jr. With later renovations the building remains central in the distillery operations today.

During the 1860s several new buildings were added to the distillery, making it the largest in the country: in 1877 it accommodated a yearly production of two million gallons of spirits. Constructed in red brick on limestone foundations, and less massive than the limestone building of 1859, they are among the finest and most striking industrial buildings of any period in Canada. The walls were divided into recessed panels, with strips or piers in between that function like buttresses to brace the verticals of the wooden structure inside. The panels, with their regularly spaced windows, are thinner than the piers and carry little but their own weight. The simple but strong rhythm of alternating piers and panels, with small windows closed by green-painted metal shutters, is majestic—especially in the warehouses at the intersection of Trinity and Mill Streets. The first of the new additions were the malting and storage buildings designed by Gundry & Langley in 1863–4 on the east side of Trinity Street, north of the 1859 distillery. To turn their roof-top cupolas (necessary for ventilation) into picturesque accents among the chimneys of the complex, the architects raised them in height, made one square and the other octagonal, and gave both arched windows.

41. *Warehouse, corner of Trinity and Mill Streets*

Across the street the Pure Spirits Building, which dates from after the fire of 1869, was designed—possibly by David Roberts Jr, the Gooderham's favourite architect—in much the same way as the adjacent warehouses. But here the plain and solid brick piers rise above the roof to support tall panels of plate glass framed in wood. As the building was used for processing extremely flammable pure alcohol, the west-facing glass wall, admitting as much natural light as possible, eliminated the need for lamps with open gas jets. An iron balcony, with a nearly transparent pattern of foliage in outline, extends across the second floor in front of French doors. Few buildings in Toronto show better how delicately beautiful Victorian architecture could be.

During the 1920s the Gooderham and Worts Distillery was purchased by the Hiram Walker Company. Only a few additions have since been made to the complex, which remains an enclosed enclave on the edge of downtown Toronto. The sign that overhangs it, the materials of the buildings, the brick paving of Trinity Street, and even the pervasive smell of alcohol in the air give the complex a unique character and identity. The twentieth century hardly intrudes at all.

Most of the Hiram Walker Company's business is handled at its traditional home in Walkerville, near Windsor, Ontario. In the next few years the Gooderham and Worts complex will likely be declared surplus to the company's needs, and Toronto will face both a challenge and an opportunity. The old buildings could be re-used—as a museum, or for offices or housing—in a way that would preserve not only their form and construction, but also the intangible atmosphere of the place, enabling a small segment of the nineteenth-century city to be handed over to the twenty-first.

XIX. *A bird's-eye view of Toronto, about 1876, looking northeast from the harbour at the foot of Spadina Avenue, showing the Canadian Northern Railway's roundhouse and lakeside grain elevator, and the Second Union Station to the right. Lithograph from a drawing by G. Gascard.*

III

HIGH VICTORIAN TORONTO

1867-1901

As the bands blared and the bells of St James' Cathedral pealed their welcome to the New Year 1867—while watchnight prayer-meetings in the city's Methodist churches meditated on the human condition—two great public events stirred the soul of Toronto. One was the defeat of the Fenians, the Irish-American Civil War veterans who had invaded the Niagara Peninsula during the year past; the other was the impending creation of the new Dominion of Canada. George Brown wrote an epic New Year's editorial on the front page of his newspaper, the Toronto *Globe*, to celebrate the Confederation that he as much as anyone had struggled to achieve. And in January the *Globe* was full of recollections of the first Sunday in June 1866, when 'the autonomy of British-America was cemented by bloodshed in battle'. On that day St James' had been packed with people when couriers burst in with the latest dispatches from the Battle of Ridgeway. The Queen's Own Rifles, the First York Cavalry, and the British troops from Fort York had been rushed by train and lake-steamer to meet the enemy. For Bishop John Strachan and other older inhabitants the event stirred memories of the border raids of 1838 and of the American occupation of 1813. But the arrival at the Yonge Street wharf of a steamer from Port Dalhousie bearing the dead and wounded, and the slow march of the half-mile-long funeral procession of gun-carriages, soldiers, and black-caparisoned horses, were engraved on the memory of even the newest and youngest of Toronto's citizens.

The 1867 mood of pride in the past and high hope for the future prevailed in the city through most of the later Victorian era. After the celebration of Her Majesty's Diamond Jubilee in 1897, the eminent Toronto jurist William Mulock, as Postmaster-General of Canada, expressed the sentiments of many of his fellow citizens when he inaugurated Imperial penny postage by issuing a big 2¢ stamp with the world map blotched in red and the inscription 'WE HOLD A VASTER EMPIRE THAN HAS BEEN'. Toronto's self-confidence was solidly based on a sober commitment to the values of British-Canadian institutions and culture, and on a remarkable record of economic progress. Even the physical growth of the city echoed the exuberance with which patrons vied to enrich their ever more elaborate new buildings. In 1867 the population of Toronto stood at 50,000, placing it between Saint John, N.B., and Quebec City in size. In 1901, at 235,000, it was already beginning to challenge that of Montreal. The city's physical area, excluding the Island and the Don estuary marshlands, had more than doubled in the 1880s when Riverdale, Yorkville, the Annex, Seaton Village, Brockton, and Parkdale were made part of Toronto. Beyond this semi-circle of inner suburbs, steam-railway service and electric trolleys had by the 1890s made such outlying communities as Mimico and Long Branch, Richmond Hill and Newmarket, and various villages in Scarborough accessible to commuters and day-trippers, preparing the way for the city's even greater expansion and economic influence in the twentieth century.

Toronto's racial and religious character in 1901 was still overwhelmingly British and Protestant, however. The only large minority, the Irish Catholics, had by now adapted to their new home and their predominantly working-class role. (But they did have a few leaders inside Toronto's business establishment, notably Senator Sir Frank Smith, the veteran Conservative cabinet minister, president of the Toronto Street Railway Company and the Dominion Bank, who had made his fortune as a London, Ontario, merchant before he moved to Toronto in 1867.) Southern and eastern Europeans, Jews, and Asians were still rare in Toronto. The black population was small and docile, grateful for their rescue from American slavery on the underground railway or for the freeing of their ancestors who had arrived as slaves of York's first families, accepting without noticeable complaint the demeaning status assigned to them by North American white society. As for the original inhabitants, they had departed the streets of Toronto for the realm of myth—'vanished races singing their death song', W.D. Lighthall wrote of them in 1889, 'as they are swept into the cataract of oblivion'.

XX. *Toronto Street looking north from King Street to the Eighth Post Office on Adelaide Street E., about 1895. The Seventh Post Office (Plate 23) is on the left; the Consumers' Gas Building (Plate 48) is barely visible on the right.*

Towards the bubbling melting-pot of American democracy, the rich cultures of continental Europe, and the 'lesser breeds without the law' whom the British race had presumed to rule and civilize, proper Torontonians maintained an attitude blended of smug superiority and happy ignorance. But when 'highest beliefs' were threatened in 1899, they roused fiercely; no city in the Dominion was more excited about the chance to send its volunteers to put down the recalcitrant South African farmers who challenged Pax Britannica in the Boer War. The hottest animosity of bourgeois Toronto was expressed against the religion and language of French Canada. Not content with sending volunteers to deal with the North West Rebellions of 1870 and 1885, and with forcing upon Prime Minister Sir John A. Macdonald the execution of Manitoba's founder, Louis Riel, Toronto Orangemen organized a mass rally in 1889, chaired by former Mayor Howland, and roared its assent as the eminent Toronto lawyer, D'Alton McCarthy, M.P., demanded that a Quebec provincial law reinstating the Jesuits be disallowed by federal authorities. 'Do you know', he cried to a crowd of 3,000 '[that instead of being assimilated] the French have been becoming more and more French? They are determined not to be British

XXI. *The family of George Taylor Denison III on the front steps of his house, Heydon Villa, 1870. He is shown in profile (centre right), aged 31, with his parents and six brothers.*

subjects!' He demanded that French Canadians be taken in hand, taught the English language, and forced to become British 'in sentiment'. They never could be, of course, but many Torontonians for years to come firmly believed they should.

Toronto's leading imperialist, Colonel George Taylor Denison III, saved his fire for other foes than papistry and French Canada, both of which bored him. Like the one hundred or more other Denisons who flourished in High Victorian Toronto, he was descended from the Yorkshire farmer upon whom vast landholdings were bestowed by President Peter Russell in the 1790s, to be greatly augmented by later acquisitions and dowries. A militia major at twenty-three in 1862, Denison was soon made colonel of his family cavalry regiment, Denison's Horse, which eventually became the Governor-General's Horseguards. Four of his brothers (there were seven sons in all) were soldiers of the Queen on the far frontiers of the Empire, and another was an admiral in the British Navy. Frustrated in his attempts to get a permanent command for himself, the Colonel had to be content with the post of senior police magistrate of Toronto for nearly half a century, and with his very limited military action against the Fenians at Ridgeway in 1866 and the Métis and Indians during the North West Rebellion of 1885.

His true role was that of author and agitator. His competent scholarly history of cavalry won him a world competition and a prize from the Tsar of Russia in 1879. He was chief organizer for the Canada First movement, the Imperial Federation League, and the United Empire Loyalists (one of whom was his grandmother, Mrs G.T. Denison I), and an inveterate promoter of such lost romantic causes as the Southern Confederacy.

Various Denison-family country homes—'Belle Vue', 'Dover Court', and 'Rush Holme', to cite only three—have given their names to streets and parks in Toronto, though the houses themselves are gone. After the Colonel had built his own red-brick 'Heydon Villa' in the West End in 1880, it became a gathering place for such local literati as the poet and Canada Firster Charles Mair, the eminent newspaperman Sir John Willison, the constitutional historian Sir John Bourinot, and Principal Maurice Hutton of University College; it was also a stopping point for visiting imperial greats, from Joseph Chamberlain to Rudyard Kipling. Heydon's high-ceilinged entrance hall displayed the head of a bison, a huge stuffed pelican under glass, and a giant Denison genealogical tree; the dining-room held portraits of General Wolseley of Red River and the defeated demigod General Robert E. Lee; on the walls of the library, besides the vast collection of military books, were a Zulu spear, a quiver of Sioux arrows used in the massacre of Custer's men at Little Big Horn, and a Union Army sword that Denison himself had picked up at the Battle of Ridgeway and used thereafter as a poker to stir his grate. His contempt for Yankees—he once described an American city as a place 'filled with disease, bad water and ruffians'—was really part of a larger quarrel he had with the brave new world of Victorian industry and commerce. Erect, keen-eyed, and bristling, he ran his magistrate's court as if, in spurs and helmet, he were leading a last great cavalry charge (he sometimes disposed of cases at the clip of one per minute). This Don Quixote of Toronto fought bravely on into the 1920s, long after the last retreat had sounded—an old man well aware that he was becoming a parody of himself, and that his antic dreams of chivalry were not for the modern era.

The new men of Toronto were a very different breed—Methodist farmers' sons such as Timothy Eaton, who moved his dry-goods business from St Mary's, Ontario, to Yonge Street in 1860; or Hart Massey, who transplanted his implements factory to King Street West from Newcastle in 1879. Sustained at first by a generous line of credit from his fellow Methodist John Macdonald of 'Oaklands', Timothy Eaton revolutionized merchandising in Toronto. The single-price cash sale, with no bartering, and prompt refunds on request, soon enabled him to expand to many lines in what became his 'department' store at Queen and Yonge. His mail-order catalogue—assisted by fast, cheap postal service and the Atlantic-to-Pacific railway service that came with the completion of the CPR in 1885—made the whole of Canada a mercantile province of Eaton's and of Toronto. Local customers were treated in the 1880s to the novel wonders of passenger elevators, telephone service, and a nurse to take care of their children while they shopped. It did no harm that another giant emerged to compete next door. Sometimes Simpson's even out-paced its larger rival in ultra-modernity: pneumatic tubes for swift, safe cash; thoroughbred dapple greys dashing through the streets with their delivery sleighs in winter and high-wheeled carts in summer; and in 1895 an elegant six-storey cast-iron-and-steel-framed store, an example of the very newest approach in architectural construction (see Plate 73). But Eaton's always managed to keep pace with the competition—except, of course, in the sale of tobacco and spirits, which the founder had banned from his premises in perpetuity. As patrons of the city, the Eaton family helped change the look of residential Toronto—with Timothy's Victorian mansion at Lowther Avenue and Spadina Road in the Annex, his daughter Josephine's 'Bellevue' at the crest of the Poplar Plains hill, Sir John and Lady Eaton's 'Ardwold' north of 'Spadina', and John David Eaton's Art Deco house on Dunvegan Road.*

Toronto became not only Canada's mercantile capital in the later nineteenth century but also the undisputed industrial leader of Ontario. Gurney's stove factory moved in from Hamilton, the John Inglis Machinery plant from Guelph, S.R. Wickett's tannery from Brooklin, Laidlaw Lumber from Barrie, Elias Rogers Coal from Newmarket—to cite only a few examples of relocations to Toronto. The Masseys of Newcastle built their giant implements factory on King Street West—still one of the architectural wonders of the city—and by the 1890s were the largest single employer in Toronto.

Between 1871 and 1891 the number of factories in the city increased five-fold, from over 500 to some 2,500, and the industrial work-force grew from 9,400 to 26,000. The great world depression that began in 1873 and lasted until about 1895 was essentially a depression in prices; it cut into profits, wages, and inefficiency rather than into industrial growth. Toronto's manufacturers—armed with Sir John A. Macdonald's national policy of tariff protection (which they vociferously supported), and boosted by the funding of the Industrial Exhibition in 1879, which became the world's largest annual fair and in 1882–3 pioneered electricity in its buildings and electric railway—moved on from strength to strength. The effects on commerce, finance, and transportation, and on such cultural amenities as

---

* In the twentieth century the Eaton's College Street store, with its elegant Art Deco Auditorium, and the Eaton Centre were other significant additions to the city's public architecture.

XXII. *Looking northwest from the tower of St James' Church, c. 1873, showing the Mechanics'*
Institute on Adelaide Street East in the foreground and the towers of Metropolitan Methodist and
St Michael's Cathedral to the west of Church Street.

the skills of master-carvers, gilders, and artists of every kind, were pro-
digious. For our purposes the most important consequence was a building
boom. Besides new stores, offices, and factories, there were cottages and
row-houses for working people, particularly in the 'The Ward' north-west
of Queen and Yonge and in large pockets of the city at either extremity of
King Street; and there were the stately homes in Rosedale and Parkdale
and on Jarvis and Sherbourne Streets. Above all there were dozens of new
neighbourhoods of solid brick middle-class houses that today, almost a
century later, express a civic character largely unaltered by time.

The pre-eminent property owner of Victorian Toronto was neither a merchant nor an industrialist, but a building contractor. Alexander Manning
had arrived as a lad from Dublin in 1834 and by the 1850s made his fortune
constructing railways and such public buildings as the Toronto Normal
School (1852; demolished to make way for the Ryerson Institute's main
campus in the 1960s). His investment in the North American Land Com-

pany, among other ventures, and his Manning Arcade on King Street West, designed by E.J. Lennox, as well as his Manning Chambers on the northwest corner of Queen and Bay, greatly expanded his worth. His role as Toronto alderman and mayor—which covered a thirty-year span, off and on, from 1856 to 1885—did nothing to diminish it. In 1876 Manning acquired the newly built Grand Opera House on Adelaide Street West. This was a business failure. But after it was reconstructed and enlarged following a fire in 1879, it became the city's foremost theatre, presenting Adelina Patti, Lillian Russell, Lily Langtry, Sara Bernhardt, Ellen Terry, Sir Henry Irving, and all the best touring companies. After Manning died in 1901 (and was laid to rest in a vast hillside monument in St James Cemetery), the Grand declined into magic shows and Irish musicals under the direction of Ambrose Small, after whose mysterious disappearance in 1919 it was demolished. (Its only memorial is the street sign 'Grand Opera Lane', marking the alley that runs south from Adelaide Street just west of Yonge). Manning not only acquired a distinguished son-in-law in Hume Blake, son of Ontario's greatest lawyer and sometime-premier Edward Blake, but literally moved into Family Compact territory in 1870 when he bought from the Boulton family 'Holland House', a crenellated Gothic fantasy inspired by Windsor Castle and built by Henry John Boulton in 1831. The last of Toronto's waterfront mansions to be occupied by one of the original families, Holland House survived Manning's move from it to Queen's Park Crescent in 1887, but not the wholesale demolitions that followed the Great Fire of 1904. Its site is now occupied by another exotic creation, the golden towers of the Royal Bank of Canada (Plate 152).

Manning's charitable instincts led him to construct and help finance the Hospital for Incurables in Parkdale—another large, picturesque building—and to participate, as president, in the good works of both the St Patrick's and the Irish Protestant Benevolent Societies. He was also president of a prosperous brewing company, however; and his long municipal career was brought to an abrupt end in 1886 by the forces of Temperance and the opposition of a young reformer, William Holmes Howland, who promised to usher in an era of 'Toronto the Good'. Howland had no municipal or political experience, but his father had been a wealthy grain merchant, a Father of Confederation, and first Lieutenant-Governor of Ontario. When the young man turned his evangelical zeal to attacking the foul water, filthy streets, and poor housing that afflicted the city's slum dwellers and took such a terrible toll of their children, he soon found he must also scourge the Tory administration at City Hall that did nothing about these conditions, nor about the proliferation of the 'groggeries' and drunkenness that accompanied them.

XXIII. *The south side of Front Street East, c. 1873. The buildings in the right foreground were demolished and replaced by the St Lawrence Centre. The Beardmore Building is visible, but there is a vacant lot where the Perkins Building would be constructed the following year. See Plate 45 for a modern view of this scene.*

Though capable of waging crusades against Mayor Manning and his unsavoury self-serving political allies, Howland was a large, cheerful, generous person who attracted a broad following, including many newly enfranchised widows and spinsters, and he won the mayoralty in 1886. With the tireless support of the City's first medical officer, Dr William Canniff, he struggled unsuccessfully to bring Toronto a pure water supply and decent garbage and sewage disposal. But his program—including the idea that drunks, instead of being jailed, should be treated in an 'asylum for dipsomaniacs'—was ahead of its time. In 1888, worn out and near personal bankruptcy, Howland retired after only two years as mayor, with little to show for his heroic efforts but the appointment of a police inspector devoted full time to the improvement of public morals. But in the long run he had helped create an expectation among the citizenry—which grew and lasted—that Toronto's civic administration should actively intervene to promote the welfare of all its people. Howland died of exhaustion six years later at the age of forty-nine.

Both Howland and Manning were involved in the long struggle to build a city hall at the head of Bay Street. However, E.J. Lennox's magnificent new fortress (Plate 76) did not finally open until well after their time, in

1899—four years after Toronto's ten-storey tallest-yet office tower, the Temple Building (demolished 1970), had appeared at the corner of Richmond to pioneer Bay Street as the financial district. Meanwhile the City, and other non-commercial bodies, were patrons to a host of new cultural buildings that dramatically changed the look of late-nineteenth-century Toronto. The Toronto Public Library system, begun in 1884 at the old Mechanics' Institute, quickly established three branches. The high school on Jarvis Street was supplemented by Parkdale in 1889 and Harbord in 1892. Upper Canada College opened its new premises above the Avenue Road hill in 1891. The Methodists and Presbyterians had already constructed their 'cathedral' churches—Metropolitan at Bond and Queen and St Andrew's at Simcoe and King. The Baptist McMaster University on Bloor, and the Presbyterian Knox College on Spadina Crescent, were both solidly established by the end of the 1880s. The Methodist Victoria University of Cobourg, now federated with the University of Toronto, moved to Queen's Park Crescent in 1892, the same year as the new Ontario Legislature (Plate 67) opened its doors. From the night of its inaugural performance in 1894 Massey Hall (Plate 70) became the city's premier concert hall.

Another maker of Toronto, John Ross Robertson—who lent the full weight of his *Evening Telegram* to the campaign to build a Hospital for Sick Children—is perhaps better remembered for publishing the newspaper that was most influential in civic politics, and for recording in his six-volume *Landmarks* the story of everything notable that Torontonians had done to shape and build their city in the nineteenth century.

Two names are particularly associated with the beginnings of Toronto's park system: the world's sculling champion and first sports superstar, Ned Hanlan, who made the Islands, including his own Hanlan's Hotel, an even more popular holiday retreat; and the ancient white-bearded tassel-toqued Ranger of High Park, John Howard—architect, engineer, and city surveyor—who had long ago laid down Muddy York's first sidewalks and taught the first drawing classes at Upper Canada College. Howard bequeathed his vast property to the citizens of Toronto and lived on there in 'Colborne Lodge' (Plate 10) until his death in 1890.

Another city park, Allan Gardens, was the gift of Toronto's grand champion of worthy causes, George William Allan. Born in 1822 to the wealthy merchant and banker William Allan, who had come to York in Simcoe's day, he was duly educated at Upper Canada College, married to a daughter of John Beverley Robinson, and called to the bar. His father gave him the northern portions of his Moss Park estate, stretching from Carlton Street up to Bloor and from Jarvis to Sherbourne. In 1849 Henry Bowyer Lane designed for him a splendid mansion called 'Homewood', familiar in the

XXIV. *Allan Gardens—between Jarvis and Sherbourne, Dundas and Gerrard—showing the pavilion (1878; demolished), which was both a conservatory for Toronto's first botanical garden and a concert hall.*

twentieth century as the building in which Herbert Bruce founded the Wellesley Hospital. Allan later developed a large portion of his property south of Bloor Street into a residential district. At one time or another he was president and benefactor of 'everything cultural and horticultural': the Ontario Historical Society, the Toronto Conservatory of Music, the Horticultural Society of Toronto, the Upper Canada Bible Society, and the Ontario Society of Artists. A friend and patron of Paul Kane, he hung a magnificent collection of the artist's paintings (now in the Royal Ontario Museum) at 'Moss Park' when he moved there after his father's death. Allan's public-service career spanned over half a century, from city council at age twenty-seven, with a year as mayor at thirty-three, to forty-four years in the Senate, of which he was eventually Speaker, and membership in the federal cabinet. He was chancellor of Trinity University for a quarter of a century. An amateur explorer and zoölogist, he travelled extensively in Europe, Egypt, and Asia, and is reputed to have been the first Canadian to climb the Great Pyramid. Allan lived until 1901, a few months longer than Queen Victoria. By then most of the Toronto boys who had gone to fight for her in South Africa were preparing to return home from the little Imperial war that had brought such excitement and satisfaction to the Queen's Own City.

THE BANK OF BRITISH NORTH AMERICA

49 Yonge Street at Wellington Street (NE)

1871–2 by Henry Langley

In the afterglow of Confederation the 1870s and 1880s in Toronto stand out as a period of confidence that gave birth to elaborate and occasionally flamboyant architecture. The scale of building changed to include a greater emphasis on height and material richness. Style changed as well. While the basic patterns remained fundamentally Classical, architects were inspired less by archaeology (as in St Lawrence Hall, Plate 16, and the Commercial Bank, Plate 14), and more by fashion and novelties, particularly those of Napolean III's Second Empire France. North American bankers, merchants, and manufacturers visited Paris, saw the new public buildings, the boulevards and opulent houses, and the Opera, and returned home with furniture, glass, and art, Worth gowns and perfume for wives and daughters, and a new taste for elaborate architecture. Henry Langley adopted the 'modern French' style for a new Government House (1866–70) at Simcoe and King Street West, and for the Eighth Post Office (1869–73) on Adelaide Street East, facing King at the top of Toronto Street. Neither building survives; but we can see the richness of the Second Empire style in Langley's next major design, the Bank of British North America, in the same commercial area of the city.

It replaced a John Howard building of 1845–6, which in its refined detail and its references to the Bank of England was ideal for a bank of its period. But thirty years later, as new commercial blocks and banks were being built nearby, it no longer expressed either contemporary fashionable taste or the Bank's view of its own importance. The basic composition of Langley's design is both traditional and simple, with a ground floor faced with horizontally channelled stone and two-storey pilasters spaced between the upper windows. But within this framework all the detail is richly elaborated.* The

high-dormered mansard roof, typical of the Second Empire, is derived from seventeenth-century French examples, constructed with a steep front slope and a nearly flat upper surface. Practical, because it gave nearly full height to the attic storey, it also made the building seem taller than its neighbours, and more imposing. The storeys of Langley's bank were tall, but with the mansard above, the building must have seemed like a skyscraper among its neighbours. The composition is crowned by eight dormers, usually described as 'bonnetted' because of the curved pediments that cap them. The building was constructed in two shades of gold-coloured Cleveland sandstone. The colours separate the detail from the flat wall, and in sunshine the façade seems to shimmer like embroidered fabric.

Langley summed up his design in the main entrance. It is round-arched, like the windows, and flanked by a double Corinthian order that supports brackets and the broad segmental pediment. Here the forms used elsewhere from ground floor to dormers are worked in greater relief to catch the eye of the passerby: full columns, panelled pilasters, swags of fruit and flowers emblematic of prosperity, and a deeper-shadowed pediment. This main door charts the history of the building. Orginally, when Wellington Street was the thoroughfare of the banking district, the door was located at the centre of the Wellington Street front. When, in 1903, the focus of business had shifted to Yonge Street, it was removed to that side of the building. The alterations—carried out by Burke, Horwood & White, successor to Langley's firm—included a redesigned banking hall, with square piers faced with coloured marble supporting a ceiling of low-sweeping plaster vaults. Except for the location of the door, the exterior remained unchanged because its cosmopolitan character continued to symbolize the values of the banking community.

In 1911 the Bank of British North America was absorbed into the Bank of Montreal; years later the former head-office building became a branch of the Canadian Imperial Bank of Commerce. In 1978 it was purchased by developer Brian Ferrier, who restored both the interior and exterior. After completion of the splendid restoration in 1981–2 it was sold to Greymac Trust, whose subsequent involvement in a financial scandal has placed the building on the market once more.

---

* Each of the round-arched ground-floor windows is set back into a deep framing embrasure, and at about shoulder height the line of the window sills is extended around the buildings to form a panelled dado like the wainscotting of a room, divided into panels inset with circles below the windows and raised panels of vermiculation (meant to give a worm-eaten appearance to the stone). The upper windows, also round-arched, are set between Corinthian pilasters. Each window is joined to its neighbours by upper and lower horizontal mouldings, which with the main pilasters create an interwoven grid of horizontals and verticals across the façades—a characteristic elaboration of the Second Empire style.

42

THE NECROPOLIS

200 Winchester Street at Sumach Street (NE)
Developed 1850–5; the gateway and chapel 1872 by Henry Langley;
altered 1933 by J. Francis Brown and Son

The Necropolis—Toronto's 'City of the Dead'—was founded in 1849–50 to provide for Toronto Presbyterians a secluded rural cemetery such as served the Anglicans in St James Cemetery (see pp. 81–3) a short distance to the north. Unlike St James, which was supported by the parish, the Necropolis was organized, like most British cemeteries before 1850, as a business operation from which the sale of plots and burial fees would yield a profit. The business venture does not seem to have been successful, and on 11 July 1855 the cemetery was purchased by William McMaster, David Paterson, and James Lesslie, all of whom were very active in Toronto politics and religious life. Though most of the purchase price of $16,000 came from their own pockets, they were not acting as private businessmen but as philanthropists convinced that they had a God-given duty to use their private wealth for the public good. The three businessmen had previously been appointed, by the provincial legislature, trustees of the Toronto General Burying Ground to administer the Potter's Field Cemetery in Yorkville, which had served Toronto since 1826 as a non-denominational burial ground. Safely removed from the city when it was established, by 1850 it was becoming over-crowded; also, the prosperous village of Yorkville was not pleased to have within its residential area a cemetery that dominated the northwest corner of Bloor and Yonge, its two most important streets. The Trustees were almost certainly appointed in the full awareness that something would have to be done about Potter's Field and that men of business like William McMaster, Toronto's leading wholesale dry-goods merchant, would bring the expertise needed to provide the best and least expensive solution to the public. Shortly after the Trustees were appointed, Yorkville successfully petitioned for the closure of Potter's Field and, as had been anticipated, the Trustees provided most of the purchase price for the Necropolis to replace the old cemetery. They were eventually completely repaid from the income of the cemetery, but there is little doubt that without their philanthropy the need for a new cemetery would not have been met so quickly, or with such a sense of style in its gatehouse and chapel. McMaster in particular had a keen interest in architecture: he also guided to completion Jarvis Street Baptist Church and McMaster College (now the Royal Conservatory of Music), both of which were designed by Henry Langley.

The Victorians required sentimental and poetic expression in a cemetery landscape. However, the 15 acres of the Necropolis—laid out before 1855—are not as picturesque as St James Cemetery. The western half of the site is almost flat and most of its narrow carriage drives are straight; only at the east end, where the property first rises and then falls in terraces towards the Don River, was a romantic landscape possible and made effective by numerous monuments. The first development of the Necropolis included a simple dead house at the centre of the grounds. This was replaced in 1872 by a chapel and superintendent's lodge—designed by Henry Langley in the Gothic style—lined up on the north side of Winchester Street and flanking the gables of the fanciful lacy gates for carriages and pedestrians. The architectural forms established by the most important part of the composition, the chapel, with its traceried south window and stone-trimmed gable, are echoed across the composition in the gates and in the many small details of the lodge. Though each element in the design is as different in scale and form as it is in function, the long line of parts is held together by the bell-tower, which rises above the chapel vestibule and is silhouetted against the pastoral landscape of the cemetery. The interior of the chapel, approached originally through a vestibule inside the gateway, is severely plain, as was appropriate at a time when most funerals were held in local churches. (The present vestibule to the chapel, facing Winchester Street, was added in 1933 when the chapel was fitted up as a crematorium.) Langley's work is often set off by delightful decorative details—here by the jig-sawn bargeboards and open framing of the entrance gates. The use of wood in religious architecture—considered unsuitably temporary in Britain—was approved in Canada because wood was seen as the most common native material. The decorative white-painted gate was deemed the perfect frame for the approach to the cemetery—guaranteed to lighten the heart of a mourner just enough, while pleasing and amusing the casual visitor.

The Necropolis was the beginning of a series of semi-rural cemeteries developed by the Toronto General Burial Ground Trustees. In 1864 they purchased land on the south side of Winchester Street from the City to expand the grounds; the area was landscaped and a few interments took place. But in 1873, in the face of public opposition to this expansion, the Trustees decided to buy land on north Yonge Street that was later developed as Mount Pleasant Cemetery (see pp.141–2). The property on the south side of Winchester was sold in 1875 to the City to form the nucleus of a new 'Eastern park' —later extended and renamed Riverdale Park. The Necropolis continues to be used today (the grounds are open to the public) and the chapel now incorporates a crematorium. The still park-like character of the grounds—which retain their original mixture of the romantic picturesque and the sentimental—proves the wisdom of the original decision to make the cemetery the responsibility of a public trust rather than a business speculation.

44. *Former warehouses at 81–7 Front Street East*

THE WAREHOUSES OF FRONT STREET EAST

From the late 1850s to the early 1870s Front Street, between Jarvis and York Streets, became the centre of warehousing, wholesaling, and light industry in Toronto because of its proximity to the harbour and the waterfront railway lines. During this quarter-century the architecture of warehouses in Toronto developed tremendously, changing from a Late Georgian plainness and sobriety to a riotous High Victorian eclecticism. The district did not evolve according to any accepted plan, and though there was a general air of uniformity in the warehouses, there was not the common agreement about their architecture that seems to have prevailed among bankers about bank buildings. But the result along Front Street was a feast for the eye that few streets in the city could match.

The building in 1844–5 of the Second City Hall on Front

Street East (Plate 11), with its market, attracted the first food wholesalers. But large-scale development of this area began in the late 1850s, after the arrival of the railways in 1853–4 had provided cheap year-round transportation; and landfill made possible the building of the Esplanade to the south and new docks on the lake. The first warehouses on the south side of Front Street East (Numbers 81 to 85, dating from 1858; Number 87 from 1865) were not unlike larger versions of the Georgian shops built along King in the 1840s and 1850s. The most distinctive feature of their plans—which took advantage of the difference in ground level between Front and the Esplanade (the result of the sloping beach of the lakefront) —was the full access at the rear given to the basements. Number 87 was built for the Leadlay Leather Company in plain

45. *Former warehouses on the south side of Front Street East*

red brick; but not long after, the company added (on what would now be part of the sidewalk) a one-storey front sales room, which gave it great visibility in the street. (This was restored in 1975, along with the rest of the building, for the Liquor Control Board of Ontario.) The three earlier shops are more elaborate, aspiring to the dignity of the Greek Revival, with heavy moulded lintels over the windows and thin pilaster strips in brick that rise from the second-floor level to brackets at the cornice level. Numbers 81 and 83 were designed as a symmetrical pair, and at the centre the pilasters frame wider pedimented windows and a semicircular attic window set under a pediment. There was originally a passage through the building at ground level that allowed wagons access to the rear, where there were hoists to raise goods to the upper floors. In the narrower plan of Number 85 there was not room for wagon access, and the loading doors (now windows) and the hoist under a pediment-like dormer (still

in place) became the centrepiece of the façade, framed by pilasters.

The character of warehouse architecture began to change dramatically in the 1860s, at the time when many of the leaders of commerce in Toronto—men like John Macdonald, William McMaster, and his nephew A.R. McMaster—were becoming involved, more or less as patrons, with the design and construction of some of the more flamboyant public and religious buildings of the period. They adopted new patterns—especially those of the Second Empire style, with its mansard roofs and decoratively enriched Classicism—both for their houses and for their business premises and warehouses. A few of the new warehouses—particularly the A.R. McMaster Building (1870-1 by William Irving; demolished)—tried to match the new banks and public buildings in size and expensive materials. Most of the buildings on Front Street, however, were constructed less expensively, though the showy Second

105

46. *The former Perkins, Ince & Co. Building*

Empire style created a panorama of elaborately fronted row warehouses, all roughly the same height, with showrooms and offices on the ground floor and open storage space above.* Each building was an effective advertisement for the company within. Because warehouses during this period could be artificially lit only by using gas jets with dangerous open flames, one priority of design was the inclusion of large windows that would admit the maximum natural light. Architects gave great prominence to the design of the windows, making their frames, divisions, and linked elements the most decorative parts of the façades.

The Griffiths Building (now known as the Beardmore Building), at 35–9 Front Street East, was built in 1871–2. One of the first commercial buildings designed by David Roberts Jr, it is perhaps the most typically Second Empire of the

* The mansard roof, which gave each building height and presence, also provided more storage space.

the warehouses surviving on Front Street. Griffiths, a wholesale grocer, planned the three units of the building to house his own premises and two rental properties. For the grandest possible effect the three units were tied together in one composition under a high dormered mansard roof, which was raised into a tower at the centre and crested with wrought-iron trim and a flag. The façade of the three-unit building is dominated by its arched windows. The original arched doors and display windows of the ground floor are gone, but the piers between—faced with panelled Corinthian pilasters in painted cast iron—remain.

In several Toronto buildings of the period—like the Griffiths Building—cast-iron decoration was used extensively because it was much cheaper than comparable work in stone. The façades of the three warehouses at 45–9 Front Street East, however, are almost totally constructed of this material. Cast iron had been widely used for the fronts of buildings in the United

47. *The former Griffiths Building, now known as the Beardmore Building*

States since the early 1850s because its lightness and strength allowed more and more of the outside walls to be taken up by light-giving windows. Whole façades could be purchased in a wide variety of patterns; or a builder could order separate components and assemble his own design, all in a short time and at a fraction of the cost of brick or stone. These three warehouses were built in 1872–3 for B. Homer Dixon, a Bostonian who, through his brother-in-law William Henry Boulton (of The Grange), had become involved in property development in Toronto. The façades are thought to have been designed by Strickland & Symon; the castings were done by the St Lawrence Foundry in Toronto. These warehouses do not aspire to the unified composition of the Griffiths Building; instead one unit design is repeated three times. Paint was necessary to preserve the ironwork. The grey, beige, and off-white stone colours—verified by paint scrapes—used on numbers 47 and 49 are unusually sedate. The vibrant red and white scheme of number 45 is more typical of Victorian taste—not unlike the colour contrasts of stone and brick found in churches, houses, and public buildings of the period.

The double warehouse at 41–3 Front Street East was designed in 1873–4 by Macdougall & Darling for the firm of Perkins, Ince & Co., wholesale grocers. (One half was rented to Beardmore and Son, wholesale dealers in leather, who shortly after bought the Griffiths Building and moved next door.) The first building completed by Frank Darling after his return from three years' training in England, it includes Gothic and Classic elements. Broad, stilted Gothic arches in stone across the ground-floor shop windows, three storeys of very different windows grouped on the second and third floors, between tall brick pilasters, and an arcade of alternating wide and narrow brick arches on the fourth floor—all topped by a cornice with two pediments in pressed metal—create a building of eccentric monumentality.

In the later nineteenth century Front Street was one of the showplaces of commercial Toronto. The constant activity between the market on the east, Old Union Station on the west, and the harbour to the south gave it a character as distinct as that of the areas to the north, with their banks, public buildings, and retail stores. Few areas showed such solid evidence of the Toronto business community's interest in architecture, or contained buildings so perfectly Victorian—laid out along a street that was wide enough to display them as a group. In the later nineteenth century there was little physical change in the street, although the rebuilding of the South St Lawrence Market intensified its business and congestion. The fire of 1904, however, levelled most of the warehouse district west of Yonge. When rebuilding began it was not on Front Street but in other parts of the city, where cheaper land and less crowding provided better opportunities for the design of new warehouses and factories. The area began a gradual decline that reached its nadir shortly after the Second World War, when new industrial areas like those in Don Mills were developed. As companies moved out, much of Front Street East was designated by City Council for urban renewal. Most of the north side was demolished with no thought of its architectural character; and the O'Keefe Centre and the St Lawrence Centre were dropped into the streetscape of the south side. Until the late 1960s, when the St Lawrence Markets were re-established as a centre of Toronto life, nothing positive was done to the warehouses that had survived demolition. But over the next ten years—beginning particularly with Janis Kravis of the Karelia shop—warehouses were renovated and restored as shops, art galleries, and architects' offices, and for other companies who found the uniform space of the city's modern buildings unsympathetic. Some of the restoration was carried out by longstanding owners like Continental Salvage, who cleaned and repaired the façade of 43-5 Front, which in 1985-6 was further restored. Most significantly, the city reversed its attitude to the area, shelving the grandiose renewal projects that had threatened it. With the renovation of the St Lawrence Markets, new park spaces, and the building of the St Lawrence Neighbourhood to the south (pages 302-5), the city became a major sponsor in the transformation of Front Street East.

Today the character of this part of the street has departed considerably from its past. Gone are the docks and railways that originally defined the area. Gone too are the wholesalers and small manufacturers. But the area is alive with an eccentric vibrancy. This comes not only from its modern businesses, but also from the sense of its affiliation with the different concerns of Victorian Toronto. Front Street East has avoided the quaint and the cute. It is not an ostentatiously discreet enclave of 'Old Toronto' next to its skyscraper equivalent, but very much part of the modern city.

48

THE CONSUMERS' GAS COMPANY BUILDING
17–19 Toronto Street (E)
1876 by Grant & Dick; addition 1899 by D.B. Dick

The building of the Seventh Post Office (Plate 23) and the York County Courthouse (Plate 22) transformed Toronto Street into one of the most important streets in the city. When the northward vista was crowned by the Eighth Post Office (1867–73, demolished) on Adelaide, the street acquired a Parisian elegance. Its various government buildings established a pattern of carefully designed and crafted architecture in a harmonious variety of styles that was followed by later commercial and office buildings. The elaborate Italianate style

of the Consumers' Gas building is one of the last reminders of the elegance and flamboyance that made the street the pride of commercial Toronto. (See Plate XX.)

The Consumers' Gas Company was founded in 1848 to provide street lighting for the City of Toronto. Its offices and the plants for making coal gas, erected over the next seventy years, showed the influence of public architecture in their sense of scale and decorative character. Consumers' Gas was one of the first commercial firms to be established on Toronto

Street, erecting in 1852 a three-storey brick building to house its offices, boardroom, and public showroom at number 17. It served the company well until the mid-1870s, when the company purchased (and demolished) the former Toronto Registry Office just to the north to provide a site for a new main office to be connected to the old.

In 1874 James Austin of 'Spadina' became president of the company. Founder of the Dominion Bank and the Queen City Fire Insurance Company, both in 1871, Austin brought an adventurous interest in architecture to the operation of all three companies. In 1876-8, as the depressed economy began to improve, he persuaded his fellow directors to signal their faith in the future by undertaking major building projects. The best commercial architects in the city were engaged: R.C. Windeyer in 1876 for the Queen City Fire Insurance building (24–6 Church Street); William Irving in 1877 for the Dominion Bank offices (1 King Street West); and D.B. Dick in 1876 for the new Consumers' Gas offices.

Born in Scotland and trained in Edinburgh before coming to Toronto in 1873, David B. Dick (1846-1925) was in partnership with Robert Grant from 1874 to early 1877, and had designed several houses and commercial buildings before receiving the Consumers' Gas commission in 1876. The windows are the most important element in Dick's design of the building's four-bay three-storey façade, and the Classical detail is organized to frame them, not as independent ornament. On the ground floor the four large windows (the southernmost one was originally a door; but this was closed when the addition of 1899 was completed) are separated by red granite columns with Ionic capitals—the contrast in colour adding to the effect of the carved ornament. The second-floor windows are set under round arches filled with carved sea shells, and framed and separated by Corinthian pilasters. On the third floor each window-frame has a keystone that turns into a carved bracket as part of the cornice above. From other brackets between the windows hang chains or disks that approximate visually the style of the lower pilasters. The piling up of such modelled forms created a tapestry-like effect.

This was the first of several new office buildings that contributed to the richness of Toronto Street, and its success led to Dick's becoming the architect for other projects of Austin's.*

---

* Dick's connection with Austin probably also led directly to his appointment as architect to the University of Toronto: he was responsible for rebuilding University College (Plate 24) after the 1890 fire.

In 1899 Consumers' Gas decided to demolish most of the 1852 building and hired Dick to design an addition to his 1876 building. It included a new entrance to expanded offices on the main floor, and a separate entrance and stairs to the rental offices on the second and third floors. The north half of the new façade repeated the window detail of the old design on the second and third floors. On the ground floor there are two elaborate doors. One (19 Toronto Street), leading to the ground-floor offices, is splendidly outlined with carved 'egg and dart' moulding, topped with scrolls and a pediment, and set between columns of red granite similar to those used in 1876. The second door (17 Toronto Street) led to the 'chambers' or rented offices on the upper floors. Above this door Dick decided not to use the established window patterns, since such windows would not light offices. Instead, to light the corridors he provided oval windows filled with grillwork and set in opulently carved 'picture frames'. The frames are in turn set off by double pilasters on the second floor and by panelled pilasters on the third. The eccentricity of this window detail, and the emphatic doors, place the new work clearly in a very different period than that of the 1876 designs.

The new addition to the Consumers' Gas offices was opened at about the time gas lamps for street lighting were being abandoned and the utility was offering mainly heating and cooking fuel for homes and energy for factories. To keep pace with increasing business the company gradually took over most of the buildings to the north, buying in 1903 the west wing of the York County Courthouse (the Courts had moved in 1899–1900) and employing F.H. Herbert to renovate it. Though the sequence of buildings developed a warren-like complexity of corridors and levels, the company was able to maintain a visible presence in the heart of the city with which it had grown. In January 1977 the site was sold and Consumers' Gas moved most of its operations to Willowdale, consigning its executives to invisibility in First Canadian Place. For several years the buildings were threatened by the wrecker's ball, but most are now leased. The glorious setting Consumers' Gas prepared for itself to indicate its position and its confidence in Toronto is now the home of the Counsel Trust Company, whose renovations have shown the same commitment to excellence in architecture James Austin displayed when he originally commissioned the building.

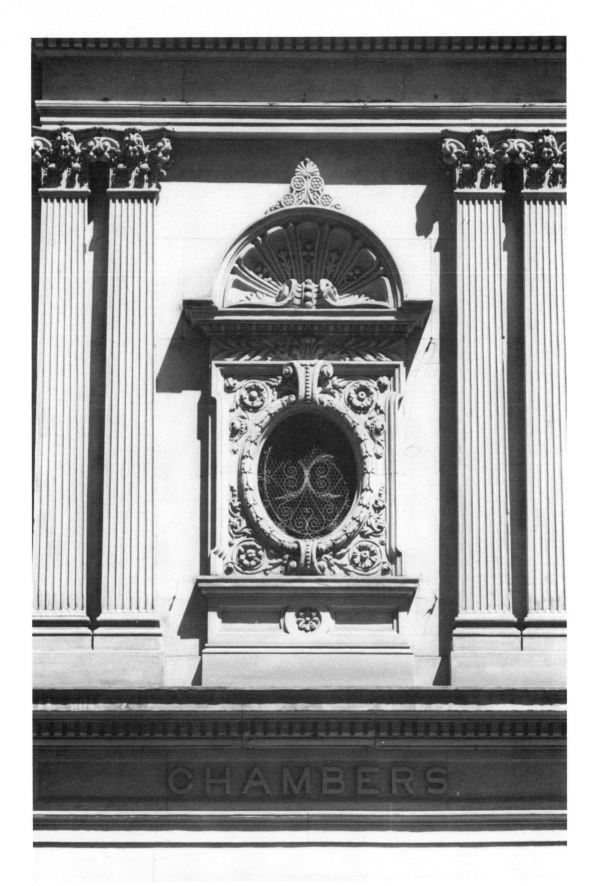

49. *Second-floor window*

50

51

THE BANK OF MONTREAL

30 Yonge Street at Front Street West (NW)
1885–6 by Darling & Curry

In nineteenth-century Canada no bank had greater power or prestige than the Bank of Montreal. Founded in 1818 with the profits of the fur trade, it became the *de facto* banker to the colonial government and then to the federal government, a position it maintained until the Bank of Canada was founded in 1935. Its architecture displayed its power. The head-office building of 1845–8 in Montreal—modelled by John Wells indirectly on the Pantheon in Rome—was once the ultimate in Canadian bank architecture, and its pedimented portico of six Corinthian columns became a corporate symbol.

The Bank's first office in Toronto was much less grand, though this Renaissance Revival building (designed by Kivas Tully in 1845) became as much an urban landmark as the head office in Montreal because it occupied a site, at the corner of Front and Yonge Streets, that was visibly in the heart of the city. By the 1880s, however, when the Bank of Montreal was beginning to enjoy the considerable profits earned from its financial support of the CPR, Tully's building was no longer adequate to express either the Bank's position in the financial community, or Toronto's growing importance in Canadian commerce. On the south side of Front Street the federal government in 1876 had rebuilt its 1845 Customs House to a florid design by R.C. Windeyer. More significantly, most of the Bank's competitors—notably the Bank of British North America (Plate 42)—had also built or rebuilt on a lavish scale. The Bank of Montreal, therefore, decided to replace Tully's building on the same site with a new and larger building, designed by Darling & Curry in 1885–6.

Frank Darling brought to the design of the new bank not only experience in the London office of Sir Arthur Blomfield, architect to the Bank of England, and in the Toronto office of Henry Langley, but also a marvellous sense of interior space and richly modelled architectural detail. Turning to the same Pantheon theme that had informed Wells' Montreal design, he created a two-storey banking hall of a size—55 feet square—and scale unprecedented in Canada. The square plan is translated into an octagon by diagonal corner arches to support a beamed and coffered ceiling that rises to a domed skylight of stained glass. The grandest commercial interior of its day in Canada, it was the first of the great banking halls that are still a preoccupation of Canadian banks and their architects. On the façades facing Front and Yonge Streets Darling echoes the portico of the Montreal head office with four piers supporting a pediment over tall arched windows that light the banking hall. These windows, and the piers, proclaim the scale of the interior space with a simplicity and largeness that was in direct contrast to the smaller, more crowded detail of its neighbours. (Such distinctness is the exact opposite of the repetitive, neutral, or mirroring finishes and patterns of today's newest banks.) The imposing entrance, set between porticoes at the corner of the building, is a small pavilion into which the richness of the whole design is condensed. Placed at the diagonal of the site and the street intersection, it brings the customer into the building at a dramatic angle to receive a striking first view of the domed hall.

More than any building since Cumberland's University College (Plate 24), Darling's Bank of Montreal shows a delight in the freely ornamental and symbolic elements of architecture. Some of the interior decorative work—by the Toronto firm of carvers, Holbrook & Mollington, to Darling's designs—is almost purely sculptural, like the Atlas figure whose straining shoulders bear the chimney stack of the manager's office and boardroom in the west wing. Other details pursue the Classical tradition of symbolism and allegory. On each pier of the portico, sculptured shields and trophies hang from carved masks to symbolize the Arts and Industries in

Canada. A plow and sheaves of wheat stand for Agriculture, a lute and clarinet for Music, palette and brushes for Painting, and a four-columned temple front for Architecture. Appropriately the piers at the southeast corner, flanking the main entrance, are dedicated to Communication and the Railway, symbolized by a telegraph pole, and to Banking, with a cornucopia spilling coins and ledgers. (Until mid-century, such detail was usually considered the prerogative of public architecture; later it was increasingly assumed by corporate architecture as a visible sign of its importance.) In the stained-glass skylight of the Bank of Montreal, manufactured by the McCausland Company of Toronto, allegory reached a climax. It was described in 1886:

> Cornucopia pour out in lavish fashion the gold and silver coin, which for centuries have been the emblem of the banker's occupation. Dragons and mythical personages in blue and crimson draperies keep guard over these treasures and defy 'the gorgons and chimaeras dire', which from other portions of the dome would ravish them away. The outer panel bears festoons of fruit and flowers, while in the centre are eight circles bearing emblems of the eight provinces of the Dominion.

The Toronto Main Branch of the Bank of Montreal occupied Darling's building until after the Second World War, when new waves of banking activity drew its main-office function away to King and Bay Streets. The building remained open until 1982, retaining the affection of staff and customers even while withstanding some egregious modernization. But it has since been sold, and redevelopment is being planned that will include adjacent vacant properties. In the discussions that lead to a new plan for the site, the city's commitment to architectural preservation, and the spirit of its planning ordonnances, will be severely tested. The building stands at present as the most perfectly conceived of Toronto's nineteenth-century banks. Strong though it is, it could be irreparably compromised and cheapened by mercenary and ill-conceived schemes to alter it—or it could be destroyed by its owners.

THE MANSIONS OF SHERBOURNE AND JARVIS STREETS

Until the end of the first decade of this century Sherbourne and Jarvis Streets were residential and synonymous with wealth and power. The houses that lined these streets were built from the late 1850s on in a multitude of different styles, both picturesque and plain. Among the later apartment buildings, hotels, commercial buildings, and parking lots a surprising number of these mansions still stand. Very few of them are now private houses, but a succession of towers, gables, high dormered roofs, and decorated façades still proclaim the magnificent past of Sherbourne and Jarvis.

James Cooper, a Toronto shoe manufacturer, built his house at 582 Sherbourne Street (on the northwest corner of Linden) in 1880–1. Designed in red brick in the Second Empire style, it is lavishly trimmed with wood, pressed metal, and expensive golden Ohio stone. The solid two-storey house (with a high mansard roof adding another full storey) was planned in a conventional manner around a wide central stairhall, but its squareness is broken by one- and two-storey bay windows and by the projecting south half of the façade. The generous use of stone for corner pilasters, window frames, and other ornaments—even to the framing of window-like panels on the faces of the north and south chimneys—makes it grander than the general run of Second Empire houses in Toronto. Though basically Classical, the forms of the stonework are as decorative as the pleatings and fancy-work of women's clothes in the period. Against the red brickwork of the walls, the stone and the cream-painted pressed-metal and carved-wood trimmings glow with life; the panelled mahogany double door, a deeper red than the walls, shines with polish and brass fittings. Inside, the rooms are high-ceilinged, spacious, and extended by bay windows. Since 1910 the house has been owned by the Knights of Columbus, who have preserved the Queen Anne decorations of the drawing-room and morning-room on the main floor. They added a large hall to the west end of the kitchen wing and placed their club rooms on the second and third floors, where the interiors were least interesting. Their sensitivity in making these and later changes—which are as important in the history of the house as Cooper's original patronage of architect and craftsman—provides an example to all institutional owners of fine buildings.

One of the most famous of the houses on Jarvis Street is Euclid Hall, at number 515 on the northeast corner of Wellesley Street, built in 1867–8 for A.R. McMaster. It was remodelled for Hart Massey, and again for his daughter Lillian Massey Treble. A baronial Gothic house of yellow brick—with a high tower and columned bay windows—it has survived a variety of alternative uses: as a convalescent home, antique gallery, and most recently as a restaurant. Accepting each change imperturbably, Euclid Hall has remained one of the most visible landmarks in downtown Toronto, presiding like a benevolent grandmother over the busy thoroughfare of upper Jarvis Street.

52. *The Cooper house, 582 Sherbourne Street*

A.R. McMaster was the head of a large wholesale dry-goods firm when work began on his house in 1867. The land came from his uncle, William McMaster, the firm's founder who went on to become a Liberal senator in 1867 and founder of the Canadian Bank of Commerce. McMaster chose a Gothic Revival design, which was fashionable for large suburban houses in the late 1860s. The name of the architect was not recorded, but it was probably William Irving, whom McMaster employed in 1871 to build his palatial business headquarters (demolished) at 12 Front Street West. Typical of the Second Empire period, the new McMaster house was built up around a proud tower that set it off in the street and declared its owner's importance to the passerby. (To McMaster's colleagues and neighbours, this would have been seen not as boastful but as public evidence of success accruing from hard work.) The main entrance—below the tower and sheltered by a *porte cochère*—led (as it still does) to a wide central hall. There was a broad staircase at the far end, and to the right a sitting-room facing the street, and further back the drawing-room. On the left was a smaller library or reception room, with the dining-room behind.

A.R. McMaster died in 1882 and the house was sold to Hart Massey for a cash payment of $12,500 (and an additional mortgage, which with interest amounted to $20,603.28 when it was discharged in July 1889). In 1870 Massey had turned the management of the Massey Manufacturing Company over to his son Charles and moved to Cleveland. There

115

53. *The Massey house, 515 Jarvis Street, c. 1900*

he engaged in speculation in land, houses, and apartments, and built for himself a large Second-Empire-style house on fashionable Euclid Avenue. In 1882 Charles's ill-health forced Hart Massey to move to Toronto to resume control of the business.

Massey renamed the Jarvis Street house Euclid Hall, in memory of his happy years in Cleveland, and almost immediately began an extensive series of alterations. The first were carried out by Langley, Langley & Burke, the architects of Metropolitan Methodist Church, where he worshipped. These included new windows in the sitting-room and decorative additions to the interior in the Queen Anne style, many of which still remain. Hart Massey was directly involved with all the architectural work he commissioned, particularly with the second set of changes made in 1885–6 by E.J. Lennox,* which included a new staircase and a veranda and greenhouse added on the south side.

After Hart Massey's death in 1896 his widow remained in residence; but control of the house passed to her daughter Lillian Massey Treble. In 1900 she engaged G.M. Miller to alter and extend it.** He rebuilt the greenhouse and veranda

and added two tall bay windows on either side of a new front porch, and a turret at the southwest corner. The new work was Gothic in style, though the intertwined foliage that decorates the porch shows the influence of Art Nouveau. Inside, Miller swept away much of the Victorian interior, moving Lennox's staircase to the north side of the hall (to connect with a coach entrance) and adding an Arabian smoking-room, with beaten brass lamps and scimitars on the walls (the style was much the rage in Toronto at the end of the century—even the staid Timothy Eaton had such a den off his front hall). The last of the renovations completed the transformation of the façade: a sunroom over the front porch, glazed with Art Nouveau coloured glass.

When Lillian Massey died in 1915 she left the house to Victoria College, and it was rented until 1924 as a convalescent home for wounded soldiers. By the 1920s society had decamped to Rosedale, Forest Hill, and Bayview. Euclid Hall was sold and became Ryan's Art Gallery; the upstairs bedrooms were rented as offices. The greenhouse and garden were sacrificed to make room for a gas station. After Ryan's closed in 1961, Euclid Hall became Julie's Mansion restaurant and it is now the Keg Mansion restaurant. The place awaits restoration and appreciation—perhaps as a luxury condominium apartment building.

The tree-lined streetscapes of Jarvis and Sherbourne can hardly be imagined today as they appeared in 1882—except for a single block, between Cawthra Square and Gloucester on the west side of Jarvis, where the houses (and trees), after many changes of use, remain much as they were in the 1890s.

---

* Lennox had been commissioned in 1883 by Charles Massey to build a house, which still stands, immediately north of Euclid Hall, at 519 Jarvis. Built in red brick in a gabled Queen Anne style, it was not finished when Charles died in 1884. It was purchased by Chester Daniel Massey, father of Vincent and Raymond, and received additions by Sproatt & Rolph in 1907.

** Miller was for some years architect to the Massey family and in 1908 designed the University of Toronto Food Sciences Building, known as the Lillian Massey Building, at Avenue Road and Bloor (SE), now the office of the Provincial Ombudsman.

From the towered Romanesque Revival house of George H. Gooderham, in glowing red Credit Valley stone, built by David Roberts in 1889 at 504 Jarvis (now Angelini's Restaurant), to the north end of the block, where the C.R. Rundle house of 1889 stands empty and neglected, the block offers a panorama of Toronto domestic architecture in one of its most inventive periods.

The most striking of these houses was built by David Roberts Jr for the twenty-one-year-old George Horace Gooderham. Within a short walk were at least six other Gooderham houses, several of them by Roberts—notably the 1883 house of Charles H. Gooderham at 592 Sherbourne, which is now the Selby Hotel. (In 1889 Roberts was also working on a house for George Sr at St George and Bloor, Plate 63.) The house at 504 Jarvis, with its rounded tower and high gable, is a fine summary, beautifully executed, of Romanesque Revival architecture, especially the second-floor loggia, with its pierced balustrade and the strong moulding that supports it.

In the 1880s and 1890s every major architectural firm in Toronto was involved in domestic architecture, providing a greater variety of the currently popular Romanesque Revival and Queen Anne styles. The J.H. McKinnon house at 506 Jarvis was designed in 1888 by Langley & Burke in a wide-proportioned Queen Anne style using fine brickwork and decorative details in terracotta; at 510 Jarvis the Thomas Taylor house was also built in 1888.

The last two houses on the block—512 and 514—were designed by E.J. Lennox and built by C.R. Rundle and Company in 1889. Rundle was one of the leading contractors in the city and worked for Lennox on the building of the Old City Hall (Plate 76). The house at 512 Jarvis was built speculatively by Rundle and sold to Edward Gallow, a stockbroker. Rundle's own house was built at 514 Jarvis, on the southwest corner of Gloucester. In this Lennox design the tower rises through the gable and the two elements are drawn together into one powerful mass. The polygonal shape of the tower, which was originally open at the top as a sleeping balcony, contrasts with the gable's precise geometry and smooth face. Lennox placed the house at the Gloucester Street edge of the narrow site and the service entrance under a large, gracefully carved arch cut through the brick wall, next to the stained-glass windows of the staircase on the north wall. The principal rooms, which needed natural light, face south, east, and west and are on either side of the entrance and stair-halls and a veranda-like porch. It is one of Lennox's best plans, making the most of a narrow site. The moulded and carved brick, and the tile and stone, that detail the strong masses of the building are of particular interest.

54. *The C.R. Rundle house, 514 Jarvis Street*

In the course of the demolitions that decimated parts of Jarvis Street after the Second World War, the block between Cawthra Square and Gloucester was preserved largely because the last family to live in the Gooderham house at 504 Jarvis was interested in the work of the Big Brothers of Toronto and helped them to buy it. The Big Brothers occupied it during most of the 1970s and then sold it to the Angelini family, who opened it to the public as a restaurant, preserving and restoring much of the interior. In 1985 they added an enclosed terrace dining-room on the south side, which replicates the original veranda. Other houses on the block have been schools, rooming houses, and students' residences. For the most part the owners have respected the original buildings, whose careful construction has supported the various uses. The fate of the Rundle house, however, has unfortunately been very different. It was bought speculatively on the assumption that the block would be cleared and built up with high-rise apartments. But the development never occurred and the Rundle house has been left to decay. During the 1970s a large dog was kept inside to scare off prowlers, and on one occasion the house was almost put up for auction to pay back taxes.

MADISON AVENUE

It was not until the late 1880s that Toronto received its first middle- and professional-class suburb, offering people of moderate means a new residential community with wide tree-lined streets close to the city and connected to it by public transit, but distinctly separate from it. This suburb—known as the Annex, because it was annexed to the city in 1887—is bounded by Bloor Street West, Avenue Road, Davenport Road, and Bathurst Street. The most attractive streets in the Annex, and those most representative of the 1880s and 1890s, are Bedford, Admiral, St George, Huron, and Madison. St George Street and the George Gooderham house (Plate 63) are not as typical of the Annex as Madison Avenue, which was laid out across land that originally belonged to the Baldwins of 'Spadina' and still retains much of its character as a residential street of the 1890s. It was purchased and subdivided by Simeon Janes, beginning in 1887. In Janes' plans the street was divided into lots that averaged about twenty-five feet wide. Its semi-detached and single houses (row houses were prohibited) were intended for Toronto's growing middle class of academics, civil servants, independent businessmen, and professionals. With very few official building regulations, the houses still respected a common setback and followed approximately the same eaves level. Open lawns separated the houses from the sidewalk and road, and trees were planted along the street, creating an unusually disciplined and civil environment that allowed considerable variety in house design. Madison Avenue is a monument to the Victorians' intelligent use of architecture and planning to achieve pleasant residential surroundings.

The lots along Madison, and the other streets in Janes' subdivision, were acquired by speculative builders who put up small groups of houses; or by private owners who contracted for individually designed houses. In either case architects better known for mansions or churches and public buildings often designed smaller houses as well. Number 37 Madison, the first house to be built on the street, was designed in 1887–8 by E.J. Lennox for Lewis Lukes, one of the contractors engaged in the building of Old City Hall (Plate 76). It is a richly textured and decorative version of the Romanesque Revival, with a few English touches, like the half-timbering in the prominent gables. The ground floor stands on a heavy basement of rock-faced stone and is massively articulated by two wide, rounded brick arches for the porch entrance and the living-room window surrounded by basket-weave brickwork. (The house is recognizably Lennox's by the monumentality of such big features as these arches.) The three floors form clearly defined levels on the façade, each lighter and more broken than the one immediately below. The entrance porch is underneath a second-floor balcony, framed in wooden lattice; another balcony on the third floor, almost completely screened by lattice, fills the triangle of the front gable.

The visitor climbs the front steps to a porch that is enclosed on two sides by heavy arches to make a cool, dark, semi-private space between the public area of the street and the privacy of the hall inside. The porch and vestibule lead into a small stairhall that is carefully designed as the centre of the ground-floor rooms, with wide arches on one side leading into them, and on the other a staircase and a large stained-glass window. The hall's squareness, its central position within the plan, and the spaciousness implied by the staircase rising in several flights from it, create an unusual feeling of space in what is fundamentally a narrow house. Similar reception halls are found in many of the houses on the street. Their details—such as oak panelling, a fireplace, built-in seats, and windows of high-quality stained glass—echo those found in many mansions of the period, and although they lacked such luxuries as a billiard room, library, or music room, the smaller houses in the Annex showed a definite attempt to make them equally comfortable.

Most Annex houses were planned without servants' quarters; the servants (almost all middle-class families of the period could afford them) usually commuted to their work from the heart of the city. In the Lukes house, like others in the Annex, the third floor contained family bedrooms. One of these opens onto the front lattice-screened balcony. Cooled by the few breezes that grace a Toronto summer and sheltered from the sight of passersby, it served as a summer sleeping porch. Another common feature of these houses is a second sleeping porch outside the main bedroom on the second floor; like the planning of the whole house around the stairhall, it indicates a preoccupation with design that could furnish convenience and comfort without sacrificing style and detail.

The Lukes house might almost have served as a model for the later houses on Madison Avenue, built through the early 1890s in the Romanesque style or the Queen Anne style. (The two styles, the first American in origin and the second English, were in their own countries very different; but in Toronto they come together with only round arches and more robust detail distinguishing Romanesque from Queen Anne.) The round arches, emphatic gables, and towers were used with great invention to give the semi-detached and single houses on the constricted Madison Avenue sites a strong identity. The pair of houses at numbers 12 and 14 are typical of many of the Romanesque houses in the Annex. Built in 1891 by T.E. Perkins, for a total cost of $9,500, they used broad round arches to frame the front windows and deep-shadowed entrance porches. The fine moulded brick of the arches, and the basket-weave pattern in brick above them, greatly enriched the narrow façades.

The Romanesque and Queen Anne styles made it relatively easy for builders and architects to individualize the houses of the Annex. In many cases, as in the semi-detached pair of houses at 24 and 26 Madison (1891), each half of a double

55. *The Lewis Lukes house, 37 Madison Avenue*

56. *Madison Avenue, west side*

house has a particular character. Number 26 has a round-arched porch and front window facing the street, two windows on the second floor, and a broad tile-hung gable at the top; number 24 is dominated by a polygonal tower with a tall pyramid roof that gives each floor a broad bay window, beside which the main entrance and second-floor balcony seem to nestle. Thus, though the plans of both are essentially the same, each has a unique appearance. The pair of houses at numbers 30 and 32 Madison, built in 1889, almost look like a mansion from the street because only one of the two entrances is visible at a time. A variation in the common plan allowed Number 32 to have a broad-arched porch facing the street, while Number 30 has a similar porch at the side. The choice of decorative details was largely at the whim of the builder and reflected his particular skills. Bricklayers and masons tended to make prominent use of carved stonework or terracotta and moulded brickwork. But the builder of 20 Madison was G.W. Turner, a carpenter by trade, and he included beautiful balcony details of carved and turned woodwork.

The development of Madison Avenue, and of most streets in the Annex, was largely completed by 1914. Walking north on Madison from Bloor today, one can easily trace the gradual changes in domestic fashion. The picturesque compositions and richly textured surfaces of the Romanesque Revival gradually gave way, first to designs incorporating features of the Georgian Revival and the English Cottage Style (see page 177) and then, south of Davenport Road, to the square-faced verandaed houses that came into fashion before the First World War and are familiar in the west and east ends of the city. Few of the houses remain in single-family occupancy; apartments, flats, and student rooming houses are the norm (contributing to serious traffic and parking problems in the area). But unlike St George Street and Spadina Road, where big houses on large lots made their replacement by high-rise apartments in the 1950s and 1960s relatively easy, streets like Madison, with smaller houses on smaller lots, escaped destruction. The most recent development on Madison has in fact used the houses as the key to the scale of a group of apartments built as infill behind number 25 and running through to Huron Street (1979–81 by Paul Martel).

The Annex displays a great variety of architectural size and style and period. Since the late nineteenth century it has undergone sometimes drastic changes in population density and character. But it is still a model urban community—the kind of place that would organize effectively to stop an expressway or a block-busting developer from threatening the character of the neighbourhood and the city. The Annex reflects the heritage of forty of the most creative years in Toronto architecture.

57. *The Army and Navy Store, with St Lawrence Hall to the east*

THE ARMY AND NAVY STORE
(Now COOPERS & LYBRAND, CHARTERED ACCOUNTANTS)
129–35 King Street East (S)
1887–9 by Langley & Burke

In the late nineteenth century King Street East was Toronto's main commercial thoroughfare. Though Yonge Street grew steadily in importance, particularly after the founding of Eaton's and Simpson's, King remained the hub of both high-fashion shops and large stores catering for the broadest possible market. When it first became commercially important it had simple three- and four-storey shops modelled on established patterns of house architecture (with shopfronts added), which were built in the 1840s and after the fire of 1849. From the 1860s on styles began to change, and none of the remaining buildings better represents the taste of the eighties and nineties than the former Army and Navy Clothing Stores at 129–35 King Street East. In that period stores became larger and showier, featuring cast iron and plate glass; and bigger shop windows whose crowded displays, often lit at night, added a new attraction to the streetscape.

William A. Thompson founded the Army and Navy Stores

in 1887. His family had been merchandising men's and boy's clothing since the early 1840s, when Thomas Thompson, William's father, opened Mammoth House—on the northeast corner of King and Francis (the first street west of Jarvis, now closed)—with the intention of providing high-quality merchandise at low prices. The first Mammoth House burned in March 1848. Business resumed immediately, but the premises were again severly damaged in the fire of 8–9 April 1849 that destroyed St James' Cathedral. However, on the morning of the 9th, before the ashes had cooled, Thompson inserted an ad in the *Globe* announcing not only that Mammoth House would, 'like the fabled Phoenix rise from its ashes and again rear its majestic form and be as HERETOFORE ''The Emporium for Cheap and Fashionable Goods'' ', but that in the meantime he would 'commence SELLING OFF his immense stock, which with the Spring Arrivals daily expected, will be as complete as any in the City.' Few retailers in the period could match the bravado of Thompson's approach to business or his appreciation of the value of advertising. Most stores were then content with having their simple business card printed in a daily or weekly paper; Thompson's ads were topical, changed frequently, and were designed to stand out from the small-type columns of the day.* During the 1870s and 1880s his ads included large eye-catching line drawings or cartoons that frequently offered comment on politics and cultural events of the day. Anti-Riel drawings appeared during the Red River Rebellion of 1870.

As it was rebuilt after the 1849 fire, the Mammoth House store was one part of a red-brick row with restrained Greek Revival detailing (the eastern section still stands at 142 King Street East). Though the design was elegant, it made little impact in the streetscape. In 1885, at the height of his success, Thompson began to make plans for a new store on the same site. In an ad in the *Globe* on 23 October he outlined the firm's history and its place in the city, and announced his plan to

> pull down our present premises and build large. Not like a certain man of old do we intend to have 'many goods laid up for many years,' and 'to take our ease and be merry'—although we don't object to being merry—but we hope to work, work, work, and to continue to stand prominently before the public, and be known as the largest, most enterprising, and most popular Retail House in the country.

But before work had begun, Thompson hit on a more adventurous plan. He decided to split the firm and allow his son and partner William to found a new establishment. The Army and Navy Store opened first at the northwest corner of Shuter, and then moved in 1887 into the new building on the south side of King Street opposite St James' Cathedral. The new firm was not, as its name suggests, a military surplus store, but a men's and boys' clothing store like Mammoth House. It was modelled on London's Army and Navy Stores, successful suppliers to members and families of England's colonial forces of everything they needed to maintain the English way of life in such distant places as India, Hong Kong, Australia—and Vancouver Island.

The new building was designed by the Toronto firm of Langley & Burke—the leaders of the architectural profession in the province at the time—in two identical sections: the east half was completed in 1887 and the west half was

added in 1888 as the business prospered. Planned to accommodate the store on the first three floors, with rental space on the fourth (the practice and club room of the Band of the Queen's Own Regiment was the most important early tenant), the four-storey building rises much higher than the three-and-a-half-storey buildings to either side. Though set off from its neighbours by its height, it is the difference in scale and the distinctive architectural form of its arched windows that make the Army and Navy Store an outstanding landmark on King Street. Built mostly of red brick and terracotta, the building is dominated by the façade, whose twin arches of glass—braced by exposed iron beams—together span the entire width, save for narrow supporting piers. Originally the ground floor had a plate-glass front display window (with a central door in each section) that was different from the present one. But the façade of the upper floors has not changed; through its expanses of metal-framed glass, natural light flooded the store during the day, and passersby could see stock and advertising displayed on three levels. Complementing the two great arches is a row of smaller arched windows—five in each section— across the fourth floor, above which a simple corbelled cornice completes the design. The spandrels above the arches are filled in with terracotta blocks decorated with a web of circles and curved squares. But it is the arched windows, both large and small, that form the dramatic element in the design, lifting it out of the ordinary among the small-scaled, plainly windowed Late Georgian shops of the 1840s that still lined the street in the 1880s.

By the turn of the century King had ceased to be a fashionable shopping street. New office buildings, and the King Edward Hotel (Plate 79), replaced several of the largest stores; the shopping district east of Church Street remained popular until 1918, when it was blighted by the same decline that had affected St Lawrence Hall (Plate 16). In 1956 York Belting took over the brightly lit spaces of the Army and Navy Store to manufacture industrial fan and pulley belts. During the 1950s, when Toronto's appreciation of Victorian design was at its nadir, the building luckily escaped demolition. Ironically the first schemes for restoring St Lawrence Hall in the 1960s posed the most serious threat to the building because they called for a plaza with high-rise towers. York Belting remained the last industrial tenant on this part of King Street until 1984–5, when the Army and Navy Store building was purchased and renovated to become office space for the accounting firm of Coopers & Lybrand—saving for the city one of the most striking commercial buildings in late nineteenth-century Canada.

---

*His closest modern counterpart might be Ed Mirvish, owner of Honest Ed's Department Store.

58

59. *The Confederation Life Building,* c. 1895

THE CONFEDERATION LIFE BUILDING

20 Richmond Street East, at Yonge (NE)

1888–90 by Knox, Elliott & Jarvis

In the late nineteenth century insurance companies, because of their size and profitability, were able to build on a scale few banks could afford. The Confederation Life Association was incorporated by Parliament in 1871. Over the next twenty years its business assets and profits—largely immune to the economic ups and downs that plagued the chartered banks, because people preferred insurance to bank deposits as a means of saving—grew tremendously, along with its interest in architecture. Covering half of its Yonge Street block,* the Confederation Life Building was one of the largest in the city, and perhaps the most romantic, with its flamboyant French Gothic and Romanesque detail.

To publicize itself and its intention to build, the Company organized an international competition for designs, which was won by a partnership, Knox & Elliott. William Knox had studied in Edinburgh and Glasgow before emigrating from Scotland to Australia and then to Chicago, where he worked first with Burnham & Root, the undoubted leaders in American skyscraper design in the 1880s, and then with Charles Ives Cobb. John Elliott, who also worked in Chicago with Cobb, was a Torontonian, educated at Upper Canada College and the Massachusetts Institute of Technology. The two formed their partnership to enter the competition. They

established their practice in Toronto and took Beaumont Jarvis as a partner; but their success caused much ill feeling among Toronto's growing architectural profession, to many of whom it seemed that plum commissions were going to Americans.

Knox & Elliott's winning design, which was erected almost without change, combines both the most basic and the most flamboyant aspects of high-rise architecture then popular in Chicago: cast-iron columns, wood and cast-iron beams, and thick structural brick and stone walling. The sheer size of the building, the thick piers and round arches of the ground floor and the arches above, which group several levels of windows, all echo the work of Burnham & Root and other Chicago architects. But much of the elongated, thin lightness of the detail comes from French Gothic work of the sixteenth century. Against the sky this detail breaks out into a towered, turreted, and steep-roofed composition reminiscent of the most fanciful of French medieval castles. The building was executed in Credit River sandstone and in brick that was closely matched in a rich, dark red. No expense was spared to secure craftsmanship for laying the brick and carving the stone. Around the ground-floor windows, and in the capitals of colonnettes beside the principal doors, the stone is lushly carved with naturalistic foliage and grotesque animal forms that complement the skyline and anticipate the stylized exoticism of Art Nouveau design.

Confederation Life was clearly delighted with its new headquarters, whose towers soared high above the city's commercial district. For several years lithographs of the building were widely distributed as part of the company's advertising. It established the architects in Toronto and they designed several houses and other buildings, although they moved to Cleveland in 1893. Originally the Confederation Life Building was divided into two sections by a small interior courtyard, with the company's offices to the east, and the Yonge Street block to the west designed to be a large department store. The store was never a success because of the presence of Eaton's and Simpson's at Yonge and Queen. In 1897–1900 the interior was reconstructed to serve as office space and the ground-floor façades were altered by John Wilson Gray, who also designed for the company's offices a large extension fronting on Victoria Street.

In 1953, when Confederation Life moved to new premises on Bloor Street East, the Richmond Street building was sold. Much of the carved detail was masked with sheets of opaque glass, concealing what changing taste could not value or admire. The recent restoration—which was endangered by a serious fire during the work—has exposed and repaired the original detail, and the building was cleaned. (Unfortunately the towers and turrets that were earlier lopped off the skyline in the name of 'simplification' have not been replaced.) The second stage of the work is far less positive. It includes the demolition of everything else in the block, including a very fine Imperial Bank of 1914 by Darling & Pearson, which stood at Queen and Yonge and was condemned because the architects declined to work with its interesting split-level plan.

---

* Extensions made over the next twenty years covered most of the rest of the block.

60. *Richmond Street façade*

61. *The Toronto Club, c. 1895*

THE TORONTO CLUB

107 Wellington Street West at York
1888 by Darling & Curry; 1911–12 additions and
alterations by Darling & Pearson

On 20 March 1837 a wholesale merchant in the import-export business, James Newbigging, summoned a group of Toronto gentlemen for the purpose of founding a society whose members and guests might engage, as its first minutes state, in 'social and friendly intercourse' and enjoy each other's company 'in the style of the best London clubs'. The Upper Canada Club, as it was first called, leased a large house at the northwest corner of King and Bay Streets. A staff of six servants was assembled, an excellent wine cellar put down, a selection of the best magazines and reviews ordered from Britain and the United States, and the place decorated handsomely and equipped with fine furniture, china, and silver plate.

If ever the city's establishment associated together in one place, this was it. The oldest families of the Compact—Jarvis, Boulton, Ridout, Macaulay—were represented, along with Chief Justice Robinson; fifteen directors of the Bank of Upper Canada (Plate 6), the Commercial Bank of the Midland District (Plate 14), and the Farmer's Joint Stock Banking Company; six directors of British American Assurance; and seven from the city's first projected railroad company, the Toronto and Lake Huron. (Newbigging was involved in both the last two enterprises.) Members included three of the five executive councillors of the province; thirteen legislative councillors; a sizeable group of the most substantial and conservative members of the Legislative Assembly; numerous officials holding office under the Crown; and at least four past and future mayors of the city. Out-of-town members included a Cartwright from Kingston, a Harris from London, and Allan McNab of Hamilton. British army officers were invited to join and some did. A few manufacturers—such as Jesse Ketchum, the tanner—were members, particularly if they held directorships in other ventures. Toronto's leading lawyers and merchants, however, represented the largest membership. Most appear to have been under fifty years of age. Archdeacon Strachan's two sons belonged, as did William Allan's successor as president of the Bank of Upper Canada, William Proudfoot. Dr Baldwin's nephew, the many-talented public servant Robert Baldwin Sullivan, was a member (see pp. 15–17), as was Sheriff William Botsford Jarvis, whose father, uncle, and father-in-law were original members of the Family Compact.

The Club's deficit soon outstripped the income from

membership fees and its affairs were wound up. But several months later, in 1842—its function being sorely missed—it was refounded as the Toronto Club. Some members' failure to pay their bills, and a general unwillingness to invest capital, confined the club to various rented premises—including for a time rooms in Toronto's grandest Victorian hotel, The Rossin House at King and York—until a decision was made to build a permanent home at York and Wellington. The present building was completed there in 1888.

Among the many clubs founded in nineteenth-century Toronto, only the United Empire Club had previously aspired to architectural grandeur. Their building of 1874 at 110 King Street West, designed by Grant & Dick, had awed members of other clubs, but its cost and maintenance drove the United Empire into bankruptcy in 1881 (the clubhouse became the offices of the North American Life Assurance Company and was demolished in 1932). Frank Darling, who had been a member, recognized the need for economy when he designed a new home for the Toronto Club, to which he also belonged. Though he drew on the rich heritage of London club architecture to establish the prestige of the organization, he chose the red brick and terracotta commonly used in Toronto, with only sparing use of decorative stone. The square mass of the three-storey building, with its deep Classical cornice, and the arched Palladian windows and balconies of the principal second-floor rooms, recall the Renaissance Revival style of the Reform Club (1837–41) and particularly the Travellers Club (1829–32) by Sir Charles Barry—far from 'modern', but plainly symbolizing the good life and companionship of clubland. (This style had been used for banks and major commercial buildings because of its associations with clubs and their members' commercial and financial power.) The round arches of parti-coloured stonework framing the entrance borrow directly from the fashionable Romanesque Revival style, and the interiors are as spacious and finely crafted as those of the best houses.

During its first two decades in the new quarters—which were inaugurated with a grand ball in 1889—the Club introduced such up-to-date features as a bicycle stand for members, electric lighting, and a 'type-writing machine'. But another financial crisis struck in 1910 when many members left to join the York Club, which had purchased the elegant Gooderham mansion (Plate 63) at St George and Bloor; however, the addition in 1911–12 of further modern facilities kept enough members involved to provide financial support. The Club was finally put on a sound footing in 1943 by J.A. 'Bud' McDougald's requirement that all members buy no-interest bonds. Creditors were also issued the bonds and were paid off as rapidly as possible.

One of the three oldest gentlemen's clubs in North America, the Toronto Club is still a retreat for the city's male establishment, in a building that is an attractive Victorian counterpoint to the giant towers of glass and steel around it.

63. *South front facing Bloor Street West*

THE GEORGE GOODERHAM HOUSE

(Now the YORK CLUB)

135 St George Street at Bloor Street West (NE)

1889–92 by David Roberts Jr

The Romanesque Revival was first introduced to Toronto in large-scale public buildings with E.J. Lennox's City Hall (Plate 76) of 1886–99 and R.A. Waite's Legislative Buildings (Plate 67) of 1886–92. But it became more popular and more successful in residences. The American architects who had the most important influence on Canadian work in the Romanesque style—Henry Hobson Richardson, Bruce Price, and the New York firm of McKim, Mead & White—had all distinguished themselves in residential design. In Toronto, apart from relatively small middle-class houses like those on Madison Avenue (Plates 55, 56), the style is most fully exploited for handsome effects in spacious mansions, and the best example is the George Gooderham house.

George Gooderham (1820–1905), who succeeded his father as president of the Gooderham and Worts distillery, was involved in a wide range of Toronto commercial and financial enterprises, including the Bank of Toronto. For much of his life he lived in his father's house (demolished) on the northeast corner of Trinity and Mill Streets, close to the distillery and his business interests. In the late 1880s, as Toronto became more clearly divided into residential and commercial areas, and as the distillery expanded, he decided to acquire property in the newly fashionable Annex and commissioned David Roberts to design his house. Roberts' father, David Roberts Sr, had been the designer in 1859 of the distillery's first important buildings (Plate 40). David Roberts Jr—after

64. *Main entrance on St George Street*

65. *West front on St George Street*

setting himself up in practice in 1870—designed several houses for family members, notably the house at 504 Jarvis Street (see p. 117).

Facing St George, but intended to be dramatically visible at the Bloor Street intersection, the Gooderham house has a corner tower that is flanked by a great gable over the main entrance, a *porte-cochère* on the left, a tall chimney-stack on the south façade, and is partially surrounded by a high stone wall. The building achieves its essential character—massive solidity—from the integrity of the geometric forms that make up the composition. There is also rich luxuriance of carved ornament. Round arches—supported visually on groups of stocky columns, colonnettes, and piers—are used to shape and frame windows and doors. Interlaced foliage and repeti-

tive geometric patterns spread across the curved surfaces of the arches, their supports, and the capitals, as well as in bands across the gables and encircling the tower. Through the foliage appear grotesque beasts and human faces (a portrait of Henry Sproatt, who worked with Roberts on the design, can be seen to the right of the main door). The carving is concentrated around the double arches of the main entrance, with their surround of rock-faced stonework, which becomes a base for an extended composition of arches and colonnettes that spreads up the height of the gable, linking the windows and transforming the entrance into a grand frontispiece for a mansion. The remarkable unity of the whole is due to the close harmony of colours in the stone, brick, and terracotta used in Toronto at the end of the nineteenth century, and to the care taken with the materials, best exemplified in the smooth curves of the brickwork around the corner tower. All the picturesque elements—gables, tower chimney, and long roof—are tied together into a seamless composition.

Inside the Gooderham house the huge central stairhall was the focus for all activity in the house.* The staircase rises in three broad flights from the hall to the private rooms above, dramatizing the act of ascent. (A small stair near the carriage entrance allowed ladies arriving for dinners and receptions to go upstairs immediately, adjust their gowns, and then make a grand entrance down the main staircase.) The hall is wainscotted in oak, with richly carved panels. Oak is also used for the beamed and coffered ceiling; for the heavily carved arches that frame the lowest flight of the staircase; and, in combination with cherry and maple, in the parquet floor. Against one wall are the mantel and fireplace, embellished with coloured marble, alabaster, and mosaic. With a roaring log fire, they became the very symbol of generous hospitality.

The hall, enveloping the visitor in a warm enclosure of richly carved oak and limestone, conveys on a grand scale an image of family wealth, comfort, and security. The other rooms that open from the hall provide more specialized living spaces: the drawing-room on the north side, and the music room that fills the southwest corner of the house and expands into the round space of the corner tower to become a sunroom, whose wide plate-glass windows follow the curve of the walls and give a panoramic view of the gardens and the entire neighbourhood.

George Gooderham died in 1905, and the house did not long remain in the family. Rising costs and taxes presented a problem even for the Gooderhams, and changing fashions must have made its Romanesque seem dark and ponderous. In 1908 the house was bought by the York Club, whose members were wealthy Toronto businessmen, professionals, and social leaders. In its scale and monumentality the Gooderham house provided the perfect setting, and only a minimum of change was necessary: in 1910–11 Darling and Pearson added

a large dining-room overlooking the south garden, and a two-storey veranda (since enclosed) next to the kitchens. The new additions were Classical, not Romanesque, in style; but with the tall arcade of the diningroom worked in the red stone of the original house, they were a perfect addition to Roberts' design.

The Gooderham house stands as a landmark introduction to the Annex. Within a few years a cluster of other Romanesque houses were built nearby. Gooderham himself had Roberts design a house next door (demolished) for his son-in-law, Thomas G. Blackstock, on the southeast corner of Prince Arthur and St George. Their gardens were contiguous, and Roberts designed a low fence of stone and wrought iron to go around both properties. Across the street James T. McCabe, a speculative builder, put up three houses in the same red stone and brick—174 (1892) and 176 and 178 (both 1891)—whose assemblage of towers, gables, and bays echo the big house as children echo their parents. The best of the later houses on St George is the Thomas Horn house on the northwest corner of Prince Arthur (180), built in 1898 by F.H. Herbert. Its compact mass of rough stone, with a swelling corner tower and bay facing St George, has the same monumental strength and simplicity as the Gooderham house.

In this setting, with its definite reference points, it is unfortunate that the new city clubhouse of the Royal Canadian Yacht Club (1984, by Crang and Boake) should be such an awkwardly designed and alien neighbour. Building on the parking lot that some forty years ago replaced the Blackstock house, and preserving what remained of the garden wall, the architects worked in dark-brown brick, stone, and concrete. Though these materials hint at the innate strength and mass of the nearby houses, the clubhouse is basically a shed onto which was tacked a symmetrical façade of several setbacks, culminating in a central gable flanked by two squared chimneys. The thin gestures of this façade, which is squeezed up against the original garden fence, do not complement the strong, solid outlines of towers and gables that enrich the neighbouring houses. The RCYC clubhouse has no presence in the neighbourhood: if it were demolished tomorrow, it would leave no memory behind.

---

* Halls of this size combined the functions of the traditional stairhall with the romantic associations of the Great Hall of late-medieval English houses, which had a strong influence on house design in the nineteenth century.

THE GOODERHAM BUILDING

(Also known as THE FLATIRON BUILDING)

49 Wellington Street East, at Church
and Front Street East

1891–2 by David Roberts Jr

The best-known building on Front Street—and certainly one of the best known in the city—is not a warehouse but an office block: the Gooderham Building. Its towered 'flatiron' shape and eclectic, flamboyant style were conceived with an eye to the same desire for image and advertising that produced the warehouse buildings on the south side of Front Street. It was commissioned by George Gooderham (see previous entry), head of the Gooderham and Worts distillery, who developed his father's company and his inherited wealth into a financial and commercial empire. As the distillery flourished and enlarged its facilities on Trinity Street (see Plate 41), Gooderham extended his own interests—into railways (the Toronto and Nipissing), insurance (Manufacturers' Life), and philanthropy (particularly the University of Toronto and the Toronto General Hospital). In 1882 he also became president of the Bank of Toronto, initiating a period of great expansion in its business and influence. Gooderham ran his affairs from an office in the Bank of Toronto building at Church and Wellington (1862, by William Kauffmann; demolished) until 1884, when he moved to a building just to the west, on Wellington Street. Finally in August 1891 Gooderham initiated plans for a new building across Wellington Street to house both his own offices and those of the distillery.

The site—an irregular triangle between Front and Wellington Streets—was the most prominent in the entire area and Gooderham bought it for its landmark possibilities.* The commission went to David Roberts Jr, who had designed Gooderham's house on St George Street (Plate 63), and he adapted the French modern Gothic style that Knox, Elliott and Jarvis had popularized in the Confederation Life Building of 1888–90 (Plate 59).

Roberts followed the site's triangular shape exactly in his five-storey building of red brick with Credit Valley stone trim. Disregarding obvious planning problems, he placed at its apex a semi-circular tower, whose large windows follow the curve of the walls. Here Gooderham had his own office, commanding a view few other Toronto businessmen could match (it included the Bank of Toronto, the St Lawrence Market, the distillery at the end of the harbour, and the railways along the waterfront). Facing Wellington Street was the second major feature of the design: a great arched portal with a

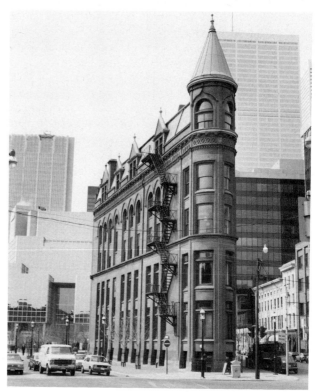

66

framing Gothic moulding. The height of the building is divided into two main levels, with the windows grouped between brick piers. Viewed from the east, the building takes its character from the tower and its conical roof. The slender proportions of the design might seem too delicate for a commercial building, had the ground-floor piers of smooth-dressed Credit Valley stone not been designed to flare out and provide an appropriately strong base for the height of the building. The fanciful pinnacle dormers and the mouldings that decorate the arch framing the main entrance are French Gothic.

When the rest of its block—west to Yonge Street—was levelled in the 1960s the Gooderham Building became an orphan in the streetscape. One wall, however, remained because it turned out that Roberts, for the sake of economy, had butted his building against the wall of the neighbouring one—and that wall had to stay or the Gooderham Building would be open to the weather.* Restoration in 1975–6, with assistance from the Ontario Heritage Foundation, highlighted the original work and made the Gooderham Building valuable office space once again. Finally, with the development of Berczy Park, and especially of the A.E. LePage Building (Plate 176), a new setting was created for the Gooderham Building that pays homage to its unique character.

---

* It had been occupied by one of the oldest commercial buildings in the city: the Coffin Block, so called because its blunted triangular shape reminded people of the end of a coffin.

* It was on the exposed outer face of this wall that Derek Besant's mural, painted in 1980, of the façade of the Griffiths Building (Plate 47) was placed as part of the development of Berczy Park.

THE ONTARIO LEGISLATIVE BUILDINGS

Queen's Park, at the top of University Avenue

1886–92 by R.A. Waite

The offices of the Province of Ontario and its tens of thousands of employees are dispersed through a dozen or more buildings in Queen's Park,* but the government's physical identity is symbolized by the Legislative Buildings. The Romanesque Revival design in ruddy-pink stone, built up around the arched façade of the high-roofed central block— whether seen from its driveway, or as the closing ceremonial vista of University Avenue—has a presence and monumentality that bespeak its important function.

Ontario has had five sets of legislative buildings, and several temporary structures in Toronto. (The first buildings were in Niagara-on-the-Lake.) In his plan for the Town of York, Governor Simcoe set aside a site at the foot of Parliament Street for a large public building. Built in 1796–7, in accordance with a project approved (and perhaps designed) by Simcoe and revised by Captain Robert Pilkington, the first Legislature in York consisted of two brick wings (the south block became Toronto's first court-house), joined by a corridor. Grandly described by John Strachan as the Palace of Government, this building was looted and burnt by the American troops that occupied York in 1813 and was not replaced until 1820, when a new brick building was erected on the southeast corner of Parliament and Front Streets. In December 1824 this too was destroyed by fire, and the government again moved into temporary quarters. Planning for the third Legislative Buildings began almost immediately on a new site in the west end: a six-acre block known as Simcoe Place, bounded by Front, John, Simcoe, and Wellington: these buildings were not completed until 1832.

The government of the United Canadas had a more active interest in public architecture than any previous administration in the provinces. A competition was held in 1852, and won by Cumberland & Storm, for a larger and more fireproof building than that of 1832. It was to be built on the site of the present Legislative Buildings, and in 1853 government leader Francis Hincks pushed through a bill expropriating for a new Legislature the central 68 acres of the University Park, where King's College (1842–5) stood, at the top of what is now University Avenue. However, nothing was done about the Cumberland & Storm designs because government monies were committed to the building of new post offices and, after 1855, of University College (Plate 24). In 1858–60 part of the expropriated land (plus adjacent acreage) became Queen's Park.

After Confederation in 1867 the legislature of the new Province of Ontario found itself occupying the 1832 Legis-

lative Buildings, which were as crowded as ever and even more at risk from fire because of deterioration. During the 1870s there were repeated calls in Toronto for new buildings. (In the spring of 1879 the roof leaked so badly that the member for Northumberland could occupy his seat only when covered by an umbrella.) The idea was supported in general by Oliver Mowat's Liberal administration (along with the Liberal *Globe*): it was on safe political ground, because by 1880 the province had accumulated a budget surplus of some seven million dollars. But repeatedly the Conservative opposition—led by William Meredith, who represented a London riding and hoped to profit by rural resentment of Toronto— refused to agree, characterizing any project for new legislative buildings as government extravagance that would deprive the average citizen of such essential services as railways.

In 1877 the Government Architect, Kivas Tully, had recommended a new building in the Classical or Renaissance style. In his annual report of January 1880 he again recommended a new building; and in February he presented a design, this time in a cheaper Gothic style, that pleased no one. Finally the Commissioner of Public Works, C.F. Fraser, announced an international competition on 27 April 1880, all designs to be submitted by 1 August 1880. Sixteen designs were judged by a committee made up of Alexander Mackenzie (federal commissioner of public works), Toronto architect W.G. Storm, and the English-born Buffalo architect R.A. Waite.*

The results of the competition were unsatisfactory to all concerned. Gordon & Helliwell were declared the winners; but two designs—by Darling & Curry and Smith & Gemmell— that obviously could not be built within the approved budget of $500,000, were considered far superior artistically. In an attempt to solve the dilemma, the government in January 1882 called for tenders on both. The bids greatly exceeded the budget, and in March 1882 the government shelved the whole project rather than face a charge of extravagance from the Opposition. It was not revived until 1885, at which time the budget was raised to $750,000. Waite was called in to choose between the two designs and he scandalized Toronto's architects by declaring that both had serious defects, and that neither should be built. Deciding that a new architect was called for, the government chose Waite himself! Even though his design, as contracted by the Toronto firm of Lionel Yorke, was estimated to cost $772,000, work began in 1886. By 1890 costs had soared to almost $1,400,000 and the building became an election issue. Nevertheless it was completed in 1892 and was occupied by the House for the session of 1893.

---

* This is also the familiar name for all the workings of the Ontario Legislature and its civil service.

* Waite had designed several large buildings in Toronto, including the Mail Building (1878), the Canada Life Building (1890), and the Canadian Bank of Commerce (1889-90)—all near King and Bay.

67

The building is complex—a series of separate units related more by proximity and the uniform use of dark-pink Credit Valley stone than by a consistent design. Waite's U-shaped plan is built up around a courtyard, with a high-roofed central block that contains a spacious main hall on the ground floor and the legislative chamber on the second—linked by a cascade of carpeted steps that form one of the grandest public staircases in Toronto. The triple arches of the main entrance and the three tall-arched windows of the chamber above, the steep slate roof, and the four domed turrets flanking it, give the building its imposing image. Scattered across the façade are heads of grotesque beasts, panels of intertwining foliage, patterned columns and colonnettes, carved parapets, and superbly crafted window frames. Leading east and west to great round-arched *porte-cochères* are side wings—planned around galleried halls rising to skylights—that contained sequences of offices and meeting rooms, and on the second floor the library and the Premier's office. The north ends of each wing were designed as more-or-less separate buildings, with their own entrances: at the end of the east wing was the Immigration Department (concerned with settling Northern and Western Ontario), and at the end of the west wing was the two-storey Speaker's apartment (used since the 1930s as an entertainment suite for the Lieutenant-Governor).

Few buildings in Toronto can match in craftsmanship and sumptuous detail Waite's design for the interior, which was influenced by H.S. Richardson's design for the interior of the New York State Capitol in Albany. The sequence of spaces through which a visitor passes—from the main entrance, across the inner hall, and up the main stairs to the Chamber—is simply planned but filled with details in carved wood and cast- and wrought-iron in the rich, sombre colours of the period. For the front hall Waite designed floors of marble and slate in mainly red tones (now covered by red plush carpeting), with pilasters painted a dull bronze and cast-iron columns. Beyond the upper hall the legislative chamber (80 feet north-south by 65 feet wide) rises more than three storeys to a coved ceiling of panels and wooden crossbeams. It is given grandeur by the deep visitors' galleries (to the east and west), separated from the well of the chamber by a tall arcade, by the arched south windows, and by the arched and drapery-hung recesses of the north wall. On the main level, members' seats are arranged in rows to the east and west, with the Speaker's dais to the south. Across the south end of the room is the Press Gallery; across the north end is the similar Speaker's Gallery. The panelling in sycamore and mahogany, and the mahogany canopy over the dais, are intricately carved with a panoply of foliage and grotesque forms. Even without the elaborate painted details Waite originally designed, the chamber still has the highly crafted jewel-box character he intended.

The discontinuity of Waite's composition—the obvious separateness of the various parts—was aggravated by later additions. On 1 September 1909 fire gutted the west wing. E.J. Lennox, Toronto's recognized authority on the Romanesque, was given the commission of rebuilding, while G.W. Gouinlock was commissioned to add a library wing on the north side, almost filling Waite's courtyard. Lennox added another floor to most of the west wing, and on the main (south) front changed the profile of the roof and introduced dormers along

its edge. The north entrance to Gouinlock's library (on Wellesley Street) is perhaps the finest Romanesque portal in the city. Its huge central arch is flanked by two small arches and surrounded by an unusually wide band of structural masonry. Above the door is an extended high-relief carving of the Ontario coat of arms, so realistic that the animals (a moose, deer, and bear) seem to be frozen in the act of springing from the wall. Though such realism was not normally part of the Romanesque style, the sculpture is a perfect complement to the powerful arrangement of the door and arched windows.

The Queen's Park home of the Legislature is not Toronto's finest Romanesque Revival building; nor do the controversies and disagreements surrounding the competition for its design, and Waite's work, present the process of government architecture in an attractive light. Yet the building has the grand presence that was called for; and it is both a major landmark of the city and a fine celebration of the crafts of architecture.

68. *The north entrance on Wellesley Street*

69. *S.R. Badgley's drawing of the façade of Massey Hall, 1892–3*

MASSEY HALL

15 Shuter Street, at Victoria (SW)

1889–94 by S.R. Badgeley

Toronto has long associations with music and theatre; but until the opening in 1894 of the Massey Music Hall, it had no permanent concert hall. With its red-brick pedimented façade and fanciful Moorish interior, Massey Hall became for many thousands of Torontonians the place where they discovered the glory of music and first heard world-famous artists.

Through most of the nineteenth century Toronto was a major stop for the recitalists, opera companies, and musical-theatre groups that toured almost continuously the northeastern United States and Eastern Canada. Concerts were first presented in churches, hotel ballrooms, and even the County Courtroom on Adelaide Street East. The opening in 1850 of St Lawrence Hall (Plate 16) provided a ballroom, which—when it was not in use for political meetings, public lectures,

and socials—could serve as a concert hall or a makeshift opera house; but it was never large enough or entirely practical for either. The music room in the Mechanics' Institute on Church Street (completed in 1861) was not much more successful. During the 1860s and 1870s several spacious theatres were built in the city. For many citizens of Toronto the Good, however, theatres were an abomination. In the absence of a proper concert hall, most concerts were held in the great new churches built after Confederation. Auditorium churches—like Metropolitan Methodist on Queen Street East—had superb acoustics, splendid organs, and employed distinguished organists and choirmasters who influenced much of the city's musical development. The role of the churches also suited nineteenth-century musical taste

71. *Interior, 1894*

in Canada, which concentrated on oratorios and organ works. But the frequent performance of non-religious music in churches, and the difficulties of presenting large orchestras in ecclesiastical surroundings, made the partnership uncomfortable.

In 1888 Hart Massey, whose love of music had developed from his appreciation of its place in worship, decided to present Toronto with a 'music hall' that could also be used for lectures, religious gatherings, and public meetings. The immediate inspiration probably came from the choirmaster of Metropolitan Methodist, F.H. Torrington; but the more personal motivation for the gift was to provide a memorial to his eldest son, Charles, who died in 1884 at age 36. Hart Massey's long semi-retirement in Cleveland, which ended in 1882, acquainted him with a fine concert hall noted for its acoustics, and with its designer, S.R. Badgeley (1857-1917). He had been born and educated in Ontario, and besides being a member of the same Methodist Church as Massey in Cleveland, had worked for Massey on several building projects there. Massey wrote to Badgeley for plans of the Cleveland

Music Hall. Using these as a model, he began to develop his own plans for a 4,000-seat balconied hall in Toronto.

Throughout the design and building process the patron seems to have been relatively unconcerned about the precipitous rise in costs for the hall, an estimated $35,000 in 1889 to over $150,000 by the time of the official opening in 1894. Much more important to him were the excellence of the acoustics and the propriety of the design. On the subject of acoustics Massey took his advice from Torrington, and he became rather alarmed when the chosen site at Shuter and Victoria Streets dictated a square rather than a rectangular plan. Massey and Torrington had a natural sympathy for the elongated horseshoe plan of Metropolitan Methodist; to calm their nerves, Badgeley had to refer Massey to the squarer plans of acoustically successful churches like Trinity Methodist on Bloor Street. During the course of his work Badgeley visited Chicago to see the new Auditorium Building (1889, by Adler & Sullivan), architecturally the most famous opera house of the period. This building may have inspired Badgeley's original scheme for the façade in the Romanesque Revival, with a high front gable. But when the exterior design was presented in January 1893 it was rejected—in part, because the plans did not include a vestibule and the round-arched front entrance was thought too open for Toronto's winter weather. In the final Classical, almost Palladian, design the façade is dominated by a four-storey pedimented centre block, with lower blocks on either side. At ground level the three main doors are grouped by stone pilasters and set against a high, severely plain brick wall. Topped by a stone frieze cut in elegant letters with 'Massey Music Hall' (the lettering was chosen by Hart Massey's daughter, Lillian), the smooth mass of the wall supports four Ionic pilasters in brick, with terracotta capitals. These in turn support the pediment. Between the pilasters are two rows of windows filled with stained glass, the upper one round-arched (the lower row is now closed). Above, the pediment originally was ornamented with relief figures emblematic of Music (since removed).

Executed in red brick, sparely trimmed in stone and terracotta, Massey Hall had a rather severe aspect in keeping with its serious purpose. Unfortunately today it is outrageously dirty; draped in shadows that are inevitable on the north-facing site, it is now commonly seen and remembered as grim and dour. Its appearance was not improved by the addition in the 1930s of fire escapes across the front, concealing much of Badgeley's detail with a veil of rusty iron.

The interior, however, was anything but dour; and even in its present state the richness and decorative eccentricity of the design can be appreciated. The auditorium is roughly square, with a raked main floor and two horseshoe balconies supported on cast-iron columns. The stage is an immense open space—originally without a real proscenium or wings, to discourage any associations with theatres. To either side were three levels of boxes (one reserved for the Massey family), now converted to broadcast booths and other uses. The most impressive feature was the Moorish decoration Badgeley designed and applied to every detail in a riot of colour—gold, red, blue, green, and yellow.* The stage boxes

and upper balcony were framed in fanciful horseshoe and ogee arches, and the shallow curved ceiling beams had thin cusped arches edged in painted detail. At the centre of the Hall hung a great chandelier (now gone) of bronze and glass, lit with 400 electric and gas lights; during the day coloured light flashed across the interior through the stained-glass windows around the hall.

Massey Hall was formally opened on 14–16 June 1894, with a three-day series of special concerts, beginning with a gargantuan performance of Handel's *Messiah* performed by soloists accompanied by a Grand Festival Orchestra of 90 musicians, the Detroit Philharmonic Club, a choir of 500 adults, and another of 1,000 schoolchildren—all conducted by F.R. Torrington. Over the next eighty-eight years the Hall (administered by a board of trustees representing the Massey family and the city) housed much of the best in Toronto's musical life. The Mendelssohn Choir was inaugurated there in 1895, and the Toronto Symphony in 1923; both called it home until 1982, when Roy Thomson Hall was opened (Plate 171). Besides orchestral and choral performances, and recitals by Melba, McCormack, Caruso, Ponselle, and many other celebrated musicians, the Hall's patrons witnessed among other non-musical events Lloyd George denouncing the Boer War, Aimee Semple McPherson saving souls, and Jack Dempsey boxing.

Massey Hall is not only part of Toronto's cultural heritage; it is also part of the fabric of the city—in an urban block that includes some of the best of its early twentieth-century banks and commercial architecture, as well as the Elgin and Wintergarden Theatres. Several proposals have been made for the careful reworking of this block and its renewal as one of the centres of life in Toronto. The restoration of Massey Hall—and the higher profile it would bring to the area—is a key factor in such plans. Its famous acoustics are unchanged (excellent for the audience, though not for the musicians). Sensitively restored, it could rejoin the mainstream of Toronto's musical culture, much as Carnegie Hall co-exists in New York with the modern concert halls of Lincoln Centre.

---

* Influenced by the extravagant Moorish-Celtic detail Louis Sullivan employed for the Chicago Auditorium Building, Badgeley consulted two expensive portfolios on the Alhambra in Granada, Spain. Hart Massey, a proper Methodist, finally accepted the extravagance of Badgeley's interior decoration because its joyous spirit expressed his own reaction to music.

72. *The Massey Tomb, Mount Pleasant Cemetery, 1894*

THE MASSEY TOMB, MOUNT PLEASANT CEMETERY

1643 Yonge Street (E)

Massey Tomb, 1890–4 by E.J. Lennox;
Cemetery laid out 1873–6 by H.A. Engelhardt

Mount Pleasant is the largest and most successful of the garden cemeteries laid out to serve late nineteenth-century Toronto. It is more elaborately planned than St James (see pp. 81–2) or the Necropolis (Plate 43), and more richly endowed than either with memorial sculpture and family tombs, of which the Massey Mausoleum is undoubtedly the finest. In 1873 the Trustees of the Toronto General Burial Grounds, led by William McMaster, purchased 200 acres with a quarter-mile frontage on Yonge Street in the ravine south of Davisville, and extending east for a mile and a quarter. To lay out the new cemetery the Trustees hired H.A. Engelhardt, who had previously designed cemeteries in Raleigh, North Carolina; Richmond, Virginia; Belleville and Port Hope, Ontario; and also prepared the early plans of High Park and the Eastern Park (now part of Riverdale Park). Engelhardt's experience was useful in the work at Mount Pleasant since the Trustees were trying to create the atmosphere of a sedate park or pleasure ground as well as a cemetery. The level eastern half of the land was left at first as pasture and woods with carriage drives. But in the western half Engelhardt exploited the ravine-crossed topography to create two valleys, one along the south side and one further north and east. In both, natural springs were diverted to create lakes connected by cascades and populated with ducks and swans. Winding across the more level plateau between the two valleys were pedestrian walks and 12 miles of wide carriage drives. The grounds were planted with exotic and native flowering and foliage trees and were scattered with beds of flowers and shrubs. Although the watercourses have been filled in, the valleys remain the focus of the cemetery's imagery. Secluded, shaded, and quiet, they were imbued with what the first commentators praised as 'natural and artificial beauty'.

Hart Massey purchased his family plot at Mount Pleasant in the early 1880s, but did not begin to plan a mausoleum until the death in 1890 of his youngest son, Fred Victor (who was commemorated publicly in the Fred Victor Mission at Queen and Jarvis Streets). For Hart Massey the tomb was a very personal project, in which all his interest in architecture was concentrated. He commissioned E.J. Lennox, with whom he had developed a close working relationship. The tomb ranks with the Old City Hall (Plate 76) among Lennox's best works; and though it is clearly his own creation, Massey contributed precise criticism and many ideas that affected the final character of the building.

The Romanesque Revival design of the tomb is based on the form of a small church with a central tower, much compressed and made asymmetrical by a circular false stair-tower with a conical roof above a window arcade. A shallow west porch leads through bronze doors into a square space that rises two storeys to form the central tower. On either side are marble-fronted loculi for coffins, while to the east the space opens into an apse through a heavily moulded arch on short columns. The apse is lit by a row of small windows set into the curve of the east wall and filled with stained glass depicting leaves and flowers: the overall effect is that of the nave and chancel of a small church. Most of the light, washing the interior in a mysterious radiance—comes, however, from windows set out of sight high in the tower. To crown the central tower Lennox designed a stepped-pyramid roof on which he intended orginally to place a very simple urn. At Hart Massey's insistence the design was amended to substitute a nine-foot female figure of Hope holding the anchor of peaceful haven after the Voyage of Life. The statue—carved, like the rest of the detail in the tomb, by the Toronto firm of Holbrook & Mollington—is a rather discordant element in the finished building, though appropriate to its sentimental purpose. Lennox's intentions in using the Romanesque Revival style were to exploit the monumental simplicity of the style. In keeping with this he restricted the use of carved detail to simple, generalized ornament around the windows and door. The character of the building comes not from detail but from the massive strength of the granite used for the walls. These are modulated in colour and finish to create thick strata through the height of the building, from the rough foundation that rises out of the ground to the smooth steps of the roof seen against the sky.

The Massey Tomb was one of the first of several large family mausoleums built in Mount Pleasant Cemetery before the First World War. The most interesting is the Chandler Tomb, built around 1900 north of the Massey Tomb on the ridge overlooking Yonge Street. A smooth, heavy cube of grey stone from which rises a low Byzantine dome, it was influenced by the Wainwright Tomb in St Louis, Missouri, designed by the Chicago architect Louis Sullivan. Most of the later tombs are more explicitly Classical in stlye. The Eaton Tomb of 1907, by W.R. Mead and Sproatt & Rolph, and the Cox Tomb of 1905, are both Roman temples—modelled on the Maison Carrée in Nîmes, France. Of the two the Eaton Tomb is more correctly designed, even though it incorporates as a recurring decorative detail an E set in a diamond that was the Eaton company logo in the period—a proud symbol of present glory commemorated in antique pattern. After the war fewer monuments of such conspicuous character and quality were built. Fewer still—like the Cutten memorial of about 1932, a long high-backed bench flanked by seated female figures with their heads draped in mourning—rise to the level of the romantic landscape in which they stand.

73

THE ROBERT SIMPSON COMPANY

Yonge Street at Queen Street West (SW)

1894–5 by Edmund Burke;
additions by Burke & Horwood (1899–1900),
Horwood & White (1922–4), Chapman & Oxley
(1928–9), and John B. Parkin Architects (1967).

Robert Simpson and Timothy Eaton were the giants of Canadian retailing in the latter part of the nineteenth century. Their department stores were the perfect symbols of Late Victorian business in Canada: expansive in scale, crowded with a multiplicity of up-to-date items, inventive in serving the customer, and above all profitable. Before Confederation the centre of retailing in Toronto was King Street. Its shops had evolved

from small, separate houselike units with display windows, to emporiums like the Golden Lion dry-goods and clothing store at 33–7 King Street East (1847 by Robert Walker; rebuilt in 1867; demolished), an immense four-storey Italianate bazaar with three-storey display windows. The local development of retailing was carried one stage further by the Toronto Arcade (1883–4 by C.A. Walton, demolished), which

74

grouped a wide variety of stores under a glass roof on the east side of Yonge, between Adelaide and Richmond. In 1883–6 Timothy Eaton built a 'department store', on the west side of Yonge north of Queen,* that combined the scale and variety of items found in the Golden Lion with the many 'departments' found in the Arcade. Robert Simpson (1834–

97) followed much the same path. Born in Scotland, he began selling quality dry goods in Toronto in 1872. By the early 1890s he had not only built an elaborate Queen Anne style store at 7–11 Queen Street West, but had expanded into three other buildings, with a total floor area of nearly three acres.

Unlike Timothy Eaton, Robert Simpson was interested in architecture and the image it could provide. In 1894 he engaged Edmund Burke, of Langley & Burke, to design a new building that would be much larger than his existing prem-

---

* This was his second store; his first, opened in 1869, was south of Queen, on a site later absorbed by the Robert Simpson Company.

144

ises and potentially expandable as more land became available. Burke's firm had built several large stores in Toronto, as well as houses for both Robert Simpson (1884–5, on Bloor Street East, demolished) and Timothy Eaton (1888–9, on Spadina Road, demolished). In 1886 Langley & Burke had made alterations to Simpson's old store. The new building was begun in the spring of 1894 and completed by Christmas. It was influenced by American—specifically Chicago—examples, just as both Simpson and Eaton had been influenced by the merchandising technique of the Chicago firms of Marshall Field (founded in the 1860s) and Sears Roebuck (founded in 1886). Like the skyscrapers going up in Chicago at the time, the Simpson building was framed in steel and cast iron: it was a cage of horizontals and verticals. Probably in an effort to simplify construction, the steel-and-iron structure was not completely fire-proofed with a surrounding skin of terracotta, brick, or stone. Unfortunately on 4 March 1895, shortly after the new store was opened, fire almost completely destroyed it, except for the ground-floor piers that had been encased—more for decoration than protection—in stone. Robert Simpson immediately commissioned the rebuilding to the original design, but took the opportunity to enlarge the frontage on Yonge Street. With improved construction, the new store was substantially more costly.

The height of the building is divided into three parts. The first and second floors form a 'base' that addresses the street and is dominated by large display windows set between massive tapering piers, with bay windows above set into a frame of mouldings. In the middle of the building the windows of the third, fourth, and fifth floors are grouped in threes, separated by spandrels between the floors, and framed by tall, plain, pilaster-like piers. The sixth floor is a more decorative 'cornice'-like level, where the triplets of windows are separated by short columns, and an overshadowing metal cornice above completes the entire composition. As the cage structure, which is clearly apparent, does all the work of supporting the building, the spaces between the horizontals and verticals were filled with windows and, at ground level, great showcases. Inside it allows the floors to be completely open, with widely spaced columns. In the tradition of much Chicago work, the exterior detail is severely plain, except for terracotta mouldings and capitals of generally Classical form, and the effects of shadow and light on the horizontals and verticals. Even with later additions of ornamental details, such as the arches at the second-floor level, the Simpson's store is the best example in Toronto of the austere tradition of the Chicago School of high-rise architecture.

Robert Simpson died suddenly in 1897, and in 1898 the company was purchased by Joseph Flavelle, Harris H. Fudger, and A.E. Ames. In 1899 and 1900 they commissioned Burke & Horwood (successors to Langley & Burke) to make exten-

sive additions along Yonge Street and Richmond Street East.* (The centre of the Yonge Street façade was delayed until an independent store on the site could be purchased.) The basic structure of the original design made this and later expansions easy. Further work in 1922–4 by Horwood & White added the arches that ornament the store's three façades. Like the earlier mouldings, they are executed in terracotta with fine Acanthus-leaf detail. They harmonize so well with the original that it is difficult to see them as additions.

In 1928–9 the Simpson's management decided to counter the Art Deco stylishness of the new Eaton's College Street store by hiring Chapman & Oxley to add a nine-storey wing at the northeast corner of Bay and Richmond, and to alter other parts of the store. In the new block the architects built in a stripped vertical idiom of brick and stone, not unlike the office buildings they were erecting elsewhere on Bay Street (see p. 214) at the time. Above the doorways at the front of the old store they added fanciful Art Deco etched glass and metal grillwork (much of it still survives) and inside finely detailed marble elements ** in a restrained Art Deco style.

After the Second World War, Simpson's entered into a corporate alliance with Sears Roebuck and devoted most of its energy to suburban shopping centres. But in the late 1960s John B. Parkin Associates added a 32-storey tower at Bay and Queen that included an extension to the store and rental office space above. This was intended to be the first stage of a scheme to wrap the entire store in light amber enamelled metal panels, with grey granite trim, that would have turned the 1894–5 building and the later additions into a replica of a suburban shopping centre. Fortunately by the time the tower was completed confusion about the role of Simpson's *vis-à-vis* the new Eaton Centre (Plate 158) put a rein on the project. As it turned out, Simpson's became in effect a part of the neighbouring Eaton Centre. By the time this was perceived, corporate taste had changed again, and under some pressure from the city Simpson's decided to restore the building, cleaning its exterior and recapturing the rich red-brown of the original materials. The ground-floor piers were refaced with granite, and the entrances given a rather flashy 'High Tech' image. The remodelling of the interior is not yet complete, but it too has been keyed to a livelier, more up-to-date image. The overall result is pleasing; and the company received the Toronto Historical Board's Award of Merit for their enlightened patronage in retaining and restoring the forms and details of the original buildings.

---

* The capitals of some of the ground-floor piers of the 1895 building and of the additions until 1924 are dated, allowing the sequence of additions to be followed around the structure.

** This is still reasonably intact in the Richmond-Yonge and Richmond-Bay vestibules.

75

HOLY BLOSSOM SYNAGOGUE
(Now the CHURCH OF HAGIOS GIORGIOS)
115 Bond Street (E)
1895–7 by John Wilson Siddall

Until the late 1880s Toronto's Jewish community was very small. Most of its members were Orthodox in observance and their first formal requirement was not for a synagogue—Sabbath services were conducted in private homes—but for a Kosher butcher (a need met by a gentile butcher in the Market, who agreed to follow the ritualistic prescriptions), and for a properly consecrated cemetery. In 1849 the Toronto Hebrew Congregation was formally established in order to purchase a burial ground on the east side of Pape Avenue,

just south of Gerrard Street East. In 1856 the trustees of a newly formed congregation, supported by some 65 men from only about 50 families, assumed management of the cemetery. (It is still maintained, although a larger memorial park has since been opened.) During the next ten years this congregation became known as Holy Blossom, using, for its meeting room and school, the second floor of a drugstore on the southeast corner of Yonge and Richmond Streets. This served as Toronto's only synagogue until 1875, when a new building

146

(demolished) was erected at 25 Richmond Street East, near Victoria. Designed in brick by Stewart & Strickland, it was extremely simple, with touches of Romanesque style in raised mouldings around its arched doors and windows, and around its rose window. The new synagogue was not unlike several of the city's simple Methodist and Baptist churches, except for the sparing decoration of the galleried interior.

During most of the next twenty years Holy Blossom, located within walking distance of the homes of both its wealthiest and poorest members, was Toronto's only synagogue. In the later 1880s, however, immigrants arriving from central and eastern Europe began to change the character of Toronto's Jewish community, and by the turn of the century several more congregations were established. To accommodate the growth of its membership—which almost doubled during this period—as well as to demonstrate the increasing importance of the city's Jewish community, the leaders of Holy Blossom began to plan a larger, more impressive building. The principal patrons were Alfred D. Benjamin (1848-1900), and his brother Frank D. Benjamin, who were partners in a metal-importing business, the M.&L. Samuel, Benjamin Co. Alfred Benjamin held a position among Toronto's Jews similar to that of John Macdonald and William McMaster among the city's Protestants. Believing that his wealth entailed social and religious responsibilities, he provided many immigrants with jobs—on condition that they attend Sabbath services at Holy Blossom. In 1889 he proposed that the congregation build a new synagogue, equipped with an organ and choir, and a lecture-room for a staff teacher. In 1893 he and his brother each contributed $5,000 to start the building fund, and from 1894 until the building's completion in 1897 he chaired the building committee.

Victorian Toronto largely ignored its Jewish community and had little knowledge of its religion and culture. Businessmen like Marcus and Samuel Rossin, Toronto jewellers who in 1857 opened the city's first luxury hotel, The Rossin House, or the Nordheimers, who established themselves in the 1840s as music dealers, publishers, and makers of fine pianos, made valuable contributions to Toronto's economic and cultural life. But few Jews had access to high society, except by marriage preceded by conversion. (Samuel Nordheimer became an Anglican before his marriage to Edith Louise Boulton in 1871.) Nevertheless the new Holy Blossom on Bond Street—still within easy walking distance from the homes of most of its members—became a worthy addition to Toronto's impressive religious buildings. During the previous fifty years several of Toronto's most important churches, including St Michael's Cathedral and Metropolitan Methodist, had been built to the south and north of the site chosen for Holy Blossom. The towers of these churches, and their associated schools and residences, dominated Bond Street, forming the most distinctive part of the city's skyline. The synagogue, constructed of beige brick and stone, was far more impressive than its predecessor in both size and scale, and stood proudly among its Gothic Revival neighbours.

The architect was John Wilson Siddall, who had previously worked for the Nordheimers. His design is broadly Romanesque Revival in style. The twin towers of brick, flanking a tall central arch, rise from spreading bases faced with smooth and rough stone. Thick outer piers, thin inner ones, and tall arched windows enhance the apparent height of the towers. The stone piers of the central arch, and pairs of inner colonnettes, frame the double doors of the main entrance, which has a row of five plain windows above and a crowning semicircular tympanum panel that was originally carved with the name and date of the synagogue in Hebrew and English. The details and the effect of the façade are not so massive as in much of the Romanesque Revival work of the period; the basic inspiration comes from the lighter patterns of Spanish Mooresque work. The key elements in this exotic style were low onion-shaped domes in copper that originally topped the front towers and their corner piers. (Moorish details were popular in synagogues because they referred to Jewish history in Spain and were uncommon in Christian churches.)

Siddall's high front arch introduces the scale of the domed interior. The ground floor, beyond the front vestibule, was designed as a large lecture-room that could be divided by sliding oak doors into eight smaller classrooms. Stairs in the front towers led up to the main temple on the second floor, an octagonal galleried space seating about 700, over which the dome rises on tall cast-iron columns. Iron gates separated the vestibule, with its windows over the main door, from the temple, whose focus was a tall arch in the east wall that framed the niche containing the Ark and the cantor's and rabbi's pulpits. Light enters the interior through stained-glass windows and through twelve arched windows cut through the curve of the dome. An architectural symbol of the Dome of Heaven, the dome was tinted blue—dark at the top, fading almost to white at the bottom—and divided into twelve sections by broad bands of white.

The building of the third Holy Blossom was an event of lasting importance in the history of Toronto's Jewish community. Though Toronto was regrettably not without prejudice, the list of donors to the project included more Christians than Jews—among them Timothy Eaton, Robert Simpson, the Masseys, and Henry Pellatt. The site, as well as the building's size and style, immediately made it a landmark in the city. Holy Blossom's form also influenced the character of several later Toronto synagogues. The congregation held its last service there on Succoth, 27 September 1937, before moving to a larger building on Bathurst Street (Plate 140). In November 1937 the first services were held in Holy Blossom of the Greek Orthodox Church of Hagios Giorgios, which was dedicated on 19 June 1938. A Greek iconostasis was added at the east end of the interior, the inscription on the tympanum panel was removed, and the distinctive onion-shaped domes were rebuilt in a Byzantine octagonal shape. But even though the building is no longer a synagogue, it remains a monument to the dignity and strength of the Jewish community in nineteenth-century Toronto.

76. *Old City Hall, looking east, with the Cadillac-Fairview Tower in the background*

77

OLD CITY HALL
Queen Street West at Bay Street (NE)
1885–99 by E.J. Lennox

The clock tower of Toronto's Old City Hall (originally called the Municipal Buildings) was for many years the downtown area's most important and visible landmark. Rising 285 feet in russet rose and beige sandstone, it no longer dominates the skyline as its architect and the city fathers intended. But even today it provides a handsome termination for the corridor of Bay Street. E.J. Lennox's Romanesque Revival building is his masterpiece. Expressing the Victorian belief that historical sources could inspire inventive, up-to-date design, it also demonstrates the monumentality, stunning detail, and superb craftsmanship possible in Late Victorian architecture. To the citizens and city councillors who championed the project through controversies about design and construction, this City Hall and its tower—whose clock chimed in the

New Year, 1900—were symbols of Toronto's strength and prosperity, its importance in Canada, and its optimism about the new century. After almost one hundred years, and another round of controversies in the late 1960s that nearly ended in its demolition, Old City Hall retains its symbolic status and the tower continues to project a powerful image. Its symbolism, however, is more complex today. Seen from the south on Bay Street; from the east at University Avenue along Queen; from Nathan Phillips Square in front of the New City Hall (Plate 143); or against the mirror-glass backdrop of the Cadillac-Fairview Building—the tower presides over a blend of nineteenth- and twentieth-century architecture that is a very Torontonian synthesis of stone, concrete, and glass, of the monumental and the unassuming.

When Toronto built its second City Hall in 1844–5 on Front Street East (Plate 11), little provision was made for the growth in civic government that would accompany the growth of the city. By the 1870s conditions had become crowded and unsanitary. During the 1870s and early 1880s various proposals were brought forward for a new city hall (including schemes to convert St Lawrence Hall into office space)—though the *Globe*, and groups like the Board of Trade, were opposed to a new building, chiefly because they feared its cost would get out of control. However, the city and the County of York faced a more compelling need: to build a new court-house. The Cumberland & Storm court-house on Adelaide Street East (Plate 22), built in 1852, was by the 1870s overcrowded, and lack of maintenance had produced unhealthy conditions, particularly in the basement cells. After lengthy negotiations York County decided to leave the problem to the City (agreeing to pick up its portion of the cost later). In 1883 the provincial legislature enabled Council to borrow $300,000 to pay for the project. After much discussion the block bounded by Queen Street West, Bay Street (then known as Teraulay), Albert, and James Streets was chosen. On 27 June 1884 Council expropriated the site. Shortly after this the Court House Committee began to plan a competition for the best designs, and called in William G. Storm as its professional adviser. The Committee had visited Buffalo's combined court-house and city hall and by late September decided to push for a similar combination of city hall and court-house. A by-law to borrow an additional $200,000 was put to the ratepayers on 30 October. Vehemently opposed by the Liberal *Globe* and the Board of Trade—they cited the potential for graft and corruption in a project run by the Conservative City Council, the expense of the chosen site at Bay and Queen Streets, and the city's greater need for a trunk-sewer and a water-works system—it was soundly defeated. The building project was then scaled down to the court-house alone, and on 24 December 1884 a design competition was announced, calling for a building of Canadian materials to cost no more than $200,000. There followed several years of political wrangling and bitter controversy. Finally a design by E.J. Lennox for a combined court-house and city hall was approved and work

began in the autumn of 1889. The cornerstone was laid on 21 November 1891.

Inspired by the work of Boston architect Henry Hobson Richardson (1838–86)—the most famous and respected North American architect of his day, particularly for his work in the Romanesque Revival style—Lennox was more heavily influenced by the Richardsonian Romanesque than any other Canadian architect of the period. His design for City Hall is unashamedly similar to that of Richardson's Allegheny Court House (1883–8) in Pittsburgh—in the outline of the solid massive shaft of the tower, and in the arrangement of the courtrooms and city offices on four levels (including a high basement) around a large courtyard. Corner pavilions with high dormer roofs accent and ornament longer outer façades with strongly shadowed features. The façades on all four sides are broken by a central gabled pavilion with flanking turrets that rise above four main entrances. Three of the four pavilions housed courtrooms; their original two-storey height—since subdivided to create two courts, one above the other—was marked by tall round-arched windows. The southeast pavilion—with its high two-storey bay window providing a panoramic view along Queen and southeast towards the centre of nineteenth-century Toronto—housed the offices of the Mayor and other city staff. On the north (above the two-storey arch leading directly to the courtyard) and on the west (facing Osgoode Hall) are courtrooms. On the east, facing the city centre of the 1880s, the pavilion housed the Council Chamber (now a courtroom), which measures 40 by 50 and rises to a height of 30 feet with an arcaded spectator's gallery. The pavilion on the south front above the main entrance contained civic offices. The curved, arched turret to the east was the office where civic property taxes were paid.

The clock tower and main entrance are the glory of City Hall. Rock-faced blocks of Credit Valley stone, and New Brunswick brownstone in shades of russet and beige, were used in the courses, whose varied height and colour are permanent decorative elements. As the tower rises its colour changes to a lighter beige, but retains its rock finish and strong appearance up to the arched bell stage and clock-faces at the top. The triple arches of the main entrance—supported on clustered columns—have elaborate capitals and wide bands of intricately carved moulding, representing lion- and dragon-like beasts breaking out through foliage on either side of the entrance. Everywhere the carved ornament (most of it done by the Toronto firm of Holbrook & Mollington) repays observation: there are caricatures of politicians, the designations 'City Hall' and 'Municipal Buildings', and letters and numbers that spell out 'E J LENNOX, ARCHITECT AD 1898'.

Lennox carried his use of stone and ornament into the building's interior. The main entrance takes the visitor into a severe stone-walled vestibule, then to a wide flight of steps through three arches similar to those of the main façade. From there one enters the galleried main hall, a two-storey rectangular space lighted by windows overlooking the central courtyard. The south half is covered by the upper gallery, supported on a long row of columns covered with imitation marble. The north half—rising the full two storeys—is dominated by the grand main stair of iron, bronze, and marble that rises to a landing and then branches to the left and right in long flights. Lennox designed the hall as both a huge waiting-room and the city's grandest indoor space, to be used as a ballroom, assembly hall, or for exhibitions. A great stained-glass window on the stairs (designed by Robert McCausland in 1898) depicts the Union of Commerce and Industry under the guidance of Britannia, with the incomplete City Hall, Toronto harbour, and the 1844–5 City Hall in the background. Allegorical murals of Toronto's history and future, painted by G.A. Reid for the Civic Guild of Arts, completed the decoration.

The building's life over the next seventy years was not as secure as its solidity might imply. Lennox's designs of 1887 had become old-fashioned by 1900; Beaux Arts and Edwardian Baroque styles had replaced Richardsonian Romanesque in popular favour. In the ensuing years the City Hall was respected more than valued, and before the First World War there were projects for a new austerely Classical building (planned for the site of the New City Hall on the west side of Bay). In the 1920s the City Hall was already overcrowded, and in 1925 Lennox drew up plans for a twelve-storey building (never presented to Council) to go up in the central court. During the 1930s and the Second World War inertia, the Depression, and scarcity of materials delayed further projects for replacement.

The idea of a new City Hall came to life again in the early 1950s—after the creation in 1953 of Metropolitan Toronto and the beginning of the post-war boom. In 1965 the Council moved into the New City Hall on the other side of Bay Street.

The old building was then sold to Metro, which rented it to the province as a court-house. Even before City Council moved, however, the Old City Hall was threatened by a series of plans formulated from 1958 on by the T. Eaton Company that eventually resulted in the Eaton Centre (Plate 158). In the early planning stages for this development, leading American architects—I.M. Pei, Victor Gruen, and Skidmore, Owings & Merrill, working with Toronto firms—called for the demolition of the Old City Hall and Holy Trinity Church (Plate 15). Vehement public protest eventually derailed these schemes. Eaton's was the first to change its mind. Metro remained obdurate until the early 1970s when the Friends of Old City Hall rallied public opposition to the proposed demolition. (At one point the Friends—rallied by Lorna Easser and Vern Burnett—gathered outside the building and began to clean a portion of its soot-blackened façade with hoses and detergent to reveal the colour that lay hidden under decades of grime.) This successful campaign initiated Toronto's appreciation of the Late Victorian and Edwardian buildings that still determine much of the city's character.

Old City Hall, which made Lennox the best-known architect in Toronto's history, is one of the city's greatest nineteenth-century buildings. A once-reluctant partner in its preservation, Metro Council has now decided to make the building its permanent home—a move that will necessitate much renovation and restoration.* If any building can provide an appropriate forum for the Metropolitan federation, it is Lennox's magnificient City Hall.

_____

* Early discussions of this move spawned a misguided suggestion that a mirror-glass office tower in the courtyard would be ideal to create more space on the site.

78

XXV. *The Canadian National Exhibition about 1908, with the Gooderham Fountain, designed by John M. Lyle. Neither the fountain nor the buildings survive.*

IV
THE EDWARDIANS AND AFTER
1901–1921

Architectural patronage in Edwardian Toronto reached its climax with the 98-room castle erected by Sir Henry Pellatt on the brow of Spadina hill. In an age impressed by battleships, giant corporations, and grand opera with elephants, Casa Loma was the most elaborate thing of its kind. Its inspiration was medieval, its materials opulent. Even the horses lived in luxury, in mahogany-stalled Spanish-tiled stables with brass nameplates. Yet with its 30 miles of electric wiring, bathroom telephones, and wine-cellar cooled by piped ammonia, it was the city's most modern house.

Pellatt's flamboyant gestures—from running to victory as a youth in the North American mile championship to shipping his whole regiment, the Queen's Own Rifles, to England for military manoeuvers in 1910—could be sniffed at by discriminating Torontonians as the strivings of an eccentric who was neither old Family Compact nor new Methodist money. But his scheme to develop and control the mighty hydro-electric resources of Niagara power, the basis of his fortune, could not. It brought Pellatt and his associates—the transit tycoon Sir William Mackenzie and the electrical magnate Frederic Nicholls—straight into the mainstream of Toronto history.

At the end of the nineteenth century a municipal reform movement spread across Europe and America. One of its leaders in Canada was a teacher of political economy at the University of Toronto named Morley Wickett, who went into his father's leather-manufacturing business in 1905 and was elected a Toronto alderman. He argued for the appointment of competent, well-paid municipal commissioners and a board of control to act as the city's executive so that its government would be better able to cope with the complexities of urban expansion and new technology. Once this system was in place, Toronto was in a position to own public utilities rather than license private operators to run them for profit.

Pellatt's rich life-style and three-hundred-pound frame and Mackenzie's intransigence made them easy targets for muckracking journalists; even many manufacturers and merchants turned against them. In 1906 a new provincial government appointed one of its members, Adam Beck, to run a monopoly for the production of electric power in Ontario. The City then went into the business of distributing power itself and running electric streetcar lines into areas that Mackenzie's transit system refused to serve. By 1921 it was ready to take complete control of all hydro and transit services.

The period gave rise to other successful reform movements as well. Dr Charles Hastings of the city's Public Health Department battled against unsanitary conditions in the slums just west of City Hall. The first systematic attempts to provide adequate housing for the working poor led to the building of Riverdale Courts (Plate 97) and Spruce Court in the east end. Ratepayers' groups marshalled the power of affluent neighbourhoods in favour of sound city planning for the future. Conservationists fought successfully to save Fort York (Plate 1) from being overrun with streetcar tracks. Two of the biggest crusades, in which medical pioneer Dr Emily Stowe and her daughter Dr Augusta Stowe-Gullen figured prominently, were the suffragist movement and the campaign for prohibition, both of which achieved their goal during the ultimate crusade—that of the Great War to save civilization and to put an end to war itself. If the High Victorian era can be compared to a patriotic pageant, the first two decades of the twentieth century resembled a great public morality play.

Through this period Toronto grew and prospered prodigiously. Between 1901 and 1921 the population increased from 208,000 to 521,000. Most of the newcomers were from the British Isles or other parts of Canada; but for the first time non-English-speaking immigrants arrived in significant numbers. The number of Jews in Toronto, mostly from eastern Europe, jumped from 3,000 to just under 35,000 and the Italian population rose from 1,000 to 8,000. Besides these two large groups of newcomers the 1921 census recorded nearly 25,000 people of other European ethnic origins and 2,000 from Asia. The city's area doubled from 17 to 35 sq. miles—the size it was to remain for the next half-century—with the annexation between 1905 and 1914 of districts to the east, west, and north, and of inner suburbs such as Bracondale, Deer Park, Moore Park, and North Rosedale. Valuable new land was created when the Harbour Commission filled in the bay between Front Street and what is now Queen's Quay.

Stimulated by the opening of the Canadian West, more railway building, and, after 1915, the demand for shells and aircraft and other war production, Toronto's labour force in manufacturing rose dramatically. Before the 1914 recession and the outbreak of war cut down on construction, the annual value of building permits soared from $3½ million in 1901 to about $27 million in both 1912 and 1913. Thousands of brick houses filled the empty lots that had surrounded the older parts of the city. The first apartment buildings appeared. But the most noticeable change in the character of Toronto came when ten- to twenty-storey skyscrapers began to soar in the business district around King and Yonge, and church spires no longer dominated Toronto's skyline. Other conspicuous results of progress and prosperity were the forests of wooden poles and wires in the streets and the thick plumes of black coal smoke rising from the factories, railway yards, and ships crowding Toronto's long waterfront.

Of all the new buildings, the grandest were the banks and insurance companies. The Bank of Toronto, for example, put up a great Roman temple, with nine giant columns marching in stately measure in both directions from the corner of King and Bay. The financial institutions, which controlled the northern Ontario mining boom and generally financed the progress of Canada's century, brought enormous wealth and power to the city.

The quintessential businessmen of the era were Edmund Walker, President of the Bank of Commerce and a heavy backer of the new transcontinental railways, and Joseph Flavelle, who used the enormous profits from his meat-packing business—along with his Methodist virtue and native acumen—in the service and control of National Trust, Canada Life, and the Robert Simpson Company, among many other enterprises. Both men were knighted for their endeavours, and both built splendid private residences. Flavelle's 'Holwood' (Plate 89) on Queen's Park Crescent now contains the University of Toronto's law school. Walker's elegant 'Long Garth' on St George Street, also given to the University, was later torn down to make

XXVI. *The Easter Parade at Sunnyside, 1909*

a parking lot. Walker became the founding patron of the Royal Ontario Museum and the Art Gallery of Toronto (he suggested to Goldwin Smith that The Grange be used for the Gallery). Flavelle, who engaged in many philanthropies, brought the Toronto General Hospital and the University of Toronto out of decades of stagnation. Under his leadership fund-raising campaigns, structural reform, and new buildings paved the way for them to become first-class institutions in health care and higher education.

Other Torontonians also helped reshape Toronto, though perhaps no innovation surpassed the elegance of the two buildings planned in the year that Edward ascended the throne: the King Edward Hotel (Plate 79) and the Royal Alexandra Theatre (Plate 80), named after the King's consort. Other fine theatres, such as the Winter Garden on Yonge Street (1914), sprang up to meet the growing demand for live entertainment in the heyday of vaudeville and for the new motion pictures, in which the local school-girl who had gone to Hollywood, Mary Pickford, was a favourite star.

Recreation took place mostly out of doors. The Bay and the Island, which had provided the military reason for the city's founding, furnished the locale for summer and winter sports. Large hotels, amusement parks, and boat-houses for rowing and sailing clubs dotted the shores of Toronto bay. The miles of Don Valley, Humber, and Garrison Creek ravines cut through the grid pattern of Toronto streets laid out by the original surveyors, affording places only a few steps from home for walks, picnics, and nature study like

XXVII. *Wintergarden Theatre (1914–26), Yonge Street, designed by Thomas Lamb to create the atmosphere of a garden restaurant. The ceiling is hung with real and fabric leaves and tiny electric lanterns. It is the best preserved of the few remaining atmospheric silent-movie theatres.*

that enjoyed by Ernest Thompson Seton. Factories and church schools organized Sunday outings in the city parks, or annual excursions on the new electric radial cars whose network fanned out into the countryside. A dozen new structures, like the Manufacturers' Building, the Women's Building, and a grandstand to hold 16,000, were added to the glass showplaces on the grounds of the Canadian National Exhibition. City dwellers built cottages on the eastern Beaches and on the islands themselves (those that remain have been turned into year-round dwellings).

Perhaps the most important influence on urban shape and space, however, was the City itself. As compulsory education came into force, primary schools sprang up as focal points of dozens of new neighbourhoods. The vast new Central Technical School between Harbord and Bloor Street West, finished in 1916, gathered together all the programs in advanced training in the arts and crafts needed by a commercial and industrial society. The crowning glory of an expanding library system was the reading room of the new main library building at College and St George Streets (Plate 83). The Prince Edward viaduct, constructed across the Don Valley at the Danforth to connect the growing population in eastern Toronto with that of the city proper, was completed during the last year of the Great War.

For all the elegance and expansion, new wealth and progress, that changed Toronto in the first two decades of the twentieth century, the city emerged from Armistice Day 1918 still a place of British loyalties, Victorian morals, and the quiet Sunday. The embodiment of civic virtue, Mayor Tommy Church, was on his way to being elected a record seven times. Motor cars, like the locally produced Russell, were frequently seen, but for everyday business—delivering coal and ice, milk or bread, or sending paddy wagons and fire engines through the quagmires or dusty ruts of Toronto's streets—horses were still relied on. The greatest ongoing public project was the improvement of Toronto harbour; the largest building in the planning stages was the giant new monument dedicated to the steam railway, Union Station (Plate 109).

As for Sir Henry Pellatt, the postwar boom and bust, the 'temporary' federal income tax, and rising land assessment were too much for him and his fortune sank like the *Titanic*. But long before that the grandiose dreams and extravagant lifestyle of Canadians like Pellatt had been deflated by a former teacher from his old school, Upper Canada College. In 1914 Stephen Leacock, who had married Pellatt's beautiful niece, published his comic masterpiece, *Arcadian Adventures of the Idle Rich*. It was Leacock who, from his academic aerie in Montreal, observed of his former home town: 'I have always found that the only thing in regard to Toronto which faraway people know for certain is that McGill University is in it.'

XXVIII. *Yonge Street looking north from Queen, 1912. The T. Eaton Company store occupies most of the west side of the street. The curved building on the corner is now being restored.*

79

THE KING EDWARD HOTEL

37 King Street East at Victoria Street (SE)

1901–3 by E.J. Lennox; alterations and additions 1917–21 by
Esenwein & Johnson of Buffalo, and Watts & Blackwell; altered
and redecorated 1979–81 by Roland Jutras of Jutras & Nobili.

The Late Victorian and Edwardian periods were the great age of hotel-building. Palatial hotels, such as the Savoy in London and the Waldorf-Astoria in New York, set high standards for architectural design, interior decoration, facilities, and services. In Canada hotel standards were set by the CPR with the chain of resort hotels it built across the country along the railway line. The first independent hotel of international consequence was the Windsor, in Montreal, built in 1876–8 and later extended by H.J. Hardenbergh, architect of the Waldorf-Astoria and the Plaza in New York. But at the turn of the century in Toronto there was no hotel to which visitors, commercial or royal, could be directed without apology or embarrassment. Opposite the old Union Station was the Queen's (demolished), which had grown by awkward additions from a row of townhouses first erected in 1838. The Rossin House (1855–6, demolished), at the southeast corner of King Street West and York, was more elaborate and had had some prestige and quality when new, but by the end of the century was desperately old-fashioned.

In these years there was much discussion about building a new hotel, and in late 1898 the Toronto Hotel Company was founded by George Aemilius Jarvis, with the support of George Cox (of Canada Life and the Bank of Commerce) and George Horace Gooderham (of Gooderham & Worts, see pp. 86–8). The chosen site on King Street East, facing Toronto Street, was that of the Golden Lion clothing store, which had closed in 1898. Along the western edge of the lot Victoria Street was extended south to Colborne. The first designs for the new hotel were drawn by Henry Ives Cobb of Chicago in 1900; but the commission ultimately went to E.J. Lennox. Permits were granted in December 1901 for a six-storey hotel, to be called the King Edward, to cost at least one million dollars; in March 1902 an additional permit was granted for two more floors.

Lennox's design had both the height and the enriched Classical detail that distinguished the best Edwardian office buildings, and Lennox was able to obtain superb craftsmanship and materials for construction and for decoration and furnishing. The result was the first hotel in Toronto whose appearance befitted the status of the society and business clientele it hoped to attract. The two-storey ground floor and lower mezzanine together form the base for the design. The grandeur of the interior is immediately conveyed by the stone columns and blocked piers that divide the street level of the façade and frame the main entrances, the bank windows at Victoria and King, and the great plate-glass windows of the Victoria Café on the northeast corner of Victoria and Colborne. Above

this base rise the floors of accommodation, arranged in three irregular blocks to permit glazed roofs over the main lobby and a second-floor restaurant (now a ballroom). The first six floors are faced in buff-coloured brick, and the corners and windows are simply framed with blocks and lintels of grey stone. The top two floors—added when the design was revised during construction—are faced in grey stone with paired pilasters and a projecting cornice.

In the crowded streetscape of King Street in 1903 the King Edward had presence and dignity, especially seen from the northwest, where a three-quarters round corner bay, supported on muscular Ionic columns, emphasized both the height and mass of the building. (Inside, the bay provides elegant space for the hotel's most important suites, as well as panoramic views. When the hotel first opened the main entrance was sheltered by a large canopy of glass and cast iron supported over the sidewalk on paired pilasters*—a perfect introduction to the interiors beyond.

Designed first to meet the needs of the business traveller, the King Edward provided a Gentleman's Café on the main floor, with a bar and buffet (later known as the Oak Room), where oak panelling and frescoes of hunting scenes suggested the décor of a private club or a personal library or smoking room. But the hotel was also designed (on the model of the Waldorf-Astoria and the Plaza in New York) as a centre of entertainment for the city's upper-middle class and its social élite. Before 1900 Toronto society rarely dined out in the evening or entertained away from home. Private clubs provided facilities for their members (though only rarely for their wives). But Toronto's few restaurants had little social cachet, especially for ladies lunching or dining away from home without a male escort; and none had the elegance Torontonians had seen in the CPR's chain of new hotels, or in New York and Montreal. The King Edward changed all that in the grandest manner.

The main lobby, known as the Rotunda (though it was neither round nor domed), with its fireplace, comfortable chairs and sofas, and massive structural columns and piers faced in scagliola (the most expensive form of artificial marble used in the period) became a major meeting place. The lobby's central space was a two-storey open court, roofed with glass and ringed at the mezzanine level with a double colonnade of Ionic columns in scagliola. Overlooking this court the mezzanine floor was designed as a Palm Room where tea and light refreshments were served. The Victoria Street entrance—

---

*The entrance has since been redesigned as a simpler canopy.

closest to King Street's most fashionable shops—was designated the Ladies' Entrance, and near it, off the lobby, was a secluded Ladies' Parlour.

On the second floor were banquet rooms, and smaller reception rooms—one in the rococo Louis XV style—that emulated the rooms of Toronto's finest houses. They provided to 'the society woman whose house is closed for decoration or repairs, the visiting actress or musician of distinction, who wishes to return hospitality' or 'the man of moderate means without a mansion in which to entertain, a charming resort for a dinner, a ball, or whatever he may advise.' Also on the second floor was the glass-vaulted room—whose great semi-circular window can be seen from the south, and which is now used for special functions—called the American Restaurant, the less expensive of the hotel's two dining-rooms. The much more expensive European restaurant (later known as the Victorian Room, and now the Victoria Café) was located on the main floor. It had the hotel's most extravagant interior: an opulent Edwardian version of the Louis XV style, with lace curtains, velvet draperies, panels hung with brocaded silk and framed in rococo mouldings, and a ceiling of heavily moulded beams and panels hung with crystal chandeliers. (Much of the plaster decoration remains.) The original ivory and green colour scheme was redone before the First World War in ivory, gold and red, with deep tufted upholstered banquettes. It was the perfect restaurant for Edwardian Toronto: historically inspired, overstuffed, boisterously detailed, and a bit vulgar. But it was the showplace of the hotel, described without irony in the brochure given to guests as 'elegant enough in style to serve as the boudoir of a Pompadour, were its dimensions not so vast.'

Even before the King Edward opened in 1903 it was apparent that Jarvis's venture was going to be a success. The first additions to the building (the seventh and eighth floors) were made even before it was completed. Others were projected in 1907; and in 1912 Lennox prepared plans for a fourteen-storey tower, to cost another million dollars; both were delayed by uncertain political and economic conditions. It was not until 1917 that the Buffalo firm of Esenwein & Johnson (designers of several office buildings in Buffalo, and of the original Statler Hotel) were called in to redecorate some of the interiors and to build a 16-storey addition east of the original building, with shops and service space on the lower floors and a two-storey ballroom on top. Though the materials and Classical detail echo Lennox's work, the addition lacks his Edwardian exuberance.

During the 1920s several hotels were built in Toronto, but only the Royal York (1929 by Ross & MacDonald) presented a serious challenge. In the fifties and sixties, as public taste in architecture changed and new hotels offered facilities hardly contemplated when the King Edward was built (swimming pools, revolving restaurants, enormous convention rooms), competition became more severe. Ultimately, however, the hotel's worst enemy was the apathy of poor management. The nadir in the King Edward's existence came in the mid-1970s, when many of its rooms were converted to house a fashion merchandising market; and finally when its owners proposed replacing it with a banal plaza and two office towers by Bregman & Hamann. Fortunately the city opposed the project. In 1979 the new owners, Trans-Nation Inc. (working with the Trusthouse-Forte hotel group from England, who now manage the hotel), undertook one of the largest and most expensive architectural renovation and restoration jobs ever attempted in Canada. The work—done by Jutras & Nobili of Bedford, Mass.—involved near-total demolition inside the upper floors, and the conversion of 470 rooms into 322 larger rooms and 30 suites. There were a few ill-conceived features: a gazebo-like structure (since removed) introduced into the Victoria Room that concealed its ceiling; the Oak Room was demolished; and gratuitous changes were made to the lobby, where new small-scaled furniture fits poorly with the muscular architecture. Completed at the same time was the re-design (around Lennox's original piers) of the interior of the Bank of Nova Scotia Branch on the corner of Victoria and King; this new work accords beautifully with the robust forms of Lennox's conception.

The hotel business is too much affected by fashion and the ups and downs of management to assume permanence. Since its reopening, however, the King Edward has regained at least part of the luxury market and social position it was built to serve in Edwardian Toronto. Like no other building in the ciy, it symbolizes the lifestyle and standards of a period that has all but vanished from living memory.

80

THE ROYAL ALEXANDRA THEATRE

260 King Street West (N)

1906–7 by John M. Lyle, initially in association
with Carrère & Hastings of New York

The Royal Alexandra is Toronto's one Beaux Arts theatre. Like many other theatres of the same period built in London and New York, it was designed in simple though elegant French taste but furnished with all the velvet and gilt opulence that for Edwardians was appropriate to the two glamorous worlds meeting within: the theatre and Society. Toronto had not suffered for lack of theatres in the late nineteenth century. The most important were the Princess, on King Street between York and Simcoe, built in 1889 as a music hall and altered as a theatre in 1895; and the Grand Opera House on Adelaide Street West, built in 1874–6. Neither, however, provided the luxury and elegance in the foyers and auditoriums that theatre-goers had become acquainted with in New York and London.

The impetus behind the Royal Alexandra Theatre Company came from Cawthra Mulock, the young president of Guardian Trust, Canada Bread, and the National Iron Works. He determined to make his new theatre what it remains today: a Toronto home for touring companies based in London and New York. Indeed, before and after the First World War it became one of the most important stops on the Canadian tours of foreign theatrical companies.

Though Mulock's personal fortune made it possible for him to finance the building alone, he associated himself in the Royal Alexandra Theatre Company with R.A. Smith, stockbroker and partner in the firm of Osler & Hammond, and Stephen Haas, a Toronto manufacturer. A fourth partner, Lawrence Solman—owner of the Hanlan's Point amuse-

81

ment park on the Island—became the manager of the theatre. The first designs were drawn by Carrère & Hastings of New York, who had recently won the competition to design the New Theatre there, which was already reputed to be the most beautiful theatre in North America. Before the Royal Alexandra project got under way, however, the commission was transferred to John M. Lyle (1872–1946), who had been brought up in Hamilton and received his training as an architect there, in Paris at the Ecole des Beaux Arts, and in New York, where he worked in the Carrère & Hastings office. Ontario law stipulated that the American firm would need a local associate for the Toronto commission, and it was probably for this reason that Lyle returned to Canada. By the time work began Lyle had developed the design, and it was he who signed the building permits, independent of Carrère & Hastings.

The site chosen for the Royal Alexandra was on King Street, about half a mile west of the King Edward Hotel (which commemorated the reigning monarch just as the theatre commemorated his consort). Lyle's design is composed in three parts: the entrance block and the symmetrically planned auditorium and high brick 'stage house' for the backdrops and other accoutrements. Lyle's inspiration for the front came from the Townsend house on Massachusetts Avenue in Washington, D.C., which Carrère & Hastings had designed in 1900. The theatre has the same general scheme as the house: the façade of grey-white limestone is arranged with a two-storey central section that rises to a dormered mansard roof set behind a low stepped parapet and is flanked by lower

wings, originally one storey (later raised in brick to two). The main entrance was sheltered by a marquee of glass and bronze supported on wall brackets and on chains. (The present one is much wider.) The three second-floor windows that light the lounge are separated by Ionic pilasters that rise to support the principle cornice and the sculpted parapet above. The middle window is wider than the side windows, each of which opens onto a balustraded balcony.

The entrance foyer, which contains the box office, is lined with green marble, with simple panelling brought to life by the glitter of electric light. On the first floor there is also a smoking-room, a ladies' retiring room, a cloak room, and office space; these public rooms are decorated in the eighteenth-century style popular in Toronto houses at the time. Polished mahogany stairs lead up to the balcony foyer and main lounge, which, with its high coved ceiling, has the air of a large private drawing-room.

Lyle's auditorium lacked for nothing in opulence and had the strong outlines basic to French Classical design. It is nearly square in plan and originally seated 1,525, including the two boxes on either side, each of which accommodated 14. All the seats are closer to the stage than was usual at the time because of the auditorium's shallowness, and the second balcony is uncomfortably steep. However, the acoustics are excellent, and sightlines are good because cantilevers were used instead of columns to support the balconies. The shallow auditorium gives unusual prominence to the proscenium. Broadly framed in a Classical moulding that curves at the corners, and surmounted by Frederick S. Challener's mural

162

82

of 'Aphrodite Discovering Adonis', it is like a window on the drama being enacted onstage. The lower parts of the side walls were panelled in oak, with mouldings picked out in gold. Above, the walls were originally hung with gold brocade set off by plaster mouldings touched with gold. The stage-drop curtain was of crimson silk ornamented with the Royal Arms, and the boxes were draped in blue and old-rose silk. With its rich texture, gilding, and soft gold tones, the scheme made the perfect background for the elaborate formal dresses theatre-going then required.

Cawthra Mulock's speculative investment was an immediate success when it opened on 26 August 1907 with Mark Swann's *Top o' the World*. Even after motion pictures became popular, the stage of the Royal Alex continued to offer the best in English and American theatre: the actors who have performed there bear the most distinguished names in theatre. After the Second World War the Royal Alex, thought too small and old-fashioned for the scale of musicals and plays that were touring North America, began to fade. Also, many Torontonians broke the habit of going to the theatre and were content for the most part with movies and television. In 1960 the O'Keefe Centre opened, and its size and modernity further undermined the Royal Alex.

In 1963 both site and theatre were put up for sale. Demolition seemed inevitable. In an act that has since assumed mythic proportions in Canadian cultural history, the theatre was purchased by Ed Mirvish (b. 1914). Better known as 'Honest' Ed for his department store, Mirvish had the theatre restored by Herbert Irvine (the auditorium colour scheme was changed to red and gold). Facilities were expanded, the number of seats reduced slightly to 1,497. Though many said Mirvish could never succeed, he almost single-handedly restored the habit of theatre-going for thousands of Torontonians. Using the assured revenue of a subscription system, he has been able to add a whole new generation of stars' photos to those that hang in the foyers and staircases. Mirvish has also made the Royal Alexandra the focal point of a restaurant empire that spreads west along the north side of King Street. He purchased several large warehouses and transformed them.* Their stained glass he collected from houses and churches that had once ornamented Toronto and were demolished with little thought in the 1960s. The combination of theatre and restaurants (Mirvish has been followed on King by other entrepreneurs) gives this section of King Street a positive image in the city, attracting many people who previously did not venture downtown. The centrepiece of the area is now Roy Thomson hall (Plate 171), but it was the reopening of the Royal Alexandra that got the rejuvenation and development underway.

---

*Oscar Wilde once praised Beerbohm Tree's Hamlet for being 'funny without being vulgar'; Honest Ed's warehouses are deliciously vulgar without being ridiculous. In fact his whole collection of flashing lights, blown-up portraits, and honky-tonk signs ('If you like home cooking, stay home') creates a crazy counterpoint not only to the ripe restoration of the theatre's interior, but also to the severe magnificence of Roy Thomson Hall and the solemn Romanesque majesty of St Andrew's Presbyterian Church to the south of the theatre.

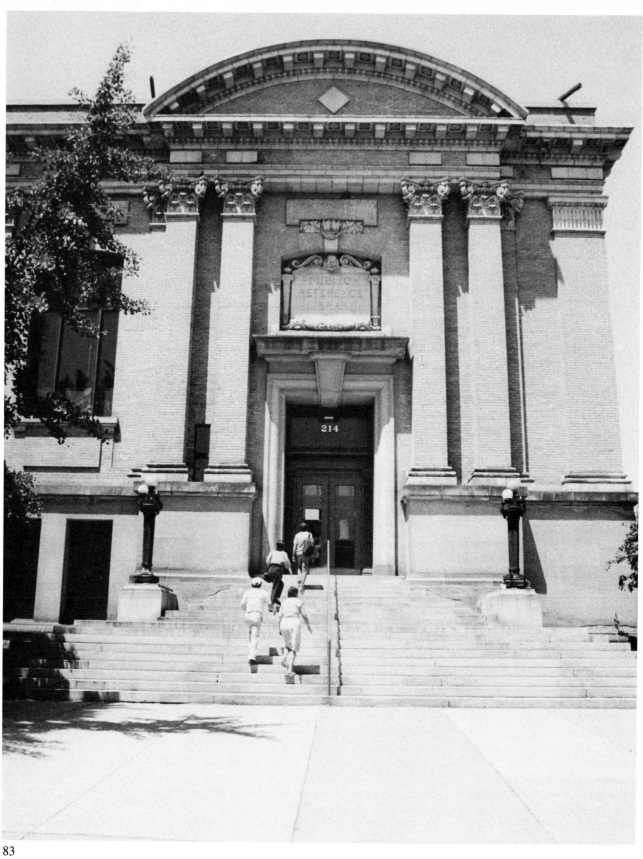

83

THE UNIVERSITY OF TORONTO BOOKROOM AND KOFFLER STUDENT CENTRE

(Formerly THE TORONTO PUBLIC REFERENCE LIBRARY)

214 College Street at St George Street (NW)

1905–9 by A.H. Chapman and Wickson & Gregg; with additions
in 1922 and 1928–9 by Chapman and Oxley and Wickson &
Gregg; and the theatre renovated in 1961 by Irving Grossman

The former College Street Reference Library and the Union Station (Plate 109), both intended to ornament the city and to provide needed public service, are the two most successful Beaux Arts public buildings in Toronto. The design of the Library is focused on a long row of two-storey windows, separated by tall Corinthian pilasters, that lighted the main reference and reading-room. With its handsome principal entrance at the top of a high stone staircase, the building has unusual presence and grandeur in the streetscape. And yet, built in a soft yellow brick above a stone basement storey, with terracotta details that catch the light, and set back from the street behind trees in a more garden-like setting than was usual in public architecture of the period, the Library remains very approachable. It is public in the best possible sense.

During most of the nineteenth century the principal lending library in Toronto was that of the Mechanics' Institute, founded in 1830, at the northeast corner of Church and Adelaide Streets (1854–61 by Cumberland & Storm; demolished). But its subscription fees, though low, were more than many residents could afford; and its total revenues were far from sufficient to maintain the collection properly. Public libraries were made possible by the Ontario Free Libraries Act of 1882, which allowed cities to finance libraries with debenture loans repaid from taxes. On 1 January 1883 a referendum approved the purchase of the assets of the Mechanics' Institute and its building to form the basis for a Toronto Public Library (originally called the Toronto Free Library).

In March 1883 the administrators of the Library recommended construction of a larger building to contain at least 100,000 volumes, as well as the immediate spending of $95,000 for new books (easily the equivalent of 3 to 4 million dollars today), all to be supported by debenture loans. Unfortunately the city was preoccupied with the expenses of building a new City Hall* (Plate 76) and numerous public schools and other projects. Instead the old Mechanics' Institute building was altered and extended; in addition, by 1900 five branch libraries had been opened across the city in space rented from private owners or borrowed in city-owned buildings. It was not until 1903—when Andrew Carnegie, as part of the Carnegie Foundation's support for public libraries, offered

$350,000 for the building of a central reference library and three branches—that the Library Board and its chief Librarian, James Bain, could begin to up-date facilities in an appropriate architectural form. Council accepted the gift on 23 February 1903, but delayed any decision on how to use the money until late October 1904. The grant was used to build a Northern Branch at 22 Yorkville Avenue (1906–7, by Robert McCallum, the City Architect) and a Western Branch on the southwest corner of Queen Street West and Lisgar Street (1908–9, also by McCallum). Funds were allocated for a new College Street Branch, which had been occupying rented premises at the corner of College and Brunswick. It was to share space with the new Reference Library, a decision that influenced the location of the building. Between the 1880s and the beginning years of this century College Street had evolved, around the twin focal points of the university and the Legislature, into an avenue lined with public and semi-public buildings. The Library site, on the northwest corner of St George Street, placed the building at the western end of the other public buildings, close to the University and to the residential area its circulating library was meant to serve, affording it a setting of shaded Olympian calm appropriate to its purposes.

Before the First World War, libraries—as repositories of knowledge—were a touchstone for high-style architectural design. They were also among the first public buildings to develop strong technical requirements in relation to stack design, fireproofing, acoustics, lighting, and security. For the design of the new Reference Library a competition was organized in 1905, open to Canadian architects, in which competitors were given detailed functional requirements and asked to present schemes of 'definite character' that would then be refined in consultation with the Library staff.

The winning scheme (which was little changed in execution) by A.H. Chapman, in association with Wickson & Gregg, was imbued with the traditions of American and French Beaux Arts public architecture, particularly the New York Public Library (Carrère & Hastings, 1897–1911). The competition directive called for the College Street Branch to be located on the ground floor of the new building. The branch entrance at the west end, framed in stone with a balcony above, balances the much more impressive reference library entrance to the east, which, because it is set between the pilasters of

---

*A proposal was made at one point to house the Library in the City Hall.

84. *Entrance hall*

the upper storey under a wide pediment, and is approached by a cascade of steps, immediately established the Library's importance.

These main-entrance steps are succeeded inside by a marble interior staircase that rises in three levels through a double row of arches—easily the most effective demonstration in Toronto of the Beaux Arts emphasis on an innately formal, processional sequence of entrance spaces that gradually introduce the visitor to the functions of a major building. The principal landing of the staircase is also the entrance hall (the Library Board's offices were on the right). The spaces in which the stair rises—first to the reading-room level and then to the third-floor level of the art rooms—was open to the reading-room, tying the whole interior into one architectural statement. Monumentality was achieved by the double arcade and piers screening the stair, repeated at the west end of the reading-room; by the pilasters that alternate with the tall south windows of the reading-room; and by the details of the foyer, with its stair balustrades and walls faced with handsome greyish-cream artificial stone, and its pale marble floor. The reading-room was high and airy. Bookcases lined the south

and far-end walls, and rows of heavy oak study tables and light spindle chairs were placed across the width of the room. Capping the whole was a beamed and panelled ceiling richly coloured in bronze-green and antique gold.

The new reference library was officially opened on 28 October 1909. In November of that year the Art Museum of Toronto (predecessor of the Art Gallery of Toronto) took over the third-floor art rooms as a gallery. From the beginning the Library Board had planned for expansion. The principal addition that gave the College Street branch more spacious quarters—designed in 1928–9 by Chapman & Oxley, with Wickson & Gregg—was the St George Street wing, extending 112 feet along the street to its own entrance, marked by a frontispiece of pilasters, and with a columned ground-floor reading-room housing the circulating library and a large auditorium on the upper floor. After the Second World War there were other changes, the most important being the conversion of the auditorium to the Central Library Theatre in 1959, with alterations by Irving Grossman.

Of much greater importance for the building was the transfer of responsibility for the reference library and its collections

85. *The former Reading Room as refitted for bookstore use*

to the Metropolitan Toronto Library Board. At the same time there were major changes in library philosophy and technology to stress informality, openness, and accessibility, as well as the new technology of computers and videos. All these changes, plus the increased space the reference library badly needed, could have been achieved through the renovation and expansion of the existing building. But Metro Council and the new Library Board, wishing to express a renewed library tradition, opted for a new building in a more central location. The result was the present Metro Library (Plate 156) designed by Raymond Moriyama and opened in 1977. Three years later the St George Street building was sold to the University of Toronto.

In 1984–5, with help from the Ontario Government and the Koffler family (founders of the Shoppers Drug Mart chain), the building was renovated by Howard Walker and Howard Chapman (son of Alfred Chapman). Part of the space, including the main reading-room, became the University bookstore, with the rest apportioned to various student services. A three-storey concourse with a glazed roof divides the two sections.

The renovation has several unfortunate elements: bookcases block the majestic ground-floor windows of the façade; the stock metal and glass partitions are unappealing; and the neo-Neo-Classical decorative details appear crude beside the strength and finesse of the original work. But the old reading-room has retained much of its original character. It was redesigned on two levels, with wooden parquet replacing the original cork flooring and bookcases at right angles to the walls dividing the space into subject areas for comfortable browsing. The demands of accommodating thousands of books inevitably clutter the lower part, but the renovation preserves the scale and grandeur of the old reading-room— particularly when viewed through the arcades of the main staircase, which have since been glazed—and the elaborately beamed and moulded ceiling has been restored in bright gold, black, and green. The best of Chapman's detailing has been retained, and students and staff find in this once-neglected building a centre of enjoyable activity and practical use.

THE TRADERS' BANK BUILDING

(Now THE MORGAN BUILDING)

61–7 Yonge Street at Colborne (NE)

1905–6 by Carrère & Hastings

The Edwardian period was a time of unparalleled prosperity in Canada. In addition to the success of such native-born industries as the Massey Manufacturing Company, the William Davies Meat Packing Company, run by Joseph Flavelle, and the Canadian Pacific Railway, foreign investment flowed into Canada from the United States and Britain, to be directed to new railways, new manufacturing, and particularly to exploiting the natural resources of northern Québec and Ontario and the timber and coal of British Columbia and Alberta. Banking benefited most from this prosperity and provided much of the guiding impetus to the country's expansion. Between 1901 and 1911—when twelve new chartered banks were founded, most with head offices in Toronto or Montreal—Canadians developed the unshakable confidence in banks that led to their prolonged love affair with savings, giving the banks enormous sums to invest in Canadian industry. Bankers continued to place great importance on architecture to establish a powerful and self-confident image. Classicism still dominated, but the Edwardian banks—given a new grandeur of form, material, and interior space—rose to greater heights in the streetscape, overtopping the church towers of the Victorian city. With their near cousins, insurance companies, they became the great public buildings of their time.

The Traders' Bank was founded in the boom that followed the completion of the CPR in 1886. Its first building on the east side of Yonge Street, at Colborne, was replaced on the same site in 1905–6 by a new building designed by Carrère & Hastings of New York (working with F.S. Baker of Toronto). Famous for the design of the New York Public Library (1897–1911), and for skyscrapers on Wall Street, Carrère & Hastings had become well known in Toronto through a design submitted for the new Union Station (see page 109) and a year later, in 1904, for the Royal Alexandra Theatre (Plate 80), which they designed in association with John M. Lyle. The Bank fully expected the firm to satisfy their desire for a building that would be both a popular and an architectural landmark.

At fifteen storeys, the building Carrère & Hastings designed was the tallest commercial building in the British Empire. Height was nothing new in banking architecture. Each generation of buildings had been taller than the last, particularly after banks realized that profits could be made by renting out the upper floors. In Toronto the invention of the elevator enabled office blocks like the Confederation Life Building of 1890 (Plate 59) to join church towers as part of the city skyline. But until the turn of the century the romance of buildings that 'scraped the sky' had not had much place in Toronto architecture. Unlike earlier banks, the Traders' Bank set out to be a skyscraper, using height to gain respect among its corporate neighbours. The design is built up in a series of levels: a ground floor faced in smooth stone; a two-storey banking hall set off by Doric columns and pilasters that frame its windows; a shadowed Doric frieze (the detail is terracotta, not stone); and then eight identical floors of rental offices articulated in four 'layers', topped by a bracketed cornice and a dormered attic storey. Today it seems absurd to call this building a skyscraper; but in 1906 it embodied a new and romantic image of height, symbolizing progress and evoking the spirit of New York, which was much admired in Toronto.

The Traders' Bank did not outlive the First World War. The building—which had expressed a new standard in Toronto architecture that valued height almost above all other architectural considerations—was in a few years no longer the tallest in the British Empire.* Its luxurious materials and dramatic interior space continued to be admired. But its early-twentieth-century expression of the power and pride of height was soon overtaken by taller buildings.

---

*The building was purchased by Montreal Trust, and the banking hall was destroyed to make more office space. The most recent owners have cleaned and restored the exterior and renamed the building.

87.   *The Dominion Bank building, 1914*

THE DOMINION BANK BUILDING

(Now THE TORONTO-DOMINION BANK)

1–5 King Street West at Yonge Street (SW)

1913–14 by Darling & Pearson

In 1913 the Dominion Bank engaged the Toronto firm of Darling & Pearson to design its new head office on the corner of King and Yonge Streets. The new building replaced a tall Second Empire office building erected for the Bank in 1877–8 by William Irving, and its towering height, completed in 1914 (at what must at the time have seemed the phenomenal cost of over $1,000,000), continued the transformation of the bank district that had been begun by the Traders' Bank building (Plate 86).

The twelve-storey design combines traditional bankerly values of formality and opulence with an almost sensuous appreciation of the visual effects of height. The three-storey base is as solid and severe as any banker could wish—its smooth surface broken by the recessed portico of Roman Doric columns facing King and the row of tall arched windows that face Yonge and provide a foretaste of the interior's monumentality. Above a cornice at the third-floor level, verticality takes over: office windows, surrounded by many sharply linear mouldings, are flanked by tall, narrow, pilaster-like panels in creamy grey terracotta. These rising verticals are continued in the highest level of the three-part façade by Ionic pilasters, until they are resolved in richly detailed round-arched and Palladian windows and a shallow Ionic cornice and parapet. Seen from the street, the Dominion Bank seems to glory in being a skyscraper, but one that achieves Classical dignity.

The splendour of the exterior is matched by the interior, with its upper and lower banking halls. Inside the King Street entrance (where wide steps lead from the foyer down to the lower-level savings bank) a palatial staircase rises, in three flights, to the main banking hall on the second floor, creating a dramatic sense of event. The character of the two-storey banking hall, borrowing from Classical temples and even Renaissance churches, is established by an arcade on piers that supports a mezzanine of office space on the south and west sides. It frames the eastern windows, modulating their light and creating a series of vistas through arches to other arches. The grandeur of the hall is completed by its beamed and coffered ceiling, ornamented with provincial crests—appropriate for a 'Dominion' Bank. The ceiling colours are rich, dark, and sober; elsewhere Darling's scheme is lighter to make the interior seem more spacious, with marble in roseate hues on walls and floors and highlights of burnished gold leaf and polished brass and bronze for the hardware, lighting standards, and service desks.

In 1955 the Dominion Bank amalgamated with the Bank of Toronto, and in 1965 completed the Toronto-Dominion Centre (Plate 149) as a new head office. Fortunately the decision was made to retain the Darling & Pearson building at a time when Beaux Arts banks were crashing like timber on King Street. Today, to the Bank's great credit, it is in magnificent condition. It is easily one of the most beautiful buildings in the city.

88. *The Banking Hall*

89

'HOLWOOD', THE SIR JOSEPH FLAVELLE HOUSE

78 Queen's Park Drive at Hoskin Avenue (NW)

1901–2 by Darling & Pearson

At the beginning of the twentieth century the character of domestic architecture in Toronto changed dramatically. The 1880s and 1890s had been dominated by the Romanesque Revival, a fashion borrowed from the United States and exploited equally for large houses such as the George Gooderham House on St George Street (Plate 63) and for smaller middle-class houses, like those on Madison Avenue (pp. 118–20). More traditional English influences dominated the first twenty years of the new century. The patterns of Georgian red-brick classicism that had been revived in England at the end of the nineteenth century provided a model for large formal houses like 'Holwood', which was built in 1901–2 by Darling and Pearson for Joseph Flavelle. With its full-scale portico facing northeast, it is the grandest of the Edwardian Georgian houses in Toronto, proclaiming itself as the home of a gentleman of both wealth and public standing.

Joseph Wesley Flavelle (1858–1939) was one of the outstanding patrons and philanthropists of Edwardian Toronto, like his near-neighbours E.R. Wood and Sir Edmund Walker. He arrived in Toronto from Peterborough in 1887, and built a meat-packing empire as part-owner of the William Davies Company, one of the predecessors of Canada Packers.* He expanded the business into the first nation-wide retail grocery chain in the country and diversified his wealth in banking and insurance, becoming a director or executive officer of the Canadian Bank of Commerce, Canada Life, Imperial Life, and National Trust. Believing that wealth was a privilege and a responsibility, he spent a good deal of his time after 1900 on public projects and charities, heading the fund-raising campaign that built the new Toronto General Hospital and the 1906 Royal Commission on the future of the University of Toronto; serving on the Board of the Toronto Housing Company, which built Riverdale Courts (Plate 97); working in his church, Sherbourne Street Methodist; and giving donations to countless charities, projects, and needy persons. Flavelle's career came to a logical climax when he was awarded a baronetcy by George V for organizing the Canadian munitions industry during the First World War. Unfortunately this was followed by virulent criticism when it was discovered that the Davies Company had made large—but not unjustified—profits, supplying British and Imperial forces with meat during the war. The furore was politically inspired, but it clouded Flavelle's public reputation. It was not until much later that he received the praise due for his imaginative benefactions.

The residential neighbourhood around Queen's Park was laid out in 1861 by the University of Toronto. Development had been slow, but by the 1890s a number of large picturesque houses had been built by industrialists with whom Flavelle had business and social connections. Flavelle's association with the University of Toronto might also have drawn him to the site. The choice of Darling & Pearson as his architects was probably influenced by their work for his colleagues, Sir Edmund Osler and Sir Edmund Walker, among others. They were also architects to the Canadian Bank of Commerce, of which Flavelle had been a director since 1897. The firm had a reputation for grandeur and style, but Flavelle thought of Holwood primarily as a family home, modelled on the spacious eighteenth-century and Edwardian houses he had visited in southern England. Darling gave his design the look and atmosphere of a country house, fronted with a portico of Corinthian columns finished in stucco and set back from the street behind tall wrought-iron gates with brick and stone piers. The house was designed in two units drawn together under a spreading roof punctuated at irregular intervals by dormers and tall rusticated chimneys. The main block, containing the principal reception and family rooms, is two storeys; on the right is a three-storey service wing. The two parts come together at an obtuse angle to define the landscaped forecourt. Between the wings the change of height is masked by a tall pedimented pavilion ornamented with paired stone Ionic pilasters that frame the arched and balconied window that lights the main stair. This pavilion is an important part of the design, but it does not compete for prominence with the monumental portico, which attracts the attention of anyone travelling south on Queen's Park from Bloor Street. The front door is equally dignified, with a crested and blocked surround framing it, and a transom and sidelights decorated with slender Ionic colonnettes. The contrast of these forms in white stone against the deep red of the walls softens their formality, combining the formal and public with the intimate and family-scaled—an ideal that wealthy Edwardians sought in their homes.

The arrangement of the interiors also juxtaposes formality and informality, each room having its own special character. At the heart of the house, behind the front portico, a corridor opens into a dark, vaulted baronial hall that was used as a music room and for large entertainments. This hall, which has not been substantially changed, is dominated by a magnificent fireplace, with a Jacobean mantel in oak. Natural light enters it through north-facing French windows. The room as a whole acquires a rather subaqueous effect from the low, groined barrel-vault ceiling, which was decorated by Gustav Hahn with Art Nouveau angels against a translucent green

---

*The enormous scale of the Davies Company, the largest pork-packer in the British Empire, gave Toronto the nickname it likes least: 'Hogtown'.

90. *The drawing-room*

background. The main living-rooms were arranged in a connected suite along the south and west fronts, opening onto a wide balustraded terrace: it extended from the Conservatory at the east end, through the drawing-room, the dining-room, and the library at the west end, and finally across a vaulted and tiled garden hall to Flavelle's study, which faced west. Next to the library, which was used as a family living-room, is another portico. Duplicating the size and details of the front portico and facing west, it stands picturesquely (rather than formally) at the top of the long sloping garden and was used as a sheltered terrace.

The drawing-room (now divided and unrecognizable) was high and spacious, painted in shades of white and enriched by elongated Corinthian columns and pilasters that supported a beamed and coved ceiling. The other rooms, which the family used more often, were less regimented and formal in design. For the dining-room, where the woodwork repeated the basic forms of the hall, Darling designed a wide double-columned mantel, a Jacobean plaster ceiling, as well as the table and Chippendale-style chairs. The library was the largest room in the house. Although the mantel, ceiling, and draperies were chosen or designed by Darling, this was the general family living-room and it reflected a strong sense of Flavelle's own taste, which could be seen in the mixture of ordinary and high-quality furniture and accessories: a cheap oak desk next to a collection of fine Chinese porcelain and numerous Holbein prints.

To some of Flavelle's associates the size and grandeur of Holwood seemed dismayingly un-Methodist. The man in the street, taking note of the source of its owner's wealth, nicknamed the house 'Porker's Palace'. Flavelle often opened the house for public events: a luncheon in 1904 that marked the beginning of talks that led eventually (in 1925) to the union of the Methodist, Presbyterian, and Congregational churches into the United Church of Canada; and annual children's parties were held after the Santa Claus Parade. But the formal parts of the house were far less important to Flavelle than those devoted to family life. He allowed Toronto's social and architectural magazines to publish only photographs of the gardens—never views of the interior, which might have seemed boastful, or revealed too much of his private life. Flavelle undoubtedly hoped that his house would remain in his family for many years. However, by the time of his death in 1939 its location and costly maintenance made that impossible. It was willed to the University of Toronto, which Flavelle had served over forty years.

The house became first the home of the Department of History, and finally—with a large but compatible library addition to the southwest—the centre of the University of Toronto's Faculty of Law. The library addition included the glazing of the rear portico as a corridor. But the grandeur of Darling's creation is still very much apparent. And in the early spring the lilacs and blue scillas of the Holwood gardens are the glory of the campus.

91. *45 Wychwood Park*

WYCHWOOD PARK

Davenport Road west of Bathurst Street

Established 1888–1907

Toronto is often lauded as a city of neighbourhoods, several of which—Chestnut Park in Rosedale, Palmerston Boulevard in the College and Bathurst area, and Collier Street bordering the Yonge/Bloor commercial district—are now, and in some cases originally were, conceived as enclaves. Wychwood Park is the most interesting of these special areas. First established as an artists' colony on the edge of the escarpment, it retains its intentionally countrified English character. On sloping treed lots, cottage-like houses are grouped around a spring-fed pond formed by Taddle Creek at the start of its southeast run across the city. The community is still administered by a corporation consisting of the property owners who, in tending to the needs of their neighbourhood, maintain a stubborn independence from the very different city surrounding them.

Wychwood Park was founded by Marmaduke Matthews (1837–1913), an English-born landscape painter who immigrated to Toronto in 1860; he eloped in 1864 with Cyrilda Barnard to New York, where he lived until his return five years later. In 1873 Matthews purchased a ten-acre estate on Davenport Road west of Bathurst, and the following year he

built 'Wychwood', a comfortably large house that still stands on the crest of the hill, facing south. With gables and a stone oriel window over the front door in the High Victorian Gothic style, it is built of yellow brick with red brick trim around the windows. Matthews was joined by Alexander Jardine, owner of the Pure Gold Baking Powder Company, who in 1877–8 bought 12 acres to the west and built 'Braemore'. Another house followed for Ambrose Goodman, Matthews' son-in-law; and in the late 1880s Sir William Gage purchased ten acres to the east, along the west side of Bathurst.

During the late eighties and the nineties Matthews' career prospered with commissions from Sir William Van Horne to execute paintings along the CPR line; and in 1888 Matthews and Jardine filed a plan to subdivide their two estates and form an artists' colony of seventeen large lots grouped around an eighteenth ravine lot reserved as park land. The plan was revised in 1891 to include 38 large and small lots; again the ravine was reserved and Taddle Creek was dammed to form a pond. Both commercial and utopian, the scheme was directly related to several other artists' communities in the United

92. *Upland Cottage, Wychwood Park*

States and Britain. For the artists and academics who moved there, Wychwood Park offered a convivial village atmosphere and a rural seclusion that few individuals could otherwise have afforded.*

The move to Wychwood Park by many Toronto artists was led by G.A. Reid (1860–1947), the premier muralist and art teacher of the period. Reid was a friend of Matthews and since 1894 had been involved with an artists' summer colony at Onteora in the Catskills of New York State. In 1905 he moved—from 435 Indian Road—to Wychwood Park, building to his own designs 'Upland Cottage' at Number 81, which backs on Alcina Avenue. (The numbering of houses in Wychwood Park does not obey any standard rule.) This large two-storey house, set back from the road, was designed to appear long and low, like an idealized English cottage, with walls finished in cream stucco under a prominent roof. A high gable draws together a wide bay of casement windows, and the line of the roof drops in a long shallow curve over the front porch to draw the front door into the composition.

This Cottage Style (as it was known) was developed from late-Medieval and vernacular English forms by such English architects as Sir Edwin Lutyens and M.H. Baillie-Scott. Rooflines were exaggerated into great sheltering sweeps, accented by tall chimneys above simple walls of plain brick, stucco, and exposed timber. Inside were spacious rooms simply finished with panelling, paint, and wallpaper; well lit by bays and rows of casements, they were made cozy by large fireplaces. The style dominated middle-class house design in Toronto from the late 1890s until the 1930s (replacing the Romanesque Revival in popular esteem). Its great proponent in Toronto was Eden Smith, for almost thirty years (until the mid-twenties) one of Toronto's most fashionable domestic architects. He created many variations on the Cottage Style in large and small private houses and in two large apartment complexes, one of which was Riverdale Courts (Plates 97–9).

For himself Smith built Number 5 Wychwood Park in 1907.

*The idea was also tried in the Indian Road area east of High Park, led by the Toronto architect Eden Smith, who built a house at 405 Indian Road in 1896. Several artists followed him over the next ten years, but as the area became divided into small lots its character quickly changed.

A large gabled house, it was made even larger by baronial additions in later years. Smith's style is better represented by Number 16 at the centre of the Park, built in 1910 for the lawyer E.A. Duvernet. A large brick-and-stucco house standing on a big lot among the area's oldest trees, it manages an air of countrified informality under a low spreading roof punctuated by assymmetrical chimneys. Among the other Smith houses in the Park are Number 15, built for Gustav Hahn around 1908; Number 7, east of the Duvernet house, built around 1911 for G.K. Howell; and Number 45, the finest evocation of the Cottage Style in the Park, built around 1910 for Michael Chapman. (Chapman's wife was the adopted daughter of the English Victorian painter and sculptor G.F. Watts and had been brought up in the heart of the Surrey countryside, where the Cottage Style had been developed for Watts and other artists.) The Chapman family moved from Poplar Plains Road to the Park, where the new house was built at the northeast corner of the development, backing onto Alcina Avenue (with a drive on that side), but almost concealed from view by trees and undergrowth. As in all of Smith's houses, the details are very simple: stuccoed walls overgrown with creepers, bays and dormers of casements (Smith never used sash windows), and spacious rooms. The L-shaped house is approached from a wooden gate up a long path bordered by high shrubbery. The smooth slopes of the roof rise in two levels, seeming to continue the contours of the site. Smith aspired to a unity of house and site in all his designs—an ideal best realized in Wychwood Park, where it greatly influenced other architects and their patrons.

Most of the development of Wychwood Park dates from after 1907, when E.A. Duvernet and G.A. Reid managed the formal creation of the Wychwood Park Corporation. Though the City annexed the Park in 1909, it has treated the area with remarkable sympathy. The Corporation still manages most of the Park's affairs, helped by purchase agreements that give it first refusal on the sale of the land and houses within the area. Since the 1930s, and particularly after the Second World War, several new houses have been added. But the original character, and the ideals of an artist's colony, are still alive and apparent.

93

CASA LOMA

1 Austin Terrace, at Walmer Road (SE)
1909–11 by E.J. Lennox

No Edwardian building in Toronto is more remarkable than Casa Loma, the largest house ever built in Canada. An architectural fantasy compiled from countless details inspired by European medieval castles, it crowns a hill-top site, majestically overlooking the workaday world of the city below. It was built by Sir Henry Pellatt (1859–1939), whose wealth grew with astute investment in the development of hydroelectric power at Niagara Falls, the provision of electricity to light Toronto, the running of electric streetcars in the city, and investment in both the CPR and land development in Manitoba and the West. Pellatt was not only a shrewd businessman but also a romantic fascinated by chivalry, the soldier's life, and military glory. His hobby and first love was the Queen's Own Rifles, in which he became a Major-General in 1921. Other Toronto patrons were richer and more influential; but none had Pellatt's flamboyance, his love of drama and effect,

94. *Main entrance*

or the self-confidence to produce such an extravagant building as Casa Loma.

In 1882 Pellatt was a successful stockbroker who had just married and settled in a house on Sherbourne Street. In 1898 he built, on the east side of the street overlooking Allan Gardens, a new house (now demolished) whose castle-like appearance betokened the taste that would inspire Casa Loma. Acquiring great wealth over the next five years with the completion of the Niagara power schemes, he planned yet another residence to be built on an unheard-of scale. Between 1903 and 1905 he purchased some twenty-five lots east of Walmer Road on the edge of the escarpment and running down its slope to Davenport Road. Pellatt's wife Mary christened the new property 'Casa Loma'—Spanish for 'House on the Hill'.

Pellatt's chosen architect, E.J. Lennox—who also relished flamboyance—worked dramatic, and at times marvellously fanciful, variations on patterns drawn from French Medieval and Early Renaissance architecture to design a complex that bears comparison with the late-nineteenth-century castles of King Ludwig of Bavaria. Work began in 1905 on the first estate buildings. These included a stable court, built around a turreted water tower on the west side of Walmer Road; a high-chimneyed boiler house that eventually provided heat for the complex; a line of spacious greenhouses (demolished); and, on the corner of Walmer Road and Austin Terrace, a

95. *Gateway to the stables*

large house known as Pellatt Lodge. Despite its low polygonal towers with pyramid roofs standing at either end of a multi-windowed façade overlooking the city, this house was intended to be a comfortable family residence as well as a showplace. The stables, however, are grandiosely overbuilt in the tradition of the equestrian aristocracy of Europe that Pellatt so much admired; and his horses lived in the same luxury as their master, in stables of mahogany, floored in Spanish tiles and decorated with iron plates set with the horses' names in brass. In the wealth of exterior detail, in white cast-stone against the red brick of the walls, the two main entrances command immediate attention, each framed by turrets with conical roofs and heavily blocked buttresses that support heraldic beasts. The stables, which cost a quarter of a million dollars, were more expensive than all but a few of the largest mansions in Toronto.

For the next few years much of the rest of the site was laid out in formal gardens and market gardens. Lennox's final plans for Casa Loma are dated 1910, when Pellatt's ambitions and wealth were at their height.* Pellatt gave Lennox virtually a free hand to build the castle. (Work began on the foundations in 1909 before the design was finished, so eager was Pellatt to have the castle completed.) He handed Lennox a sheaf of sketches and photographs illustrating his ideas about castle architecture. Working from these, Lennox designed the building—in grey-brown Credit Valley sandstone laid in random courses, with trimmings of white cast stone and a roof of red tiles—to stand on a battlemented terrace at the edge of the hill. Above the three main floors rise three towers: a squared north tower above the entrance hall; a round west tower five storeys high with an open roof terrace, known as the Norman Tower; and to the east, the far more dramatic Scottish Tower rising to a stepped conical roof, which from the city below is the focus and most recognizable part of Lennox's design. Between the towers is a series of bays, turrets, oriels, balconies, and banks of casement windows; punctuated by chimneys, they create façades that appear haphazard but are actually carefully controlled to give each room behind a unique space, character, and outlook.

There are at least 98 rooms. The amazing range of accommodation includes three bowling alleys, a shooting gallery, a wine cellar, and a marble-panelled swimming pool; there are thirty bathrooms and at least twenty-five working fireplaces. Most of the principal rooms are arranged in a connected row facing the south terrace and the view; the service rooms, the main staircase, and the less-important rooms face north. Between them a corridor runs east-west along the length of the house. Pellatt's visitors entered through the north *porte-cochère* (as visitors do today) and passed through a long vestibule into the corridor. To the right—in a space the size of the average large house—is the great oak stair that rises in three flights past a bay window overlooking the north drive.

96.   *The stables*

Facing visitors as they enter is the Great Hall, which Pellatt used as a setting for military banquets.* The most evocatively medieval room in the castle, it has a 45-foot-high oriel window looking onto the south terrace, a high stone mantel, and an oaken hammerbeam roof arching 60 feet above the floor. A pipe organ was built into the west wall, and above the east fireplace a balcony allowed Pellatt to survey the Hall from his bedroom.

Beyond the Hall to the west are two splendid rooms for more everyday life. North of the corridor is the spacious billiard room with a semi-circular bay window and two floor levels that allowed spectators to watch the game being played a few steps below. On the south side of the corridor, opening onto the terrace, is the Oak Drawing Room, probably the most beautiful room of its period in Toronto. Lennox designed its dark oak panelling in the late seventeenth-century style of Grinling Gibbons. The deeply coved ceiling is enriched with carved plaster mouldings and was designed for one of the first uses in Toronto of indirect lighting. The rectangular room is extended to the west by a wide semi-circular bay that fills the base of the Norman tower.

On the east side of the Hall, and also opening out onto the south terrace, is the Library, walled with glazed bookcases for 10,000 books; and the Dining Room beyond, panelled in walnut in a late eighteenth-century style—which is actually two rooms, for Lennox added to the rectangular main space a

---

*That summer Pellatt took the Queen's Own to manoeuvres in England at his own expense.

*The grandeur and immense scale of Casa Loma express Pellatt's hope that it would become the City of Toronto's military museum, dedicated to the Queen's Own.

circular bay (the base of the Scottish tower) of tall windows where the family could dine overlooking the garden.

In this part of the house the long corridor, with its doors leading into the Library and the Dining Room, is known as Peacock Alley. Oak-panelled by Lennox (in imitation of the principal corridor of the royal apartments of Windsor Castle), it served as a display space for Pellatt's large collection of medieval and early-renaissance armour. To support the weight, the concrete floor was reinforced and boarded with teak planks held in place by wedges and pegs of rosewood. Pellatt's study is on the north side of the corridor, next to the rooms of the service wing. From the east end of Peacock Alley and the Dining Room, doors of glass and heavy polished bronze lead into the Conservatory. (Pellatt loved rare and fine plants and filled the greenhouses with them; at their peak they were moved into the Conservatory for display.) Inset into the pale beige stone walls are wide Gothic windows set off by Doric columns with capitals entwined with floral garlands. The floor is paved with pink and green marble, and planting boxes (equipped with steam pipes to warm the soil) are faced with grey Canadian marble. Over the centre of the space rises a coved glass ceiling ornamented with a pattern of grape vines in stained glass. The ceiling, made in Italy, is now covered on the outside to protect the glazing.

On Casa Loma's more intimate second floor are a round sitting-room in the west Norman tower, and adjoining suites for Pellatt and his wife above the Library and Dining Room. By the time the Pellatts moved into the house, Mary Pellatt was a semi-invalid; her suite was designed with sitting-room, bedroom, a sunroom in the Scottish tower, and a balcony overlooking the gardens. The second-floor private and guest rooms are Georgian Revival in decoration and show an unfamiliar domestic side to the Pellatts' life. But even here, Edwardian extravagance was given full play: the bathrooms are walled in marble and tile and equipped with telephones. Pellatt's chrome-plated shower surrounded him with hundreds of jets, and Lennox designed Mrs Pellatt's bathroom so that she could, at the turn of a dial, choose one of four perfumes to scent her shower automatically.

Casa Loma was meant to be not simply the grandest house in Toronto but the most up-to-date in technology. Compressed ammonia was piped in to cool the wine cellar to the right temperature; a built-in vacuum system reached all the rooms to make cleaning easier; and 150,000 feet of wiring was laid for the electrical system of 5,000 lights inside and out, designed to be controlled from a basement room lined with white marble switchboards. Everything was executed in the finest materials with an eye to permanence. The main rooms all have parquet floors in different patterns, laid over concrete

framed in steel; these and thick walls made the house totally fireproof. The house was complete enough by the summer of 1913 for the Pellatts to move in. The final costs for construction and decoration are said to have come to $3.5 million. Even so, neither the Great Hall nor the billiard room received their panelling, and the staff and guest rooms on the third floor were not finished as Lennox intended. Pellatt is said to have spent another $1.5 million on furniture for the house, much of which appears in photographs to have been of museum quality.

Like the Edwardian age itself, Pellatt's world perished in the social and economic changes wrought by the First World War. Toronto's suburbs advanced around the castle, changing its pastoral setting and raising the taxes on the house to punishing levels. Inflation and a changed economic climate cut into Pellatt's wealth; and in 1923 the collapse of the Home Bank of Canada, in which Pellatt was heavily involved, nearly bankrupted him. Casa Loma had been mortgaged to support other investments; and as the costs of maintenance skyrocketed, Pellatt reluctantly agreed to move out. In the last week of June 1924 the interior was stripped and virtually everything was sold at auction for a total of $131,600. Toronto, which had never understood Pellatt, clucked smugly. However, even after these disasters Pellatt was still far better off than many of its leading citizens.

The fate of Casa Loma was much more problematic. In 1928 several investors, including Pellatt himself, leased the house to operate it as an exclusive apartment hotel, with suites for both permanent and temporary residents. In the renovations the Library and Dining Room were thrown together as one room, to serve as the residents' dining-room. The hotel was never really successful and the Great Depression killed the project. Other schemes were proposed, including Mary Pickford's idea of converting the building into a movie studio. Ultimately the castle and its grounds reverted to the city for unpaid taxes; the stables became a local firehall. In 1936 the Kiwanis Club leased the castle, and for almost fifty years it has been the romantic setting for graduation dances and wedding receptions. The third floor is operated as a museum of militaria and changing exhibits. Casa Loma has also become one of Toronto's principal tourist attractions. Over the last few years the Club has begun to restore the main and family rooms to recapture some of their original flavour—a difficult endeavour, given their character and the furniture needed. Though the effect is at times strange and haphazard, Casa Loma still represents Henry Pellatt much as he would have liked—as a man who never made small plans and hired one of Toronto's greatest architects to build him Canada's most spectacular house.

97. *Riverdale Courts looking southwest*

RIVERDALE COURTS

Bain Avenue

1914 by Eden Smith & Sons

Toronto's politicians and philanthropists first became involved with housing because of the crowded conditions in which the city's wage-earning working and lower-middle classes were forced to live at the turn of the century. While the upper-middle classes had never been better housed, the same cannot be said for the families and single men and women of the classes immediately below: salespeople in the city's large shops and department stores, office clerks and secretaries, and senior factory workers. The building boom in the early years of the century had provided little in new housing that they could afford to buy; and inflation and the housing shortage had pushed rents up by an average of 95 per cent between 1897 and 1907. With the recession in 1907 the situation became even worse; and when the economy picked up a few years later, building costs and house prices again rose faster than wages. Most of these workers were employed south of

College Street and had to live reasonably close by. But in this part of the city rental accommodation was often decrepit, crowded, unsanitary—and, because of rising land values, expensive.

In 1907 the Canadian Manufacturers' Association sponsored a scheme to produce small houses that could be sold profitably but at reasonable prices. The recession that year killed the scheme, and when it was revived in early 1912 both land and financing costs made it prohibitively expensive. However, in May 1912 the Association—together with the Toronto Board of Trade, the Toronto City Council, the Guild of Civic Art (the principal group sponsoring various City Beautiful schemes for Toronto), and the Local Council of Women (who were especially concerned about the welfare of working single mothers)—conceived the Toronto Housing Company to provide proper accommodation.

From the beginning the leaders of Toronto society and business lent their support to the Company. Its patron was HRH The Duke of Connaught, in his role as Governor-General, and the Honorary President was Sir John Gibson, Lt-Governor of Ontario. The three members of the Advisory Board were Zebulon A. Lash, Sir Edmund Osler, and Joseph Flavelle (later Sir Joseph), all of whom were capable of mobilizing support from the city's largest banks and brought to the Company experience gained from other philanthropic and architectural projects. But the working force behind the project was G. Frank Beer; he more than anyone devised the system under which the Company achieved its goal. The main problem was financing, and Beer was able to secure passage of the first Ontario Housing Act in 1913, which gave Ontario municipalities the power to guarantee bonds for a housing company of up to 85 per cent of its working capital, as long as the remaining 15 per cent was directly invested by the public. In return the municipality received representation on the Company's board and considerable control over the type and character of buildings erected. With a working capital of $1,000,000 assured at a low interest rate, the Toronto Housing Company first purchased two suburban sites, intending to build houses for sale and rental at low cost. Neither was developed, however, because it decided instead to concentrate on rental housing closer to the industrial heart of the city.

Two developments of 'cottage flats'* were planned and carried through. Spruce Court, at Spruce and Sumach Streets north of Cabbagetown, was built on a plot of land originally occupied by the Toronto General Hospital, which was acquired at reasonable terms when the Hospital moved to its new location at College Street and University Avenue. The second and much larger complex was Riverdale Courts, located east of the Don River in Riverdale (almost within sight of Spruce Court) on both sides of Bain Avenue, west of Logan. Fifteen minutes by streetcar from the industries and offices of downtown, it was only one block from Riverdale

and Withrow Parks in a stable, solidly built middle-class neighbourhood. The location was important because the surrounding neighbourhood dispelled any associations with indigence. So too was the choice of Eden Smith as architect. The 'Cottage Style' that he had perfected for domestic architecture provided the right image for these flats. Popularly and romantically associated with a simple country life, this style featured rough brick and stucco walls, half-timbered gables and bay windows, with verandas and porches that stepped out into gardens. Smith had also developed the use of a limited range of standardized details for windows, doors, staircases, and decorative mouldings, and encouraged his suppliers to mass-produce them. Their availability as stock details made the quality finishes and interesting design that were part of his work economical.

At Riverdale Courts the Company originally built 204 cottage flats for which it provided a central steam-heating plant and took care of repairs, grounds maintenance, and snow removal. They were arranged in three-storey blocks around quadrangles (the courts) in order to accommodate as many families as possible while still leaving much of the site open for lawns and play yards. There are three spacious front courts, 80 feet wide, and two narrower service yards that extend north-south on both sides of the street. On the north and south edges of the site there are more blocks of flats looking towards Bain Avenue. The courtyards, which give the complex an agreeably planned, spacious character that sets it apart from the regular streetscape of long ordinary blocks, are an essential part of the development. Both Riverdale Courts and Spruce Court were conceived as family housing and the quadrangles were grassed as recreation areas, particularly for younger children who, safely removed from the dangers of street traffic, could easily be supervised from within.

Eden Smith clearly devoted considerable time and effort to giving the flats pleasant domestic associations that immediately dispelled any taint of 'public housing' or 'charity'. As he did in his private houses, he designed steep shingled roofs with broad shadowed eaves that clearly symbolized the comfort of a good home. The long roof-slopes overhang two-storey porches and are punctuated by hipped dormers. On the south side of Bain Avenue, to enliven the north-facing façades that would normally be veiled in shadows, Smith detailed the gables with half-timbering to stand out against white stucco walls.

The courts were the focus of the sense of community Smith fostered with his planning. Each entrance has a broad stoop facing the lawn for socializing and sitting out, just as each apartment has a balcony or veranda. But he also sought the same privacy that his wealthy clients demanded. The ground-floor apartments have both front and back entrances. Though the arched front entrances lead to apartments one above the other, the two doors are neither side by side nor directly opposite one another: one entrance is always set in an angled wall, ensuring privacy even when both doors are left open to allow children to come and go, or for ventilation during hot,

---

*A cottage flat was described by the Company as a 'modern apartment with its own front door to the street'.

99. *Riverdale Courts, looking southwest from the corner of Logan and Bain*

98. *Riverdale Courts, looking north across Bain Avenue*

sticky Toronto summers. The size of the apartments was intentionally varied to accommodate a full range of residents, from one-bedroom second-floor flats to four-bedroom two-storey flats for large families. The rooms were not large (a living-room 14 feet square is usual), but each flat was lighted with electricity (gas was still normal in Toronto), centrally heated, and had a separate kitchen and bath. There were hardwood floors, and decorative details like picture- and plate-rails in moulded and stained Georgian pine—in fact everything except fireplaces that Torontonians of the period expected in a well-built, comfortable house.

The Toronto Housing Company's work represented the finest spirit in philanthropy and architectural patronage of its time. Originally rents ranged from $14.50 to $26 a month (approximately $290 to $520 today), including heat and utilities, with a security deposit of $12 to $15. Though beyond the means of Toronto's poorest families, the project was an immediate success. At these rents (which were raised after the war) the Company itself was only marginally profitable.

Dividends of 5 per cent and 6 per cent were declared between 1923 and 1933, and there was sufficient profit to allow the expansion of Spruce Court in 1926. However, after 1933 there were no more dividends and the Company eventually sold its assets to a private owner.

The Toronto Housing Company marked an important beginning for the involvement of both Toronto and Ontario in publicly supported housing. After several false starts, symbolized by the rather grim character of the province's Regent Park project, public involvement through the newly created City of Toronto Housing Company (now called Cityhome) again assumed social and architectural importance in the 1970s with the building of the Dundas-Sherbourne (Plate 163) and Hydro Block projects, and the 7000-resident complex called Crombie Park. Public funding also allowed the Spruce Court and Riverdale Courts complexes to be saved from luxury renovation and sale as individual condominiums. Instead they became co-operatives, run by and for the residents.

100

ST ANNE'S CHURCH

Gladstone Avenue

1907–8, Ford Howland; decorated 1923–5

by William Rae, J.E.H. MacDonald, and others

St Anne's Church is one of the few Canadian public buildings whose internal design included a complete program of decoration. This Anglican parish was founded in 1862 to serve the western suburbs of Toronto, and the first building erected was an evocation of an English medieval parish church, carefully Gothic in form. As the mainly working-class neighbourhood surrounding it expanded, the church was extended several times. Finally in 1907 there was a need for a still larger church, and the decision was made to rebuild completely. A competition was held and the winning design by Ford Howland was in the Byzantine Revival style. The new church, which seats close to 1,400, was built in 1908 on a large Greek Cross plan with a very plain exterior set off by two towers flanking the east entrance. Over the centre of the church floats a vast dome 55 feet in diameter and 60 feet high supported on four great arches. These arches open to the north and south into wide transepts, and to the east into a narthex-like extension of the nave. The west arch opens into the sanctuary and choir, set in a semi-domed apse. Because the floor here is raised five steps above the nave and is separated from it by a parapet, the apse forms a theatrical setting for the mysteries of the liturgy. Although the proportions of the arches and piers are broad, thick, and massive, the interior is never sombre or oppressive because it is flooded with light—

101. *Nave and sanctuary*

from the transepts and narthex, from a crescent of five windows in the apse, and particularly from eight semi-circular lunettes that pierce the dome.

Decoration was very much a part of the Byzantine Revival style, which was strongly influenced by St Mark's in Venice and the churches of Ravenna and Constantinople. At St Anne's little decoration had been possible during the initial building campaign. Not until 1923 did a donation of $5,000 lead to the completion of a consistent decorative scheme for the interior. To direct the program Canon Skey, rector from 1902 to 1933, called in William Rae as architect and J.E.H. MacDonald, a member of the Group of Seven, as overall designer. Rae rearranged the background, altering the galleries, enlarging the organ-loft arches, and improving the lighting, while MacDonald marshalled a force of ten painters and two sculptors to work within an overall conception. Artists in the 1920s were increasingly aware of their social responsibilities, and MacDonald and his workmen endeavoured to brighten the lives of the average 'man in the street', for whom Old Masters in galleries and the allegorical sculpture of public buildings had little meaning.

MacDonald's decorative program was harmonized by a carefully limited palette of earth-tone colours, plus gold and ultramarine blue. In the apse the curve of the vaulting is decorated with a flat ornamental of twining grape vines, symbolizing the Eucharist, with Venetian red leaves and gold grape clusters. Geometric stencils with stylized flowers in red and blue curve along the lower faces of the four main arches, while sun and star signs and religious insignia are scattered across the rise of the dome. The panels in the apse are devoted to the life of Christ, with large scenes by Frank Carmichael of 'The Adoration of the Magi' and 'The Entry into Jerusalem' over the organ lofts, and a cycle of smaller panels over the five windows. They include, from left to right: 'Jesus in the Temple' by Arthur Martin; 'The Raising of Lazarus' by Thoreau MacDonald; 'The Transfiguration' by J.E.H. MacDonald in the centre over the altar; 'The Tempest', also by MacDonald; and 'The Palsied Man' by Neil Mackechnie. But the most important figural works fill the pendentives that rise from the corner piers of the nave to support the dome, their figures seeming to carry its weight while looking down on the congregation: facing the altar, are 'The Ascension' by H.S. Stansfield and 'The Resurrection' by H.S. Palmer. Flanking the chancel and facing the congregation are

102.   The Nativity *by F.H. Varley*

'The Crucifixion' by MacDonald and 'The Nativity' by F.H. Varley, with its breathtakingly beautiful portrait of the Virgin (and an adoring, humble shepherd, for which Varley himself was the model). The program is completed in the vaults of the north and south transepts by panels of St George (above the war memorial window) and St Anne by Thoreau MacDonald. To complement the image of the heavens recreated in the dome, MacDonald placed around its base four gigantic heads of the Old Testament prophets Moses, Isaiah, Jeremiah, and Daniel, painted by F.H. Varley, and sculpted plaques of the symbols of the four Evangelists, by Frances Loring and Florence Wyle, to represent the spread of the word of God through all the ages.

MacDonald's avowed goal in the figure painting at St Anne's was to move beyond the hierarchic patterns of Byzantium to incorporate the calm purity and superior realism of the fourteenth-century work of Giotto. The earth-toned background of the figure paintings is lined in red to create a vague impression of Byzantine mosaic work and the serene expression and pose of the figures suggest Giotto. The final effect is clearly related to the work of the English artist Eric Gill, particularly in MacDonald's own 'Crucifixion'. The rich tones of the colours, however, and the handling of water, drapery, and foliage in the scenes, are all characteristic of the classic Group of Seven style.

The completion of MacDonald's program for St Anne's gave Toronto, and Canada, one of its very few public monuments that could be described as finished, both artistically and architecturally. Until 1960 little more was done to the church. In that year the threat of demolition activated cleaning and restoration work, during which some rather debatable changes were made—notably the gilding of the dome's interior to replace MacDonald's deep red, and the reversal of the colour values in the chancel, giving it blue vines over a buff ground instead of white on blue. In 1960 also a mosaic reredos in a marvelous blue and gold was added to the chancel and new paintings were added to the nave vault, an area MacDonald thought was under-detailed. But the colour changes do not compromise the experience of the interior. Washed with natural light and rich colour, it is mystical and transcendent.

189

103

TIMOTHY EATON MEMORIAL CHURCH

230 St Clair Avenue West (N) between Warren and Dunvegan Roads

1909–14 by Wickson & Gregg; sanctuary altered and chancel added, 1938, by
W.L. Somerville and Hardie Phillip (of New York)

The dynasty founded by Timothy Eaton (1834–1907) still maintains one of the largest family-controlled corporations in the country. Its importance to the city of Toronto is memorialized in the College Street department store, opened in 1929 (now an apartment, office, and shopping complex) and the downtown Eaton Centre (Plate 158). There are two monuments to Timothy Eaton. The best known—a bronze statue portraying him as a severe patriarch seated in Edwardian majesty—was installed first in the Queen Street store (demolished) and then moved to the north entrance of the new Eaton Centre store. (A tradition of touching the toe of his shoe for good luck has kept that part of the bronze as shiny as a new penny.) The other is Timothy Eaton Memorial Church, one of the most impressive of Canada's twentieth-century Gothic churches, and the centre for a United Church congregation that is one of the largest and wealthiest in Canada.

Timothy Eaton was a devout Methodist, and after his death his widow and his son, John Craig Eaton, decided it would

be appropriate to continue his philanthropy by supporting, with a gift of land and building funds, the founding of a new Methodist Church on The Hill, the area soon to be known as Forest Hill Village. The gift was announced in May 1909 and substantially increased in the summer of 1910 to include the present block-wide site and a larger building fund. No stipulation or request was made that the church be named after Timothy Eaton. That was the decision of the congregation in late 1911. In later years the church was sometimes dubbed 'St Timothy and All Eatons', partly because many members of the family and senior employees of the store were involved in its affairs. Whatever the irony intended, the congregation accepted the connection without demur, and indeed with considerable pride.

The architects chosen for the project, the Toronto firm of Wickson & Gregg, were best known for their Classical or Georgian Revival public buildings and houses (in 1909 they began work on 'Ardwold', John Craig Eaton's Georgian man-

190

sion overlooking the city from the crest of the Escarpment). They were appointed in 1909 and the Sunday School was opened on 19 November 1911. The final design of the church itself was approved in September 1912 and Mrs Timothy Eaton laid the cornerstone below the main windows of the south façade on 28 August 1913. On 20 December 1914 the completed church was dedicated.

The choice of the Gothic style, popular in Canada since the 1860s, was appropriate for Anglicans and Roman Catholics because the history of their churches could be linked directly to the Middle Ages; and the accepted liturgy—with the focus of the service shared between pulpit and altar—could fit easily into the traditional Gothic plan of nave, aisles, chancel, and transepts. Though this plan was not suitable for those Protestant denominations whose liturgy focused on pulpit and choir, rather than altar, many of them, in accordance with the prevailing fashion, chose Gothic Revival for their churches—with interiors that were galleried auditoriums, often with brilliantly coloured fresco decorations and eccentric Gothic detail.

The Gothic style of Timothy Eaton Memorial is based on English cathedral architecture of the fifteenth century. Given solid monumentality by great buttresses and the rough-finished Credit Valley stone of the exterior walls, it is ornamented by the elaborate use of stone tracery. Most of Toronto's early twentieth-century churches were pinched and constrained by small sites and low budgets. Here the immense site—238 feet wide along the north side of St Clair Avenue West and 134 deep along the side streets—allowed the elements of the design to be spaciously planned. The two-storey Sunday School is a massive corner-buttressed block. Joining it to the church is a block of reception rooms and offices, also two storeys, that is domestic in character—with a broad bay window and rows of leaded casements across each floor. Nothing, however, could be more publicly conceived and scaled than the grouping of the tower and the gable of the high auditorium, which make the church the most important landmark in its neighbourhood. The tower, which rises 100 feet to support a carillon of 21 bells, is squared and strengthened by stepped corner buttresses. The walls of the two lower stages are of rough masonry; those of the bell-stage are smooth and opened with pairs of traceried windows. At the base of the tower the east entrance is set in a tall arch at the top of a flight of steps and outlined by multiple mouldings and a blind parapet of heraldic panels. Next to the tower are three powerful buttresses that rise up to support arches, and the gable and parapet of the façade. Their exaggerated massiveness creates deep recesses framing the two majestic traceried windows of the south front that light the auditorium. A final, and unexpected, element in the composition—the *porte-cochère* sheltering the west entrance—is a low, arched structure in cut stone that balances the height of the tower and the mass of the Sunday School to the east and effects a smooth transition from the ornamented south façade to the plainer forms of the west front.

Wickson & Gregg designed Timothy Eaton Church with a galleried auditorium that was T-shaped in plan, focused on a pulpit set before a huge oak-panelled choir-loft and the centrally placed console of the Casavant organ.* Above rose an immense window designed in honour of Timothy Eaton by Robert McCausland around a stained-glass copy of Holman Hunt's 'The Light of the World'. This plan was traditional in Methodist churches from the 1860s on. However, during the 1920s the liturgy used at Timothy Eaton underwent a change: the sacrament of communion began to assume more importance and the role of the choir in the service began to take on an element of pageantry. A major influence was the growing affection of Lady Eaton** for all things English, and particularly for Anglican usages. A more ritualistic communion service was first celebrated at the church in December 1925. In 1929 Lady Eaton asked the church's Board to institute a choir processional and recessional, a suggestion that could not be taken up because the auditorium lacked a centre aisle. Early in 1936 she proposed, and the Board accepted, that a chancel be added to the auditorium, as a memorial to her husband. The incumbent minister, Dr David MacLennan, supported the change; there was some shock, but no concerted opposition among traditionally Protestant members of the congregation. The design, by W.L. Somerville of Toronto and Hardie Phillip of New York, was approved in early 1938 and the renovated church was opened on 1 December 1938.

The renovations gave the church a nave 117 feet long and just over 45 feet wide (it is extended on the east by a chapel). The south gallery, with its oak balustrade, was not changed, but the east and west galleries were replaced by balcony seating areas set behind narrow arches, with stained-glass windows above. The pews and other woodwork were executed in oak as before, but the original wall panelling was removed; the walls today are smooth cream-painted plaster. Divided from the nave by a tall, plain arch, the new chancel—45 feet wide and 63 feet deep—has much the same air of Spartan simplicity. The lower third of the walls is panelled in light oak, in a simple pattern of squares, relieved only by luxurious textiles that are hung behind the altar on special occasions. Above the panelling on the east and west sides are latticed plaster grilles covering the organ chambers, while at the north end Somerville and Hardie re-installed the great memorial window. They shaped the wooden roof of the chancel into a five-sided panelled vault sparingly decorated in brilliant colours. The altar that is now the focus for the interior has only a cross, candelabra, and side standards of flowers for ornament. It sums up the special character of Timothy Eaton Memorial Church as a combination of Methodist simplicity and more formal elements that evoke the historical beginnings of Christianity: neither has lost any power by close association with the other.

_____

*(Sir) Ernest Macmillan was the first organist, from 1920 to 1925.

**The widow of Sir John Craig Eaton, who was knighted in 1915 and died in 1922.

104. *The station as completed in 1916*

THE NORTH TORONTO STATION OF THE CANADIAN PACIFIC RAILWAY

1121 Yonge Street (E)

1915–16 by Darling & Pearson

This is one of Toronto's great 'lost' buildings. Familiar as the 'Yonge Street liquor store', it is known to few for what it originally was: a railway station. With a tower modelled on the Campanile of St Mark's Square in Venice, it is a perfect Toronto landmark—whether seen from the east, rising elegantly in buff stone with a green copper roof above the trees of Rosedale Valley, or from the north and south, above the Yonge Street traffic.

In the nineteenth century Toronto was crossed by several railway lines and dotted with numerous stations; most were on main lines leading to the waterfront and the old Union Station. Except for the stations in suburban Riverdale and Parkdale, the smaller stations disappeared in the early years of this century with the planning and construction of the new Union Station (Plate 109). But the CPR also controlled a line across the city, below the ridge of the escarpment (it served the West Toronto stockyards), and maintained at Summerhill Avenue, where the line crosses Yonge Street, a small passenger station and a small hotel (last known as the Ports of Call, and recently demolished). This station probably would have been phased out in the early years of this century but for the long delays that occurred in building the new Union Station. In 1912, to protest the delays and provide a better setting for the services connecting Toronto to Montreal and Ottawa, the CPR moved these services to Summerhill.

The original Summerhill Station was not grand enough to be an important city terminal. Accordingly, in 1914 the CPR commissioned Darling & Pearson (the firm had just completed the CPR's skyscraper offices at Yonge and King) to design a new passenger station. The design they produced—simple but imposing—was an exquisite miniature, not really a full-sized station (there was no adequate provision for freight). The waiting-room was a block-like three-storey pavilion, flanked by lower wings, set back from Yonge Street to face south and linked to a 140-foot clock tower. (The present parking lot in front of the building was in 1916 the workyard of a maker of cemetery monuments.) The façade—in mottled beige Tyndall limestone from Manitoba, with some cast-stone detailing—is shadowed by a deep canopy that shelters the main entrance and the side vestibule in the base of the tower. Above the canopy rise three two-storey arched windows flanked by wide pilaster-like panels, on which hang stone-carved railway crests draped with swags. A simplified frieze, cornice, and parapet extending round the building emphasize

the pavilion's blockish shape. The main waiting-room—70 feet wide and 51 feet deep—filled most of the building and rose to its full height; faced with marble, it was flooded with light through large south windows. Occupying the low east wing were the ladies' waiting-room, the smoking-room, and lavatories; to the west were the ticket offices.

The clock tower was—and remains—the great picturesque feature of the design. It is typical of the lavish gestures made by both Beaux Arts and Edwardian Baroque architects (and accepted enthusiastically by their patrons) to make buildings of importance stand out as landmarks in the streetscape and on the skyline of the 'City Beautiful'. The design owes something—particularly in its profile—to the tower of E.J. Lennox's City Hall (Plate 76), completed in 1899–1900. But from the Campanile of St Mark's comes the sheer rise of the tower to a colonnade, topped by a clock stage and a crowning pyramid roof. The St Mark's Campanile had collapsed in 1902; the disaster, and the subsequent rebuilding, were commemorated in several versions by North American architects. Darling's tower, while by no means the tallest, has the great advantage of standing among relatively low neighbours and being visible from several directions. The best view is from the east, from the Glen Road Bridge in Rosedale, where it identified and located the station to its most frequent users.

The cornerstone was laid on 9 September 1915 and the station was opened on 14 June 1916—one of the few large projects to be completed in Toronto during the First World War. Until the new Union Station opened in 1927, the North Toronto Station provided the most elegant and aesthetically satisfying gateway to Toronto. After 1926, however, its role became less important, and in 1929 it was closed as an economy measure. Shortly afterwards the building was leased to the Liquor Control Board of Ontario.

The station has not been well treated over the last fifty years. The main sales area of the liquor store occupies the waiting hall; but all sense of the original space, light, and marble of Darling's design has been obscured by the dropped ceiling and masked walls. Fortunately the scale of the façade and the height of the tower have defied philistine and insensitive alteration (although the tower has lost its clock). Over the last thirty years several development plans for the site have been proposed, but nothing has materialized. The LCBO might consider opening up the entire hall to view and replacing the clock.

105

HART HOUSE

The University of Toronto

1910–19 by Sproatt & Rolph

When Hart Massey died in 1896 he left to charity the greater part of his personal fortune, most of which was invested in shares of the Massey Manufacturing Company. Several bequests went to organizations in Canada and the United States—like the Fred Victor Mission in Toronto—with which he had long been associated. But the bulk of it was not specifically dedicated; his executors were instructed to liquidate the estate within twenty years, spending the assets on projects that would continue Hart Massey's philanthropy. For the next twelve years the fund was administered mainly by Massey's surviving son, Chester Daniel Massey, with the assistance of other members of the family. They had their own pet projects: Lillian Massey built the Food Sciences Building at the University of Toronto (1890–12 by G.M. Miller); and Chester Daniel Massey gave Metropolitan Methodist Church the Memorial Parsonage at Bond and Shuter Streets (1906–7 by Curry, Sproatt & Rolph). The Estate made possible the building of Massey Hall at the University of Guelph (1901 by G.M. Miller) and Annesley Hall, the women's residence of Victoria College, Toronto (1901–3 by G.M. Miller). Large and small sums were given to an incredible variety of projects—especially colleges, hospitals, and churches—and in almost every case money was pledged to a building project, usually on condition that a substantial sum be raised from other donors; but only rarely did the Massey name appear on a building. During these years—and particularly after 1901, when Massey-Harris was formed by merger—the trustees of Hart Massey's estate created the Massey Foundation on the model of the Rockefeller Foundation (Chester Daniel Massey's adviser was his nephew George Vincent, first head of the Rockefeller Foundation) to extend the philanthropy beyond the 1916 deadline mandated in Hart Massey's will. Finally, in 1919, the Massey Foundation was formally chartered and endowed, the first of its kind in Canada.

The work of the Massey Estate, and then of the Massey Foundation, was wide-ranging, supporting education, music, drama, and the fine arts. But its great monuments were architectural. Both Hart Massey and his son Chester were interested in quality and efficiency in design. However, in 1909-10, when Vincent Massey (Chester's son) became the principal influence over the Estate's architectural patronage, there was a definite change. Vincent Massey had a sensitivity to architecture that was rare in a layman. (In his autobiography, *What's Past is Prologue*, he wrote that had his situation been slightly different he would probably have become an architect.) Far more than his father or grandfather, he was concerned that buildings should exercise a positive influence over those who use them. This Victorian ideal was part of the ideology of the City Beautiful Movement that dominated so much progressive thought about American and Canadian architecture at the turn of the century. The projects with which Vincent Massey was associated were invigorated, in both design and concept, by a firm belief in the ability of fine architecture—and the historical and cultural legacy it represents—to influence for the better men's lives and character.

After graduation from University College in 1910, Vincent Massey earned a second degree from Balliol College, Oxford, in 1913; and much of his patronage in architecture was shaped by a vision of English university life that was both romantic and practical. He placed a supreme value on British traditions in democracy, politics, responsible social service, and cultural excellence, and he saw Oxford and Cambridge as the cornerstones of these ideals and as continuing formative influences on them. The buildings with which he was most intimately involved—Burwash Hall for Victoria College; Hart House and Massey College (Plate 146) for the University of Toronto; and several additions to Upper Canada College—were conceived to provide an environment in which the English traditions of education that had long been adapted for Canadian institutions could flourish. The first of these, Burwash Hall (1909-11 by Sproatt & Rolph), provided for Victoria College the accoutrements of an Oxbridge college: residence and common rooms for male students and some staff, dining-hall and kitchens arranged to form a quadrangle next to the college building of 1892. Creating a traditional college image and atmosphere for Victoria, its Gothic style (Massey disliked the Romanesque Revival of the main building) was solid and domestic. A tower, gables, and extended

bay windows created the unpretentious atmosphere of history and permanence Massey wanted, and was able to foster personally as Dean of Men from 1913 to 1915.

Hart House (named for Hart Massey) is not only architecturally important but still fulfils its original goal of fostering and housing some of the best aspects of life in the University of Toronto. In 1910 the University (as distinct from its colleges) provided few non-academic facilities for students. It seemed to many, but especially to Vincent Massey, that it would never acquire the coherence necessary for a great institution without a central facility where students and staff from all colleges and faculties could come together.

Planning for Hart House began in mid-February 1910, spurred by the YMCA's decision to rebuild its campus gymnasium. On February 14th a request from the YMCA, which had often received subsidies from the Masseys, for support for their new university building crystallized Vincent Massey's ideas for a different kind of campus centre. The first of several meetings to define and plan a new complex was held on the 16th. In a letter of the 21st, Chester Massey, on behalf of the Massey Estate, wrote to Edmund Walker, Chairman of the Board of Governors, offering to build and equip the new YMCA as well as a Student Union, the two to be connected by an 'Assembly Hall'. The gift was accepted by the YMCA on March 3rd and by the University a day later. Thereafter—although there would be constant communication between the University and the Massey Estate—the project was effectively controlled in every detail by Vincent Massey. From the spring of 1910 until Hart House officially opened in 1919, Massey worked with the chosen architects, Sproatt & Rolph—particularly with Henry Sproatt, whom Massey later described as 'a man of real genius and a master of the Gothic form'. During the late summer and fall of 1910 the project was held up while Massey recuperated from typhoid (contracted when he was with the Queen's Own Rifles on annual manoeuvres with the British Army in England). But in this period he supervised a revision of the plan, refining the complex scheme of function and forms that were to make up the building, as well as the system by which Hart House would later be run by students, alumni, and the University staff.

Hart House stands northeast of University College; its south front is aligned with the north end of the College's east wing. The two buildings seem to form two sides of an immense quadrangle, in the centre of which stands the former Dominion Observatory (1854-6 by Cumberland & Storm). The space between the two buildings is closed by the Soldiers' Tower (completed 1924), whose carillon of bells was the University's memorial to the First World War. Next to the Tower a cloister screen bears the inscribed names of the University's war dead. Designed by Sproatt & Rolph as a free adaptation of the tower of Magdalen College, Oxford, the Tower—the base of which is cut through by a gate-like vaulted passage—is very much part of the completed design, though not formally part of Hart House. Its height and Gothic pinnacles provide a unifying

106. *East entrance and exterior of the Great Hall*

architectural symbol of the University's many other towers and buildings.

Hart House is perhaps the finest example of Beaux Arts Gothic Revival in Canada. The main features of this architecture—clear, carefully organized planning, precise historical references, and grand spaces—are usually associated with Classical buildings like the Union Station (Plate 109). But the same design principles were also applied to Gothic architecture as Beaux Arts designers simplified the traditions of nineteenth-century church-builders. The plan of Hart House successfully unites many diverse functions, arranged around a quadrangle: common rooms in the south and west wings, athletic facilities in the north wing, the Great Hall and kitchens on the east, and a full theatre underground, below the quadrangle. There are large picturesque university buildings all across North America that evoke the architectural glories and patterns of Oxford and Cambridge, many of them as dry and lifeless as museum wax works. Hart House, however, has an authentic 'living' atmosphere—the legacy of both its architect and its patron. Henry Sproatt worked in stone, brick, stucco, and wood to replicate the slowly ageing atmosphere of his English prototypes. And all his design activities were informed and guided by Vincent Massey, who ensured that the building's English architectural allusions were not too elaborate to provide a comfortable setting for recreational and cultural activities in a modern North American university.

The balanced composition of the long south front of Hart House—framed by the majestic Soldiers' Tower at the west end and at the east end by the high, arched window of the Great Hall set between two turrets—announces both the character of the building and the grandeur of its individual elements. The centre of this façade is a wide three-storey block that houses most of the principal rooms. With its enclosed entrance-porches at each end, and symmetrically spaced mullioned and transomed windows in casements and bays between, it borrows its forms—particularly the four groups of tall stone chimneys rising through the smooth sweep of the slated roof—from large English houses of the sixteenth and early seventeenth centuries. The central block is connected to the Great Hall by a short cloister of Gothic arches. To the west a lower block with two-storey bay windows—housing the reading room and the second-floor barrel-vaulted Library—connects the main block to the base of Soldiers' Tower. All the elements in this south façade—windows, bays, cloister, and porch—are related harmoniously. This characteristic of Beaux Arts design extends to the interior, where common rooms, Library, Great Hall, and the adjoining spaces are all smoothly interrelated, while possessing their own integrity and individuality.

The formality of the south façade is continued in the central quadrangle—a long, rather narrow space, with raised terraces at each end, that is overlooked on the south side by the third-floor guest room available for the use of House members, and on the west by the rooms of the Warden's Apartment and those of student employees. The visitor's attention is inevitably drawn to the relationship between the arch at the west end, leading to the campus, and the glazed cloister at the east end whose broad arches lead to the Lower Gallery and the Great Hall. Because the quadrangle is directly above the Theatre, there are no trees to soften the formal outlines of the space with dense overhanging foliage; it is therefore unexpectedly severe.

The north side of the quadrangle is defined by the Athletic Wing, with its running track and Upper and Lower Gymnasiums. This wing is of particular interest because instead of creating an incongruous, but historically correct, Gothic Revival gym (they are legion in North America), Sproatt & Rolph refined the Gothic system of arch and buttress to support the steel trusses of the roof: the buttresses are linked with almost flat arches and the walls are pierced with windows in tall slits and broad groups of panels. (Inside the gym the lighting was supplemented by great skylights.) This ability to extend the principles of Gothic design to solve problems of structure and expression raised by modern functions and materials—perhaps best expressed in the articulated meeting of these steel trusses with the brick and stone of the Upper Gymnasium walls—led Vincent Massey to describe Sproatt as a designer to whom Gothic was not just a language to be learned but a vernacular to be used.

107. *The Great Hall*

The most important space in Hart House is the Great Hall, used daily as a dining-hall, as well as for concerts, meetings, and large entertainments. Its two most striking features are the modified hammer beam roof, built in oak (but with a considerable amount of steel in its structure), and the windows, which are placed high in the walls—especially the great traceried south window, which is fitted with armorial glass honouring ten of the benefactors of the University and founders of its colleges. The lower walls are simply panelled in oak squares, painted at the south or High Table end with the Royal Arms and the crests of universities of Britain, Canada, and the Commonwealth. At the north end the fireplace is surrounded by the crests of universities in countries that were allied in the First World War. (These include both Japanese and Italian universities; during the Second World War there was considerable agitation in Toronto's newspapers for their removal, a suggestion Vincent Massey rejected as jingoism.) Around the cornice of the panelling is inscribed a passage chosen by Massey from Milton's *Areopagitica*, an eloquent attack on censorship of the press that enjoins freedom in the pursuit of learning. At the south end the High Table stands on a dais from which rises a corkscrew stair set in a Gothic windowed tower, like a miniature of Soldiers' Tower, that leads to the Senior Common Room on the second floor. (A second similar tower in the Lower Gallery connects the basement and second-floor kitchens.) The climax of the interior of Hart House, just as the Soldiers' Tower is the climax of the exterior, the Great Hall has both atmosphere and vitality—provided by its flawless expression of the British cultural and historical traditions that inspired it, and by its constant use. The Great Hall and Hart House itself always feel alive, and they have developed their own history.

The basic work on Hart House was largely completed before the beginning of the First World War, but it continued into 1919, even though the House and much of the University were occupied by the armed forces as a training centre (the Front Campus became an airfield). Progress was hampered by both the difficulty and increased costs of building during wartime, and by a drop in the income of the Massey Foundation as the company's factories were converted to war work. But Vincent Massey's devotion to the project ensured its completion. When construction was finished the Foundation, through him, endowed Hart House with art, books, and fine objects (including a Gutenburg Bible and a consort of Renaissance viols). Massey and Warden Burgon Bickersteth evolved a system of government based on committees that enabled students to work together with staff and faculty to administer the House and its programs. In over half a century the system has been extraordinarily responsive to change. Membership of Hart House has grown tenfold; women are now active members, no longer simply honoured guests; the athletics department has migrated across campus, leaving the North Wing to serve mainly the current fitness boom; and a new climate-controlled art gallery has been created in the West Wing. But Hart House remains true to the humanist

spirit that gave it birth—in the concerts given by the Music Committee; in productions of plays given in the Theatre; in the writing, and writers, encouraged by the Library Committee; and in the collection of Canadian art (one of the best in Canada) assembled over a long period by the Art Committee. It is a lively, independent, and necessary part of the University—continuing to be a fine setting for fellowship, while also honouring the University's highest ideals.

108 *Soldiers' Tower and east front of University College*

XXIX. *Bay Street, looking north towards the City Hall, December 1924*

MODERN TORONTO
FROM THE TWENTIES TO THE FIFTIES

For a long time nothing seemed to change. Toronto went quietly about its business—passing through post-war boom and bust, the excitement of the twenties, the bleakness of the great Depression, the trials of war and post-war once again—without changing character. Though many Torontonians suffered the long absence or permanent loss of family members during wartime, and though the poor and most new immigrants suffered disproportionately to other citizens, this smug provincial Canadian city was a haven of peace and security in a difficult and dangerous world. Empty buildings and vacant lots existed for most of the period, but high-rise apartments with their acres of sterile lawn, and the asphalt expanses and sprawling shops of suburban malls, had not yet arrived. Night life and hot spots were things to be discovered by way of a weekend in Buffalo.

The automobile was suddenly everywhere; many of Toronto's notoriously muddy streets were paved in the twenties, though few were widened.

XXX. *The Princes' Gates, Exhibition Grounds, c. 1927*

With the creation of the Toronto Transportation Commission in 1921 the price of a streetcar ticket was fixed for over thirty years at four for 25¢; yet the TTC gave good service and paid its way through the fare box until subsidies were provided for capital projects in 1959 and for operations in 1971. The boundaries of the city proper were not expanded for over half a century (1912–67) and its population growth slowed drastically: 521,000 in 1921, it was only 672,000 forty years later. The suburban fringes grew, of course, but until the 1950s at nothing like the pace of urban growth in the nineteenth and early twentieth centuries.

The dominant elements of the city skyline for over thirty-five years were the Bank of Commerce tower (Plate 117), 'the tallest building in the British Empire', completed in 1931, and the Royal York Hotel, 'the largest hotel in the British etc.', which opened in 1929. The magnificent Union Station (Plate 109) was finally declared finished by the Prince of Wales in 1927, though no trains arrived on its elevated tracks for another three

XXXI. *Sunnyside Pavilion, c. 1924*

years. Together with the long sweeping curve of the new Dominion Public Building, redolent of London's Regent Street, the giant columns and mass of the Station gave monumental definition to a quarter-mile of Front Street, where once the waters of the bay had lapped. The Bay Street Canyon (Plate 112) was completed in the late twenties and, like the department-store twins—Eaton's (bigger, with more variety) and Simpson's (smaller, but slightly more fashionable)—took its place among the established verities of Toronto's downtown. The Canadian National Exhibition entered its golden era in the twenties, and was provided with a ceremonial grand entrance, the Princes' Gates, to mark the Dominion of Canada's Jubilee in 1927. Within the CNE grounds the annual Royal Winter Fair began in 1922 and its horse shows and livestock were judged in the new Coliseum. Just to the east rose Sunnyside Amusement Park, of which only the Bathing Pavilion (Plate 139) survived the construction of the Gardiner Expressway in 1959. A new baseball stadium by the Western

XXXII. *The Wood Street façade of Maple Leaf Gardens, built in 1931*

Gap was built in time for Toronto's victory in the Little World Series of 1926. Defying the Depression, hockey impresario Conn Smyth took the Toronto St Pats out of the Mutual Street Arena and re-named them to suit his rapidly built Maple Leaf Gardens in 1931—which soon became a fixture in Toronto public life as the arena for a wonderful variety of events besides hockey: the protest rallies of the Depression, Youth for Christ, Ringling Brothers Circus, and in the 1950s the Metropolitan Opera. Foster Hewitt, already a veteran of hockey broadcasting, continued his half-century career in radio from the Gardens' gondola. Among other prominent sports figures were Lionel Conacher—superstar of hockey, lacrosse, and football in the twenties and thirties—who reappeared later as a popular politician; and Bobbie Rosenfeld, the Olympic athlete who went on to enjoy a long career as a Toronto sports writer. By the 1940s American radio comedies and programs such as Andrew Allan's CBC Stage series had changed Toronto's Sunday evening church-going habits. Radio's chief rival, the motion pictures, had brought before the end of the thirties dozens of theatres like the Hollywood and the Fox to Toronto's neighbourhoods, to supplement the older grand palaces of vaudeville and film like the Imperial and Loew's and Shea's Hippodrome in the city's centre.

XXXIII. *The auditorium of the Eglinton Theatre, 1936—the best-preserved Art Deco interior in Toronto that is still in continuous public use.*

The fixed points of modern Toronto culture were provided for most of these forty years by Dora Mavor Moore in theatre, Ernest MacMillan and Healey Willan in music, Morley Callaghan and Ned Pratt in literature. Bert Niosi was Canada's King of Swing, Mart Kenney's Western Gentlemen eventually moved to Toronto, and Horace Lapp survived his first career as pianist for the silent movies and went on to play at the Royal York. Lady Eaton—along with the formidable Mackay sisters, Mrs F.N.G. Starr and Mrs W.D. Ross, widow of the Lieutenant-Governor—presided over almost every worthy cause and social event one could think of, and herself became a controversial patron of architecture in the conversion of Timothy Eaton Memorial Church (Plate 103) to a modern and Catholic interior plan in 1938. From the late twenties on, some members of the Group of Seven, who had been trained in design, as well as younger painters such as Charles Comfort and sculptors such as Frances Loring and Florence Wyle, made a substantial contribution to the decoration of Toronto's newest buildings. A major patron of the arts and architecture throughout this period and into the 1960s had, by 1919, already given his greatest single gift to Toronto. While still a senior at university in 1910, Vincent Massey conceived and commissioned Hart House (Plate 105, named for his industrialist grandfather Hart Massey) as a student union dedicated to all aspects of humane culture and recreation. He then worked with his architects on every detail until its completion.

In medicine the triumphant success of Doctors Banting and Best in the treatment of diabetes did much for medical research in other fields. Dr Allan Brown brought 'science' to the Sick Children's Hospital and the practice of pediatrics. Dr William Blatz developed a new approach to child raising at his Windy Ridge School. Dr Marion Hilliard set a high standard as one of Toronto's finest general practitioners. Even the most important Lieutenant-Governor of the period was a medical man: Dr Herbert Bruce, founder of the Wellesley Hospital and an advocate of social reform during the Depression.

Following a career in politics as Ontario's Minister of Education, and serving as Rector of St Paul's, the largest Anglican church in Canada, Canon H.J. Cody became President of the University of Toronto in 1932. Cody, however, did little to defend academic freedom when Ontario politicians and other leading members of society attacked it. Professor Frank Underhill in particular was in continual trouble for his sharp criticism of conventional wisdom during the Depression and wartime, and only the vigorous intervention of a couple of members of Toronto's Establishment, led by Stanley McLean of Canada Packers, prevented his being fired.

The conservative *Evening Telegram* still had by far the most influence of the Toronto newspapers in choosing candidates for City Hall. In 1930 the *Telegram* even helped its managing editor Bert Wemp become Mayor. The city's first Jewish politician was Nathan Phillips, a Conservative whose career spanned the whole modern period from 1924 on, first as an alderman and then into the 1960s as self-styled Mayor of all the People. Except for Phillips and a few Communist members of City Council (until the last of them was defeated in 1951), Toronto's non-Wasp population was not vigorously or even noticeably represented. As for Toronto's newly enfranchised women electors, they did not provide the outspoken and effective Adelaide Plumptre with even a token female colleague during most of her long incumbency as alderman.

Modern times in Toronto possessed a certain architectural style that set them off from the preceding period and the one to follow. The Victorian look had a vigour and vulgarity that expressed optimism and eclectic enthusiasm, to which the Edwardian era added its own grace-notes of opulence and splendour. Half a century later, in post-modern Toronto, there was once more an outburst of flamboyance and asymmetry. But the intervening modern era strikes a more restrained note: its buildings clad in grey concrete or stone, its sober plans and streetscapes sound a minor key, in counterpoint to the major chords and lush orchestration of its

XXXIV. *Two of the new streamlined streetcars introduced in 1938, at the City Hall loop, 1941*

predecessors. This was essentially a classical period between two romantic ones. Its newest and most creative approaches to design—Art Deco and Art Moderne (c. 1928–42) and the International Style in the 1950s—were, at their best, clear and serene, beautifully measured and understated. The former styles can be seen in the Toronto Stock Exchange building of 1936 (Plate 123), the Eaton Auditorium in the new College Street store, the Eglinton Theatre, the Lawren Harris house (Plate 135), the Garden Court Apartments (Plate 137), and the Eaton house at 120 Dunvegan Road; or, for that matter, in the streamlining of automobiles and of the new streetcars introduced in 1938, in such street furniture as the beer-stein street lamps, in the typography of signage, and in all manner of interior design.

The International Style arrived in Toronto with John C. Parkin* and such post-war buildings (in their original form) as his George Harvey Secondary School on Keele Street, and reached an early serene perfection in the design

---

* The John B. Parkin partnership, in which John C. Parkin was the senior design architect, did not conform to one particular style or school, however. It gave birth to the IBM building and the Bata building in Don Mills, the Imperial Oil building on St Clair Avenue West, and Terminal One of the Toronto International Airport—all of which are distinguished by fine detailing well used and by their monumental presence.

XXXV. *The Ortho Pharmaceutical building, 19 Green Belt Drive, Don Mills,*
1953, by John B. Parkin Associates; John C. Parkin, senior design partner.

of his house on the Bridle Path and of the Ortho Pharmaceutical plant on
Eglinton Avenue East. The International Style's greatest achievement in
Toronto is undoubtedly that of the master himself, Mies van der Rohe, in
the Toronto Dominion Centre (Plate 149), with which Parkin was associated,
as he was with Viljo Revell's New City Hall (Plate 143). Even more pro-
lific, though not the equal of Parkin at his best, was Peter Dickinson, who,
within the brief span of his life—he died of cancer at the age of 39 in
1961—showered Toronto with a range of such buildings as the Four Seasons
Motel (now the Hampton Court) on Jarvis Street, and the Benvenuto and
other Avenue Road apartment buildings. Just as the vocabulary of the
International Style remained long after the 1950s, when it all too easily
degenerated into repetitive empty gesture, the styles of earlier periods were
imitated or quoted (often quite effectively) in modern Toronto—Gothic for
new colleges and chapels at the university, for example, and Georgian in
domestic architecture.

In spite of what they had in common, each of the decades from the
twenties through the fifties did witness dramatic change. In the 1920s small

XXXVI. Benvenuto (1956), a concrete apartment building on Edmund Avenue at Avenue Road. Designed by Peter Dickenson, it was built in the former gardens of 'Benvenuto', the home of S.H. Janes, developer of the Annex. The garden wall is visible in the foreground.

apartment buildings became fashionable and popular; the number of Torontonians living in them increased dramatically. The modernization and expansion of the harbour paid off; the tonnage of freight passing through Toronto increased five times in the decade. Toronto Hydro pushed electric rates down and volume up. The 1930s saw some practical city plans develop and at the end of the decade the first comprehensive zoning laws adopted by City Council. The first Commissioner of Planning, Tracy LeMay, struggled to improve traffic flow with the many bridges, road extensions, and jog eliminations that brought the city's grid street plan a little closer to completion. No government acted on the Bruce Commission's recommendations for new public housing, but City Hall insisted effectively on the upgrading of old housing stock. In 1937 two new airports were built by the city and the federal government at Malton and on Toronto Island. Because of its stock-market, insurance, and banking facilities, and the concentration of such service industries as publishing and advertising, Toronto survived the Depression relatively well. The 1940s brought an enormous variety of war industries to the city. And the armed forces' temporary housing at Little Norway and on the grounds of the Eglinton Hunt Club, as well as the 7,000 permanent residents crowding into Toronto Island cottages, were signs of the times.

The 1950s saw tremendous change, not all for the good. The federal government's fast depreciation to encourage capital investment and avoid a post-war return of the great Depression resulted in the destruction of many of Toronto's finest buildings. Don Mills, a thoroughly planned model suburb, was to be imitated later in a vast area of new developments around the city. The suburbs' prodigal use of land created a strain on municipal services and a heavy dependency on the automobile. But the city itself maintained a population density exceeded in North America only by New York, as vast numbers of European immigrants arrived, bringing new life and a healthy concern for the fabric of Toronto's older houses. The city that was 80 per cent British in 1931 and 1941 was less than 70 per cent so in 1951; and by 1971 half of Toronto's population was of non-British origin, and Roman Catholics actually outnumbered Protestants. In 1953 the city was joined to twelve surrounding suburban municipalities in the federation of Metropolitan Toronto. Metro's first chairman, Frederick Gardiner, was said to act more like the head of a construction company than a leader of government as he battled to create the water and sewage and road services that the post-war population explosion required. The wise planning for a subway system, prepared for years by Norman Wilson, led to the opening of the Yonge Street subway in 1954.

Perhaps the person who summed up the best of Toronto's spirit in the planning of its space and style throughout this period was Eric Arthur, a New Zealand architect who arrived in Toronto in the 1920s by way of Liverpool to teach at the University of Toronto. He helped to write the Bruce Commission's report on housing. He was the moving spirit in the founding of the Architectural Conservancy of Ontario and insisted on recognition of the quality of the city's fine historic buildings. And it was he who enabled Mayor Nathan Phillips to carry Toronto into the post-modern era at the end of the 1950s by initiating, and presiding over, the international competition for a new City Hall.

109

UNION STATION

Front Street West (S), between Bay and York Streets
1913–27 by John M. Lyle, Ross & Macdonald, and Hugh G. Jones

Railway stations hold a special place among the monumental buildings of urban North America. Their importance in the nineteenth century stemmed partly from their mundane value as centres for the passenger and freight traffic serving the growing cities and their hinterlands. But railway stations were also romanticized as gateways to the city for visitors and immigrants, and as access points to the rest of the world. Unlike airports, railway stations steadily developed grander and more complex architectural forms, borrowing patterns from Classical architecture to stress their civic importance.

The first train from Toronto—four cars and an engine symbolically named 'Toronto'—left on 16 May 1853 bound for Aurora. To encourage the rail development essential to its economic growth, Toronto cheerfully gave over The Esplanade and much of the waterfront to railway tracks, and during the next 100 years filled in large parts of the harbour to create what are now known as the Railway Lands. The first Union Station—so named because more than one railroad shared its facilities—was built in 1855–8 on the south side of Front Street, west of Bay. It was little more than a shed with spreading roofs to cover the platforms next to the trains. (Several other stations were soon built in Toronto, to serve specific neighbourhoods as well as individual rail lines.) A second Union Station was built in 1871–3, close to the water

110. *The colonnade, with ramps leading down to the lower concourse of the station*

on the south side of Station Street west of York, to designs by E. P. Hannaford, Chief Engineer of the Grand Trunk Railway. Second Empire in style, it had a partially glazed train-shed arching over the tracks and three domed towers. In 1892–4 the station was extended by a concourse and an office building by Strickland & Symons that faced Front Street with a great Romanesque Revival arch. Modelled on the Illinois Central Station in Chicago (1892–3), it had a tower that shared the downtown skyline with the spire of the St James' Cathedral (Plate 19) and the clock-tower of Lennox's City Hall (Plate 76). The additions almost doubled the facilities of the old station. But almost immediately, before 1900, passenger and freight traffic in and out of Toronto had grown so much that there were calls for an even larger and more efficiently organized station.

In the late 1890s railway stations grew even larger as traffic increased, and more complex with the addition of restaurants, waiting-rooms, shops, and other services. The preeminent models for the new stations were both in New York: Pennsylvania Station (1902–13 by McKim, Mead & White; demolished) and Grand Central Station (1903–13 by Warren & Wetmore). Each possessed Roman grandeur and was built in the finest materials; both were also key elements in the monumental streetscapes being developed for Manhattan. All these factors were influential in the design of a new station for Toronto.

The final steps in the process that led to building the new Union Station began with the fire of 19 April 1904. The city acquired the burnt-over lots on the south side of Front Street between Bay and York; by April 1905 an agreement had been made with the railways on crucial design points; and in 1906 the Toronto Terminals Railway Company (owned jointly by the CPR and the Grand Trunk Railway) was incorporated to build and operate the new station. The first design proposals, including one by Carrère & Hastings of New York, were made in 1906. However, the final designs developed slowly, partly because of complex suggestions from engineering firms regarding the new station's technical requirements and its arrangement of tracks and platforms. Three firms were directly involved: Ross & Macdonald of Montreal; Hugh G. Jones, also of Montreal; and John M. Lyle of Toronto, who had earlier been associated with Carrère & Hastings. Lyle had gained experience designing stations for the Temiskaming and Northern Ontario Railway in 1909; and in 1911, in his plans for a proposed Federal Avenue extending north from a new station on Front to Queen Street West, he established much of the basic character of the present Union Station. Ross & Macdonald, who represented the interests of the Grand Trunk, had just completed the new Union Station in Ottawa (1908–12) and were known for their ability to handle large projects. Hugh G. Jones was one of the CPR's principal architects.

Work on the final design was begun in 1913 and it was approved on 26 April 1914; construction began on 26 September 1914. Material and labour shortages during the war, and financing problems that led to the collapse of the Grand Trunk Railway in 1919 (and the creation of the Canadian National in 1923), delayed completion of the station until 1927. Arguments about whether the tracks should approach the station at grade, or at a level above the streets leading to the harbour, dragged on until late 1924, and only after agreement had been reached on the present raised tracks were the platforms finished. The station was officially opened by Edward, Prince of Wales, on 6 August 1927. In May 1930 the last viaduct connections were completed and the new Union Station became fully operative twenty-six years after the project began.

Lyle is considered the architect mainly responsible for the design. Much of its character—particularly the long Front Street façade that fills the entire block and is divided into three parts by pavilions—can be seen in his 1911 drawing for the Federal Avenue scheme. It is difficult to ascertain the exact contributions of Hugh G. Jones and Ross & Macdonald. Given their previous experience, their work might have centred on the planning of the complex functions of the station. Ross & Macdonald thought enough of their contribution to display the façade design prominently in their own offices. In any event, all three firms were wedded to the principles of the Beaux Arts, and the station is the quintessence of that style.

All railway stations have two basic parts: the concourse/platform area that provides access to the trains, and the 'headhouse'—the reception building that includes waiting-rooms, ticket and baggage offices, and freight-storage and other service areas. The austere monumental scale and Greek Doric detail of the façade probably reflect Lyle's work more than any other part of the design. Pavilions divide the length of the façade into three parts, but it is dominated by the continuous horizontal of a severely plain cornice, with an almost undetailed attic above. The east wing was originally occupied by the Post Office (it is now office space); the west-wing section contains Terminal offices. Across the middle third of the façade Lyle placed a colonnade of 18 Doric columns of colossal scale. Four columns at each end step forward in front of piers to mark the high-arched main entrances to the station. The main part of the colonnade is set back in line with the side façades; behind its columns, under a shallow vault, two ramps allow arriving passengers direct access to the street. Above this section of the portico the name of the building, its dates, and crests of the railways are displayed. Behind the colonnade is the Great Hall and above the long cornice of the façade rises the attic storey that covers its vault.* To allow the composition's balanced symmetry and its relation of horizontals and verticals to be appreciated at a glance, the street was widened by 25 feet and the building

---

*Lyle designed sculptural groups to stand above the entrances that would have ornamented the façade and softened the severe horizontal outline of the composition had they been executed.

111.   *The Great Hall looking west*

line was set back 47 feet further. To arriving passengers, even today, stepping out into the portico is a memorable experience: much of the skyline, and many buildings along Front Street, suddenly come into view framed by tall columns.

Joining a façade of this grandeur to the complex functions of the station required careful planning. The design of Union Station placed the headhouse along Front Street, with the platforms running parallel behind because most trains arriving in Toronto went on to other cities on through-lines. Connecting the two parts underground is the concourse. The arrangement of the headhouse gives the plan its special character. To handle most of the business of the terminal, the architects provided the Great Hall, which is entered through the Front Street portico. Around this space, originally designated the ticket lobby, are the essential services of the station; from there, travellers descend a ramp to the concourse, which leads to the tracks and trains. Below the Great Hall, on the basement level, is another large circulation space. The two levels were planned to work together at peak periods; travellers arriving in Toronto were directed to the lower level, where they could collect luggage, meet friends, and then pick up cabs in a sunken driveway that joins Bay and York Streets. They could also reach the Royal York Hotel through a tunnel under Front Street. (The hotel was not built until 1928–9, but was almost certainly part of the project from the beginning.) Today, with Via Rail services for inter-city passenger travel concentrated in the upper station, the subway and GO Transit commuter services in the lower, the plan's luxurious provision of space has been amply justified.

The teachings of the Ecole des Beaux Arts that informed the planning of Union Station, and the severe monumentality of its columned exterior, emphasized dramatic interior spaces as settings for the important functions of the buildings. The Great Hall—where passengers purchased tickets, checked luggage, and then departed for trains—is grandly Roman (its antecedents the halls of Imperial baths or the naves of early Christian basilicas). In grandeur and space it is without peer in Canada. A plain entablature that runs around the walls, related to Corinthian columns that frame the entrance to the concourse, echoes the portico of the façade, whose monochrome colours are repeated inside in large squares of pale marble parquet on the floor, and walls of grey-beige stone, and in the coffered vault of Guastavino tiles. Lyle's manipulation of natural light gives the Hall its special character as light floods in through windows set high above the cornice on the south and north sides, and especially through the four-storey-high windows framed by vaulted arches at the east and west ends. The passage of the sun through these windows is traced across the floor of the hall as on a sun dial. Lyle indulged his interest in ornament based on Canadian themes only once in Union Station in the frieze of the cornice that runs around the room, which he inscribed with the names of the cities connected by the CPR and the CNR. Running from

east to west, ocean to ocean, in geographical sequence, they are like an incantation to the transcontinental nation the station was built to serve.

Compared with the Great Hall, the other interior spaces of Union Station are almost Spartan. The concourse leading to the tracks is even simpler, and the platforms upstairs are roofed in low concrete canopies. But even here the dimensions are impressive: the sheds—temporary spaces for users of the station—are 1,200 feet long; there are four miles of platforms, more than two miles of which are covered. The lower station is related to the Great Hall by the extent of its spaces and the use of fine materials; but it is the most altered part of the complex, changed to accommodate both the subway and GO transit, as well as many commercial outlets.

When the Union Station became fully operative in 1930 railways were already beginning to be undermined by the automobile. But its greatest hour came in the 1940s and early 1950s when it served Canadian soldiers and their families and the first flood of postwar immigrants. Less than twenty years later its days as a gateway to Toronto seemed numbered. The vast growth in air travel during the 1960s erased much of the market for which it had been designed. Railway stations across the United States (including the greatest of all, Pennsylvania Station), fell to wreckers as their owners saw greater potential and profit in the land on which they stood. In Canada, Marathon Realty, the CPR's development arm, was wreaking similar havoc, almost always to the permanent loss of the cities concerned. Union Station would likely have disappeared had not the land underneath, which was still owned by the City, been the key to proposals for redeveloping the railway yards to the south. Until the City agreed to the removal or rebuilding of the station, none of the railways' schemes for profitable real estate could go ahead. In April 1967 CN and CP presented a plan to develop the Railway Lands (in later form to be known as Metro Centre), calling for the demolition of Union Station and labelling it inefficient and outmoded. However, Torontonians had already been awakened to the city's architectural heritage by development schemes endangering Old City Hall, Holy Trinity Church (Plate 15), and many of the city's inner neighbourhoods. Led by John Caulfield Smith, the Union Station Committee was formed, and over the next eight years a group of determined citizens and experts marshalled the facts and opinion necessary to preserve the station. Since 1975 the expansion of subway and GO traffic to and from the centre of the city has given Union Station the functional vitality necessary to convince even the most skeptical observers. Though it has a commanding position on the Railway Lands, no one now proposes demolition.

Eighty years after planning for it began, Union Station—a majestic reminder of a time when Canada's and Toronto's futures seemed boundless—hums with activity and remains the open gate it was designed to be.

THE BAY STREET CANYON

Much as Wall Street is shorthand for New York's financial centre, Bay Street stands for Toronto's, spreading its aura over the blocks from Front Street north to Queen, and west from Yonge to University, where the streets are peopled by the power-brokers of Canadian politics and business, and lined with banks. King Street is the district's main artery; King and Bay is its heart. But Bay and its side streets—with their towers and smaller palatial buildings, constructed over the last sixty years—provide the image.

Laid out in 1797 as part of Peter Russell's first extension of the Town of York, Bay Street developed slowly and took its mid-nineteenth century character from towered churches, small shops, and a few row-houses. The King and Bay intersection has always been the hub. In 1840 the Bank of Montreal opened its first successful Toronto office on the northwest corner (the site of its present Toronto Main Branch), and in 1852 William Cawthra, Toronto's first notable property magnate, built a palatial house on the northeast corner, where the Bank of Nova Scotia now stands.

Through much of the late nineteenth century King and Bay was the centre of Toronto's newspaper community. The towered building (almost a skyscraper) built by *The Mail* (1878 by William Irving), with its public look-out platform, first raised the street to importance on the skyline. But Bay Street did not assume an identity of its own until the City Hall (Plate 76), with its clock-tower, was completed in 1899 on a Queen Street site that closed the northward vista.* The City Hall was a magnet for commercial development: the nine-storey Temple Building, on the northwest corner of Bay and Richmond (1895 and 1901 by G.W. Gouinlock; demolished), began the evolution of Bay Street into one of Toronto's prime office districts. The fire of 1904 hastened redevelopment, which was also spurred by the banking district's gradual move west along King Street. The Bank of Toronto's palatial office on the southwest corner of Bay and King (1911–13 by Carrère & Hastings, demolished) and the Toronto Stock Exchange (1912 by John M. Lyle, rebuilt 1936–7; Plate 123) brought rapid development to Bay Street, though the area was still dotted with mid-nineteenth-century houses, stores, and other buildings. The Graphic Arts Building (now a restaurant) at 71–3 Richmond West was built in 1913 by *Saturday Night* magazine to designs by F.S. Baker. Strong rusticated piers define the corners of the two colonnaded façades in a simple Ionic order. The temple form celebrates not just the glories of commerce but also the older image of humanist culture that *Saturday Night* sought to encourage in Canada.

The 1920s brought more dramatic changes with a series of towers (15 to 20-or-more storeys high) replacing earlier buildings. Chapman & Oxley's Northern Ontario Building of 1925–6 at Adelaide and Bay (NW) is severely simple,

rising in smooth yellow brick from a base defined by two-storey piers with a wide cornice, worked in cast stone. The Crown Trust Building at 302 Bay Street was originally designed as a columned temple in 1916 by Curry & Sparling and was given in 1929 an equally plain tower rising 14 storeys to a deep overhanging cornice.

Easy to plan and build, and very profitable to rent, these straight towers covered their sites almost completely. The higher they rose, the more they cut off sunlight and air from the surrounding streets, transforming them into 'canyons'. The alternative was to design towers whose height rose in steps, with successive floors set back to allow light to reach the street below. Changes in building codes in New York were the first to require such setbacks. In Toronto, as in most North American cities, there were few regulations for skycrapers. But some Toronto architects—like Alfred Chapman, and others, who had been trained in New York or admired New York design—adopted the setback tower whole-heartedly, as in the queen of Toronto's Art Deco skyscrapers, the Canada Permanent Trust Company Building at 320 Bay Street on the southwest corner of Adelaide, designed in 1928–9 by F. Hilton Wilkes and Mackenzie Waters in association with Mathers & Haldenby. Much in the design is Classical—notably the pilasters framing the ground-floor windows, the cornice above inscribed with the trust company's name, and the high main entrance that leads under a coffered vault, like that of a Roman triumphal arch, into the banking hall. At the entrance the eye is drawn up the height of the building—past setbacks that narrow its width and make it seem taller—to a sculpted roofline that resembles the crest of a towering crag. The details—especially the floral and leaf forms—are characteristic of Art Deco, more reminiscent of engraved metal-work than of modelled sculpture. As the sun catches the forms, the building seems to glitter. Inside, the glitter is authentic. The elevator doors are bronze, polished to look like gold. Among their panels of stylized foliage and flowers are two kneeling figures, one solemnly displaying a model of the Permanent's former headquarters on Toronto Street (the former Masonic Hall of 1857–8; demolished), the other holding a model of the new building. (The pattern comes from the golden throne found in the tomb of King Tutankhamen in 1922). Virtually all the interior detail is worked in polished bronze and brass—cast, chased, and engraved—set against neutral tones of polished marble surfaces. The arrangement of the interior, with its parallel rows of piers, leads the eye, as down the nave of a church, towards the sanctity of the safe-deposit vault, secure behind its gleaming protective grille.

Chapman & Oxley created their masterpiece in the Star Building at 60 King Street West (completed in 1929; demolished). This was thoroughly abstract Art Deco in detail; but their work was more conservative in the speculative office buildings they designed for Bay Street. The twenty-storey Sterling Building (1928)—372 Bay at Richmond Street West

---

*New York's Wall Street, which is about the same length, gains similar definition from the tower of Trinity Church at its west end.

112. *The Bay Street Canyon looking south from the Old City Hall*

113.   *Canada Permanent Trust Company*

114. *Relief sculpture ornamenting the main entrance.*

(SW)—which rises from a Classical base through fifteen storeys, has tall squared piers. The pastel pinkish tones of the slightly Venetian Gothic cast-stone detail is strongly influenced by the taste of the late 1920s. The top five floors, which lift the building into the skyline, are scalloped at the corners into a tower crowned by a row of framed windows with elegant arches and a modelled parapet.

More inventive in design are the Concourse Building, at 100 Adelaide Street West, on the northeast corner of Shepherd, designed in 1928 by Baldwin & Greene, and its sister building of 1929–30 by the same firm: the Victory Building at 80 Richmond Street West. Both are speculative office towers of medium height—the first 16 storeys, the second 20—designed with a central elevator-hall flanked by retail space that could be rented for shops or restaurants. Neither makes use of setbacks—the economics of floor rentals were against them—and neither building is tall enough to achieve landmark status. But the architects exploited fully the stylized detail popular at the time to give each a distinctive image. For the Concourse Building the firm engaged J.E.H. MacDonald (1873–1932). MacDonald is best known as a painter and as a member of the Group of Seven, but he was also interested in applying design (some of which was specifically Canadian in theme) to architecture and manufactured goods. For the side façade of the Concourse Building he designed spandrel panels of cast stone with a stylized pattern of pyramidal mountain peaks to go between the windows. The arch of the ground floor is generally Romanesque, with lively entwined foliage. But the coffers of the arch are filled with mosaics of airplanes and ships depicting historic and modern means of transportation. The semi-circular panel above the door is also finished in mosaic, with a riotous abstract landscape dominated by a flaring sun and crossed by a stylized stream filled with fish. The vertical piers between the windows are crowned with abstract flame-like motifs borrowed from American Indian art and executed in coloured tiles. The scheme expresses the 1920s' admiration for architecture both as a symbol of the period and as a manifestation of its vitality, because architecture manipulated technology into a form that could dominate the natural landscape.

The Victory Building—with its coloured-brick, marble, and cast-stone detail—suggests the mannered streamlining of the 1930s more than the bold, direct design of the 1920s. The ground floor is faced with polished black marble in alter-

115. *The Concourse Building*

116. *The Concourse Building: mosaics by J.E.H. MacDonald over the main entrance*

nating wide and narrow courses, into which shop-front doors and bay windows are recessed. These windows are shaped like those of eighteenth-century shop-fronts—and appeal to tradition in the midst of the conscious modernity that was appropriate to the jewellery and clothing stores located there. Above the wide brick band displaying the building's name in sanserif metal letters are horizontal bands of reddish-brown and yellow brick (repeated around the building's flat crest), and then—to exaggerate the height—tall strips of windows between yellow brick piers. The window spandrels are red-brown cast stone inset with a pyramid of vertical strips.

The lineaments of the Bay Street Canyon were established by the time the Depression put an end to the building boom of the late 1920s. During most of the 1930s Toronto was greatly overstocked with vacant office space. Completion of the Victory Building was delayed into 1931 and it stood empty until 1938. After the Second World War renewed construction began on King Street and only gradually spread to Bay, replacing first the surviving nineteenth-century buildings. The

last to go, the Temple Building of 1895 on the northwest corner of Richmond and Bay, was a grievous loss; it was replaced by the dreary Thomson complex at 390 Bay. When King Street was redeveloped with vast projects set in plazas, Bay Street fortunately remained a continuous streetscape. By the 1970s City Council, deciding that Bay Street was a unique and valuable feature of the downtown, set out to preserve its form with inventive planning regulations. Only at the south end, where the commonplace one-storey banking hall of First Canadian Place has weakened the King and Bay intersection, has the streetscape been breached. Elsewhere the new construction (more often renovation and in-fill) has respected the street—even the uninteresting large addition to the Ontario Northern Building (1982 by Webb Zerafa Menkes & Housden). Throughout the recent transformations of downtown Toronto, the Bay Street Canyon has endured both as architecture and as a traditional focus for the life and work of the city.

117.   *The Canadian Bank of Commerce Building next to the main tower of Commerce Court*

118

THE CANADIAN BANK OF COMMERCE BUILDING

(Now part of COMMERCE COURT NORTH)

25 King Street West, at Jordan Street (SW)

1929–31 by York & Sawyer; Darling & Pearson, associate architects

The Canadian Bank of Commerce (now united with the Imperial Bank of Canada to form the Canadian Imperial Bank of Commerce) was founded in 1867 by William McMaster, who had made his fortune in wholesale dry goods. Its first head office was in the former Bank of Upper Canada building at Yonge and Colborne Streets (1856 by William

Thomas; demolished). But in the late nineteenth and early twentieth centuries, under the guidance of Byron Edmund Walker—Toronto General Manager from 1886 and President after 1907—the Bank of Commerce developed the most elaborate and widespread architectural program of any bank in Canada. Beginning with a new Toronto head office at 25

King Street West, built in 1889–90 to designs by R.A. Waite, it built large and small branches from coast to coast: each building was both a well-designed local landmark and a corporate symbol. After many years of discussion, planning was begun in 1927–8 for a larger main office building. To provide for projected expansion (it was assumed that a major bank would double its space needs in ten years), and to take advantage of the property boom in downtown Toronto, the Bank decided to surpass the scale of the banking district with a skyscraper taller than any previously erected in the city—or the country. The commission went to York & Sawyer of New York—one of several American firms that had combined traditional historical style with modern techniques to create distinguished bank towers and interiors. The firm was just completing an elegant classical tower in Montreal for the Royal Bank that would become the 'Tallest Building in the British Empire'. The decision by the Bank of Commerce to use the same firm as its competitors, and to surpass them, is a quirk of architectural patronage that is not unusual in commercial circles.

When completed, the new Bank of Commerce building, rising 434 feet, itself became the Empire's tallest, and the best-known landmark in Toronto. The shaft of 34 office floors gains strength from wide, smooth piers at the corners and between the windows, and narrows gracefully into terraced set-backs as it ascends. The tall seven-storey base, containing the main Banking Hall and the corporation's offices, is aligned with the street, and a complex decorative scheme on the façade projects the Bank's image to the passerby. With its arched entrance on King Street and its office tower rising above, this building was a contemporary evocation of a medieval cathedral. The great arch of the main entrance is banded by an interlaced garland of bears, squirrels, roosters, bees and their hives—all emblems of thrift and industry. In the semicircular sculptured panel above the main doors, female figures of Industry and Commerce are joined by Mercury, patron deity of bankers; in the background a grain elevator and an outline of the new building itself combine with a flight of five Canada geese. Such symbolism fitted easily into the decoration of 1920s architecture, as did the historical murals by Arthur Crisp that adorn the original savings and foreign-exchange banks to the left and right of the front vestibule.

The U-shaped Banking Hall wraps around the entrance and elevator lobby. The main part of the hall to the south (now used for corporate banking), is 145 feet long, 85 feet wide, and 65 feet high to the apex of the vault. It is modelled on the Baths of Caracalla in Rome, but the design is richer and has more atmosphere than a standard archaeological reproduction: the walls are of deep plum-coloured limestone, and the coffered vault is painted deep blue on buff, with gilt mouldings.*

The top of the building was designed as a look-out across the city, with tall arched windows and a surrounding terrace. Crowning each of the main piers at this level are enormous stone heads of guardian deities that look out—in the manner of gargoyles on medieval cathedrals—across the modern city. From the observation platform Torontonians and tourists were able for the first time to get an aerial view of the city below. By day, and even at night, when the crest was floodlit, the tower transformed the skyline and image of the city.

The tower became one of the best-loved buildings in Toronto. It was fortunately also loved by its owners. After the Commerce amalgamated with the Imperial Bank of Canada in 1961 the directors decided to retain the building as the centrepiece for the new Commerce Court development (Plate 151) designed by I.M. Pei—though most architects of the period considered its Beaux Arts grandeur and historicism laughably old-fashioned and out of tune with the modern city that Toronto was becoming. The cost of the restoration and renovation was phenomenal—nearly equal to the expense of the new complex itself. Though some of the changes made were unfortunate, especially the closing of the observation deck and the removal of the banking counter from the main hall, the end result is surely one of the most generous examples of corporate architectural patronage in Toronto's history. The restoration, and the setting that Pei created for it, underline the elegant richness of the 1920s Beaux Arts architecture. Even the casual passerby—looking in through the King Street entrance to the vaulted foyer, or up through the Banking Hall windows at the gilded vault—can experience architectural pleasures here that are unmatched elsewhere in the city.

---

*Such a derivative approach to design had long been criticized. But in the late 1920s architecture was less hampered by a need for consistency, perfect historicism, or 'modernity', and was increasingly admired for creating a desired effect with mixed styles.

119.   *The Banking Hall*

120

THE DOMINION BANK, YONGE AND GERRARD BRANCH

(Now THE TORONTO-DOMINION BANK)

380 Yonge Street at Gerrard (SW)

1929 by John M. Lyle

The Gerrard and Yonge Street Branch of the Dominion Bank is a Classical Beaux Arts pavilion, in the tradition that was passed on to North American architects from the Ecole des Beaux Arts in Paris and that made its first dramatic appearance in Toronto with the Union Station (Plate 109) and the Trader's Bank (Plate 86). Though John Lyle used Classical pilasters and cornices to give his building presence and a sense of controlled monumentality, he was also influenced by the fashion for simplified, often flattened linear forms (loosely described as Art Deco) that swept the decorative arts and commercial design in the late 1920s and the 1930s. He

smoothed and stripped the curves and projections into a sleek, linear pattern.*

The Dominion Bank was founded in 1871 by a syndicate led by James Austin. The Bank's original corporate interest in architecture continued under the presidency of Sir Edmund Osler, who employed Darling & Pearson to build the head-

---

*Among the more exotic products of the style were the streamlined 'Airflow' Chrysler and the ocean liner *Normandie*. In Toronto, architecture influenced by Art Deco included the Eaton's College Street store and the Eaton house at 120 Dunvegan Road.

224

office tower at 1 King Street West (Plate 87), and most of the Bank's new branch buildings. When Lyle was commissioned in 1929 to design a new branch for the southwest corner of Gerrard and Yonge, he had already designed or altered several other branches. Yonge Street, between College and Dundas, was undergoing extensive rebuilding, spurred by the construction of Eaton's new College Street Store. As part of this development the street was widened between College and Gerrard; accordingly the Bank decided to build on a grander scale than was usual for their branches. The street-widening to the north would give the new branch an unusual prominence—which Lyle turned to architectural advantage with a design of solid monumentality adapted to a narrow corner lot.

The three-storey height of the bank is faced in limestone and divided into two levels: a two-storey Banking Hall, with its main entrance on Yonge Street, and a single storey of offices above, entered by a door at the west end of the Gerrard Street façade. For the Yonge Street façade, Lyle grouped the actual entrance, with its bronze pilasters,* and a window above as a single unit set between quarter-columns to proclaim the high open space of the Banking Hall beyond. To either side of the portal there are normally scaled windows that light private offices; and above, on the third floor, a three-part window is flanked by circular carved plaques that in fact depict coins of Louis XIV and Queen Victoria. The whole composition suggests Roman triumphal arches—a motif often used to express the importance of banking, though here the pattern is stylized and simplified. The Gerrard Street façade continues the large scale of the main façade with a row of five tall windows that light the Banking Hall, each framed with quarter-columns set within a row of taller smooth pilasters. With the front quarter-columns, these pilasters support a flat-simplified entablature (across which, on the front and side, originally appeared the name of the bank in elegant bronze letters). Above its slightly projecting cornice the third floor is more an 'attic' storey than an independent part of the design. Against its smooth walls are reliefs of urns filled with flowers.

The interior is one long room, dominated by the size and spacing of the windows facing Gerrard Street. As on the outside, there are pilasters between the windows. The interior space used to be divided roughly in half by the banking counter; the working area was backed against the windows to give the staff natural light behind them. In the 1960s this arrangement was reversed and the original marble counter, with its light bronze work, was replaced by another, also in marble but crudely designed. At the same time the polished bronze Art Deco hanging lamps were removed. The interior has been disfigured by office partitions, creating a narrow corridor at the entrance, and by brown paint on the travertine walls.

121

Art Deco favoured stylized natural details derived from flowers and animals for architectural decoration. Here, as in several of his other buildings, Lyle incorporated into the decoration native flowers, plants, birds, and animals that were identifiably Canadian. The Gerrard Street façade has swans and pigeons set in pairs back to back to approximate the curving symmetry of Corinthian capitals. The eight urns above are each filled with Ontario flowers. Lilies and sunflowers form the capitals of the quarter-columns that flank the main portal and fox heads the capitals of the bronze jambs of the front door. The round eyes of owls' heads on the triple window above recreate the volutes of an Ionic or Corinthian capital. On the Gerrard Street façade the decoration is completed by two octagonal reliefs representing the industries of Toronto and a crowded harbour scene. (The panel closest to Yonge Street has been obscured by the blatant illuminated sign with which the Toronto-Dominion Bank disfigures its buildings.)

The decorative results of Lyle's Canadianism are often whimsical but are well worth examination. Unfortunately the Bank, which had earlier supported Lyle's work as his patron, has treated the building badly over the past twenty years. The clock over the main door went out for repair in 1975 and has not been seen since; signs disfigure the exterior; and the most recent interior changes are of poor quality. Here is a perfect restoration project for a corporation that elsewhere has shown its sympathy and love for the arts.

*The original glass doors, now replaced, were also framed in bronze and elaborately decorated with floral motifs cast in the same metal.

122. *Detail of cut-stone frieze designed by Charles Comfort*

The Former
TORONTO STOCK EXCHANGE

230 Bay Street

1936–7 by George & Moorhouse; S.H. Maw, associate architect

The financial power in which Toronto takes pride is only partly represented by the great bank buildings of King and Bay Streets. Another significant aspect of that power is represented by the Toronto Stock Exchange. Founded in 1852 and incorporated in 1878, the Toronto Stock Exchange has been, and remains, a major agent in the foreign and local investment that has supported Canadian industrial and resource growth over the last hundred years. Much of the wealth invested through the Exchange came from the same wholesale and manufacturing businesses that had created the Dominion Bank, the Bank of Toronto, and the National Trust; and many of the men who dominated the Exchange—Henry Pellatt, A.E. Ames, E.R. Wood, and E.B. Osler—used their wealth (which partly resulted from this association) to become important figures in Toronto society and philanthropy. For almost fifty years, from 1937 to 1983, the home of the Toronto Stock Exchange was the splendid building on Bay Street that is still standing but now unoccupied. The formality of the building

evokes the traditions of bankers' architecture; and its smoothed surfaces, fine materials, and a decorative program that dramatically combines both the Art Deco and streamlined Moderne styles, express the astonishingly optimistic spirit of renewed industry and prosperity towards the end of the Depression.

There have been several exchanges in Toronto—the Toronto Exchange, founded in 1854 as a produce exchange; the Standard Stock Exchange and the Mining Exchange, both founded to exploit the boom of the 1890s—all of which were more or less subsumed into the Toronto Stock Exchange. Its first headquarters—a palatial stone building at 34 Wellington Street East (1855 by James Grand; demolished)—more than matched large banks in size and ornamental character. Begun at 20 King Street East in quarters shared with the National Trust and the A.E. Ames brokerage firm, the Toronto Stock Exchange in 1911 acquired the Bay Street site from Henry Pellatt (one of its most important members), and after a

123

competition erected a new building designed by John M. Lyle to house its own facilities and rental office space. During the boom of the 1920s—when the numbers of shares traded, and their value, increased enormously—the facilities of the Exchange, and particularly the Trading Floor, became overcrowded. The Crash of 1929 upset this growth for several years (although the Exchange, like Canada's banking and brokerage system, emerged relatively unscathed). By 1935–6 a sense of the pre-1929 prosperity had returned and the Exchange decided to rebuild its premises, engaging George & Moorhouse as architects, with S.H. Maw as associate architect.

During the twenties and thirties the business of the Stock Exchange was transformed by new technical developments. In the first premises on King Street, floor traders from A.E. Ames had communicated with their offices downstairs by dropping notes through a hole in the floor. By the 1930s communication by telephone, telegraph, tickertape, pneumatic tubes, and Translux displays of trading prices in New York had revolutionized the trading methods, just as the volume of shares had changed its scope. With the completion of its new building the Toronto Stock Exchange became the first major financial institution in the city to sponsor a thorough modernization of its image in the world of banking and finance.

The plan was simplicity itself. The trading floor, devoted to technical and spatial needs, was the dominant element of both the interior and the exterior; its tall windows are the most important feature of the façade. The building is effectively five storeys high; but the functions were arranged on three levels over a basement devoted originally to mechanical equipment. The ground floor contained cloakrooms, a members' dining-room, vestibules, and stairs to the upper floors. The second level was almost entirely taken up by the trading floor—an open space three storeys high. The third level, carried on special trusses over the trading floor, housed the Exchange's executive offices. On a relatively small site, the need to obtain the maximum interior space meant that the façade rose smooth from the streetline, with no place for the porticos and plastic modelling of bankers' classicism—though strong vertical piers between the front windows, rising to support a simple cornice-like moulding across the façade, suggest those of a Classical portico. A base of smokey pink granite, textured to pick out the courses, supports the upper façade of pale Indiana limestone. The trading floor inside—

with a central space 72 by 105 rising 39 feet, and galleries at the east and west ends—has much the same air of stylized formality; but the forms are dramatically modernistic. The lower five feet of the walls are faced in pale marble, and the upper walls in acoustic tile horizontally striped with bands of polished silver metal and thin wooden strips. Stretched across this pattern—up the east wall, across the ceiling, and down the west wall—are broad bands of opal glass in metal frames that cover both the long east and west windows and the lighting fixtures across the ceiling. The bands of light thus provided are the strongest decorative feature of the interior, creating an effect that expresses an architectural sensibility that borrows artistically from technology and is as futuristic as a science-fiction movie set.

To complete the decoration of the Stock Exchange the architects called in Charles Comfort, who brilliantly adapted his skills as an illustrator to create descriptive art that reinforced the public character of the building and underlined its modernity. For the strongly architectural setting of the trading floor, Comfort painted a suite of eight murals, sixteen feet high, that depict the industries of Canada in a Cubist style. On the exterior he ornamented the doors with roundels of stainless steel on which are engraved figures representing individual industries. And to span the façade above the two main entrances he designed a frieze, but in gold-coloured stone, that represents the workers in Canadian industries: flat, linear, mechanistic figures united with their machines by a dynamic zigzag pattern. This is the most striking piece of sculpture from the period in Toronto.

In the last decade the Stock Exchange began to adopt new technology that was not even thought of when the 1937 building was opened. To accommodate this, and to provide expanded facilities, it moved in 1983 into new headquarters on the southeast corner of York and Adelaide Streets in First Canadian Place. The old building was transferred to the Olympia and York developers. They have proposed to fund the establishment of a design centre in the old building and the raising of a tower of rental offices above it, but the plans are not yet finalized. The idea is not in itself terrible, though the density bonuses demanded by Olympia and York in return for saving the Exchange may not be approved by City Council. The immediate considerations are those of material, scale, style, and the relationship of the new top to the old bottom. If the plan is insensitively carried out, both Bay Street and one of its finest buildings will suffer.

124. *Glendon Hall*

THE BAYVIEW HOUSES

In 1925 the financier E.R. Wood* presented 'Wymilwood', his house on Queen's Park Crescent West next to Sir Joseph Flavelle's 'Holwood' (Plate 89), to Victoria College and moved to 'Glendon Hall', his new country house on Bayview Avenue, designed by Molesworth, West & Secord. Opening out across terraced gardens to a seemingly endless Don Valley landscape, Glendon is a low, rambling country house of Italian inspiration, different in character from most of Toronto's domestic architecture. It is clearly the country home of an urbane connoisseur.

Around this time many of Toronto's wealthiest men—like E.R. Wood—were on the verge of retirement and ready to build more expansive houses further from the city. Thus

*Originally a telegraph operator, Wood joined the Central Canada Loan & Savings Co. in 1884. He later became Managing Director and Vice-President, and was elected President in 1914. He was also a Vice-President of National Trust; Brazilian Traction, Light and Power; Canada Life Assurance; and the Canadian Bank of Commerce.

developed a new type of country house, and new areas with picturesque landscapes close to Toronto were set aside for country estates. One of these was the scenic Bayview district that extends east from Lawrence Park across Bayview Avenue and the valleys of the Don River to Leslie Street. An advertisement from *Canadian Homes and Gardens* (May 1929) gives the tone of this new suburb:

> Bayview. Your country estate within twenty-five minutes by Motor from Toronto's business centre . . . 900 acres of beautiful rolling and ravine land are being developed into the most exclusive and high class residential district in Canada. . . . Carefully planned restrictions (on design) offer permanent protection. Location—beauty—accessible remoteness—Does this not suggest a site for the home of your dream? Areas of two acres and upward (nothing less) are available.

Though it was not the first of the Bayview houses, Glendon Hall set a standard of stylishness and scale for both house

125. *The Frank Wood house: garden front*

126. *The Frank Wood house: entrance front*

and garden that influenced later houses, many of which were built for Wood's business associates. The estate is entered from Bayview Avenue, between monumental Classical gate posts in a fine stone wall. Invisible from the road, the house is set back on the edge of the Don Valley ravine, and at first sight appears simple in form and detail. Two storeys high with a green tile roof, it consists of a main block with an angled service wing to the west, and its design elements are homelike rather than pretentious: rough grey stucco-covered walls, a broad low roof with deep eaves, covered by mottled green tiles, large shuttered windows, and floor-length French doors east of the main entrance, indicating the main living-rooms. The house faces southeast; but the service wing creates a forecourt where the drive curves around a sunken garden and under a glazed *porte-cochère* framed in cast- and wrought-iron. The front lawns sweep to the south and a boundary of trees, forming a landscape in the tradition of English country houses, contrived to seem limitless.

On the other sides of the house the principal rooms open onto terraces set into the steep edge of the ravine (so steep that the basement recreation room facing north has its own terrace). To the east the terraces form a partially enclosed garden; beyond are a pair of low-roofed summerhouses of white trellis work. These terraces especially give the house its Italianate character, derived from the terraced villas outside Renaissance Rome. The entire house is dedicated to the magnificent view across the Don Valley.*

The land on the north side of the Don Ravine (then known as Bayview Heights), which overlooked Glendon Hall, was purchased by E.R. Wood's brother, Frank P. Wood, who was a leading Bay Street stockbroker. To design the new house he engaged the New York firm of Delano & Aldrich; both partners were members of New York's highest society, and the firm had built town and country houses for the Astors, Rockefellers, and Whitneys, among others. They were noted for their skill in manipulating Colonial American and Georgian prototypes to create grand houses featuring unaffected design and domestic comfort. Their Georgian-style design for Wood, completed in 1930, is American in character: cleanly precise in smooth stone, it avoids the romantic, soft-focus qualities of

*After Wood's death in 1941 Glendon Hall passed to the University of Toronto. The Ontario College of Art used it in the 1950s, and finally it was transferred to the newly founded York University. Beginning in 1960, several new buildings were constructed (none of them an ornament to the setting), and the whole complex became York's Glendon College when the main campus of the university was constructed on Keele Street.

127. *Donningvale*

English-style houses such as Gerald Larkin's in Rosedale (Plate 129). Two-and-a-half storeys high, seven bays wide, and crowned with a slender octagonal cupola that lights the main stair, the house is visible from all sides and commands its setting through its symmetry and precise proportions. In front of the house a forecourt, paved in brick and walled in by the stable block on the north, focuses attention on the main entrance, with its pedimented and columned doorcase. Above the door an octagonal window—plainly of the Art Deco period—firmly dates the house. The character, colour, and detailing of the materials are precise and fastidious. The smooth limestone façade—carried up to a full stone cornice—displays the proportions of the house; it is laid in random courses that give the surface a fine linear pattern. The pale gold-grey of the walls is complemented by the grey-green slate roof and the grey-blue louvred shutters that frame all the windows.

The Frank Wood house is planned around a central hall that runs through the building, past the main stair, and opens to the main rooms on the south side and along the east or garden front. The symmetrical façades are almost identical, though the east windows open through French doors onto a broad terrace. Beyond the terrace, towards the edge of the Don Ravine, the lawn—surrounded by tall clipped hedges—extends east to a semi-circle of columns that frames the view of the woods beyond. The landscape design, like that of the house, is simple almost to the point of austerity, in contrast to the wildness of the valley woods. From the east front the garden terrace wraps around to the south, where a conservatory opens from the drawing-room to overlook the ravine towards Glendon Hall. Here a fringed Regency-style roof is supported on thin verticals of weathered bronze, in-filled with great plate-glass panels.

Frank Wood built his Bayview house partly as a setting for a splendid collection of English and European art. After his death in 1955, most of the collection went to the Art Gallery of Toronto, to which Wood also left the house, with instructions that it be sold to provide funds for future acquisitions. At the sale it was bought by George Weston, who lived there until the 1970s. It was then sold to Crescent School, a private boys' school. Several buildings have since been put up to the north and west, and a few changes have been made inside, but the house has been allowed to stand clear in its original landscape as one of the finest Georgian Revival houses in Canada.

South from Glendon Hall, along Bayview Avenue (which was little more than a country lane in the 1930s), are two stone gateposts inscribed 'Donningvale' that mark the entrance to a straight drive leading back along the grounds of Sunnybrook Hospital to the J.J. Vaughan house. John J. Vaughan (1882–1966) joined Eaton's in 1903 and rose through the firm as the trusted right-hand man of John Craig Eaton. When Sir John Eaton died, and his cousin R.Y. Eaton assumed leadership of the firm, a great deal of responsibility for the business fell to Vaughan as a Director and Secretary-Treasurer. Vaughan lived at 135 Glen Road until 1930–1, when he moved to Bayview.

Designed by the Toronto firm of Burden & Gouinlock, with grounds laid out by Gordon Culham, Donningvale is in a simple Elizabethan style, planned around a gabled main entrance with higher gables at each end of the façade. The effect is straightforward and homelike, with the gables repeated on the side façades; on the east side an arched loggia next to the hall looks out across the tops of the trees on the valley floor. (The interiors are not consistent with the exterior: the main rooms are Georgian in style.) The grounds complement the simplicity of the house: the direct approach to it is softened by artfully random clumps and plantings of trees that gradually give way to the circle of lawn before the front door. To the south Culham laid out a vista that frames the bay window of the library and suggests from there a limitless extension of the grounds. Like 'Bay View' to the south, Donningvale was expropriated after Vaughan's death to provide land for Sunnybrook Medical Centre, which accounts for this hospital's almost rural setting. The house was neglected for many years, but has now been taken over by the Renascent Foundation as a rehabilitation centre affiliated with the hospital.

Several of the houses built in Bayview along other sections of the Don Valley have perished completely, and almost without record, to make way for the expansion of hospitals and parks, or for subdivisions to accommodate smaller houses. However, philanthropic donations and sensitive re-use ensured the preservation of Glendon Hall, the Frank Wood house, and Donningvale. The story of 'Bay View', however, was nearly one of neglect leading to demolition.

'Bay View' was designed and built for J.S. McLean in 1928–31 by Eric Arthur, with twenty hectares of gardens and surrounding landscape planned by Gordon Culham. McLean (1876–1954) made his fortune in meat-packing: from his own company and from others interests he created Canada Packers. His chosen architect, Eric Arthur (1898–1982), was born in New Zealand and trained at the University of Liverpool, the leading English school of architecture in the period. The author of *Toronto: No Mean City* (1963) and Toronto's first

serious architectural historian, he was also a keen student of Ontario's colonial architecture, and of the Georgian tradition as it was transferred to Ontario. In the late twenties and the thirties Arthur created several inventive designs for houses inspired by Georgian or colonial themes.

The two-storey Bay View, with its high dormered roof, borrows directly from the Georgian traditions that interested Arthur in this period. Unlike the Wood house, which is also Georgian but in the American manner, the Bay View design—especially in its walls of rough-hewn parti-coloured fieldstone—draws on the patterns of Scottish houses in the eighteenth century and on houses that were built in Ontario by Scottish stonemasons as late as the 1850s. Bay View is approached from the west, but the main entrance—sheltered by an arched porch with simple Corinthian columns—faces east across the trees of the Don Valley. Two wings step forward: the one on the first ends in a curved bay window that lights the mahogany- and walnut-panelled dining-room; the one on the left ends in a heavily arched loggia that is open to both the valley view and the gardens to the south. Between the entrance and the dining-room wing, a tall arched window lights the main hall's graceful spiral staircase.

The garden front, which looks southwest across a terrace and down a lawn enclosed by hedges and flower borders to a fountain, is simpler in plan, with single windows and two-storey bays symmetrically flanking a garden door. On one side of the door is the library; on the other is the drawing-room; and beyond the drawing-room is a large sunroom surrounded by wide windows, with a bay window commanding the south view of the lawns. The second floor of this wing is one large sitting-room for the master-bedroom suite, fitted with arched sash windows. On the exterior of this garden wing the upper walls and roof-top parapet are covered with white fancifully elaborate trellis-work.

The colour and texture of the fieldstone walls and the strong, simple outlines of the house first catch the eye. But the smaller-scale detailing—like that of the garden-wing trellis—show the full range of Arthur's skill and inventiveness as a designer. Despite its size, Bay View has the grace and intimacy of a family home, and seems neither too large nor too formal. Essential to the success of the house—as in all the Bayview houses—was its appropriately scaled and detailed garden setting. Though the area of Maclean's estate was relatively modest, Culham's design creates an impression of immense size, partly by exploiting the view across the Valley, as was done at Glendon Hall.

The landscape that Gordon Culham designed as a setting for Bay View has today reached the magnificent maturity that was planned for it in the 1930s. The driveway from Bayview Avenue approaches the house through a densely wooded ravine before sweeping up to the plateau on which the house stands at the edge of the valley. The gardens (used by the family for relaxation and sports) are on the southwest side of the house, sheltered by tall hedges. For most of the

128. *Bay View*

estate, however, Culham planned a lawn—spreading away to the southeast between banks of trees—that was inspired by eighteenth-century English work and designed to be seen from the windows of the sunroom and the terrace just outside. By using trees that change to brilliant colour in the autumn, and evergreens for accents in the expanse of winter snow, Culham adapted the traditional English characteristics of his design to the Canadian setting.

Bay View remained the McLean family home until 1967, when J.S. McLean's widow died. It was then expropriated so that the grounds could be used to expand the Sunnybrook Medical Centre. For five years the house was the temporary home of the Donwoods Institute and then, on the assumption that it would be demolished, it was used as makeshift office space for Sunnybrook. The fate of the house was not reconsidered until the early 1980s, when the hospital's new additions had been completed. Plans were then made jointly by the Junior League of Toronto and the Interior Designers of Ontario to restore the house and part of the gardens, and to open it briefly as an elaborately decorated showcase house. Work began in January 1982, and in the early summer of 1983 a formal ball celebrated the return of Bay View to a state that architect, landscape architect, and patron would have appreciated. This decorator's showcase was temporary, however. Bay View is today the Sunnybrook Conference Centre, used for medical gatherings and occasionally for special entertainments and charity functions. But even without the magnificent furniture that was installed for the showcase, it is still possible to appreciate in the Centre the original character of the house and to imagine the way of life for which it was designed.

It is doubtful whether houses and estates on the scale of Glendon Hall, the Frank Wood house, Donningvale, and Bay View will ever be created again. For a brief period of about thirty years, from 1925 to 1955, the Bayview area was a delightful pastoral suburb on the edge of a burgeoning city. New roads had made it easily accessible to downtown, and taxes on land there had not yet risen to levels that would make estates and spacious mansions prohibitively expensive to maintain. The Bayview district is still home to many of Toronto's business leaders and patrons of the arts, but today its mansions do not aspire to their original splendour and seclusion. Although the way of life they once represented has vanished, these magnificent houses and gardens—commemorating the elegance of a bygone era—fortunately remain to be seen and enjoyed.

129

THE GERALD LARKIN HOUSE

7 Castle Frank Road (N)

1926 by George, Moorhouse & King

In the first decades of the twentieth century Toronto turned abruptly away from the architectural monuments of the Late Victorian period. Nowhere were the changes more dramatic than in domestic architecture. As Toronto became more sophisticated and formal in its social and business relationships it was believed that domestic architecture should develop in the same way. The most popular style for large, expensive houses was Georgian Revival, which came to epitomize elegant comfort for the business and professional classes during the 1920s and 1930s. Forest Hill, Lawrence Park, and other fashionable districts are dotted with handsome neo-Georgian houses. None, however, is a finer evocation of the English eighteenth century than the Gerald Larkin house on Castle Frank. Built in 1926 of mellow, soft-textured red brick, it was designed and crafted with such accuracy in proportions and details that it is a revival in the truest and most complimentary sense of the word.

Gerald Larkin—the son of Peter C. Larkin, founder of the Salada Tea Company, who was also Canada's first High Commissioner to London—succeeded his father as head of the firm and used his wealth to accumulate an opulent collection of European and English art and furniture, for which his house was designed as background. As his architects Larkin chose George, Moorhouse & King—an interesting choice because Allan George (1874–1961) was the English-trained son of Sir Ernest George, one of the leaders of the revival in England of evocative Georgian forms for clients who were connois-seurs of both art and architecture. The Larkin house is spacious, but simple in design: two storeys high, seven windows wide, with the central three bays stepping forward under a sculpted pediment to set off the main entrance. In its formal symmetry, the carefully arranged proportions of the windows, the superb quality of its brickwork, the white-painted doorcase that frames the main entrance with its broken pediment, Corinthian pilasters, fan-lighted transom, and overhanging wrought-iron lantern, it is clearly a gentleman's house, secure and comfortable. A brick wall in front opens through two wrought-iron crested carriage gates that lead to a curving front drive. The house seems to require a landscape setting and in fact it stands on a wide but shallow formally landscaped Rosedale lot overlooking the much larger Osler estate of Craigleigh (now a public park), which gives the principal rooms a country-like prospect.

Gerald Larkin lived on Castle Frank Road until his death in 1961. His interest in art and architecture was expressed in his sponsorship of the Trinity College Chapel (built in 1953–5 to designs by Sir Giles Gilbert Scott, architect of Liverpool Cathedral and the most important Gothic Revival architect of the twentieth century); and in the endowment of St Thomas's Anglican Church with lavish vestments and religious art. When Larkin died his fortune, and much of his collection, were divided between Trinity College and St Thomas's. The house was sold to Kenneth Thomson, the second Baron Thomson of Fleet.

130. *The Balmoral*

THE BALMORAL
150 Balmoral Avenue at Avenue road (NE)
1927–8 by S.B. Coon & Son

THE CLARENDON
2 Clarendon Avenue at Avenue Road (NW)
1927 by Charles B. Dolphin

THE CLARIDGE
1 Clarendon Avenue at Avenue Road (SW)
1927–8 by Baldwin & Greene

The late 1920s and the 1930s were the heyday of apartment construction in Toronto. Coinciding with the development of the skycraper, the period featured apartment buildings with the same distinctive and eclectic sense of architectural form and historic style. Few structures better represent the contemporary taste in luxury apartment design than those on both sides of Avenue Road at the crest of the hill overlooking the city to the south: the Balmoral on Balmoral Avenue, the Clarendon on the northwest corner of Clarendon Avenue and Avenue Road, and the Claridge opposite, on the southwest

corner. Each is built of brick and stone, in historical styles associated with gracious living: Tudor in The Balmoral and The Clarendon, and in The Claridge a medieval style reminiscent of Venetian *palazzi* of the Gothic period. These styles inspired designs that express luxury in their scale and elaboration of details, and suggest domesticity in their many windows arranged in groups and bays and overhanging oriels.

Toronto's first luxury apartment buildings were constructed in the 1890s. Though spacious and comfortable, they lacked the impressive size and opulence of the New York or Boston

131. *The Clarendon*

buildings that were the models for North American apartment life. Most of Toronto, however, was still wedded to the single-family house, and few Toronto apartment buildings were considered sufficiently convenient or fashionable to justify a move from a separate house on a quiet side street. During the 1920s these circumstances began to change dramatically. After the war, houses became expensive to buy and maintain and good servants difficult to find; and in Toronto's developing economy there were more moderately wealthy people for whom a luxurious apartment became a viable alternative to a house. New areas that were almost as fashionable as the best of the established neighbourhoods opened up to apartment development. This was especially true of the Avenue Road area south of St Clair Avenue West.

In late nineteenth-century Toronto this escarpment, with its spectacular views south across the city, was lined by country estates. Senator John Macdonald's 'Oaklands' (see Plate XV) claimed most of the east side of Avenue Road. Senator William McMaster's 'Rathnelly', and Simeon Janes's 'Benvenuto' on the crest of the hill, claimed the west side. After the turn of

the century a few other mansions were built on the same scale; but large sections of the district were subdivided into lots for smaller, though still very fashionable, houses. The major change came in 1924 when the Benvenuto estate was broken up after the death of its second owner, Sir William Mackenzie. Apartments in a near-Georgian style were built at 400 Avenue Road in 1926; and, on the southwest corner of Avenue Road and Edmund in 1927, three six-storey blocks by Catto & Catto in a simpler design with fashionable Art Deco touches. Far more luxurious and stylish (not only in their regal British names) are The Balmoral, The Clarendon, and The Claridge, built in 1928–9.

The Balmoral is the most stately. For the developers Wilkie and Delamere, S.B. Coon & Son designed a six-storey H-shaped block around a narrow front courtyard that shelters the entrance and admits light and air to the inner rooms. This conventional plan blossomed into a giant Tudor palace of tan brick trimmed with white stone, entered from Balmoral through a two-storey stone arch, with a carved gable and a pendant lantern. The most important elements in the design

132. *The Claridge*

are the banks of casement windows grouped in tall bays under gables that rise above the flat roof; these windows are the central homelike feature of apartments that stretch across the entire width of the façade. Stone parapets at the second-floor level and around the roof draw the design together. Though plainly an apartment building, The Balmoral still has much of the romantic grandeur its first residents considered desirable.

The 4-storey Clarendon is also a Tudor palace, but smaller and less flamboyant. As in The Balmoral, the wide bays of casements on the upper floors are the focal points of the façades, to which are added spiral fluted colonnettes beside the main door, and carved panels around the entrance and set into the faces of the bay windows. But the greatest attention was lavished on the planning and decoration of the interior, which is entered through an oak-panelled reception hall, 30 by 60 feet, which fills the centre of the ground floor. The Clarendon is planned in three blocks separated by narrow courts open to the street. The central block is shorter than the ones to the east and west; and the rear apartments look down on a sheltered court. Each block has its own central elevator, to avoid long connecting corridors. The apartments

originally ranged in size from one bedroom to four bedrooms, with living-rooms averaging 14½ feet by 25 feet, and separate dining-rooms averaging 11½ feet by 12½ feet. Each had a fireplace in the living-room, windows facing at least two directions to permit cross-ventilation, bathrooms with marble shower stalls as well as tubs, and rear service stairs. Many apartments had a maid's room; and the building originally included additional servants' rooms in the central block. The Clarendon suites included all the features of a Forest Hill house, plus some enticing extras: the ground floor reception hall was designed to be used for private parties, and off it was a restaurant for residents who did not wish to cook for themselves; the basement provided underground parking for 46 cars; there were separate men's and women's exercise rooms, a laundry room, and a fully equipped billiard room; and the rear court was originally laid out with a miniature golf course. The Clarendon provided a residential environment matched in few Toronto buildings prior to the development of luxury condominiums in the 1980s.

The last of these three apartment buildings to be completed was The Claridge. Its designer, Martin Baldwin of Baldwin & Greene (he later became director of The Art Gallery of

133.   *The Claridge: front entrance*

134. *The Claridge: reception hall*

Toronto), employed the full range of Venetian Gothic detail to create the queen of Toronto apartment buildings—comparable in luxurious finish and eccentric vitality to the firm's Victory and Concourse Buildings in the Bay Street Canyon (Plate 112). The H-shaped plan is similar in size to The Balmoral—six storeys high—but unlike The Balmoral (and to a lesser extent The Clarendon), which is all show on the exterior, The Claridge possesses an entrance hall that must be the most beautiful in the city. From the street a narrow courtyard leads between wrought-iron lamp standards to an arched entrance door, which is flanked by Corinthian pilasters decorated with a vine scroll. More scrollwork covers the lintel and, in wrought iron, fills the arch above the door. An iron interlace of circles fills the front door itself, to either side of which a simple Corinthian arcade stands in front of the hall's triple-arched casement windows.

To design the reception hall Baldwin engaged the well-known painter and designer J.E.H. MacDonald, who employed patterns and colours developed from Spanish-American and Indian motifs. The openness of the hall is immediately apparent: walls of glazed doors and arched casements, leaded in overlapping circles and squares, face north towards the street and south into a courtyard. Moorish arches, a heavily beamed painted ceiling, and a generous use of tiles create an interior filled with light and warm, rich colour. Every detail is precisely planned and executed. Art Deco chandeliers and sconces were specially designed. The walls are buff adobe-finished plaster, and the ceiling is arranged with intricate designs in muted colours (painted by Carl Schaefer) that include zodiac symbols (painted by the designer's son Thoreau MacDonald) and stars on the panels between the beams, which are painted with geometric patterns. The elevator halls on either side are reached through wide arches framed in panels of tiles in greyed tones of pinkish-brown, blue, and green, and up steps with colourfully tiled risers. The richness of the colours and the light provided by the glass-wall effect of the doors and casement windows create the atmosphere of a sunny patio cooled by surrounding shade.

On the exterior the decorative detail is sometimes playful in its eclectic references to architectural history, but always shows precision and care in the execution. The effect is totally individual and unforgettable. Grey-buff brick is used on the two lower floors in a checkerboard of light and dark tones, and above in a diamond-pattern grid. Stone is used sparingly, but for strong details: in ogee arches over windows, in the basecourse and cornice, as well as for gargoyles at the corners of the block. As in the other two apartment buildings, the windows are grouped for interior effect in rows and bays, sometimes opening onto balconies; the most fanciful are three overhanging bays on the third floor, supported on the backs of carved angels, as if above a quiet canal in Venice. Few buildings in Toronto better demonstrate the rich effects and the beauty made possible by the eclectic spirit of the 1920s—though there is far less history here than in The Balmoral and The Clarendon: Baldwin made his own history and imbued it with the romance of apartment life as the 1920s saw it.

The Claridge was praised for its fireproof construction and the first use of automatic elevators in a Toronto apartment building—as The Clarendon and The Balmoral were praised for *their* facilities, which were important attractions for the first tenants. Almost sixty years later such conveniences are expected. But these three buildings are the jewels among Toronto's apartments and condominums. The virtuoso qualities of their design, the care and skill that went into their construction, and the resulting pleasures of beautiful detail and effects are the very qualities lacking in many of the city's most expensive recent buildings—for all their saunas, Florida rooms, and gold-plated fixtures. A study of The Balmoral, The Clarendon, and The Claridge may provide useful models for new apartment buildings that seek to offer true luxury in the midst of a plethora of mere facilities.

135

THE LAWREN HARRIS HOUSE

2 Ava Crescent (N)

1930 by Alexandra Biriukova

In the twenties and thirties the European ideal of the modern house—sharp geometric outlines, flat roofs, and broad window panels—had little influence in Toronto. For most Torontonians modernity meant such interior features as elaborately fitted bathrooms and kitchens, and air-conditioning. The romantic image of 'home' continued to be expressed in Colonial, Georgian American, or Olde English architecture; modern European designs were considered 'unhomelike' and lacking in resale value. The few identifiably modern houses built in Toronto at this time were the result of special artistic patronage. Of these the Lawren Harris house—which would have been seen to have distinction even in Paris—is probably the best example.

Harris, a founder of the Group of Seven, was one of Canada's best-known landscape painters. His early paintings of streetscapes show a strong sympathy with architecture—with houses especially, and with their geometrical forms. His landscape painting in the twenties, concentrating on the stark outlines of northern terrains and snow-covered mountains, was also geometrical; in the thirties it became abstract. A private income allowed Harris to take a direct interest in architecture. In 1913 he commissioned Eden Smith to design for him the Studio Building on Severn Street in the Rosedale Valley—an unstyled, almost factory-like structure containing six double-height studios, including Harris's own. The house on Ava Crescent was intended for the domestic side of his life, not only for day-to-day living and entertaining but for displaying his paintings and the works of his artist friends. This time he chose as his designer Alexandra Biriukova, a Russian-born architect who had come to Canada via Paris and supported herself by teaching art at Upper Canada College. Post-revolutionary Russia, where she received the first part of her training, had been preoccupied with a stark modern architecture, reduced to dramatically bare essentials; but her design for the Harris house is much more influenced by sophisticated Parisian expressions of Art Deco.

The flat-roofed white stucco house is composed of two wings radiating from a central block with a three-storey frontispiece in which the entrance and the elongated windows above rise together in a tall, narrow arch inset in the smooth wall. (The frontispiece faces southwest and through most of the year the white façade gleams in the light of the evening sun.) The main block contains the hall, stairs, and other rooms, while the living-room wing to the right and the dining-room wing to the left (both with bedrooms on the second floor) are arranged in a butterfly plan. On the ground floor long French windows grouped with simpler second-floor windows in shallow recessed panels give the design linear elegance. In a conscious attempt to provide a Canadian motif, the cast-metal spandrels between the windows above the front door, and in the front-terrace railings across the main windows, were patterned on pine needles—fairly realistic sprays in the window panels, but only delicate curving lines in the railings. The Harris house is an example of the interest shown by many Canadian artists—not only Harris, but J.E.H. MacDonald and the architect John Lyle among them—in applying Canadian motifs to the ideas and forms of European modernism.

For the ground-floor interior Biriukova designed a suite of rooms with a strong French flavour, each having a different shape: the dining-room a square octagon, the living-room a rectangular one; the hall an elongated oval; the library five-sided. These rooms are high-ceilinged, simply detailed, light-filled, and open to vistas across the hall. They were the perfect setting for Harris's paintings (many are quite large) and for the works of his friends. The Lawren Harris house, immaculately cared for and filled with art, was for many years afterwards the home of Mrs Harry Davidson, one of Eric Arthur's first architecture students at the University of Toronto, who with her husband was a leading advocate of contemporary art and architecture in the city.

136.   *The stylized form of the entrance and balconies in one of the smaller blocks*

246

GARDEN COURT APARTMENTS

1477 Bayview Avenue (E)

1939–42 by Forsey Page & Steele

Before the Second World War, middle-class Torontonians considered apartments unsuitable for family life. Although social commentators had long since seen apartments and flats as the best solution to housing reform for the city's lower classes, and increasing numbers of the rich had embraced luxurious apartment life in buildings like The Balmoral and its neighbours on Avenue Road hill (see pages 238–43), 'home' for most of Toronto's middle classes was a detached house with a front and back garden on a quiet side street. Economic conditions during the 1930s made this ideal almost unattainable. Under the Dominion Housing Act of 1935, and the National Housing Act of 1938, government-sponsored mortgages became available; but their effects were modest. In the same period many developers were saddled with large suburban properties—originally planned for detached houses —for which there was little or no market. Apartment construction was an obvious solution. But architects were challenged to create apartments whose plan and surroundings would satisfy the precise image of 'home' cherished by the middle classes. In Toronto this challenge was met most effectively by Garden Court.

Fronting on the east side of Bayview Avenue, Garden Court runs east to Berney Crescent. It stands about three-and-a-half miles from the city's centre in the heart of Leaside, which was incorporated as a separate municipality in 1913 and became Toronto's quintessential middle-class suburb in the period between the wars. New houses sold for $8,000 to $11,000. If they were ordinary, and their physical setting unspectacular, there was no denying the comfort and convenience of Leaside. However, large tracts of land were still undeveloped, and it was on one of these that Garden Court was built.

Page & Steele—one of Toronto's most successful and fashionable residential firms—were the best possible architects for the new development. To their repertoire of Georgian and English Cottage Style residential designs they added in the early 1930s a streamlined Moderne style; and, unlike many of Toronto's leading architects, they had expanded into apartment design, becoming proficient at working with speculative builders. The immediate inspiration for Garden Court was a scheme presented in 1934 to the Bruce Commission on Housing Conditions in Toronto by a committee from the Toronto Chapter of the Ontario Association of Architects*. As a plan for publicly funded downtown housing (which was never actually built) to replace a block of slums in what is now the Regent Park area, it called for a large courtyard surrounded

137.   *Northern block facing the interior courtyard*

by low-rise apartments. Page & Steele adapted this plan, designing the buildings in yellow brick, with curved balconies and strong horizontal and vertical details—for most Torontonians a first introduction to the Moderne style in architecture. An important contributor to the scheme was the landscape architect H.B. Dunnington-Grubb, who designed the interior court. He laid out gently formal spaces that through scale and the use of terraces are related both to the units of the complex and to the development as a whole.

The long rectangular garden court, running north-south and secluded from the traffic of the surrounding streets, is the centrepiece of the plan. Around it the apartments are arranged in a series of connected blocks. Most of these are entered from the garden, but there are three- and two-storey blocks flanking the porticoed Bayview entrance with front doors on that street, and three-storey blocks and rows of connected two-storey town houses facing Berney and flanking the simpler open entrance there. To eliminate the need for noisy and anonymous corridors, the blocks of one- and two-bedroom apartments are arranged around stairhalls opening directly to the outside; the front doors of the two units on each floor open directly onto the landing.* The doorways to each block of apartments—framed in cast stone or brick mouldings and sheltered by porch roofs—and the staircases are the most emphatic elements in the exterior design. The staircases are lit by tall strip windows (filled with glass blocks in some of the larger buildings), and to either side of these windows the apartment balconies branch out, each with a curved brick parapet or metal railing.

---

* This committee included Eric Arthur, Anthony Adamson, R.A. Fisher, J.A. Craig, and landscape architect Gordon Culham.

---

* A service stair behind each apartment connects with the kitchen.

138. *A block of four apartments*

Though the design of Garden Court is Moderne—with clean lines, bold emphases, and the occasional use of metal trim—it is also basically traditional: the sloping roofs of the larger blocks visible above their parapets, and the use of yellow brick with quoined corners, are as much Modernized Georgian (a popular style of the period) as Moderne. In Garden Court a convincing balance was struck between the image of the house and the patterns of residential apartment design. Dunnington-Grubb's landscaping completed the environment, giving Garden Court the atmosphere of a real home—totally unlike an apartment block to be endured until a house could be purchased. The Bayview portico—whose stylized cornice bears the name of the complex in sanserif letters of silvery Monel metal—offers the visitor a long vista that leads down three short flights of wide steps into a garden. Axial walkways across the garden, and another walkway around the edge of the terrace, connect with each of the apartment blocks. Ordered plantings of trees, shrubs, and flowers, and symmetrical plots of lawn, define this as a formal space that is also

relatively public, because it belongs to the community of residents in the surrounding buildings. But the large flower beds on the terrace level can be seen by the occupants of the ground-floor apartments almost as a personal possession.

As an experiment in residential design Garden Court was an immediate success; today it is still difficult to obtain an apartment there. Despite some disrepair (the result of postponed maintenance), it is a landmark in the community, its Moderne details giving distinction to the dull commercial strip of Bayview Avenue. But Garden Court is also important as a model for satisfying the ideals of home living and privacy in what is essentially apartment architecture. It has given food for thought to many architects of apartment complexes—most recently in the planning that developed the St Lawrence Neighbourhood (Plate 166)—and is a constant source of visual pleasure to its neighbours, and to passersby. Unfortunately there have been recent signs that it is threatened by developers of luxury condominiums.

THE SUNNYSIDE BATHING PAVILION
Lakeshore Boulevard West, at the foot of Colborne Lodge Drive
1921–3 by Chapman, Oxley & Bishop

Any photograph of downtown Toronto in the 1920s shows sedately dressed women, and men wearing hats and tightly-buttoned dark suits. Equally formal, and in most cases symmetrical and classical, was the architecture of its public buildings. The Sunnyside Bathing Pavilion—the centrepiece of a recreation area badly needed in the industrial city—is one such building, even though it was designed as a background for pleasure: swimming, strolling, courtship, or tea on the upper terraces. In grey-white stucco, which blurs the precision of line and moulding, and with arches and colonnades framing the vistas of the man-made beach on which it stands, the Pavilion has an almost magical quality. Its Italianate white columns, arches, and overhanging eaves were meant to foster a romantic mood and provide a generous scale to the lives of those who crowded Sunnyside Park and its beaches on summer weekends. Though the image it created, and the city's role as architectural patron, were perhaps aggressively paternalistic, the Pavilion was a popular recreational environment. (See Plate XXII.)

Until the beginning of the twentieth century the commercial and recreational uses of Toronto's lakefront and harbour were chaotically intertwined. The fire of 1904, however, provided an opportunity for reshaping the waterfront. The Harbour Commission, established in 1850, was reformed in May 1911 and vested with both ownership of, and responsibility for, twelve miles of lakefront property. In September 1912 the Commission submitted a scheme (expanding a 1909 plan of the Toronto Guild of Civic Art) for new commercial and recreational areas around the harbour, and new parkways. The First World War delayed most of the work at Sunnyside Park (named for a Gothic Revival villa erected by John Howard in 1845 on the eastern edge of his High Park estate), and the first major building, the Pavilion Restaurant, was not finished until 1917. Work began on the Bathing Pavilion in 1921, after landfill had created an immense level area and a sandy beach along the lakefront.

The Pavilion was planned with changing rooms for the swimmers around open courtyards on the lower beach level. (In the latest renovation the facilities have been replanned and the courtyards redesigned as tiled patios, with a fountain and plantings to create a Mediterranean atmosphere.) A long terrace-loggia above, with a covered centre section, provided seating space and a tea garden overlooking the lake. Finished in painted stucco over a brick and concrete structure, and open on three sides, with elegantly detailed high Palladian arches, the Sunnyside Bathing Pavilion is a palatial space cooled by shade as well as by passing breezes.

It was opened on 28 June 1922; a 300-foot pool (the ancestor of the present one) was added the next year. The Pavilion was one of several buildings along the Sunnyside section of the lakeshore that included the Palais Royale (1922), several buildings of an amusement park, and the Palace Pier (1927–32, by Craig & Madill). Sunnyside—called 'the city of light' in its heyday—prospered until the early 1950s, when urban expansion and the increase in easy car transportation drew away its clientele. By 1956 most of the buildings were derelict, and in 1957 the widening of Lakeshore Boulevard led to the demolition of everything but the Palais Royale and the Bathing Pavilion. The beginning of the Gardiner Expressway in 1959 added to the ruination of Sunnyside Park. For the next twenty years most of the Bathing Pavilion was unused and there were frequent proposals to tear it down, while the Parks Department allowed it to become more and more decrepit (stucco needs frequent care in Toronto's climate). Finally in the late 1970s the city decided to restore the building and to provide new facilities for the adjacent pool; only the upper terraces await restoration. The Sunnyside Bathing Pavilion is once more a popular summer haven.

140

HOLY BLOSSOM SYNAGOGUE

Bathurst Street at Ava Road (NW)
1936–7 by Chapman & Oxley, Maurice D. Klein,
Associate Architect

Holy Blossom is one of the most impressive religious buildings in Toronto. Its Romanesque style recalls the form of the third Holy Blossom on Bond Street (Plate 75) and the Mooresque style traditional for synagogues. But the eloquent severity of its arched façade and plain side elevations in poured concrete are rivalled by few other twentieth-century buildings.

By the end of the First World War the size of the congregation of the third Holy Blossom Synagogue had outstripped the available space. At the same time, so many of the members had moved to the city's northern suburbs that a larger building in a more convenient location was called for. The first plans were made in the early 1920s, and in 1926 Sigmund Samuel, son of Louis Samuel, one of the founders of the congregation, raised enough money to pay the outstanding mortgage and debts and start a new building fund. The Depression upset plans for a new building, and it was not until 1936 that rebuilding was possible. The major force at this time was Nathan L. Nathanson who, at a dinner party, encouraged his friends to match his own pledges and raised almost half the money needed. On Friday, 20 May 1937, the new temple was dedicated. The ceremony took place in the presence of Lord Tweedsmuir, Governer-General of Canada.

The new Holy Blossom was built on Bathurst Street in Forest Hill Village on the northwest edge of the city, where the crest of the hill north of St Clair Avenue offered panoramic views. The surrounding area—partly rural land in the process of development—promised to become a convenient centre for the congregation. Land was relatively cheap, and the site between Ava Road and Dewbourne Crescent allowed for a sprawling, free-standing building with room for later expansion. To display the entrance dramatically, and to provide sunlight on the main façade through most of the day, Chapman & Oxley placed the main block at a 45-degree angle to Bathurst Street, facing southeast. The classrooms and administration offices were located behind the auditorium, as well as in a two-storey classroom and assembly-room block running parallel to Bathurst Street that is connected to the auditorium at an angle marked by a five-storey bell-tower.

Chapman & Oxley—using an arrangement also found in the earlier Royal Ontario Museum façade—grouped the three entrance doors, and the rose window above that lights the auditorium, under a three-storey arch set deeply into a plain wall. The arrangement and the style owe much to John Wilson Siddall's early Holy Blossom on Bond Street, but the contemporary character of the design comes from the use of concrete. The exterior walls are built up in layers, with the rough bonding between them visible; both the colour and the texture of the concrete suggest the effects of stone. All the windows are straightforward cuts in the wall, made without elaborate

framing and mouldings while the concrete was being poured, but with interesting shapes, proportions, and groupings in pairs and triplets. Only around the entrance and the rose window was the concrete used to create decorative detail. Above the main arch a simple corbel cornice outlines the low gable, and a menorah cast in concrete ornaments the smooth wall. To either side of the arch a pierced lattice covers a stair window. The piers between the doors are topped by rampant lions, and the multiple circles of the rose window are set into a fine lattice of tracery filled with stained glass.

The Romanesque style of Holy Blossom is almost free of decorative and Mooresque elements, and alludes to its historical roots through simple forms. Nowhere is this more evident than in the galleried auditorium. This rectangular space—approximately twice as long as it is wide—has the stark simplicity of a Late Classicial basilica, with a tall arched apse at the west end and five unadorned, deeply arched bays dividing the side walls. Inset into each are side galleries, with narrow aisles on both levels. The tall upper passages are arched, complementing the taller arched stained-glass windows in the centre of each bay. Across the east end of the temple the gallery widens above the main floor vestibule; and in the southwest corner a transept, two bays wide, forms a chapel on the ground floor and a wider gallery above. The lower walls of the nave are finished in smooth plaster, lined in imitation of masonry; above, the surface is roughly stippled. The colour throughout is a pale creamy pink, varied on sunny days by splashes of transparent colour from the stained glass. The heavily beamed wooden roof provides a sheltering cover for the space. Based on actual Late Classical examples, it has open trusses set against a boarded inner roof, and its red-brown stain—with stencilled details on the beams in blue-red and white—gives it a presence that suits the strength and monumentality of the arched side walls. The western apse is neither wide nor deep, but its tall arch is set off and framed by a simple layered moulding. A flight of steps leading between the pulpits to the Ark, and a lattice screen of fine concrete framing the pierced oak doors of the Ark, give it the architectural importance its religious significance demands. The pulpits and steps, finished in a polished pink-beige marble, complement the lighter colours of the auditorium. Behind, on the screen, are relief panels of religious symbols with backgrounds of an intense sky blue—the colour of the vault of the apse, which is a metaphor for the Dome of Heaven.

Behind Holy Blossom is a distinct sense of history, expressed in simple, almost abstract forms. But its spirit and materials are also modern. The success of Chapman & Oxley's design lies in the serene austerity of its setting for celebration and worship.

141

THE BANK OF NOVA SCOTIA

44 King Street West at Bay Street (NW)

Conceived by John M. Lyle, 1929–36; erected after
redesign, 1946–51, by Mathers & Haldenby, with
Beck & Eadie as associates

The Toronto architect John Lyle was fascinated by skyscraper design. In 1922 he was one of four Canadian architects in the most famous architectural competition of the twentieth century, for the design of the Tribune Tower in Chicago. As Lyle became interested in a Canadian architectural style he con-cluded that Canadian architects were not being given suffi-cient opportunities to work, particularly in skyscraper design. Most of the plum commissions—especially for bank towers, such as the Bank of Commerce (Plate 117)—seemed to go to American firms. The Bank of Nova Scotia head office was for Lyle 'The Big Job', the design that would prove his faith both in the viability of Canadian architecture and in a Canadian style for skyscrapers.

The Bank of Nova Scotia was something of an outsider in Toronto banking circles because it had been founded in Halifax and did not establish its head office in Toronto until 1902. The first office was on the south side of King Street West, near Jordan. The chance to move to a location of real prominence at King and Bay came in 1929 when Canada Life announced plans to move to University Avenue. The building Lyle designed for the new site was 24 storeys high, rising cliff-like from Bay Street for maximum effect, with the height modelled into picturesque set-backs along the Bay Street façade. Like many towers of the period, the windows were grouped between tall buttress-like piers, and Lyle exploited the smooth stone surfaces as the background for an elaborate sculptural program of Canadian themes and subjects, styled in the Art Deco manner he had used in the decoration of smaller bank buildings, such as the Dominion Bank at Yonge and Gerrard (Plate 120).

Lyle's plans were presented in July 1930; but in the face of the Depression and the glut of rental office space in the downtown area, the project was first delayed and then shelved. Lyle continued to refine the design, but he died in December 1945 just as the project was being revived. In 1946 the Bank announced that it was at last in a position to carry out the project. It was handed over to Mathers & Haldenby, working in association with Beck & Eadie, Lyle's successor firm formed by his two principal assistants. After Mathers & Haldenby brought the technical aspects—the air conditioning and plumbing, etc.—up to date, they restyled the exterior almost completely. The basic massing of the 24-storey building remains as Lyle designed it, though Mathers & Haldenby smoothed away his Art Deco flourishes, leaving sleek vertical piers of smooth stone that were clearly influenced by buildings of the late 1930s, particularly Rockefeller Center in New York. The lower four storeys, housing the Banking Hall and some of the executive offices, address King Street with a pair of tall squared portals, while a long row of equally tall banking-hall windows and another entrance faced Bay Street. The height of the Bay Street façade is modelled to create overlapping layers that step forward at each end to form 13-storey pavilions. Facing King, the sheer rise of the façade is precipitously monumental and is crowned by the windows of the top floors, which are deeply recessed behind the surface of the piers to form a shadowed colonnade. Above the windows of the Banking Hall and the main entrances are sculptures of classical deities executed in the muscular style of late-1930s heroic realism.

Outside, the design is streamlined. Inside, the high entrance foyer that extends across the main façade and the long colonnaded Banking Hall form the most magnificent and sophisticated banking interior of the period in Toronto. In the vestibule, reliefs portray Canadian totem poles and symbols of industry, the crest of the Bank of Nova Scotia and of the

142. *The Banking Hall*

smaller independent banks it had absorbed; and a monumental inscription recording the Bank's history is placed high on the marble walls like a temple dedication. The hall is coloured in the beiges, browns, and sunset-mauve tones of marble, travertine, and modelled plaster, touched with the glitter of gold, silvery Monel metal, polished brass, and engraved glass. The climax of the space is a noble relief filling the north wall, designed by Donald Stuart, that commemorates the men and women and the industries of Canada and the foreign countries served by the Bank.

In 1983 the Bank of Nova Scotia announced plans to rebuild much of the surrounding city block. The complex, to be called Scotia Plaza on completion in 1986–7, preserves the Lyle-Mathers & Haldenby building next to a new 66-storey tower (838 feet), designed by Webb Zerafa Menkes & Housden, with a faceted façade clad in reddish brown granite and copper-tinted glass. The development is huge—1.6 million square feet, or 16 times the area of the lot.*

---

*By preserving the existing building, saving the adjacent National Club, re-using the terracotta façade of the Kay furniture store (1898 by G.S. Curry) that stood at 36–8 King, transferring already approved density from the Lakeshore area, and agreeing to assist the City in the building of low-cost housing, the Campeau Corporation as developer was able to accumulate floor-area bonuses that have made the new project the most densely designed in the city.

XXXVII. *The Toronto skyline in 1983. The most prominent buildings from left to right are: the CN Tower; the Sun Life Centre, shown here under construction; the renovated Queen's Quay Terminal Warehouse (Plate 160); the Royal York Hotel; the Toronto-Dominion Centre (Plate 149); First Canadian Place; the Royal Bank Plaza (Plate 152); Commerce Court (Plate 150); the condominium and hotel towers of the Harbourside/Harbour Castle development; and the Toronto Star Building at the foot of Yonge Street.*

THE CITY
IN THE LATER TWENTIETH CENTURY

Over the last quarter-century Toronto has undergone more visible changes than in any other short period of its history. Hundreds of fine old buildings vanished and the mid-century skyline of church spires, banks, offices, and two large hotels was engulfed and almost hidden by a dazzling downtown sculpture garden of towering shapes—black, silver, gold, and brilliant white. And scattered among the older blocks of brick and cement still standing were forms in mirror glass or metal sheathing or exposed structurals. But, thanks in part to a fiercely competent group of senior administrators at City Hall—half of them Scotch, it seemed—there were some ways in which Toronto did not change. It was still a relatively safe, clean, uncorrupted place, a city that worked, if not exactly like clockwork, then at least to the rhythm of the Protestant ethic that had prevailed since the time of Queen Victoria. (You can still find pedestrians who, if you step on their toes, will stare fixedly away pretending it never happened or even utter a nervous polite 'Sorry!') In most of its myriad cultures Toronto is a community of more or less middle-class domesticity, slightly repressed but comfortable. It is a good place to live, to visit, or just to look at. One visitor, Peter Ustinov, remarked that Toronto seemed to be a New York City run by the Swiss.

Toronto's recent urban history can conveniently be divided into three parts: a thesis of expansion and unrestricted growth from the late 1950s into the early 1970s; an antithesis of protest in favour of conservation in the balance of the seventies; and the synthesis that emerged from the interaction and conflict between the two during the 1980s.

In the first period the prevailing winds brought progress and a major restructuring of the urban landscape. Fuelled by population growth and the expanding economy, driven by the need to be liberated from the dead hand of conventional wisdom and the restricting exigencies of Depression, war, and post-war, the city's patrons, architects, planners, designers, and even *avant garde* visual artists such as Painters Eleven sought radical change in a new look, new buildings, a new community style for Toronto. 'Make no little plans' was their byword. If established traditions and old buildings had to be sacrificed in the process, then so be it. The vast fortress of the University Armouries was destroyed to make way for an addition to Osgoode Hall; the Dominion Bank's magnificent Roman temple at King and Bay and many other fine buildings were removed to provide the site for the Toronto Dominion Centre; the classic Registry Office and the heart of Chinatown gave way to the land for a new civic square and City Hall. For other demolitions there was usually no such excuse. The elegant Temple Building, Toronto's first skyscraper, for example, was replaced by the dull, near-anonymous Thomson Building; St Jamestown's hundreds of fine Victorian houses and large working-class community by a dozen bleak apartment towers and acres of dubious green space and concrete; and the fine early Victorian shops at the foot of Toronto Street by an appalling two-storey parking platform.

In 1965 the annual value of buildings erected in the city of Toronto alone had doubled from the over $100 million of 1960, and it more than doubled again in the 1970s to over half-a-billion dollars. Hungry for development and increased tax assessment, city councils of the 1960s eagerly assisted developers in their land assembly. 'Urban renewal' became synonymous with indiscriminate community destruction. As long as progress seemed to promise jobs and wealth, little concern was shown for neighbourhoods, the environment, or historic preservation. At its crudest the prevailing attitude was 'If something's old, tear it down; if green, pave it over.' In the

XXXVIII. *The Toronto skyline about 1953. The most prominent buildings from left to right are the Queen's Quay Terminal Warehouse (Plate 160), with its now-demolished west wing; the Royal York Hotel; the Toronto Star Building (demolished) on King Street West; the Bank of Nova Scotia (Plate 141); the Bank of Commerce (Plate 117); a cluster of banks at the intersection of King and Yonge, including the Dominion Bank (Plate 87) and the Traders' Bank (Plate 86); the King Edward Hotel (Plate 79); and the tower and spire of St James' Cathedral (Plate 19).*

name of economic necessity parking lots erupted like bombsites in the city core, a thousand petty festivals of free enterprise broke out along the main arteries, and the suburbs were turned into a dispiriting landscape of bland single-use tidiness on the one hand, and commercial-industrial chaos on the other—sprawling far into the lovely countryside, which became 'not city not country, but either spoiled', as Dickens first described such blight.

Toronto's subway was being expanded in three directions. The first part of the east-west line on Bloor opened in 1964 and the Yonge Street line was extended north from Eglinton. But the pride of the city's transportation system were the four great bypass highways ringing Toronto: the 401, the 427, the Gardiner, and the Don Valley Parkway, which enabled automobile and truck traffic to move quickly on the periphery of the city. The plan for the 1970s was to pierce the heart of residential areas in the centre of the city with expressways—the Spadina, the Crosstown, the Scarborough, and the Leslie Street extension—until no citizen's car would be more than a quarter-mile from six-lane speed and mobility.

Such rapid and indiscriminate change did not sit well with the spirit of Toronto's past or with that of the late sixties' culture, both of which were essentially conservative and conservationist. Community groups representing well-established professionals and old families, and those animated by community organizers in the poorer districts, joined forces in their common desire to save neighbourhoods and to prevent the loss of cherished landmarks. Affluent areas on the fringe of the city core, such as South Rosedale and the Annex, bullied their aldermen into giving them some of the controls they needed to protect themselves from the developers. Poorer neighbourhoods, if they could not fight City Hall and the developers to a standstill, made sure their blockbusting activities were as slow and expensive as possible. Pressure groups formed to stop the destruction of old buildings standing in the projected route of expressways. The preservation of the Old City Hall, which was scheduled for demolition in the first plans for Eaton Centre (Plate 158), and the cancellation of the Spadina Expressway in 1971, were the early crucial victories of these groups, and they were indicative of more to come.

In the 1972 election a loose coalition of community representatives—tory and radical alike—succeeded in gaining majority control of City Council, which put a temporary hold on the construction of all buildings over 45 feet in height and 40,000 square feet in area, until the Central Area Plan of 1976 imposed a set of permanent guidelines. The whole city became a demolition-control area, which meant that no residential building could be torn down without a specific vote of City Council, thus gaining time for negotiations that might lead to its being saved. Crucial to the city's well-being, of course, was that many great heirlooms of the past—such as the Royal Alexandra Theatre (Plate 80) and the Bank of Upper Canada (Plate 6)—were saved from destruction and rehabilitated for a new and vital existence by enlightened patrons of the post-modern era. But perhaps just as important was the new belief that not only the best century-old buildings should be deemed 'historical', but that recent streetscapes and ordinary buildings were worth cherishing to prevent the collective memory from being lost. With Council's support, the Toronto Historical Board increased their list of old buildings worthy of preservation from a few dozen to many hundreds—reflecting a fundamental change in approach from that of conserving only architectural masterpieces to that of finding new economic and social uses for every possible building and streetscape from all periods, including the contemporary.

In most of these actions the city was assisted by the provincial government, along with at least two provincial agencies: the Ontario Municipal Board and the Ontario Heritage Foundation. To stop a Metropolitan Council that was intent on building a network of expressways, Premier Davis simply ordered the cancellation of the Spadina. To prevent the federal government from distorting the city's growth and the ecology of a vast region to the northeast by the construction of a second airport at Pickering even grander than Montreal's Mirabel, the Premier—at the urging of a coalition of community groups and elected councillors from Toronto to Oshawa—withdrew provincial services from the proposed airport. The largest of all projected developments, that for the railway lands known as Metro Centre, foundered because the City owned the land under Union Station and therefore Metro Centre Developments was not free to tear it down.

Besides the provincial premier, with his final decision-making power over the city ('Mayor Bill', Davis was often called), and a small number of leading municipal politicians and developers, there are at least three persons whose crucial role in shaping Toronto of the 1970s and after should be noted. The 'red tory' David Crombie, mayor from 1973 to 1978, led City Council to adopt the new Central Area Plan of 1976 and seemed popular enough to have stayed in office forever had he chosen to. His successor as mayor (1979-80), John Sewell—community organizer, alderman, and writer on urban affairs for over twenty years now—had a vision of Toronto, a mastery of detail, and an ability to cut to the heart of an issue that made him one of the most influential city councillors in Toronto's history, though his absolute inner certainty contributed to his defeat as mayor. A New Yorker who became a Torontonian, the great urbanist Jane Jacobs—the most widely read author in her field in North America—gave to her adopted city the full benefit of her tough mind, generous heart, and consummate skill in community animation.

The work of these three people, along with that of their allies and followers, resulted in halting the march of mindless and destructive progress and channelling its energy towards more humane ends. All over Toronto in the later seventies there began a kind of microsurgery or invisible mending, filling in and sewing up the torn fabric of the city, almost imperceptibly renewing blighted areas and empty spaces and buildings. Set into the centre of the city were large condominium buildings that sometimes—as in the Renaissance Centre at Bloor and Avenue Road, with the hundred-year-old Church of the Redeemer nestled in the arms of its L—derived elegance from neighbouring structures and in turn dramatized older ones by providing new contexts. Sidewalks, not roadways, were now being widened, many of them dotted with planters and benches. Yonge, the central spine of the city—along most of its length, from Front Street to the city limits—became an attractive street for pedestrians. Another important reversal of urban history took place in 1974 when City Council, refusing to let Yonge Street be bathed in the bright glow of state-of-the-art sodium vapour lighting, opted to keep its old-fashioned incandescence. Toronto is thus one of the few remaining North American cities that shows soft lighting in the centre, even if wild midnight blazes of blue and orange are spotted throughout the suburbs.

XXXIX. *The Barton Myers house on Berryman Street, an innovative high-tech insertion into the Victorian streetscape of Yorkville.*

In the name of 'small is beautiful' and 'less is more' the city encouraged the construction of small apartment buildings and clusters of semi-detached houses instead of highrise towers. Parking lots gave way to miniature parks, large backyards were partly filled in with dwelling units (Dundas/ Sherbourne, Plate 163), industrial warehouses and factories were converted into offices (Berkeley Castle, Plate 169), or institutions like George Brown Community College. Canada's largest vaudeville and film theatre, the Imperial, was transformed by architect Mandel Sprachman, with its elegant original décor intact, into six smaller movie houses. Surplus firehalls, churches, and other public buildings, instead of being demolished, became theatres, daycare centers, community halls, and artists' studios. The city suspended its own set-back and minimum frontage by-laws so that architect Barton Myers could construct his experimental modern house among the old cottages of Yorkville on Berryman Street. Two new developments of the sixties— Boris Zerafa's miniature two-storey courtyard, Lothian Mews, and Gerald Robinson's shopping-cum-apartment building, The Colonnade—

unique at the time, were the forerunners of a host of experiments in multiple-use enclosed space.

Two of the city's traditional forms of transportation were given a new lease of life. Bicycles were provided with paths in Metropolitan parks and with a few designated routes on city streets. Instead of being phased out in favour of buses, Toronto's familiar 1938 PCC streetcars—the largest fleet of them in the world—were scheduled for replacement by a similar but more energy-efficient generation of 'red rockets' that would preserve this urban vehicle into the twenty-first century. It was an appropriate decision for the city that had originated the world's first electric streetcar, and whose financiers had prospered so mightily from exporting electric transit systems to other cities and countries. The subway system, along with more and better public-transit and service vehicles, and the establishment of the first few reserved bus lanes, all kept the TTC in the forefront of public transportation in North America. In 1984, for example, Toronto had 220 riders per capita on its system, Montreal 185, and New York and Chicago about 100 each; all other large cities, according to American Public Transit Association figures, rated below these four.

Private automobile traffic also increased steadily through the seventies and eighties, but—thanks in part to the huge computer for controlling traffic lights—never reached the proportions of E.B. White's nightmare: 'It was rush hour. Nothing stirred.' This traffic growth occurred chiefly in the suburban and exurban fringes of the city. While North York and Scarborough achieved some success in attracting new office development around their city halls, the great bulk of new construction was still occurring in central Toronto. And after a pause in the later seventies, development was speeding ahead faster than ever. The Central Area Plan of 1976, with its opportunities to developers for transferring density, its bonuses for preserving historic buildings and for providing assisted housing in conjunction with their new office towers, shaped and redirected the nature of development but did nothing to slow it down. A remarkable example of this was the proposed Bank of Nova Scotia development at King and Bay. With density transferred from its developer's land on the waterfront, and bonuses provided for incorporating the Bank's 1951 headquarters office building (Plate 141) in the new complex, the developer in 1985 gained fifty per cent more density than even the maximum 12-times coverage allowed under the old city plan of the 1960s. He can thus build to an unprecedented total floor footage of eighteen times the area of his site. The Bank of Nova Scotia development and proposals for the vast railway lands west of Union Station over to Bathurst Street revived the old debate about whether Toronto's public and private transportation systems—even with the many improvements proposed by

XL. *The Sun Life Centre—designed by Webb Zerafa Menkes & Housden and completed in 1985—on both sides of University Avenue at King Street West. Sculpture by Sorel Etrog.*

traffic engineers—could possibly handle the volume of goods and people seeking access, without destroying both old downtown neighbourhoods and traffic mobility in the city's core. The possibility of Toronto's still being a viable and humane city by the end of the century seemed once again precarious.*

In the meantime a host of other developments were initiated or completed in the 1970s and 1980s. There were glittering mirror-wall buildings on insurance alley—Bloor Street East near Church Street; the two towers at opposite ends of the Eaton Centre; the Hydro building and the Sun Life complex, more or less at either end of University Avenue; and the A.E. LePage building (Plate 176) east of Yonge and Wellington. A whole new wall of condominiums arose at Harbourfront (see p. 295). The CN Communications Tower, the world's tallest free-standing structure—at least for its first decade or so of existence—symbolized the energy, wealth, and expansion of the new Toronto. Each of Canada's five great chartered banks

---

*The ideas and program of the City reform movement of the seventies, far from losing their impact and relevance in the 1980s, pretty much became the conventional wisdom. Arthur Eggleton, the successor to Crombie and Sewell and well on his way to being the longest-serving mayor in Toronto's history, while rightly perceived as a careful politician of the extreme centre, is committed to the main goals that brought the reformers to power in 1972: neighbourhood protection and nourishment, mixed-use developments in the city core, an end to inner-city expressways, strong public transit, and the preservation of Toronto's past.

made a major change in the city's skyline with their towers near the corner of King and Bay.

Not all indications of growth pointed upwards, however. Manufacturing was increasingly driven out of the city, and even beyond Metro itself, as the price of land and other expenses of doing business soared. The growth in the service sectors in some ways more than compensated for this loss by maintaining a variety and quantity of employment in the central city—particularly important for those who lived there. But the search for new light industries was meeting only modest success in the 1980s. As expected, the City of Toronto's population, even with the thousands of new dwelling units being constructed, remained stable or possibly in slight decline, as it had from the 1960s, since the number of occupants per household was dropping steadily. But official projections for a huge increase in the population of Metropolitan Toronto proved to be excessive: it stabilized at around 2.1 million in the 1970s and 1980s. The chief growth areas were now in the outer edges of the greater Toronto urban region. Because of the low-density sprawl there, and because growth tended to outdistance sound planning in the provision of services, serious problems loomed not only for the suburbs but for the older inner city.

The most noticeable demographic change in post-modern Toronto was the increase in non-European immigrants. In 1981 the number of people of English ethnic origin in Metropolitan Toronto stood at 28 per cent, and of Italian at 12 per cent—still the two largest individual groups. They were followed by the Scots at 6.8 per cent, Irish at 5.4 per cent, Jewish 4.9 per cent, Portuguese 3.5 per cent, Greek 3 per cent, German 2.6 per cent, French 2.5 per cent, and Ukrainian and Polish almost 2 per cent each. But the 4-per-cent Chinese, the 3-per-cent Caribbean, and the 2½-per-cent Indo-Pakistani groups recorded in the 1981 census were certain to show the largest proportional increase in 1991. In the mid-1980s Toronto's sizeable numbers of Korean, Arab, Latin American, Filipino, Maltese, and Vietnamese immigrants, of Japanese-Canadians, of Canadian native peoples, and of peoples from many other countries clearly established the city as one of the most racially and culturally varied in the world. Among the noticeable effects of this was the mélange of languages to be heard on the streets and on radio and television; the numerous ethnic presses; the wealth of pavilions in the annual June multicultural festival (Caravan); the increasingly elaborate ethnic community events, such as the annual Caribana parade; and the appearance of a great variety of excellent restaurants.

Perhaps the most remarkable growth industry in the first quarter-century of post-modern Toronto has been that of culture and entertainment. The era has produced new television and radio stations, the only recent successful new North American daily newspaper founded in a metropolitan region, a major-league baseball franchise, at least two dozen professional theatres whose standard fare was Canadian plays (an unthinkable development even as late as 1960), and an increase in both the number of private art galleries and of merchants specializing in some aspect of service to the various cultural industries. In the city's future was a projected opera house and an enormous domed stadium.

All this naturally affected the patronage of architecture. The largest patron was the provincial government, whose contributions ranged from building the bland civil-service offices south of Wellesley and east of Queen's Park, and destroying early Toronto's finest large building, John Howard's 999 Queen Street West, to the creation of the popular Ontario Science Centre and Ontario Place (Plate 155), as well as the large public-housing ghettos in the Dundas-Parliament area. The province enlarged the Art Gallery of Ontario five-fold in the 1970s, added extensive new facilities to the Royal Ontario Museum in 1981, and contributed the biggest share of funds and much of the initiative to many of Metropolitan Toronto's cultural developments, including the Metro Zoo on the northeast fringe of the city.

The city's patronage included the brilliantly successful New City Hall (p. 143), the total reconstruction and rehabilitation of the St Lawrence Hall (p. 16), the two new theatres of the St Lawrence Centre, and the recovery of the old TTC building on Front Street for the Young People's Theatre. The city's most important contribution was the creation of Cityhome, the housing corporation designed to rehabilitate old buildings, to provide infill where necessary, and to construct whole new communities such as the St Lawrence Neighbourhood (Plate 166).

Apart from government, the largest employer and institution in the city was the University, whose mixed record of patronage was also important for shaping Toronto's character. In concert with the Massey Foundation, the University of Toronto was patron to one of the great new buildings of the period, Massey College (Plate 146). Among many other fine buildings, the University was directly responsible for the brilliant, brutal architecture of Scarborough College, for the knitting together of a group of old houses on the St George Campus into Innis College, and for the preservation of the old Toronto Public Reference Library and its rebirth as the University bookstore and student centre (Plate 83). But it was also possibly the most destructive developer of the 1960s in its assault on neighbouring areas to make room for the giant Robarts Library, the new Athletics complex, and various other buildings. 'Long Garth', the magnificent house given to the University by Sir Edmund Walker, was demolished for parking space.

XLI. *The Central YMCA (1984) on Grosvenor Street, designed by A.J. Diamond Architects.*

Through the work of private and public patrons, superb new facilities were built for the Central YMCA; for Toronto Symphony concerts and other musical events, the Roy Thomson Hall (Plate 171); and for the Canadian Opera Company, the Tanenbaum Centre, created from the shell of the old Consumers' Gas Works on Front Street. The extensive restoration and use by George Brown College of old factories and warehouses in the old Town of York was a great boon to the area. Several developers showed—in Hazelton Lanes and in the rest of Yorkville, for example—that by working in conjunction with the city it is possible to serve the needs of people in a humane way rather than by mindless acceptance of the demands of unrestricted profit or the exigencies of old city by-laws.

One of the best things Toronto did in the post-modern era was to turn again to the Bay and the Lake. The site had been chosen by Simcoe for his naval base and capital because of its protected harbour and the fine ship timber of the Don Valley. Peter Russell and his associates placed their homes and public buildings along the water's edge. For over a century Toronto's chief forms of outdoor recreation were sailing, canoeing, and sculling in the summer, and ice-boating, skating, and sleighing in the winter, when the unpolluted bay was always frozen; and the lake boats were Toronto's chief link with the outside world for both commerce and passenger traffic. But in the last third of the nineteenth century the railways sliced across the waterfront and cut the city off from it. After 1912 the Harbour Commission's filling of the Bay between Front Street and Queen's Quay made the waterfront even more inaccessible to pedestrians. Except for the Island ferry and pleasure boats, there was little recreational activity or interest for citizens in the waters of the Bay. Matters were made worse by the construction of the elevated Gardiner Expressway in 1959. Only on the Island and in the eastern Beaches did people maintain a vital and continuous relationship with their lakefront.

About 1972 when Harbourfront, Canada's first national urban park, was created (see page 295), Toronto's attitude to the potential of its waterfront changed. The pleasure park and leisure grounds of Ontario Place (Plate 155) and the Leslie Street spit attracted throngs of visitors. The community on Ward's Island, almost wiped out by deliberate municipal policy in the fifties and sixties, was given a stay of execution and a hopeful promise for its future by the city and the province. Into the vicinity of the harbour were clustered a new Convention Centre, two new hotels, the Toronto Star building, and a host of condominiums from Harbour Square to Arthur Erickson's King's Landing. The transformed Terminal Warehouse (Plate 160)—with its shops, apartments, restaurants, and Canada's first dance theatre—was one of the most exciting mixed-use complexes. At the western boundary of Peter Russell's Town of York a vast dome was planned—a shape echoing the clam-shell of Viljo Revell's council chamber in his New City Hall. And among the hundreds of boats skimming the Bay there appeared like a miracle the old Island ferry that had rotted for years in an Island lagoon. The *Trillium*, restored to life, once again carried holidayers out into the sweet air of the Lake and around the Island where Elizabeth Simcoe had once enjoyed the pleasures of the natural wilderness— and where for centuries before her the Indians had found it a soothing retreat and a place of magic healing powers.

143

NEW CITY HALL

Queen Street West at Bay Street (NW)
1958–65 by Viljo Revell;
John B. Parkin Associates, associate architects

The most important project a city undertakes is the building of its city hall. Toronto's present civic home—after more than twenty years still known as 'New City Hall'—is its fourth. The first, built in 1830–1, was little more than an adaptable meeting-room over a market, inherited from the Town of York when the city was incorporated in 1834. The second (Plate 11), built in 1844–5 by Henry Bowyer Lane, was a conservative Late Georgian building that provided an impressive image for a struggling young city, with its tower, public clock, and pedimented façades looking out on both the city and the harbour. The Romanesque third City Hall with its tower (Plate 76)—designed by E.J. Lennox, and the largest, most complex, most expensive building ever erected in the city when it opened in 1899—represented the functioning heart of the turn-of-the-century city. Viljo Revell's New City Hall was commissioned in 1958, when Toronto was well into an economic boom and an era of self-confidence comparable to that which began in the late 1890s when Lennox's building was completed. Its impressionist melding of modern technology and material with a semi-abstract aesthetic was completed just as the construction of new skyscrapers like the Toronto-Dominion Centre (Plate 149) began to transform the city's business core. The New City Hall is a worthy successor to the monuments of the Victorians and the Edwardians—an enduring civic symbol that is also one of the world's great buildings.

Despite some initial disputes, E.J. Lennox's City Hall was immensely popular with Torontonians. Even before the building was completed, however, the city had begun to extend its functions into new areas of planning, services, and social welfare and it soon became clear that more civic office space would be needed. There was also a growing feeling that Lennox's Romanesque Revival building was old-fashioned for a city that was striving to be a modern Canadian metropolis.

The first agitation for a new city hall came from the architects, patrons, and civic politicians associated with Toronto's support for the international City Beautiful Movement. John M. Lyle crystallized the idea in his 1911 proposal (prepared for the city-sponsored Civic Improvement Committee) for Federal Avenue, to run north from Union Station (see page 211) to Queen Street West. Here a great plaza was to be opened on the north side of the block between Bay and Elizabeth Streets, between Lennox's City Hall and the east fence of the Osgoode Hall garden—the site today occupied by the New City Hall. The ideas behind Lyle's scheme, however, produced only the new Registry Office on the west side of the site in 1914–17 to designs by Charles S. Cobb. Fully Beaux Arts in its marble walls and Ionic portico, it was designed to

fit eventually into a future city hall scheme, such as the one Lyle had proposed. But City Council concentrated on its other projects for schools, bridges, roads, and services until finally the dislocation caused by the First World War made such an immense project impossible.

During the next fifty years thoughts of a new city hall were never abandoned; both the growth of the city bureaucracy and periods of prosperity encouraged new proposals. In 1927 Alfred Chapman presented a design for the same Queen Street site that Lyle had outlined; and in 1929 the Report of the Advisory City Planning Commission (which was more concerned with road- and transportation-planning) made the same suggestion. With the onset of the Depression, the building of a new city hall became an impossibility, and so it remained throughout the years of the Second World War. During the war, however, City Council began to anticipate the possibility of a boom that might follow the coming of peace, making the first plans for the subway system, and returning to active consideration of a new city hall.

In 1946 Toronto's voters approved in a plebiscite the purchase of the land bounded by Bay, Queen, Chestnut, and Hagerman Streets—the site originally proposed by Lyle in 1911—for a new city hall fronted by a civic square. Architectural planning began in June 1953, when three of Toronto's leading architectural firms—Marani & Morris, Mathers & Haldenby, and Shore & Moffat—were engaged to co-operate on a design for a new building. Marani & Morris and Mathers & Haldenby both represented the conservative side in Canadian architecture and the design presented in 1955 was in the dry, stripped Classical style that both firms were providing to banks and government departments at the same time. Although City Council had asked for something 'bold' and 'fresh' when they retained their architects, the immediate opinion was that the design was exactly the opposite: dull, heavy, and monotonous, and uninteresting in both structure and materials—more suitable for an insurance company than a city hall. The proposed design was budgeted at a fairly conservative 18 million dollars; but the entire project had to be approved by a general plebiscite of Toronto voters.

The controversy that greeted the designs prepared by Marani & Morris *et al.* stemmed less from the design itself than from the dissatisfaction felt by many people in the Toronto arts community at the extremely slow acceptance of Modernism and its forms in Toronto. The design's stripped Classical monumentality and conservative inspiration seemed to typify the 'Old Guard' that dominated painting, architecture, and the other arts in the city. Nowhere was this feeling stronger than among the young members of the architectural profession—especially in the University of Toronto's School of Architecture, where architectural Modernism, particularly the International Style, was presented not only as the most rational of architectural systems but as the best solution to all social and cultural needs. The Modernists were astute propagandists and the logic of their ideas made their criticism difficult to refute. When the principal Toronto daily papers took up the argument, there was little City Council could do to support its case for the proposed design. In the plebiscite that followed in 1955, the whole scheme was rejected. However, Mayor Nathan Phillips and a majority of City Council remained convinced of the need for a new city hall, and had been persuaded by the controversy that a Modern design was the only possible solution. Another plebiscite was held in December 1956, and thanks to Phillips' tireless campaigning, and a scaling down of the projected costs from $18 to $13 millions, approval was finally given by a narrow majority.

Since there was no consensus on who should design the new city hall, Council had adopted a resolution to establish a competition open to the architects of the world to find a striking design. This was Toronto's third competition for a city hall and it had the great advantage of creating tremendous publicity for the city itself, putting it on the architectural map in a way that perfectly matched the boosterism of contemporary politics. The professional assessor, the guide for the Mayor and Council through the by-ways of Modernism, was Professor Eric Arthur of the School of Architecture. The choice implicitly signified that a winning design would have to adopt a modern vocabulary, while also seeking to give the mundane facts of government and bureaucracy an unmistakeable image. Image and form were paramount, since the design was certain to stand or fall on public reactions as influenced by the press and other opinion-makers.

Accordingly, the conditions for the competition called for only a few expressive drawings, and emphasized the use of a scale model that would be both immediately understandable to the general public and easy to display or present through photographs. Submissions were requested by 18 April 1958 (a generous time period to allow as many foreign entries as possible), and the jury was chosen with a careful eye to the international status of the competition. It included Eric Arthur and Gordon Stephenson, representing the local architectural and planning professions, the Vancouver architect C.E. Pratt, as well as three architects of international reputation: Eero Saarinen (USA), Ernesto Rogers (Italy), and Sir William Holford (Great Britain). While Council and Nathan Phillips hoped the competition would make a major splash in the architectural world, they and the jury could hardly have foreseen that the competition would become one of the largest in modern times, with a final list of entries totalling 510 submissions from 42 countries. Seven designs were chosen from the first round of the selection process and the architects were asked to refine their design and elaborate their presentations. This group included I.M. Pei, who was later

to have dramatic impact on Toronto with the design of Commerce Court (Plate 151), and Australian architect John Andrews and Macy Dubois working together, both of whom later made major contributions to Toronto architecture.* The winner in the second stage of the competition was Viljo Rewell (1910–64),** working with Bengt Lundstein, Heikki Castren, and Seppo Valjus.

All of the winning first-round designs showed strong unforgettable architectural character, but offered very different solutions to the requirement for a public square over underground parking in front of the building, and to the question of dynamic symbolism for the main features of city government: Council Chamber, offices, and public areas. Revell's design was greeted with some dismay when it was announced as the final choice on 26 September 1958; it was clearly the most abstract of the seven semi-finalists—both in concept, with the paired office towers partially wrapping the saucer-shaped Council Chamber, and in the actual presentation, where the drawings and the model made only the basic ideas clear and ignored the multitude of specifics necessary for a working building. But thanks to the design's sculptural quality, the building could be seen and understood both as a striking landmark and as an ideal symbol for the city that chose to build it—one that could not be forgotten once it had been seen, and could never be dwarfed by the growing city, no matter how high the surrounding buildings might become. The Modernists had done their job well in preparing both the press and the public to accept a building the likes of which they had never seen before.

Formal agreements were signed with Revell in April 1959 and he opened an office in Toronto in association with the John B. Parkin Partnership to handle the construction. During the next two years Revell made several refinements to his design, rearranging office accommodation that had originally been placed around the Council Chamber, reshaping the office towers, and replanning the civic square. Some of these changes were made in response to criticism voiced during the final stage of the competition, but the central character of the design remained intact. Finally on 7 November 1961 (Nathan Phillips' birthday) the first sod was turned. During construction a second competition was held for the design of furniture appropriate to the new building's interior. Eric Arthur was again chairman of the committee. The costs involved made the special commission of furniture one of the most controversial aspects of the project, but ultimately the furniture, produced in Canada by the American firm of Knoll International, proved indispensable to the effect of the overall design.

Revell died a few months before the completion of the building. Nathan Phillips, who was retired by the electorate

---

* Andrews later designed Scarborough College (1966); Dubois, in partnership with Robert Fairfield, designed New College, University of Toronto (1964 and 1967).

**His name was later respelt Revell so Canadians could pronounce it correctly.

before the opening, had already received the ultimate honour in return for his devotion to the project: in 1961, as construction on the new civic square proceeded, Council unanimously designated it Nathan Phillips Square. The New City Hall was officially opened on 13 September 1965 by Governor-General Georges Vanier; and the final touch was added on 27 October 1966, when Henry Moore's 'Three-Way Piece No. 2' (better known as 'The Archer') was unveiled in the square.* This last gesture was just as controversial as the first steps towards construction had been. Council was tentative about abstract sculture and even more so about what the public would say. But ultimately, the affection of Torontonians for both Revell's building and the sculpture in front speak eloquently of the City's coming of artistic age—discarding the smug narrowness of the 1950s for the more sophisticated (though often equally smug) attitudes it has cultivated since.

The New City Hall was startlingly unlike anything that Torontonians expected a city hall to look like. And yet its abstract, sculptural qualities co-exist with a fine understanding of the way cities like Toronto operate with regard to the public, and with a superbly rational sense of arrangement and planning. The building is divided into three basic parts: a podium, a council chamber, and two office towers. The two floors of the podium house the offices of the mayor, the aldermen, and such services as the Births and Deaths and Weddings Registry and the Municipal Reference Library, to which the public need everyday access. Virtually all of the outside walls are floor-to-ceiling glass panels. The long curve of the south front, with the two main entrances, is set back under an overhanging roof supported by tall concrete columns to form a protected entrance at ground level and a covered walkway from east to west along the north side of the square. Visitors approaching the main door can look up and see the mayor at work in his suite of offices, and through massive wooden doors (hung so that they can be easily opened) enter a great foyer whose openness and accessibility characterize the civic process in Toronto. The foyer widens to a square, with high clerestory windows, surrounded by open balconies that lead to second-floor offices and committee rooms. Though there is little detail, and the over-all grey colour** is uninteresting, the eye is attracted and held by the column that grows and spreads like a great mushroom from a sunken and carpeted amphitheatre at the centre of the space to support the Council Chamber overhead. Here certainly is the structural and material virtuosity that the Modernist critics of the Marani design desired. To either side curving stairs with massive handrails of multi-ply wood lead up to the sec-

144. *The Council Chamber*

ond floor; beyond are banks of elevators that service the office towers.

Like many other designers in the competition, Revell was fascinated by the possibility of dramatic changes in level. The podium became a stage on which was poised the free-standing saucer-like council chamber—housing the representative functions of City Hall—embraced by two curving glass-faced office towers containing its administrative functions. A wide ramp* swoops up from the civic square to the top of the podium, providing ceremonial access to doors that lead directly into the Council Chamber, which is commonly approached from elevators in the foyer. The interior is arranged like an amphitheatre under a 155-foot-wide low concrete dome and echoes the unforgettable image of the exterior. Three quarters of the pod is devoted to the council chamber. Revell designed it as a Greek theatre** whose curved perimeter rises in tiers of public seating that focus on the horse-shoe arrangement of alderman's desks, which in turn focus on the mayor's desk, raised slightly higher on a dais. A broad walkway runs around the top of the amphitheatre past boxes reserved for the press and offers a continuous view through the chamber's perimeter windows of the podium and the city beyond. (Few council chambers provide such an expanse of

---

* City Council refused to pay for the sculpture and the other art Revell had planned as an integral and necessary part of the building and the square; but fortunately a number of Toronto philanthropists, led by Mrs Amy Stewart, both personally and through her involvement with the McLean Foundation, arranged to donate the Moore piece itself.

** Revell intended it to provide a background for colourful works of art.

---

* The ramp is rarely used today except by strollers who find that the roof of the podium is a spacious platform from which to view the city centre. This platform unfortunately lacks creative landscaping and most of it is now used for a fitness-training facility. A summer wine garden or an all-year restaurant have been suggested for the space.

** Its Classical Greek heritage was considered by Revell to be particularly appropriate for the meeting-place of a civic democracy.

window without distracting from the business meetings at hand.) The south wall, ornamented by black wrought-iron representations of the crests of the City of Toronto and Metropolitan Toronto, neither rises fully to the curving concrete ceiling, nor extends to the side walls, where it would interrupt the perimeter windows; instead it divides—like a theatrical backdrop—the chamber from the lower-level alderman's foyer and the upper-level aldermen's lounge, without intruding on the visitor's sense of the structure's unusual shape.

The form and position of the Council Chamber represent in romantic and idealistic terms the importance of the institution of City Council. The paired office towers, which house the civic bureaucracy, curve to shelter the Chamber. They are unequal in height: the east tower rises 326.5 feet above street level in 27 storeys, and the west tower rises 260.5 feet above street level in 20 storeys. Along its curve the west tower is approximately 225 feet long—about 100 feet shorter than the curve of the east tower. The arrangement allows maximum western sunlight to flood into the space between the towers and reach the façade of the east tower. The outer faces of the towers are entirely of poured-in-place concrete, ribbed vertically to create a shell-like structure that is immensely strong: the walls were specifically designed to resist wind stresses and the curves increased their strength. The individual floors extend from the curved walls as immense shelves of space, with supporting beams braced by a row of piers. This arrangement allows the inside walls of the towers to be an uninterrupted curtain of glass where no structure can obscure the light or the view. Few architects in Canada have since dared to exploit the possibilities of modern concrete and modern structural dynamics in such an adventurous way. The private offices coveted by senior staff are placed along the windowless back wall of each tower, where they receive their natural light indirectly through glass partitions hung with mesh draperies. The panorama of light and view belongs to secretaries and junior staff, who in traditional office design are usually cut off from windows. Unfortunately on sunny afternoons the public servants in the east tower are cooked by extreme heat that no air-conditioning or improvised baffles have yet been able to moderate.

Classical architectural ideas freely inspired the amphitheatre of the Council Chamber and the long curved colonnade sheltering the front entrances of the podium. Though Revell had little interest in Classical forms *per se*, he had a great interest in the society that had given birth to them. This indirect interest is prominent in the design of Nathan Phillips Square; no architectural comparison in Toronto could be more instructive about the importance of an architect's attitudes to his buildings than that of Nathan Phillips Square and its near contemporary, the plaza of the Toronto-Dominion Centre. Mies was even more a Classicist than Revell, but his vision of a Modern architecture imbued with Classical ideas was formalist; it had relatively little to do with the welfare of the people who used

his buildings on a regular basis, as the severity of the T-D Centre's plaza amply demonstrates. In Nathan Phillips Square Revell placed the City Hall podium at the far north end of the site in order to leave as much open area in the Square as possible and to allow a clear view of Old City Hall on the east side of Bay Street. The abstract stillness of the City Hall's composition is complemented by the comings and goings of citizens in the square and, at the south end, by the play of fountains on the rectangular pool in summer and the steady circling of skaters when the pool becomes a wintertime rink. Meanwhile, the three giant concrete arches overhead echo the curves of the building and its towers. With its benches, sculpture, and 'Peace Garden,' the square also affords a pleasant space for people to stop awhile to meditate or watch the passing scene. Unlike most designers competing in 1958, Revell did not let the square flow onto the surrounding sidewalks, but set it back from Queen and Bay beyond areas of lawn. Outlining it is a walkway raised on concrete columns (it is now connected by a bridge to the Sheraton Centre on the south side of Queen).

The structure of the colonnade, which has very little detail and is easily missed, functions exactly as did the colonnades surrounding the market-places and forums of ancient Greece and Rome. Its summer shade, and winter shelter from wind, snow, and rain are important amenities. Like its Classical forebears it outlines the space and gives it a positive identity. To this is added a particularly North American purpose, for without tightly enclosing the square and cutting it off from the surrounding city—which would reduce the Square's value as a civic meeting space—the colonnade manages to keep street traffic and chaos at bay, at least visually. Along the west side of the square, both inside and outside the line of the colonnade, Revell developed dense plantings of low trees, the most interesting of which provides a secluded seating area washed with sunlight but effectively secluded from the activity of the square. The result is one of the few civic plazas created in a modern city to capture the hearts of citizens. During the summer much of the passing show that our winters confine to the interiors of the Eaton Centre and the underground mall system moves outside to Nathan Phillips Square. And year round it is the focus for ethnic festivals, civic and artistic events, and rallies of celebration or protest. The City Council of 1958 almost certainly envisioned a more formal, calmer and duller space. It is to Viljo Revell and his humanistic concept of ancient and modern city forms, and of urban life itself, that Toronto owes the success of its civic square. Without it the building would have been forever incomplete.

The New City Hall is Revell's masterpiece. But it is far more important as a civic symbol. Virtually from the day it opened it has attracted people as an agreeable place to be, as the natural setting for civic activities, and as the quintessential Toronto image. It is truly the living centre of the city.

145. *The components of Revell's design for the New City Hall—plaza, podium, Council Chamber, and towers—seen from the top of First Canadian Place.*

271

146. *Massey College, looking north-east.*

MASSEY COLLEGE

6 Devonshire Place, at Hoskin Avenue (NW)

1960–3 by Ron Thom

Massey College was the last gift of the Massey family and the Massey Foundation to the University of Toronto. Its quadrangle of ruddy orange brick and soft beige stone, overhung with trees and vines, provides the ideal shelter for a community of established scholars and graduate students engaged in research; one that tempers and quiets, but never excludes, the invigorating and sometimes disturbing influences of the campus, the city, and the twentieth century. Partly inspired by the colleges of Oxford and Cambridge, the plan includes a quadrangle, whose fountains mask the traffic noise and cool the summer air; a gate house and bell tower; and a dining-hall on the second floor that becomes the dominant feature because of its corona of stained glass set in a cage of concrete and stone. But the unique modern detail created by its

architect, Ron Thom—from an admixture of references to Japan, Britain, modern West Coast houses, and to the early-twentieth-century work of Frank Lloyd Wright— firmly locate it in the twentieth century it was meant to serve.

From the beginning it was Vincent Massey who defined the image of the college. The sources were English, but the purposes were more general, as outlined in a statement given to the competing architects:

> It is of great importance that [the College] should in its form reflect the life which will go on inside it, and should possess certain qualities—dignity, grace, beauty, warmth. Such a college as we have in mind possesses antecedents in various countries, and whatever their physical forms may be or the date of their erection, they have a character in common. What we

272

wish is a home for a community of scholars whose life will have intimacy but at the same time, academic dignity.

The formal donation of Massey College to the University was made on 14 December 1959. But its creation had been considered as early as 1 April 1957 (in a letter from Vincent Massey to his brother Raymond), and active planning had begun in January 1959. The gift was accepted on 17 December 1959—though not without criticism from those who thought its basic ideals anachronistic in the modern multiversity that the University of Toronto was becoming, if not 'colonial' or fundamentally élitist. Since its function in the university was rather like that of All Souls College, Oxford, critics dubbed it 'Half Souls College, Toronto'. As had been the case with Hart House (Plate 105), the question of design was left to the Foundation, on which Vincent Massey's son Hart and his nephew Geoffrey—both of whom were practising architects—now served. The program was defined fairly exactly. The site was 100 feet by 150 feet; the building was to be arranged around a quadrangle with suites for Senior Fellows drawn from the University faculty, spacious rooms for the Junior Fellow graduate students, a dining-hall seating 100, a large and small chapel (only one was built), plus library, common rooms, Master's Lodge, and other spaces.

What was not clear from the beginning was the overall character of the College: was it to be traditional Gothic or Georgian Revival, like other Massey commissions, or more modern and experimental? Both Geoffrey and Hart Massey wanted the College to have a distinctly modern look, and a proposal was made that they should design the building together—an idea that was quickly rejected because of 'legal and practical problems'. Finally on 1 February 1960 a limited, very private competition was organized, and four architects were invited to submit designs: Ron Thom (then working with the Vancouver firm of Thompson, Berwick & Pratt), Arthur Erickson (also practising on the West Coast), Carmen Corneil from Toronto, and John B. Parkin Associates (also from Toronto, and the leading firm in the country). Each architect was to receive $3,000 for his work on the designs, and each was brought to Toronto to meet with the Foundation. Designs were to be presented at Vincent Massey's Port Hope estate by June 1960. After each design was considered, Carmen Corneil and Ron Thom were asked to submit revised plans (which were now to include a bell tower, as well as two special guest rooms), with a scale model and elaborate perspective of the principal interiors.

Only Thom's designs fleshed out the functional program with an architecture that would foster the spirit Massey College was meant to represent. His first version was strongly influenced by the broad-roofed forms and overhanging eaves of Frank Lloyd Wright's early domestic work—the same patterns that influenced Thom's first houses on the West Coast. In the final revision many such references were smoothed away to create a design with an enjoyable ambiguity that was immediately evident when the building was opened. Massey

147. *The west side of the quadrangle.*

College is both modern and traditional, public and private. Its scale can seem large (almost monumental) in the public rooms, or intimate—particularly in the houses of the residence, with their mullioned casements and walls of warm brick with details of wood.

The key to the spirit of Massey College as laid down by Vincent Massey—and also to the plan of the finished building—is the north-south quadrangle. Long and relatively narrow, it rises slightly towards the north, and three of its sides are defined by the five interconnected blocks or houses of suites and rooms, each unit having a façade that steps back irregularly from a central doorway. Along the south side of the quad are the main Common Room, with the Dining Hall above, as well as the libraries, kitchens, and other subsidiary rooms, with the Master's Lodge, and the main gate and porter's lodge, tucked in at the southeast corner. In front of the windowed north wall of the Common Room the lower part of the quadrangle forms an irregular plaza paved in limestone slabs that wraps around and bridges the pool, whose fountains add movement and sound to the architectural forms in both summer and winter. Rising out of the pool and supporting part of the porch roof of the Common Room and Dining Hall is the bell tower, which regulates much of the College life and schedule. It consists of a series of juxtaposed but separate walls or planes of brick. Clustered together, each at right angles to its neighbour, they rise higher and higher towards the centre, the tallest two becoming a pierced lattice of stone that supports the College bell. Like much of Thom's detail in the College, the bell tower is clearly modern, though picturesque in a traditional way: it is the pivotal feature at the intersection of the paths leading into the complex from the outside and from the houses into the Dining Hall and Common Room.

Behind the tower the Common Room overlooking the fountain pools, the Dining Hall above, and the two-storey stairhall between them form the heart of the College. The Common Room—warm and comfortable in brick, wood, and leather—is very much a living-room. It is influenced by the domestic work of Frank Lloyd Wright, particularly in the design of the raised ceiling over the central section, and of the two seating areas on either side, which are placed two steps lower and overlook the enclosed garden to the south and the pools and quadrangle to the north. The stone staircase to the Dining Hall—with its slow, dignified rise around the free-standing fireplaces—also owes much to Wright, as does the second-floor fireplace, with its abstract sculptural arrangement of brick and stone masses. But the spirit of the Dining Hall is romantic, surrounded as it is by a stone lattice of clear and coloured glass that fills the upper half of the walls. As the campus darkens in the evening the Dining Hall, elevated above its surroundings, shines from within the walls of the College as a beacon in the community.

The quadrangle is completely separated from the surrounding streets, and indeed seems separate from the rest of the campus. Yet the outer walls of the College are not forbidding. A series of wall sections, or planes, step in and out to form a broken perimeter line, and tall window slots break up the planes into smaller units—adding at night accents of light along the smooth, dark façade. Where the College looks out on the University (on Devonshire Place at Hoskin) the main gate of wrought iron frames an enticing view of fountains and quad. Above the gate is the bull's-head crest of the College, and at the top of the gate-tower, to make it a landmark on the street, Thom provided a metal grille that is back-lit at night. On Hoskin Avenue vines and overhanging branches from the gardens of the Master's Lodge spill over the top of the wall, providing abundant greenery along the traffic-laden streets.

Massey College was the final monument created by the patronage of Vincent Massey, who approached architecture with a deeply felt belief in its potential to shape perceptions and to influence lives. Since the early 1960s the whole idea of patronage—particularly when it is based on a well-defined program and on detailed criticism of proposed designs—has been frequently rejected by architects and critics, who believe that only trained professionals should influence the basic aesthetics of a design. When it was completed in 1963 Massey College was criticized as old-fashioned and retrogressive—even as an evil influence that set back Canadian architecture fifty years. But in 1986 there can be little doubt that it has stood the test of time. Far more than other Toronto buildings of its period, it is entirely functional; it is beautiful in a way that is immediately understandable and enjoyable; and it stands as a serene and pleasing addition to the urban landscape. Vincent Massey could have had no better memorial than Ron Thom's masterpiece, Massey College, a marvellous place in which to live and study. In the 1980s, when Canadian architecture is opening up as never before to a wide range of historical, personal, and theoretical influences, Massey College is one of the best examples in Toronto of architecture's creative possibilities.

148. *The bell tower.*

149. *The Toronto-Dominion Centre, with the Bank of Montreal tower in the upper left, Commerce Court (Plate 150), and the towers of the Royal Bank Plaza (Plate 152) on the right behind the Royal York Hotel.*

THE TORONTO-DOMINION CENTRE

King Street West at Bay Street (SW)
1963–9 by John B. Parkin Associates, Bregman & Hamann;
Mies van der Rohe, Architectural Consultant

Ludwig Mies van der Rohe (1886–1969), one of the heroes of modern architecture, is listed only as a design consultant* for the first stages of the Toronto-Dominion Centre. But its towers of black steel and dark bronze-tinted glass—precisely proportioned, and set like minimalist sculpture on a podium—declare his influence.

Working with the elements of high-rise architecture developed in the U.S.—a supporting steel skeleton with an infill of glass or window—Mies (as he is usually known) achieved an abstract purity in his structural system of horizontals and verticals to create open interior spaces than can be manipulated to serve almost any need. He insisted on the finest materials; and his belief in the principles 'less is more' and 'God is in the details' led to scrupulous attention to planning and execution. Thanks to the patronage of Phyllis Bronfman Lambert, Mies was chosen to design New York's world-famous Seagram Building (1954–8), which revolutionized corporate architecture in North America. Seagram's owners were the Montreal-based Bronfman family, who also controlled the Fairview Corporation (now Cadillac-Fairview), one of the largest property developers in North America. Fairview was beginning to reshape the centres of several Canadian cities and their plans included a major project for downtown Toronto. At the same time the Bank of Toronto, which had amalgamated with the Dominion Bank in 1955 to create the Toronto-Dominion Bank, decided to highlight the change by developing a new head-office complex. This followed bank practice: the Bank of Toronto's 1862 office at Wellington and Church Streets (by William Kauffman, demolished) had marked its initial prosperity, and its 1911–13 temple by Carrère & Hastings, on the southwest corner of King and Bay, had announced its status as a leader of Edwardian banking. In the early 1960s Mies was (as Carrère & Hastings had been fifty years before) one of the most famous and respected architects in the world: the Bank and Fairview gave him virtually a free hand to create the Toronto-Dominion Centre.

The developers assembled most of the surrounding city block—the largest land assembly to that date in Toronto—and the magnificent Carrère & Hastings building was demolished. A plaza paved in grey granite was laid out across the site, serving as a platform for the development; underneath is a network of shopping corridors, underground parking, and provision for all necessary services. Atop the plaza, like geometrical sculpture on a display table, rise a three-storey banking pavilion near the intersection of King and Bay, and, to the south-west, a 54-storey tower, 725 feet high. Broad steps approach the tower from Wellington Street, and on the north side the plaza spreads out level with King Street. The ambitious scale of these buildings helped to trigger a cycle of redevelopment that transformed the physical character of downtown Toronto, reshaped its skyline, altered the city's image, and set new models for urban architecture across Canada.

In phase two of the project the Royal Trust Tower was built on the west side of the forecourt, its mass and height balancing the transparent pavilion of the banking hall to the east. A third tower (the Commercial Union) was added later at the north-east corner of Wellington and York, and in 1985 a fourth, the IBM Tower, on the south side of Wellington. (This last tower repeats the forms of the first three, but it is an extraneous element because of its site.)

Although he used the most modern technology to build his steel-and-glass skyscrapers, Mies was greatly influenced by the character and discipline of Classical design. The podium of grey granite forms a base of rough texture and manifest strength for the towers above, while throughout the buildings the component parts of post and beam display the integrity and structural importance of the columns and cornices of a Classical temple. The Classical influence is most apparent in the single-storey banking pavilion; but the spare and elegant balance of verticals that support and horizontals that brace and connect is also fundamental to the soaring towers. Mies related the height of each tower to its width and depth in a strict proportional system, and all the other features of the design are similarly balanced. The roughness and strength of the grey granite floors and of the beige travertine walls in the ground-floor lobbies complement the transparent glass-curtain walls and strong but smooth load-bearing black-painted steel frame. Within this frame the details are worked out with a precision that surpasses the requirements of structural support in order to highlight the parts that are most important. The main verticals—the ones that stand for essential structure—are smooth and unencumbered; the window mullions, which carry only the weight of the glass panes, are more ornamental, overlaid with steel I-beams that throw shadow patterns across the smooth surfaces. The glass-curtain walls are sleekly neutral—bronze-tinted to appear almost black from a distance—and each panel of glass is fitted with integral

Venetian blinds to conceal the various drapery patterns in the interior.

Because no detail was too small for the attention of Mies and his design team, the Toronto-Dominion Centre shows—as few other large buildings in Toronto do—a modern architect's superb control over his materials and architectural vocabulary. The T-D Centre more than amply repays observation of its composition and design. Unfortunately it is less successful as a major addition to a functioning city whose downtown depends in large part on pedestrian traffic. The dark towers cast gloomy, chilling shadows, and produce unnaturally strong winds through the spaces between, making the plaza uncomfortable on all but the warmest and calmest days of summer. In addition the plaza weakens the definition of the streetscape, in some places obliterating it altogether, substituting for a well-defined sidewalk a vast open space of vague dimensions that dwarfs all who attempt to cross it. Only on the steps and the upper terrace to the south (facing Wellington Street) does the architecture show an affinity with the street, allowing visitors to establish a clear relationship between their own size and that of the building. The plaza environment can be so daunting that even in fine weather many people walk close to the banking pavilion and the towers—not simply for protection but for reassuring proximity to the walls and the semi-reflections in the windows.

In 1985 the Toronto-Dominion Bank and Cadillac-Fairview Corporation made a concerted effort to mitigate the bleakness of the plaza and alter its aura of a sterile no-man's land. The plaza had many times been used for temporary sculpture exhibitions (Mies had intended it to be so used); and during completion of the IBM Tower the corporation commissioned two major permanent sculptures. Joe Fafard's 'The Pasture' was the first to be installed—on the small patch of lawn west of the IBM Tower. It consists of a group of seven larger-than-life bronze cows, apparently resting out the heat of a summer's day on the grass. Few contemporary patrons or sculptors have had the self-confidence to introduce so pastoral and realistic a note into Toronto's downtown. Fafard has described his work as a reminder to all city dwellers of the often forgotten country on which their urban lives depend. 'The Pasture' may be regarded by sophisticated observers as a witty response to Mies' Modernist Classicism; but the reactions of many Torontonians to its simple theme indicate that it may, like 'The Archer' in Nathan Phillips Square, eventually become a well-loved work of public art. The second piece, designed in bronze by Al McWilliams, is situated on the plaza facing King Street. Composed of a nine-foot-high circle of wall interrupted in three places, and three out-sized chairs arranged around it at some distance, the arrangement seems to invite contemplation of the vistas through the openings. McWilliams' work has a certain mysterious grandeur, but it does not succeed in controlling its space. The scale and sheer size of Mies's own sculptural composition for the Centre itself totally dominate any smaller piece in the environment. The third group of art works is composed of five sets of tapestries that hang in the foyers of the four towers. In their vertical proportions and rough textures they complement beautifully the shapes and materials of the foyers and bring them new colour.

The Toronto-Dominion Centre is Toronto's quintessential expression of the Modernism of the International style. Along with the New City Hall (Plate 143), it introduced the forms and ideas of architectural Modernism to a city that had previously given them little acceptance—indeed, their impact on Toronto's public consciousness had been negligible. It was the most important of the new commercial complexes of Toronto's postwar construction boom, and within several years the T-D Centre's influence could be seen in buildings on two of the other corners at King and Bay and elsewhere across the city and the country.

150. *The Plaza, looking east, past one of the chairs of Al McWilliams' sculpture group. The building on the right is the main tower of the T-D Centre.*

151

COMMERCE COURT

6 King Street West at Bay Street (SE)

Completed 1972 by I.M. Pei & Associates; Page &
Steele associated architects

The Canadian Bank of Commerce amalgamated with the Imperial Bank of Canada in 1961 to form the Canadian Imperial Bank of Commerce. As in a similar amalgamation that created the Toronto-Dominion Bank (see p.277), the corporation decided to participate in the 1960s construction boom by building a new head-office skyscraper. Also like the Toronto-Dominion, the CIBC chose a major American architect to guide the design and to work in association with a Toronto firm of architects.* The resulting 57-storey tower of glass and stainless steel appears at first glance to be merely one more standard tower, differing from its black neighbour, the tallest building in the Toronto-Dominion Centre, only in having a silvery appearance and a couple of additional storeys. But it represents certain positive alternatives—in architecture, development patterns, and urban form—to those exemplified in the T-D Centre (Plate 149). As the developer of the complex the CIBC chose to influence purely economic decisions by reference to its own history. It decided to preserve and renovate the 1929-31 Bank of Commerce (Plate 117)—for more than three decades the tallest and most distinctive building in the Toronto skyline—as the showpiece at the heart of the development. The preservation of the older tower complicated the design of the new one. Instead of having a clear site that could be freely planned and excavated, the architect had to work around the older building and find a way of integrating old and new in one composition.

Pei designed a sleek tower clad in a thin skin of stainless steel, sandblasted to preserve a warm silver finish against weather stains, and glass that takes its silvery colour from a thin layer of mercury laminated into its thickness. His skyscraper is set back from King Street, leaving the 1929-31 building uncompromised in the streetscape. From the intersection of King and Bay, and from closer up, the tower's glass and steel, and the exaggerated airiness and transparency of the lower three floors, are a perfect counterpoint to the solidity of the older stone building; and the rectilinear skeleton of the new building—despite the immense spans of its beams—complements the high arch and Romanesque detail of the older neighbour. In Pei's design the contrast of both material and detail was so important that it included construction of a new arched side entrance to the 1929 building

(directly facing the tower) that repeats, in a slightly simplified manner, the form and detail of the York & Sawyer work.

The studied relationship of old and new assumes greatest importance in the middle of the complex, where the architects created a terraced fountain court. Unlike the plazas of most new downtown skyscrapers, which are completely exposed to view, this court is sheltered from the surrounding traffic to make it both a new part of the city and a retreat within it. Defining the south and east edges of the space are low office blocks—five and fourteen storeys high respectively and faced, like the older tower, with limestone; colonnaded passages shelter shopfronts along their ground floors. There are clear views to the east towards the Dominion Bank (Plate 87) and the Traders' Bank Building (Plate 86), and from the corners of the space—towards Wellington, Bay, and King Streets—to the surrounding streetscapes. But the court is also sheltering. The relatively low height of the south and east office blocks allows the sun to reach the court even in December. On the terraces locust trees provide patterns of foliage and shade, and a circular fountain tempers the sounds of the city with falling water. On warm days this provides a popular outdoor lunchtime gathering-place in the banking district.

The plan of Pei's great tower is a rectangle, twice as long as it is wide, whose ground floor rises the equivalent of three storeys. The south half contains free-standing elevator banks. In the centre of the north half, facing both King and Bay, is a great circular well through which an escalator descends to the main banking hall below on the same level as the shopping concourse. The design of this banking space has none of the handsome detailing and monumentality one might expect. But it is connected to the main hall of the 1929 building by a new escalator, and on the ride up, the older space unfolds dramatically. The shopping concourse is a vast improvement over the corridors below the Toronto-Dominion Centre. The shop-fronts are framed in glittering stainless steel, the signage is recessed behind the glass, and the high concourse ceilings prevent the claustrophobia that inflicts many users of underground malls.

Commerce Court conveys an awareness of time in the city, of a gradual accumulation of buildings, and of urban space—extended or reshaped by changing uses and new construction. Standing here—as in Nathan Phillips Square in front of New City Hall and between Osgoode and the Old City Hall—it is possible to feel that this is a city whose past, present, and future go hand-in-hand.

---

* I.M. Pei was hired by the Canadian Imperial Bank of Commerce after the success of his Place Ville Marie project (1956-65) in Montreal, which was built for the Royal Bank. There was a nice symmetry to this commission, since the Bank of Commerce tower of 1929-31 was designed by the American firm of York & Sawyer, which had also come to prominence in Canada with a Royal Bank tower in Montreal.

152

THE ROYAL BANK PLAZA

Bay Street at Wellington (SW)

1972–6 by Webb Zerafa Menkes & Housden

The Royal Bank, founded in 1869, was an outsider in Toronto banking circles until 1976, when many of its central operations, though not its head office, were moved to Toronto from Montreal. However, it had spared no effort to make its presence felt in Toronto early in the century with an Italian Renaissance-style building (demolished) on King Street East, designed by Carrère & Hastings of New York in 1907–8. This was replaced in 1914 by a skyscraper (still standing) on the north-east corner of King and Yonge, also designed by Carrère & Hastings (in association with Eustace G. Bird of Toronto and Ross & Macdonald of Montreal). In 1964 the Bank moved its Toronto offices to 20 King Street West, between Yonge and Bay. Designed by Marani, Morris & Allan in the International Style, this building (also standing) is embellished with Carrara marble and gold mosaic; inside, a pair of Gobelin tapestries illustrate the four seasons.

In the early 1970s, when the Bank was planning for the present building, there was no large site available in the centre of the banking district at King and Bay. The Bank wisely chose to build on the south-west corner of Wellington and Bay, on a site that extended south to Front Street. Though slightly outside the bankers' Valhalla it had the advantage not only of size but of location—between the Union Station, with its subway and commuter rail traffic, and King and Bay. Unlike other banks, the Royal chose not to compete for the title of tallest building. First Canadian Place—which was then being built by Olympia & York for the Bank of Montreal on the north-west corner of King and Bay (1973–83, designed by Edward Durrell Stone and Bregman & Hamann)—was, at 74 stories, about as tall as such a building could go and still make economic sense. (With its uninteresting design and ersatz monumentality, it removed whatever appeal was left to the notion of being 'Tallest Building in the British Commonwealth'.) The Royal Bank sought to create instead a complex that aspired to architectural drama, and whose location made it an impressive gateway to the entire downtown—and to the financial district itself. Perhaps no other building in Toronto better represents the exuberant materialism that has replaced the minimalist and intellectual refinement of the pure International Style in North American corporate architecture.

The basic arrangement of the Royal Bank Plaza is very simple: the two triangular towers, their outer skin broken by vertical facets and cased in gold-leafed mirror glass, rise 26 and 41 storeys and flank an atrium space that makes a diagonal passageway across the site—NE to SW connecting the corner of Wellington and Bay Streets with Front Street opposite Union Station (Plate 109). The upper levels of this space are the principal banking areas for the Royal Bank; the lower two levels are an underground shopping mall. Both banking halls

and shopping levels are centred on a vertical well that rises from a garden-like fountain on the lowest level past sets of escalators into the highest space of the atrium, visually uniting all levels. The traditional tower-on-a-plaza form of the banks at King and Bay might have given the complex more office space. But by avoiding that formula the architects were able to give the Royal Bank the architectural presence and distinctiveness it wanted.

The atrium that forms the central core of the complex rises 130 feet to the girdered and skylit ceiling. From the outside the exposed cantilevered structure of its end walls has an undisciplined vitality; the finishing panels of glass at ground level are tinted but transparent to encourage passers-by to look in, and particularly at Bay and Wellington to enter with a casual freedom largely unknown in the head offices of other major banks such as the Bank of Commerce (Plate 118), the Bank of Nova Scotia (Plate 141), or even the equally transparent glass banking pavilion of the T-D Centre (Plate 149).* Once inside, the visitor can only be struck by the static character of the banking hall levels. Earlier banks combined perfection of materials, cathedral-like space, and an everything-in-its-place precision to create a sense of whispering awe. The Royal Bank has size and unusual space and structure to create its impression, but the result is dull rather than imposing. Lacking here is the formality of the T-D banking hall, with its fine marbles, granite, leather and wood finishes, exactly placed chairs and fittings, and thoroughly detailed structure. In the push to create a wonderful space, the details that are a central part of the experience of any fine building have been neglected in the Royal. The materials—polished granite, chrome, and arborite—are curiously proletarian and ordinary, the upper windows are merely squares punched through the nondescript beige facing of the walls, and the arrangement of counters and furniture is uninteresting.

The problems of the basic design for the banking hall are especially unfortunate because the Royal Bank took the trouble to commission and purchase a wide variety of art to ornament and complement the building. After choosing appropriate sites for art, the selection committee requested ideas from a number of artists for each of them. Five works were finally installed both inside the building and on the outside terraces. The largest and most important was designed by the Venezuelan artist Jesús Raphael Soto to hang from the ceiling of the banking hall. A suspended structure of 8,000 metal rods enamelled white and yellow (though in the light of the interior it appears to be multi-coloured), it is titled *Urban Span* and is meant to recall with shimmering lines of

---

* The same device of transparent glass panels was used in the lobbies of the two towers to indicate the way into the buildings.

153. *The cantilevered glass wall of the atrium set between the two office towers, seen from the corner of Wellington and Bay.*

colour and filtered light the immensity of the outdoors, of the forests and seas left behind in the city. The manner and medium are abstract in both colour and presentation: the sculpture accentuates the static character of the interior instead of complementing it (as for example realistic pieces or even great Calder mobiles do in other equally still settings). But its linearity gives the interior a soaring elegance that it would otherwise lack. Two of the other pieces are more successful. Both Rita Letendre's *Irowakan*, a mural in acrylics, and Mariette Rousseau-Vermette's tapestry *Reflection of the Sun*, on the lower and upper levels of the banking hall respectively, display a dynamic range of colour and an uncompromised individuality that turn their relatively low-ceiling settings into dramatic focuses of interest. Because the eye is quickly drawn from the atrium to these side spaces, they assume particular importance. This is surely one of the best things art can do for such a setting.

In the two-storey shopping mall below, the unabashed commercial variety of the many shops and restaurants provides a haphazard vitality that is enhanced by the fountain and garden— never far from sight or hearing—that form their centrepiece. Architecture intrudes at times on one's enjoyment, however, particularly around the fountain where steeply sloped floors (designed to obviate the need for steps that are dangerous in winter and inaccessible to the handicapped) make it difficult to stroll comfortably through or to pause to admire the atrium above. But elsewhere the architects have given the most ordinary functions a grandeur unusual in Toronto. Like most shopping malls in the city, the Plaza has an area where all the fast-food counters are grouped together. (At the Eaton Centre they are in an out-of-the-way low-ceiling backwater.) The two-storey court reserved for the counters and tables is entered from Bay and Wellington down a stone staircase that winds around the upper wall before spreading out into the space below. Most of the daytime illumination comes from a great pyramid skylight that creates dramatic effects and contrasts of light and shade as the sun rises and sets, creating all the character and dynamic interest that one would have liked to see in the much larger banking hall upstairs.

The exterior of the Royal Bank Plaza is one of the most beautiful ornaments of the city. The towers are faceted like

154. *The interior of the atrium, with Soto's 'Urban Space'.*

great basalt crystals and glazed with golden mirror-glass—gold has been laminated into the glass panels. While the facets give the interior variety and unpredictability, and some extra prime corner offices (and the gold tinting is useful as a heat reflector), on the exterior they create a spectrum of colours—from burnished gold or copper to clouded blue-pink—as they are played upon by the changing light. Magically transforming itself into a glistening flat rectangle when seen from Toronto Bay, or a dazzling many-faceted tower when seen from Front or Bay Streets, the Royal Bank Plaza is an exciting addition to the skyline of Toronto. Few buildings in the city can match it for dramatic effect, and no other so well embodies the romantic excitement of modern urban life.

155. *The entire expanse of Ontario Place, looking northeast, with the business core of Toronto and the CN Tower behind.*

ONTARIO PLACE

Lakeshore Boulevard at Exhibition Place
Completed 1971 by Craig, Zeidler & Strong

Ontario Place is an oddity among Toronto's important modern buildings: it was designed to amuse rather than impress. Strung out across three artificial islands and five pod-like structures poised on long legs above the waters of the lake, this combination amusement park, children's playground, marina, and trade-tourism pavilion, created and run by the Province of Ontario, is a postscript to the exuberance of Montreal's Expo 67, where Canadians first discovered that architecture could be both interesting and enjoyable. In the spirit of the Tivoli Gardens in Copenhagen or the Prater in Vienna, it creates an environment where the pressure of the city is suspended, and provides—without the aggressive commercialism of Disneyland and modern theme parks—a variety of entertainments for a modest admission price. At night, when its various parts are lit up and the geodesic dome of the Cinesphere is studded with small lights, it is the perfect fanciful counterpoint to the illuminated bank towers that dominate the skyline from the lake.

In the 1960s Ontario set out to provide the cultural and social facilities that its status as Canada's biggest and wealthiest province demanded. Along with the restoration and construction of several buildings, Toronto's share of the bounty included the Ontario Science Centre, and extensions to the Art Gallery of Toronto (renamed the Art Gallery of Ontario at the time). But the most exuberantly frivolous, and by far the most distinguished architecturally, was Ontario Place. The project was initially intended to give the province a new pavilion for the annual Canadian National Exhibition, but became a longer-term many-faceted entertainment and exhibition facility, administered by a Crown Corporation. Three islands were created just off shore by sinking several ageing lake steamers and surrounding them with landfill. The islands shelter three lagoons and the entire site covers 96 acres of land and enclosed water.

Since the late 1920s Ontario has had a pavilion at Exhibition Place. Still standing among the jumble of CNE buildings is the badly altered but elegant Classical multi-domed building in buff stucco and concrete designed by Chapman & Oxley around a triangular court. Neither its size nor its Beaux Arts style suited the image sought in the sixties: Ontario Place was to be as modern as the province's tomorrow. When Craig, Zeidler & Strong received the commission for Ontario Place the firm was experimenting with a much wider range of modern architectural elements than was usual in the severe, rather humourless work common in Toronto at the time. In Ontario Place the mechanical side of the architecture—the pipes and girders and services—are exposed for all to see as the brightly painted detailing of the pods. Parts of the building have the fascinating character of a giant Meccano set. Eberhard Zeidler (b. 1926, educated at the Bauhaus and the University of Karlsruhe) summed up the ideas that inspired Ontario Place in his description of architecture as a two-part process: first the technology and design must satisfy the functions and stability of the building, and then the image of the whole must meet its emotional purposes by providing a variety of form, colour, and shape that will delight and satisfy the user.

In Ontario Place each area has a different character adapted to its specific purpose. The most striking parts of the design are the five three-storey pods standing on legs above the lagoons—square in plan with both solid and fully glazed walls, designed to house changing exhibits and restaurants. Supported on thick guywires from the pylons, connected by open and glazed walkways, and fitted with fragile openwork stairs at the corners, they are as modern as a science-fiction movie. After many visits the technology still projects an otherwordly quality that suggests a floating place a million miles away from ordinary Toronto. The concession area is completely different—a crowded waterside village of interlocking huts of plywood, glass, and painted canvas away from the more serious educational exhibits in the main pods. Restaurants with covered terraces reach out over the lagoon, and irregular traffic patterns, bright colours, and changing levels create a small-scale confusion totally appropriate to the boutiques,

restaurants, and bars near the marina and the boats on the lagoons. The Forum, designed as a covered concert bowl with revolving stage, is dug into the centre of the smallest island. Its seating surrounds the performance area, under a tent-like roof of tongue-and-groove plywood sheathed in copper. Though the roof conveys the simplicity of an outdoor camp erected on the spur of the moment, its shape is that of a hyperbolic paraboloid, the most complex of computer-designed geometrical figures.

The showpiece of Ontario Place is the Cinesphere theatre, an inner triodetic dome 56 feet in radius that seats 800 in front of an 80-by-60-foot curved screen. The outer geodesic dome, with a 61-foot radius, has a framework of extruded aluminum tubes. At night a network of large and small lights picks out the structure and turns the theatre into a jewel box reflected in the surrounding water. Like the IMAX process of 70 mm cinematography that the theatre is designed to exploit, the design uses available technology to create a dramatic form in which delight and enjoyment transcend technique.

Ontario Place also includes a Children's Village playground (no adults allowed, unfortunately) that is unmatched for its innovative approach to play on water slides, rooms filled with rubber balls, and a continuously changing assortment of amusements. The result is a complex like no other in Toronto, and few in North America, with none of the commercialism of conventional amusement parks.

In Zeidler's work, Ontario Place was the first of a series of designs for powerfully technical buildings. Here, as in the McMaster University Medical Centre in Hamilton, and in the Eaton Centre (Plate 157) and the Queen's Quay Terminal Warehouse (Plate 159), the structural features generally used in buildings that create the modern city have been exposed, elaborated, and turned into features of interest in their own right. These elements usually seem cold, impersonal, and dehumanized. In Ontario Place—with colour and exaggerated size and detail, in a fantasy setting by the lake—they become objects of delight.

156

METROPOLITAN TORONTO
REFERENCE LIBRARY

789 Yonge Street at Asquith Avenue (NE)

1970–7 by Raymond Moriyama

Public architecture is concerned as much with the use of images and forms as with the functions of buildings. The nineteenth century developed a varied repertoire of forms for public buildings, which the first half of the twentieth century largely accepted and, with simplifications, continued to use. The tower and carved detail of E.J. Lennox's City Hall (Plate 76) announce its presence to all the city's visitors and residents; in the former Central Reference Library at College and St George (Plate 83), the Corinthian pilasters, rising stair, and spacious reading-room proclaimed the august cultural tradition perpetuated by the library. However, since the 1950s there has been no real agreement about the imagery appropriate for any public building. The discontent with old patterns arose from a desire for new forms to express late-twentieth-century conditions and needs, and—more significantly—from the poor quality of many traditionalizing designs. With Viljo Revell's design for the New City Hall (Plate 143) and Eberhard Zeidler's for Ontario Place (Plate 155), Toronto received new buildings whose exploration of forms achieved unique expressions of modernity that were also comprehensible to the ordinary user. The building of the Metro Reference Library on Yonge Street was guided by a similar desire for a new sense of form.

When Metropolitan Toronto was formed in the federation of the City of Toronto with the municipalities on its perimeter, certain functions, like policing, were delegated to the central government. Others, like the library systems serving local neighbourhoods through branches, remained with the separate municipalities. The Central Reference Library on College Street, with its rapidly growing special collections and different concerns, at first remained the responsibility of the City, but by 1968 had been handed over to Metro. The period after 1950 was one of rapid diversification within the reference system of the Library; and because of space problems in the College Street building the new departments were scattered to quarters in various parts of Metro, to the dissatisfaction of staff, users, and politicians alike. This period also saw rapid technological changes in library management—with, in particular, the introduction of computers into the system. But more important was a general change in attitudes about the ideal character of a library and its role in the community, which called for interior space that was open and welcoming and where knowledge in many forms could be sampled with few controlling strictures. Instead of expanding and renovating—which was both economically and architecturally feasible—the members of the Metropolitan Toronto Library Board opted for a large new building. The

chosen site on Yonge north of Bloor was close to both the main subway lines and gave convenient access from all corners of Metro. The chosen architect was Raymond Moriyama, who had designed the immensely popular Ontario Science Centre. His Scarborough Town Centre (1973)—grouping the municipality's offices and its board of education on opposite sides of a high, circular atrium—provided this sprawling suburban city with an identifiable focus, as well as a dramatic modern image. The Centre is monumental but welcoming enough to provide an attractive public meeting space.

Moriyama's first designs for the Library, presented in 1973–4, provided for the now-familiar arrangement of spaces and functions on several floors around a skylighted atrium. But the exterior was to be a sharply cornered scaleless rectangle faced with mirrored glass. One of the first of many mirrored buildings proposed for Toronto, the design was in startling contrast to the small units of the surrounding area but was justified on the grounds that the walls would attractively reflect the late-nineteenth-century shops on the west side of Yonge. However, under pressure from public opinion and Toronto City Council, the Library Board instructed Moriyama to revise his designs. The building's bulk was reduced by setting back the upper floors along both Yonge Street and Asquith Avenue and reworking the south-west and north-east corners as ranges of stepped floors. To soften the relationship between the library and the street, and to encourage pedestrian traffic along Yonge, considerable planting was installed and a covered promenade designed for the main frontage from Asquith north to Collier Street; the main entrance at Asquith and Yonge was recessed on an angle under a glass canopy and the corner in front paved as a miniature public square. The windows of the upper floors are still glazed with mirror panels, but the brown brick covering the other wall surfaces does not accord with the yellow and red brick that predominates in the nineteenth-century buildings of Yonge Street and Yorkville. At one time shops had been planned for the ground floor of the Yonge Street frontage, and that space is now used as the Library's art gallery, while on Collier Street near the corner of Yonge a greenhouse projects from the façade, creating an informal periodical and newspaper reading-room filled with plants and sunshine. On the east side low staff-office windows overlook a small amphitheatre and sunken garden. These changes do not give the Library a strong identity from the street because Moriyama has not really responded to the implicit call for a new public imagery. The simple bulk of the building is what chiefly attracts the attention of passers-by on Yonge Street. There is nothing about the exterior that declares it to be an important public building or that compels admiration.

The interior of the Metro Library is a different story. Moriyama opened up the inside of the Library with a great central atrium that widens as it rises. The five public floors (between them are mezzanine levels used as stacks for book storage) are given over to reading and working areas, as well as to open stack storage, and are arranged like shelves or trays of space. Long banners hang in the open area of the atrium to indicate the subject matter of the individual floors, whose low carpeted parapets, overhung in many places with plants, allow casual day-dreaming views across the central space and up and down to other floors. The structure of the library is based on a regular grid of concrete columns placed thirty feet apart; but the engineering makes little impact on visitors because the irregularity of the atrium and the spaciousness of the open floor arrangement dominate the interior.

Moriyama is unusual among Canadian architects in being unafraid to express his ideas in romantic and religious terms. Influenced in his thinking by both Japanese Buddhism and a personal Catholic humanism, he is concerned about the use made of his buildings by the average visitor and about the perceptions that will be carried away. He views the interior of the Library as an 'empty cup', which the activities of the user, not vacuous monumentality and imagery, will fill; or as 'a defined emptiness' in which the architect guides but does not compel the user. Against this background many of the elements in Moriyama's design—features that have been employed gratuitously in other buildings—make a positive contribution to the pleasure of using the Metro Library. Moriyama welcomes visitors to the study environment by bringing them past falling water in a small pool, by taking them to the upper floors in a glass elevator that allows the atrium to unfold and be fully appreciated, and finally by making them agreeably conscious of that space, and of the presence of fellow users. In this interior the function of a library is expressed in a new imagery (missing on the exterior), though several practical problems have arisen. The staff complain that the atrium and the diagonal arrangements of floors create awkward and often inefficiently located working areas, which are too small and are separated by great distances. Many of the Library's most basic functions fit uncomfortably into the scheme—especially on the ground floor, where book stacks, shelves of catalogues, and bulletin boards make it difficult to appreciate the space Moriyama designed. The two pools that were incorporated into the ground floor—one with a trivial water-fall, the other functioning primarily as a security

157

barrier—are poorly detailed and the security facilities are inconveniently located.

Nevertheless the enthusiasm of the great majority of its frequent users must be accepted as a confirmation of the Metro Library's success. Since the building opened, the most optimistic predictions by members of the Library Board have been exceeded: attendance has skyrocketed. Many of the users are school children who seem to feel, as Moriyama wished them to, completely at home in a public reference library. The strength and immediate effect of Moriyama's building come from the interior, which is totally unlike that of a traditional library and more than compensates for the unimpressive character of the exterior. Its colour and light, its sensuous curving forms, and even the silent movement of the elevators all provide a soothing contrast to the busy streets and nondescript skyscrapers outside. Precisely because it is impressive, as well as casually accessible and non-threatening, it draws people to it who might never think of entering a great reference library.

THE EATON CENTRE

Yonge Street (W) between Queen and Dundas

1973–9 by Bregman & Hamann, and the Zeidler Partnership/Architects

The Eaton Centre is Toronto's most-visited tourist attraction, a high-roofed multi-level street lined with shops that runs north along Yonge from Queen and the Simpson's store to Dundas and Eaton's. It might have been a mundane shopping plaza, but distinctive architecture has transformed it into a glazed galleria filled with shops, trees, and fountains. Though the Centre is not without flaws, to most of the people who crowd it every day—shopping, strolling, meeting friends, walking through on their way to somewhere else—the building and the passing show sum up the energy and excitement of modern Toronto.

The T. Eaton Company Ltd.—founded in 1869 and still family-owned—is historically the leader in Canadian retailing. Its coast-to-coast chain of department stores, and its famous mail-order catalogue, published twice a year from 1884 to 1976, made it as much a Canadian institution as the chartered banks, the CPR, and the CBC. Timothy Eaton opened his first store on Yonge Street south of Queen, but soon moved north of the intersection, leaving the south side of Queen to Simpson's (Plate 73). On the new site the store expanded into a disjointed but internally impressive collection of existing and new buildings until it covered the city block bounded by Yonge, Queen, Albert, and James. In a cluster of factories to the north, around Trinity Square, the company pioneered production of house-brand merchandise in order to control prices and quality. A plan to replace the old store gave birth to the Eaton's College Street store (now the core of the College Park Development), constructed in 1928–30. Because of the Depression that plan was only partially completed, although the College Street store was maintained until 1976. In the late 1950s and early 1960s planning began for a new store that eventually resulted in the present Eaton Centre.

Coinciding with the rise of the urban preservation movement, which involved much citizen activism,* the erection of the Eaton Centre followed the longest and most complex design and consultative process in the history of Toronto. The first schemes proposed a huge complex of retail space and office towers covering the entire area from Queen Street north to Dundas between Yonge and Bay. Toronto's city government was to move, in 1965, into the New City Hall (Plate 143), and Eaton's proposed demolishing the Old City Hall (Plate 76) in order to include its site in their own development. Fortunately the same Torontonians who were resisting new expressways and saving neighbourhoods like the Annex (see page 118) demanded preservation of the Old City Hall.

At the same time the congregation of the Church of the Holy Trinity (Plate 15) refused to abandon their downtown ministry and their site on Trinity Square. Several redesigned plans were presented before enough support could be secured to allow the present scheme to proceed around both Old City Hall and Trinity Square.

The Eaton's store—by E.L. Hankinson, with Blake Millar and the Parkin Partnership as associates—exists within this complex as the largest department store in Canada, a million square feet on ten levels. The elegance and flair of the main floors have been rivalled only by the design of the College Street store. Its centrepiece is a high open space, like that of the Bon Marché (1876) in Paris and other fashionable nineteenth-century department stores*, that is frequently filled with huge fanciful displays keyed to the seasons of the year. However, little of the store's activity registers on the exterior, where the architects chose to play down the traditional importance of display-windows that in the old Eaton's, as in Simpson's, had enticed people from their homes and offices to stroll and window-shop along Yonge Street. Indeed, the basic principle behind the planning of the Centre was that all shoppers, and even casual pedestrians, would be drawn inside, leaving the city's streets and sidewalk-oriented businesses behind. Since potential visitors to the centre—arriving often by subway and spending all their time within the multi-level mall—would never see the exterior of the building, and probably never enter it while simply walking along Yonge Street, the next-to-last designs for it in 1972 presented a mall and store that essentially disregarded Yonge and the vibrant life associated with commerce on the street. The present exterior of the store—sheathed above the recessed band of windows in featureless enamelled metal of a dreary caramel colour—is an indication of what was proposed for the rest of the Yonge Street façade.

In 1972 the basic concept was approved with only three dissenting votes by a City Council anxious to encourage this and other downtown developments. But public objections to the effects of its bland and sterile exterior—on the pedestrian life necessary for other businesses along Yonge Street, and on the mixed old-new character of Toronto—and the fact that the proposal was attacked by a majority of aldermen elected to the 1973–4 City Council helped to convince Fairview (Eaton's partners in the development), with the support of Phyllis Bronfman Lambert, to call in the Zeidler Partnership. The new Council passed a holding by-law that enabled the City to require changes to improve the character of the

---

*The process and the result established the foundations of a new development-approval procedure for the city that is now far more sensitive to the needs of Toronto than ever before.

---

*The Eaton's store of that period had a similar multi-storey space at its centre.

development—such as the amount of sunlight for the new Trinity Square.

Zeidler's design, with exposed and exaggerated structural detail and greenhouse glazing, created an airy high-roofed shopping street reminiscent of the Galleria (1865–7) in Milan. Cutting east-west across it, the high transepts of the Trinity and Albert Ways follow the line of now-vanished nineteenth-century streets and provide connections between Yonge and the Old and New City Halls to the west—as well as to the restored Scadding House, old Rectory, and Holy Trinity Church in Trinity Square.* The dimensions of the galleria are, and were intended to be, impressive: 866 feet long, with 1,566,700 square feet of space, and at least 305 shops. The Eaton Centre is visited by almost twenty million shoppers and tourists each year.

At the Dundas and Yonge entrance a huge multi-level glazed space joins two floors of the mall to the subway and street. Overhung by part of the structure of the building above, the Eaton's office tower, it is filled with foliage and the constant movement of people on escalators and stairs. It has a wonderfully uncontrived informality. The virtue of the Zeidler work is that here, and in the long galleria south of the Eaton's store —under a vault 127 feet high—the marketing scheme that placed moderate-price stores and chains on the lower levels, and luxury and specialty shops above, has been transformed into a series of identifiable spaces. On Level Three, among the Benjamina trees, there is even a sense of seclusion in the midst of the Centre's artfully disordered busyness. Equally pleasing in an architectural way is the space at the south end of the galleria, where the Canada geese in Michael Snow's 'Step Flight' head south under the vault. To the west, rising right out of the galleria, is the curving glass of the Cadillac-Fairview Tower, which from outside the development can be seen to echo Eaton's office tower at the north end. Zeidler changed the earlier Eaton Centre plan to place shops along Yonge Street. A system of walkways and balconies built up from metal beams and railings animates the façade and supports an array of neon signs that add light and movement. Unfortunately, though the exterior walks and balconies were designed for public use, people tend to stay inside, so that some shop-owners with doors on the mall and on Yonge prefer to keep the Yonge entrances closed.

The Eaton Centre is undeniably an architectural event.

---

*To complete the plan of the Centre there should have been a public walkway from Dundas Street into the galleria that could have remained open when the store itself was closed. However, such a public amenity would have been awkward to incorporate into the store, and Eaton's decided to reject the suggestion during initial discussions with the Zeidler design team.

159. *The north entrance, corner of Dundas and Yonge.*

However, its construction wiped out a whole section of nineteenth and early twentieth-century buildings on the west side of Yonge Street that might have been incorporated, and it weakened—though it did not destroy, as many sceptics expected—the everyday life of Yonge between Dundas and Queen. Nor is it the composite development that was once envisioned—with housing, a library, and genuine public space inside (the Centre controls access and can exclude at will). But the Eaton Centre already has become what its boosters claimed for it all along: one of the attractions that sustain the continued life of the central city. As its popularity spawns imitative developments across Canada, one of the most important achievements associated with the Eaton Centre may be the example it provides of a city's demanding a positive and formative role in decisions affecting its development, environment, and future. In Toronto itself, the outstanding fact about the Eaton Centre is the powerful contribution its architecture have made to downtown city life.

160

THE QUEEN'S QUAY TERMINAL
WAREHOUSE, HARBOURFRONT

207 Queen's Quay West at the foot of York Street

1927 by Moores & Dunford of New York; renovated 1981–3 by
The Zeidler, Roberts Partnership, as part of Harbourfront

Harbourfront, Canada's first urban national park, was created in 1972 on almost 100 acres of land stretching along Toronto's lakeshore south of the Gardiner Expressway from York Street on the east to just beyond Bathurst Street on the west. Over the last eleven years it has developed into a lively extension of the downtown. More significantly, it has responded to the aspirations of many urban reformers for a playground that would convince Torontonians that the lake should be—for the first time in years—a genuine part of the city. While the idealism behind the project meets with general approval, there is no final agreement on the character of the area. Even as the development nears completion and traffic problems increase, the debate continues about how best to combine public, commercial, and recreational space with much-needed housing, so that Torontonians will draw the utmost pleasure and use from their waterfront.

The first of the major buildings to be completed was the renovated Terminal Warehouse, a glittering showplace combining two levels of shops, a theatre, parking, and several floors of offices (all within the original building), with 72 apartments built on the roof, arranged on four levels around three garden-courts. The renovation—frankly palatial and ostentatiously chic—has been designed with a flair and bravado rare in the city's architecture. Though few Torontonians can afford to own the apartments with their panoramic lake views, or to shop here on a regular basis, it embodies—like two earlier Zeidler buildings, Ontario Place (Plate 154) and the Eaton Centre (Plate 157)—the architect's belief that his creation should be constantly interesting and entertaining. With views of the lake and harbour from interior atriums, surprising architectural effects, and careful details surrounding expensive boutiques, it captures so well the spirit of fun sought by Harbourfront that it may be forgiven its opulence and the irrelevance to most Torontonians of the life-style for which it was designed.

As early as 1818 the council of the Town of York made an attempt to preserve the waterfront by designating as a public promenade the area that is now The Esplanade and the St Lawrence Neighbourhood (Plate 166). Around the same time the first of a series of garden villas enjoying views across the water, and cooling summer breezes, was erected west of Yonge almost to Bathurst Street. However, by the 1840s the private and public wharves and landfill caused by the gradual westward spread of the commercial harbour began to separate the lake from the city. In 1852 City Surveyor John Howard presented a plan to restore and extend the recreational use of the shoreline with a scheme for 'Pleasure Drives, Walks and Shrubbery for the Recreation of the Citizens' on the original sloping beach and landfill south of Front Street West, between York and Bathurst. * But within a year the situation was changed by the arrival of the railway. To ensure its commercial importance, Toronto gave over the harbourfront to the railways, funding more landfill along The Esplanade and allowing private wharves to close in much of the waterfront. By the turn of the century, factories and storage yards lined the shore from the Don River to Bathurst Street. Recreational uses were crowded—often dangerously—into the spaces between, while the railways occupied more than 200 acres of land.

Little attempt was made to co-ordinate the waterfront and to open more land for recreation until 1912, when the Toronto Harbour Commission—established in 1911 and vested with ownership of the public land along the lake—sponsored an ambitious plan for the shoreline that included 50 miles of pleasure drives, and the re-organization and extension of industrial land, housing, parkland, and recreational facilities. Lakeshore Boulevard West and the Sunnyside Bathing Pavilion (Plate 139) are lasting remnants of that plan; but in the central harbour area, where the Harbour Commission and several private owners controlled the land, it seemed impossible to reconcile recreation and waterfront living with the conditions and needs of a working harbour. After the St Lawrence Seaway opened in 1959, planning was dedicated solely to commercial and industrial uses, and parkland was developed only on the Toronto Islands and the eastern and western lakeshores. By the late 1960s, however, changes in

the character of lakeside industry and in shipping technology had reduced Toronto's need for vast harbour facilities. Meanwhile Torontonians were being encouraged by politicians and urban reformers to consider the waterfront an integral part of the city. (The railway lands north of the Gardiner Expressway were a separate concern.) In 1972 the federal Liberal government announced a plan to create a park on land south of the expressway, between York Street and just west of Bathurst. This was not only a proposal of great significance—there were no urban national parks in Canada—but it offered, through the government funding of a Crown corporation, a chance to reclaim the recreational aspect of Toronto's harbour.

The project was christened Harbourfront, and the first plans were almost completely oriented to recreation. Many existing buildings were adapted to a variety of uses—with cycling and jogging paths winding through the area, antique flea-markets, coffee houses, art galleries, and makeshift theatres —but there was relatively little new development. The atmosphere was informal, almost countrified. Meanwhile the land to the east of York Street, developed by the Campeau Corporation, had assumed a dense urban character with a high-rise hotel, condominium towers, and a convention centre. The plan for Harbourfront, to be largely completed in 1987, now extends high residential density several hundred metres further west. While such development can be seen as partly cutting the city off from the water once again, it does serve as a buffer between the waterside park and the expressway and rail lines, which still form the chief barrier between the bay and the city. The best sites have gone to the most expensive housing developments, and few of the condominiums being built are moderately priced. The quality of the buildings is undistinguished, with two notable exceptions: Arthur Erickson's understated King's Landing apartments at the foot of Spadina, and Zeidler's Terminal Warehouse renovation.

The Terminal Warehouse was built in 1927, when harbour traffic was expanding tremendously and central warehousing and cold-storage facilities seemed essential to its efficient operation. The architects, Moores & Dunford of New York—noted for their large warehouses—created a dramatically simple concrete building eight storeys high (with a west wing that has since been demolished), its façade a simple grid of horizontals and verticals following the internal structure. The side and lake façades had straightforward industrial glazing; on the north front, visible from the city, are touches of Art Deco linear detail, and rising above the façade at the centre is a clock-tower ornamented by thin overlapping concrete planes. At the four corners are similar but lower stair-towers. Inside, the principal feature was—and remains—the exposed thick 'mushroom' form of the concrete columns that spread out at the top to support horizontal beams.

During the 1970s parts of the Terminal were renovated for office space, but Harbourfront wished to make it a showplace for the entire area. A limited competition for architectural firms, in association with specific developers, was won

---

* This location was immediately north of Harbourfront. Howard's idea of piers and major streets reaching into the lake, with landscaped parkland threaded with walks and drives between, was similar to the original plan of Harbourfront.

by the Zeidler, Roberts Partnership, working with Olympia & York. Dividing the building horizontally—with shops, the Premier Dance Theatre, indoor parking on the lower three levels, and offices on five floors above—the interior was arranged around two inner courts connected by a spacious shopping concourse. The principal entrances are on the north side under the clock tower, and at the northeast corner, where terraces lead up from York Street and Queen's Quay. The north part of the foyer, with its escalators, is partly open through two storeys and extends back to the small north atrium, formed by removing floors through the height of the building. Walking towards the lake, the visitor enters a more complex space. The great south atrium is bounded by ten columns and contains escalators rising from between fountain pools to the second level; visitors are also carried upwards in glazed elevators. In the upper part of the atrium, skylights and windows in bays and oriels look down from the office levels. Even more dramatic are the lower levels, where the skeleton of the building has been exposed. To the southeast the floors have been removed, leaving only the three-dimensional grid of columns and horizontal beams, painted white and flooded with light through an inset curving window. No other Toronto renovation has been as daring or as sensitive to the sculptural qualities of architectural structure; at the southeast corner stand the visible bones of the building, sometimes dissolved in glare or filled with shadow. On the southwest corner is a greenhouse-like projection that allows the ground-floor restaurants and upper-level offices to spread out beyond the original walls of the warehouse to embrace the bay. The building is finished in creamy white, and the glass addition is tinted a pale grey-green, a combination suited to the lakefront setting. The cool elegance of this colour scheme suffuses the entire project—furniture, paintwork, permanent fixtures, windows, and the metal cladding and railings of the four levels of rooftop apartments. These are arranged around three garden courts, with centre skylights lighting lower floors, a seven-metre waterfall, and a two-storey glazed pool enclosure.

161. *The south atrium.*

Like both the Eaton Centre and Ontario Place, Queen's Quay Terminal is immensely popular with Torontonians and tourists alike. Its success rests on Zeidler's daring idea of removing large sections of the floors and turning the interior structure into a strong and dynamic motif. Though Zeidler took great chances—he risked endangering the physical integrity of the building—he followed his initial inspiration through to a triumphant conclusion. It is very easy to like the Terminal Warehouse building, and to acknowledge the artistry that went into its design.

162. *The Avenue Road front of York Square, showing the renovated Victorian buildings. Hazelton Lanes is on the left.*

YORK SQUARE

Yorkville Avenue at Avenue Road (NE)

1968 by A.J. Diamond & Barton Myers

Since the 1960s the growth of Toronto's several commercial districts has tended to result from the gradual conversion of existing houses, warehouses, and occasionally churches—for use as restaurants, offices, and stores—rather than from replacing old buildings with new. This tendency has created new commercial space while preserving much of the local character that originally drew businessmen and their customers to a particular area. Nowhere in Toronto has the trend resulted in a wider range of solutions than in Yorkville, along the streets immediately north of Bloor West, between Yonge and Avenue Road—a district long associated with luxury retailing. York Square, with its mix of new construction and renovation, is the most attractive of these modern extensions of Yorkville.

Originally a village just north of the toll-gate at Bloor, Yorkville was annexed to the city in 1883 and became a comfortable middle- and working-class suburb, crowded with houses dating from the 1850s through to the First World War.

Between the wars it acquired a vaguely artistic and Bohemian reputation, and in the late 1950s—when redevelopment began to destroy the artistic community of Toronto's 'Greenwich Village' on Gerrard Street—it blossomed with art galleries, restaurants, antique stores, and coffee houses. Though still a residential neighbourhood, Yorkville played host first to the folk-music culture (from which came Gordon Lightfoot, Malka and Joso, Ian and Sylvia, and Joni Mitchell) and then, in the late sixties, to Flower Power and hippie culture.

During most of this time Bloor Street, only two blocks away, was becoming the centre of fashionable retailing. The large stores along Bloor presented one aspect of this enterprise. The other aspect—established first by art galleries and antique dealers, and then by a variety of modish purveyors—was seen in the boutique, the small specialty shop, often located in an old house and informally grouped with similar stores along Cumberland, Yorkville, and Hazelton. Here trees and small-scale buildings preserved the village atmosphere (like that of New York's Greenwich Village, which many Torontonians knew and appreciated), though the district was clearly becoming commercial. An early and effective attempt to complement the old flavour of Yorkville in a new commercial complex was Lothian Mews (1963, by Webb, Zerafa & Housden; mostly destroyed by later renovation), between Bloor and Cumberland—shops grouped around a galleried court, with a fountain and a restaurant.

Of the new developments York Square, which still retains much of its original character, was the most successful. The site, at the north corner of Yorkville and Avenue Road—owned by Laver Investments, whose president was Richard Wookey—was originally occupied by seven Late Victorian brick houses facing Avenue Road. Current theory would likely have proposed a monolithic high-rise building. But Wookey was attuned to the village ambience of Yorkville and hired as his architects Jack Diamond and Barton Myers. Though new to Toronto, they were well acquainted with American, English, and European architecture and to them, Toronto's nineteenth-century buildings (which many Toronto architects of the previous generation had been taught to despise or ignore) were aesthetically pleasing and offered possibilities for combining new functions with old architectural forms.

The four brick houses on the corner of the site were retained and renovated with ground-floor additions for shops, and offices upstairs; the three other houses were completely refaced. Behind them a U-shaped two-storey building was erected to contain shops and restaurants around a brick-paved square, entered from both Yorkville and Avenue Road. Constructed of red brick, in homage to the old houses, it has stark rectilinear windows on the upper floors, and circular shop windows that were originally tied together with large-scale two-dimensional super-graphics that spread across the sidewall of the corner house. The old houses were painted white, and their bays and tile-hung gables became a decorative part of the complex. Inside the square the exterior window forms were repeated on the ground floor; on the second floor a light grid of windows was framed in thin steel. The square itself, shaded by a rangy maple tree, is a quiet haven similar to an urban backyard.

York Square succeeded largely because of its stylized village atmosphere and air of casual commercialism. Some of its basic ideas were borrowed for the larger Hazelton Lanes development to the north, also completed in 1976 (by Webb Zerafa Menkes & Housden, again for a consortium headed

by Richard Wookey). In the early 1970s Wookey had purchased many of the Late Victorian houses on Hazelton Avenue and renovated them as luxurious shops and apartments. On the west side they form a screen for Hazelton Lanes: two long blocks of brick apartments, stepped back with spacious balconies, that rise above two levels of shops. The eastern block is almost invisible from the street; the western acts as a buffer against the Avenue Road traffic. Between is a courtyard—in summer a restaurant and in winter a skating rink—that, unlike the one in York Square, is not casually accessible because of the building's design; and the shopping corridors, though sumptuous, are so labyrinthine as to be disorienting and confining. Unfortunately this development led to the removal of the super-graphics from the walls of York Square, which for much of the year is now merely a passageway to Hazelton Lanes.

York Square provided an object lesson for renovators by successfully using modern materials in the restoration of old buildings—reworking but preserving the original atmosphere of Yorkville—but it was ignored by property owners in the area. Shortly after, a long row of houses on the north side of Yorkville Street was veneered with rough brick and fronted with phony Victorian lamp-posts. Also slotted into the streetscape were three-storey split-level structures that tried to imitate the pattern of bay windows under a gable—traditional in Toronto houses of the 1880s and 1890s. Such changes have given Yorkville a synthetic period flavour—appreciated more by tourists and suburban visitors than by those who are aware of its history and enjoy such authentic architecture as York Square.

163. The central walkway of Sherbourne Lanes. The backs of the renovated houses are on the right.

SHERBOURNE LANES

(The Dundas-Sherbourne Project) 241-285 Sherbourne Street (E)
1973-6 by Diamond & Myers (Barton Myers, partner-in-charge)

One of the most remarkable developments in the social and architectural history of Toronto is the Dundas-Sherbourne Project. It consists of a dozen substantial Victorian and Edwardian houses and a grouping, in what was once their backyards, of six-storey modern apartment buildings, with a connected series of brick courtyards in between. Pedestrian walkways afford passage from the front of the project on the east side of Sherbourne Street, above Dundas, to the north-south lane that also serves as a back entrance to Seaton street houses at the rear of the project. The mature chestnuts on Sherbourne, along with other trees preserved in the courtyards, provide a graceful counterpoint to the beige-and-red

brick houses that face the street and the flying-form, cast-in-place, slab-and-column concrete apartment buildings that rise unobtrusively behind them.

The Dundas-Sherbourne Project was an ambitious experiment, both as architecture and as publicly supported housing. Toronto has long accepted a basic responsibility to provide housing for at least some of its low-income citizens. Beginning with Regent Park, planned in the early 1930s and built in 1947-8, and continuing with the fourteen- and fifteen-storey towers and town houses of Regent Park South (1957) and Moss Park (1961), new apartments—usually linked to slum clearance and urban renewal—were built in relatively large numbers. In almost every case thriving but run-down communities were replaced by buildings that few architects or planners would have wanted to inhabit. But Modernist social and architectural theories assured them and the politicians they advised that towers and occasional town houses with minimal living quarters, surrounded by spreading open space and built in clusters set apart from the city's established routines and patterns, would provide a better life for the people being rehoused. Toronto's projects were less huge and alienating than those in many other cities; but by the late 1960s it was alarmingly clear to some social scientists and architects, a few politicians, and many residents that such designs caused more problems than they solved. Families with small children were lodged in apartments high above the parks and playgrounds necessary for their daily life; but worst of all, the projects had become ghettos for the poor, cut off from every other economic and social class.

The first impetus for change originated with the people the city had meant to assist. Though some help came from urban preservationists interested in saving downtown nineteenth-century architecture, the real drive came from the people who were being forced by urban-renewal projects to give up the homes and communities of generations. Opposition— beginning in Trefann Court north-east of Queen and Parliament Streets, where planners and politicians had decreed the clearance of the existing houses (many of which could have been renovated) and the building of a sanitized project—launched the public career of a young lawyer named John Sewell. Over the next ten years Sewell, with other Reform aldermen and Mayor David Crombie, championed a new vision of publicly supported housing that would mix people from several economic levels; combine subsidized housing with units renting at near-market levels in complexes integrated into the community fabric; and preserve and renovate the existing architecture, while building new on a similar scale when necessary. The climax of this vision—and the ultimate proof that it could work—was the St Lawrence Neighbourhood (Plates 166-8). But the first real test for the new ideas in Toronto was Dundas-Sherbourne.

The architecture preserved by the Dundas-Sherbourne project along the length of Sherbourne between Dundas and Carlton Streets exists like a microcosm of the street's fashionable Victorian past. The oldest house was built in 1856 for the brewer and philanthropist Enoch Turner, who built Toronto's first free school.* He called the two-storey red and yellow brick house, with its Regency-style wooden veranda, 'Allandale' after William Allan, squire of the Moss Park Estate to the south. A farmhouse, rather than a city house, it recalls the rural atmosphere of this part of Toronto in the middle of the last century. More urbane are numbers 283-5, a pair of three-storey town houses built in 1956-7, and distinguished by simple Greek Revival details such as lintels

164

over the windows and doors. Between are a pair of bow-windowed houses with dormered mansard roofs that were built in the late 1860s, and a group of houses from the late 1880s, the 1890s, and the first decade of this century, whose designers borrowed freely both from the Queen Anne fashions for elaborate wooden porches and gable detail and from the Romanesque Revival taste for monumental stonework.

Like the large houses of Jarvis and St George Streets, those on Sherbourne ceased to be viable as family homes in the late 1920s. Many were demolished, a few became institutions, but most were simply rearranged into small apartments or rooming-houses; they were largely dismissed as architecturally uninteresting and of minor significance for their historical associations. But in the late 1960s a growing awareness of their architectural heritage opened the eyes of many Torontonians to the interesting features of these houses; and in 1972 the election of a Reform city council created a political climate in which the rights and character of the neighbourhood could be respected and defended. And defence was crucial, because in the same year a major developer proposed razing the houses and replacing them with two high-rise apartment towers, designed to satisfy Toronto's burgeoning middle-class market. By the time Council turned its attention to the problem a demolition permit had been granted, and it took an act of illegal intervention to gain the time necessary to find a solution. When the developer's demolition crews arrived at 7:00 a.m. one late-winter morning in 1973, about 100 people (including 7 aldermen) were there waiting. They trespassed onto the site and swiftly removed the hoardings around it—

---

*The school was located immediately south of Little Trinity, the Anglican church he belonged to.

which meant that no further demolition work could be done that day. Major David Crombie, while dissociating himself from the act of trespass, was afforded further time to negotiate with the developer, and with the provincial and federal authorities who were needed to assist the city in funding the purchase of the property.

In the belief that new housing should no longer be based on wholesale redevelopment, Council wished to renovate the old houses along the street frontage and provide new accommodation by building in the spacious backyards that backed onto a public lane. New apartments and the renovated houses were then to be made available not only to families who could afford to pay rents close to market value but also to families who needed public support to obtain proper housing. To administer the project, Council created the city housing corporation, later named Cityhome; and to solve the building problems they turned to the Toronto firm of Diamond & Myers (with Barton Myers as partner-in-charge), whose earlier works, such as York Square (Plate 162), had shown a fine sympathy with the character of the existing neighbourhood. In the final plans, and at an ultimate cost of $7 million, seventeen of the eighteen houses were renovated and subdivided, and five blocks of new suites were built. There are 376 units of various types for about 900 residents; the spacious square rooms of the Enoch Turner House were fitted out as bed-sitting rooms, while other houses contained apartments with as many as five bedrooms. Thanks to the public lane and the deep back yards behind the original houses, there was room to build without offensively cramming them, and to ease them into a new development scaled to the neighbourhood and to family living. Barton Myers managed in the end to provide for more people than would have been accommodated in the developer's towers. Cityhome's policy insists on a social mix of middle- and lower-income people. Only about one quarter of the residents in any one project receive rental assistance, though provincial authorities seem determined to greatly increase assisted tenancy and thus alter the social balance.

The walkway functioned almost as a private street for the development, linking the apartments in both the old and new sections and providing supervised play areas for children. The new apartments, in five different-sized blocks, rise no more than six storeys above one level of below-ground parking, nor more than one-and-a-half storeys above the front gables of the original houses. Four of the blocks are placed in a staggered row along the rear lane, with the fifth—the northernmost block, which is only five storeys high—running east-west out to Sherbourne Street. The suites entered at ground level are mostly two-storey town houses and, appropriately for family use, have direct access to both the front walkway and the rear lane. The apartments on the upper floors are planned as one- and two-level suites; those on the third and fourth floors all have access from a third-floor corridor-balcony that overlooks the walkway and leads to a central elevator and stairs. The modern form of the fifth unit, which

165. 'Allandale'—the former Enoch Turner house (1856).

replaces the one house that was too dilapidated to restore, shelters the entrance to the basement parking and service area.

The careful paint work, which approximates original finishes, and the restoration of other details return this section of Sherbourne to much of its original glory. The new buildings, of concrete faced in yellow and red brick, are free of the ersatz period details and artificial quaintness that are common in new construction in a Victorian setting. Throughout, the brick forms are robustly geometrical, and the patterns of red brick and concrete across the yellow-brick wall surfaces are strongly linear. Along the central walkway the same features characterize the paired entrance porches and second-floor balconies, giving each town-house suite its own identity.

Prior to the creation of Dundas-Sherbourne little effort went into the preservation and rehabilitation of non-middle-class neighbourhoods. Although not everything met the hopes of architects and politicians—financial exigencies dictated more crowding than is ideal and sacrificing some of the architectural finishes and features—socially, and as part of the living city, Dundas-Sherbourne is an almost unqualified success and has been a model for most later Cityhome developments. A survey done by the City, when it considered applying the ideas used here to other developments, indicates that the residents are happy with their accommodation. The ideal of a mixed community with both supported rents and market-value rents has been maintained, and there is a constant demand for the apartments. Architecturally as well, the design has presented a powerful lesson. Attention to the streetscape, to providing varied accommodation, and to use of a cleanly contemporary idiom in housing design can be seen in many developments by other architects; and what was once thought of as radicalism is now fundamental to much good design.

THE ST LAWRENCE NEIGHBOURHOOD
The Esplanade between Jarvis and Berkeley Streets

The City of Toronto's participation in development usually takes the form of providing general advice, zoning controls, and basic services. In the St Lawrence Neighbourhood, however, the City itself was the developer. The housing there—apartments and town houses—was designed to create a new residential neighbourhood on what was originally the southern edge of the Town of York, where no housing had previously existed. St Lawrence was not only a social and political experiment but an architectural one as well. In a city and country where innovative architecture for multi-family housing had been given little chance to prove itself, St Lawrence was to be an attempt to provide working models that would set positive examples for private developers in the city. Some of the new buildings and streets work well; others are less successful. Overall, however, St Lawrence is a noble on-going experiment.

Nineteenth-century Toronto, like most cities of the period, was a patchwork quilt of large and small buildings of all types, both commercial and residential. Because transportation was costly and slow, all but the wealthiest of Toronto's residents lived as close as possible to their places of work. For convenience, public buildings and working and shopping areas were centrally situated. There were distinct districts and neighbourhoods; but as Toronto grew, even new neighbourhoods such as the Annex were still within easy walking distance of downtown, which for many people was actually home. As transportation improved in the early decades of this century, the city became divided into separate parts—industry here, shopping there, and houses often far from downtown. Only the poor or the eccentrically bohemian remained in the centre of the city. Modernist planning from the 1920s on supported such separation, and developers presented the subdivision as the ideal residential community.

By the 1960s it was apparent that this arrangement was beginning to create suburbs devoid of activity by day, and a downtown that was empty of life and interest in the evening. Toronto escaped the most severe consequences of such planning; but changes in its character were noticeable by the 1960s, when expressways designed to carry commuters downtown threatened neighbourhoods that had retained their vitality and identity on the fringe of downtown. Activists from these areas—the Annex, Rosedale, Don Vale, Grange Park, and North Jarvis—elected in the 1970s city politicians who would protect the character of their own neighbourhoods. One thing the reform-minded city councillors did was to influence the creation of neighbourhoods in the city core that were both similar to the older ones they represented and yet more varied and mixed in character.

In the St Lawrence Neighbourhood the City was planner, organizer, and client. The land chosen for the development stretches north from the intertwined barrier of the railway tracks and the Gardiner/Lakeshore Boulevard expressways to the south side of Front Street East. The buildings completed to date lie on either side of The Esplanade, from Jarvis to just east of Berkeley Street. A further triangle of undeveloped land extends west from Jarvis almost to Yonge Street.

The new neighbourhood was envisaged as a residential component of the renewed and commercially important Town of York and St Lawrence Market areas. Its centrepiece is The Esplanade, on land that as early as 1818 was reserved for public promenade along the waterfront. Landfill pushed the lakeshore further south, and by the mid-1850s Toronto had given over The Esplanade to the railways as a convenient right-of-way bounded by a narrow street. By the 1970s, however, the functioning rail lines were mostly further south. The new plan aimed to reconstitute The Esplanade in name and spirit as a wide double street (The Esplanade on the north, with Wilton Street and Scadding Avenue* on the south), with a strip of parkland running down the centre. Crossing this strip the main streets of the Town of York were extended south to create the large rectangular blocks of the community's basic subdivisions. The continuous street system was designed to connect the area with the established city to the north and to prevent the separation that was common in earlier large-scale projects like Regent Park and St Jamestown. Along part of the south side of Front Street, and east of The Esplanade where A.J. Diamond Associates developed the Berkeley Castle (Plate 169), there were old buildings to be preserved. But elsewhere the area was a blank slate on which many of Toronto's most inventive architectural firms were given a chance to work out their ideas about multi-family housing. The City, through Cityhome—the agency established to handle this and other housing schemes, such as the Dundas-Sherbourne Project (Plate163)—outlined certain conditions, the most important of which concerned the number, cost, and family-size of the new units; their division among row houses, apartments, and other units for rent and sale; as well as the general layout. Large buildings were to be built along the north and south boundaries and east-west streets in order to shelter rows of smaller independent houses on the blocks between them. Brick was to be used as the basic material because its colour and texture suggested intimacy and hominess.

The St Lawrence Neighbourhood proposal was announced in 1974 when David Crombie was mayor, and work began in

---

* Named after the Rev. Henry Scadding, first Rector of Holy Trinity (Plate 15) and first historian of Toronto.

166. *Crombie Park.*

1976 with the Crombie Park complex (this includes shops and two schools as well as apartments) on the south side of Wilton Street, between Jarvis and George, to designs by Irving Grossman. In 1976–7 the David B. Archer Co-op by Jerome Markson Architects was started on the north side of The Esplanade between George and Frederick, with the Labour Council Development Foundation working as patron within the Cityhome guidelines. At the same time the Woodsworth Co-op was begun directly opposite, on the south side of Wilton, to designs by Sillaste & Nakashima. The next stages

of construction included the co-op at 176 The Esplanade, between Frederick and Sherbourne, by the Zeidler Roberts Partnership, with Alan Littlewood; a large building (with houses behind) by Ron Thom on the south side of Scadding, east of Princess; and the Windmill Line Co-op and the Caroline Co-op townhouses further east, by Matsui Baer Vanstone & Freeman. Almost everything was completed by 1982–3 when federal austerity caused the mortgage funds that had supported the work to dry up. During seven years of work 3,500 units were built to ease Toronto's continuing shortage of affordable and publicly supported housing. Though the number was small in relation to the city's need for such housing, it stands as a nearly miraculous accomplishment in the context of the difficulties of building publicly supported housing in Canada.

When St Lawrence was being planned, the City decided that the Neighbourhood required the integration of government-assisted units with others renting at market value. To prevent St Lawrence from becoming either a welfare ghetto or an inner-city enclave of upwardly mobile professionals, the buildings were conceived as co-operatives that would welcome tenants from all walks of life and all income levels. The architects were encouraged to create designs that would give each co-op a definite identity, while providing a range of accommodation and services.

Using brick in several warm colours, the buildings show a variety of form, detail, inspiration, and planning invention.* With few exceptions the townhouse rows are the least interesting parts of the neighbourhood. In the big blocks—seven-to-nine-floors high—there are references to nineteenth-century warehouses, the Classicism of the Italian and English Renaissance, and the more mundane speculative buildings of the 1950s. Irving Grossman's Crombie Park, which was the first to be built, is one of the most complex, for it contains not only townhouses and apartments but public and separate elementary schools and a row of shops and restaurants along Jarvis Street. Its L-shaped mass rises six storeys to shield the separate townhouses behind from the worst traffic noise in the area. Along Jarvis Street, above a walkway/colonnade in front of the commercial space on the ground floor, the brick façade is a regular grid of horizontals and verticals with expensive glazing. The colonnade, raised one storey higher, is continued on the façade facing The Esplanade. The schools occupy the lower floors; above, between the piers, angular bay windows and balconies step forward to establish the domestic character of the upper floors of the buildings.

The Woodsworth Co-op by Sillaste & Nakshima is more simply arranged as a narrow eight-storey building set off on the north or principal façade by four massive smooth pylons containing elevators and service stairs. The walls between are divided by a grid of horizontals and verticals, filled in with a taut surface of window and brick wall. The floors are grouped in pairs: one level with conventional windows, the other with wide semicircular panels of glass fronting corridors. The south façade is more regular, divided into tall panels by thin piers; but the arches recur on the ground floor, where two-storey townhouse units are fitted into them. The arched windows are a contrivance designed to distinguish

167. *The townhouses of the David B. Archer Co-op.*

the building from its neighbours; such eccentric detail is a failing of other buildings in the Neighbourhood as well. The nine-storey façades of Ron Thom's building on Scadding Avenue, modelled with groups of irregularly angular bays and balconies, create interesting interior effects and avoid the awkwardness of the Woodsworth design; the same is generally true of the arches that echo a Roman arcade, screening the enclosed parking garage and supporting a raised garden terrace along Sherbourne Street. But Thom capped his façades with thin pre-cast concrete arches, one of which stands out against the sky like a mammoth rib-bone, while others—built into the brick wall—canopy windows behind. Such features accomplish little and would not be missed.

From the beginning St Lawrence was seen as the residential extension of the Town of York, where—as in the Berkeley Castle (Plate 169)—late-nineteenth-century warehouses and factories are being renovated for other uses. The Windmill Line Co-op borrowed directly from these buildings. Across the ground floor stretches a two-storey arcade of wide arches inset into the thickness of the wall. The seven storeys of window above are grouped vertically between pairs of narrower arches set on tall piers. Despite the use of ordinary windows throughout, the rhythm of the pattern and the apparent thickness of the brickwork give character and validity to the borrowings from warehouse design. Unfortunately the majestic row of arches relates awkwardly to the nondescript two-storey façades of the units behind.

The Caroline Co-op (situated behind Windmill Line), by the same firm, is much more successful. The best and most attractive townhouses in the entire neighbourhood, they are

---

* They express the current preoccupation of many architects with the controversial ideas that have been loosely labelled Post Modernism, which—unlike the austere simplicity of the International Style in such buildings as the Toronto Dominion Centre—have encouraged architects to explore historical references and decorative and picturesque forms.

arranged with one-storey units on the ground floor and two-storey units above. A steep mansard roof, prominent and varied dormers, high party-walls with tall chimneys, as well as massive porch/vestibules set the units apart from one another and establish a comfortable image of 'home' and domesticity. The roofline, the soft pinkish brick, and the windows gracefully echo Georgian and Victorian traditions. The porches—the finest invention of the design—strongly define the length of an otherwise boring long straight street. A tall arch in front shelters steps that lead to the doors of the upper units; smaller arches highlight the doors of the lower units, where the porch roof becomes a balcony overlooking the street from the third-floor bedrooms.

The large L-shaped block on the northwest corner of Sherbourne and The Esplanade—designed by the Zeidler, Roberts Partnership with Alan Littlewood,—shelters two rows of townhouses. At the north end of the site, on the southwest corner of Front and Sherbourne, another block forms a quadrangle. Along Sherbourne and Front there is ground-floor commercial space, and the north façade tries to accord with the older buildings to the west. The result is the most varied and ambitious design in St Lawrence. Entrance from The Esplanade is through a Palladian gate with round windows to either side. In front is an enclosed courtyard paved in concrete and red brick, with a triple stair at the far north end leading up between concrete columns to a quadrangle. (Here there is a branch of the Toronto Public Library designed by Philip Carter, who used shiny modern materials and pastel colours—the epitome of Canadian Post-Modernism.) The plan, which refers to large European housing complexes of the beginning of the century and borrows many details from the Classical traditions of architecture, creates an insular world sheltered from street traffic and noise. The apartments on two levels overlook both the street and the courtyards; but except for their grand Classical forms and reminiscences, the details of the façades—standard windows and stacked-up ugly metal balconies—are of little interest.

The finest of the St Lawrence buildings, the David B. Archer Co-op by Jerome Markson Architects, would stand out in any setting. Like other buildings in the area it is arranged with a seven-storey block facing The Esplanade and, behind, four parallel rows of two- and three-storey townhouses and apartments. Immediately behind the main block is a T-shaped courtyard—entered through bridged driveways from George and Frederick Streets—that acts as a laneway to the inner houses and creates a private enclave for the co-op community. There are no specific historical references in the Markson design and no eccentric details. The mass of the building is clearly set off by strong horizontals and by the recessed apartment balconies, with their solid brick parapets. The height of the main block is stepped down to five storeys over the bridged lane entrances to join the three-storey houses along

168. *The main block of the David B. Archer Co-op.*

George and Frederick. Here the entrances are paired under wide arches at the top of steps; and the windows in bays, standard panels, and extra-wide units are set off by white frames and surrounds. Above the entrances, at third-floor level, are white-painted wooden balconies with open beamed roofs. Their projections—the reverse of the dark shadowed recessed balconies of the main building—break the smooth line of the row façade with shadow and accents of white against red brick, creating a picturesque varied streetscape. Along the inner lane the Archer townhouses are simpler, with mansards added to form two- and three-storey units in broken lines. All of these rows, even with their prettier detail, have a comfortable family relationship to the main block in material and basic forms.

In general the results of the City's effort to create a new neighbourhood in the St Lawrence area have been positive. People of many occupations and several income levels feel at home in the district and enjoy benefits of life close to the heart of the city. Although many of the buildings lack the richness of detail and the warmth of character that were hoped for in the beginning, the Archer Co-op and the Caroline Co-op of townhouses have proved that there are definite alternatives to the merely bleak and drab reasonably priced multi-family housing. In these two developments, and to a lesser extent in the other designs, St Lawrence has fulfilled the City's initial expectations. By creating interesting housing it has provided an environment in which a neighbourhood community can take pride.

169

BERKELEY CASTLE

Berkeley Street at The Esplanade

Renovated 1980–4 by A.J. Diamond and Partners

When John Graves Simcoe founded York he laid out, as the first town site, the blocks bounded by Front Street on the south, George on the west, Adelaide on the north, and Berkeley on the east. This is the core of the area known today as the Town of York, which was gradually extended south to The Esplanade, west to Jarvis and the St Lawrence Market, north to Queen, and east to Parliament. Very few buildings remain here that have any connection with the city's history before 1850—the Bank of Upper Canada (Plate 6) and the Fourth Post Office next door are the most important. Today the area acquires its character from industrial and commercial buildings built after the 1870s, and particularly from brick and stone factories and warehouses of the 1890s and the Edwardian period.

Until the 1950s most of these buildings retained their original, or similar, uses. In the next decade, however, the district was ripe for redevelopment and it suffered several losses. Fortunately inertia protected it long enough for the preservation movement of the early 1970s to convince the City that it possessed a distinctive character worth saving. Seeing the value of keeping first the industry housed in these large downtown warehouses and, second, the buildings themselves and the character of the area, the City adopted preservation as standard policy. When the first plans were being drawn for the St Lawrence Neighbourhood (Plates 000–0), industrial buildings that ten years before would have been destroyed were included in the total scheme.

Several nineteenth-century industrial buildings* on the edges of the St Lawrence Neighbourhood have been renovated since the early 1970s, but the most ambitious project of rehabilitation in the area is Berkeley Castle, as it is called by its owners, carried through by A.J. Diamond and Partners. This complex grew out of the derelict buildings of the former Joseph Simpson Knitting Mill. Dating from the mid-1870s, with extensive additions in the 1890s, the buildings were irregularly grouped around a central court filled in with lower structures. Though little effort seems to have been made in this once thoroughly industrial area to give the factory a formal or architectural image, even the earliest buildings—particularly the Mill, which forms the north side of the central court—have smoothly accomplished brickwork and a regular arrangement of sashed windows, each with a shallow arched lintel worked in yellow brick that contrasts with the red of the walls. The Keep—a free-standing block in the centre of the court that now houses a restaurant on the ground floor—is more elaborate, with the windows of the two upper floors grouped in slightly recessed panels. The four-storey block facing The Esplanade, known in the renovation as the Hall, is more elaborate still, with arched third-floor windows. The last of the units—the six-storey block on the corner of The Esplanade and Berkeley, now known as the Tower—has the straightforward factory aesthetic of the early twentieth century, with large square windows grouped between tall, plain brick piers.

In working though the rehabilitation of this complex, the designers of the Diamond firm have shown a sensitivity to the character of the existing buildings that is unusual in Toronto renovations. New windows, sealed to allow air conditioning, have preserved the multi-paned patterns of the nineteenth-century glazing and avoided the stark, staring panels of thermopane that are the norm in renovation work. Along Berkeley Street, where wide shop fronts have replaced a jumble of windows and doors, the new large-paned windows framed in coloured metal and sheltered by roll-down awnings have a subtle modernism, their clean lines and simple patterns drawing on the factory aesthetic of the nineteenth century. Devoid of ersatz Neo-Victorianism, the effect is completely in harmony with the period of the building. Inside the complex, the courtyard—which originally contained one-storey buildings—is the focus of the project and the key to its character. The space is cleanly designed, calm and balanced,

170. *The inner courtyard.*

almost Classical in its geometry, with a carefully placed walkway and spare plantings.

Diamond's first proposals for rehabilitation called for parts of the buildings to be arranged as studio and loft apartments (on the model of loft conversions in New York City), with ground-floor space devoted to commercial uses keyed to the street traffic of the area, and upper floors to offices. This plan required a zoning change that would have been nominally inconsistent with official policy for industrial buildings downtown. Only after it became apparent that the building was unlikely to be used industrially again were partial zoning changes made to permit office and commercial space—but not, unfortunately, a residential component. Its absence has the unfortunate effect of making the development a 9-to-5 complex that lacks diversity of use.

The purity of conception and detail of Berkeley Castle partly results from the fact that the architects were their own clients, for Jack Diamond's firm became the first major tenant and occupies a large part of the Tower. Diamond's belief in the value and merits of the buildings as he envisaged and then carried out his renovation attracted other tenants with connections to architecture and the design industries. They now help to fill the complex, whose ongoing life enriches this downtown neighbourhood.

---

* For example, the Young Peoples' Theatre was created from the power-house of the Toronto Street Railway at Front and Frederick Streets, and theatre spaces for both the Toronto Free Theatre and the Canadian Opera Company were carved out of former gas-production facilities of the Consumers' Gas Company, at Front and Berkeley Streets.

171

ROY THOMSON HALL

Simcoe Street at King Street West (SW)

1972–82 by Arthur Erickson with Mathers &
Haldenby as Associate Architects

Named in memory of the newspaper magnate Baron Thomson of Fleet, Roy Thomson Hall has succeeded Massey Hall (Plate 70) as Toronto's chief venue for concerts and the home of the Toronto Symphony and the Mendelssohn Choir. Unlike Massey Hall, with its dour façade and cramped interior spaces, Thomson Hall is a glittering pleasure pavilion. The sheen of the web of glass enclosing the building and the multiple reflections of the lobby's mirrored walls provide a dramatic introduction to the restful elegance of the handsome oval concert hall with its austere grey concrete and upholstery.

Very few concert halls built in Canada have been able to match the overall acoustic excellence of Massey Hall. What it has lacked is a proper lobby or other accessory space and adequate backstage and rehearsal facilities. Agitation for a new concert hall in Toronto began in the late 1960s; but it was not until 1972 that the architectural design process led by Erickson, Mathers & Haldenby, and the acousticians Bolt, Baranek & Newman, began. From the beginning it was the wish of the Massey Hall Board of Governors, who today administer both the original hall and the new building, that the acoustics should be the determining factor at all stages of the design. The acoustics, and the possibility of varying them to suit different types of music and instrumentation, were provided by the oval shape and arrangement of the auditorium, and by the ceiling with its clear plastic disks that can be raised, lowered, and adjusted for everything from pop concerts and large vocal and orchestral classics to intimate chamber works. Even movies can be shown on a screen that drops from the ceiling. It was Erickson's responsibility to clothe the concert hall both inside and out in an architectural formality and elegance that would provide an appropriate setting for the cultural and social events to which the hall was dedicated.

The site of Thomson Hall, provided by Marathon Realty with the encouragement of City Council, is one of the most historic in downtown Toronto. This was the heart of Victorian Toronto's social and official life. Upper Canada College stood on the north-west corner of Simcoe and King, on land designated as Russell Square in 1797; immediately south, between Wellington and Front Streets, stood Upper Canada's third Legislative Buildings; while on the south-east corner of King and Simcoe stands St Andrew's, the city's premier Presbyterian church since it was built in 1875. The land chosen for Thomson Hall at the south-west corner of Simcoe and King was from the 1830s until 1912 the site of the first two formal Government Houses in Toronto. After 1912 it was occupied by the tracks, sheds, and shipping building of the CPR's express services. These buildings were declared surplus in the early 1970s and Marathon Realty, the railway's real-estate development company, offered the choice corner site for a new concert hall in return for concessions in the development of the rest of the site. The concert hall was to be only part of a much larger scheme to include office towers, apartment buildings, and a three-acre park around a large pond.

The irregular oval of the concert hall rests on a four-storey square block that spreads out beneath it. This supporting block includes two levels of underground parking, one level of service and rehearsal-room space that is above grade on all but the east and north sides, a mostly glass-roofed main-floor foyer entered from Simcoe Street, and lobby space arranged on several interlocking levels. Each of these elements is designed to insulate the hall from outside noise and vibration. Unfortunately Erickson also chose to isolate Thomson Hall from the fact of King Street as well, by placing the sunken pool and terrace of the Dunnington-Grubb Court between the Hall and King Street. The least likeable part of the whole design, and rarely used by most patrons, it cuts off the building from its most logical approach and prevents the street and sidewalk from having a real connection with the Hall.

Three-quarters of the height of the auditorium rises through the surrounding square, giving the complex its unique silhouette. In Erickson's presentation scheme the glass roof of the foyer was to be stretched like a tent of mirroring membrane—without visible supports or glazing bars—from the curving edge of the auditorium to the square edge of the outer walls.* It was a scheme that would have required virtually every pane of glass to be individually designed and fabricated in a manufacturing process guided by computer. No glass manufacturer could be found willing to undertake the considerable bother and expense, and the design was finally modified. Erickson describes the existing roof, with its outer surface divided by thick glazing bars into diamonds and triangles and supported on an inner skeleton of steel tubes, as 'stiffer' and 'clumsier' that the original mirror-finished design. But the effect inside the foyer, surrounded by glass and a constantly changing view of the city, is very close to that of the original. Between the foyer and the auditorium are two walls, ensuring separation of sound. Against the foyer wall broad stairways rise to the several levels of the auditorium. In keeping with the nineteenth-century tradition of grand staircases in concert halls and opera houses, these stairs are broken into broad terraces as meeting-places and resting spots for the social intermissions that are part of concert-going. Each of the upper terrace landings, supported on thin columns of concrete, seems to float under the glass roof. The effect is intensified by the panels of mirror that almost cover the inner wall surface, doubling the image of the city outside and the crowds inside. In very few concert halls does the outdoor setting form such a large part of the interior—until the moment of entering the auditorium. Erickson's buildings are famous for such effects, although they are usually designed to incorporate images of nature's wilder aspects.

The foyer wall is designed with a series of overlapping folds that shelter the doors to the auditorium, through which the concert-goer leaves behind an exciting space of varied levels, and of crystalline and refracted light, for one muted in light and colour that focuses on the stage. With an area of thirty thousand square feet, the auditorium rises to a height of eighty feet and seats 2,875. Its size was largely dictated by the economics of concert-hall management, but architect and acoustician together avoided the usual arrangement of orchestra level overhung by first and second balconies by dividing the balcony seating into a series of small sloped units. Each is entered from one of the landings on the main stairs; the largest (opposite the stage) seat as many as 75, while the smallest (to either side of the stage) seat as few as 12. The interior effect resembles the traditional division of a baroque theatre into boxes. Each unit has its own special character and relation to the music, and together they tend to dissolve the huge audience into intimate and companionable parts. At the first level a U-shaped arrangement for choir seating surrounds the back of the stage, and on certain occasions this area is sold as rush seats to the general public. The complexity of the auditorium's design is subdued by Erickson's use of fine silver grey concrete for wall, balustrade, and parapet surfaces, a matching grey for carpets and upholstery, and

---

* In execution the design of the glass roof was simplified to give it a base with the same shape as the upper outline, standing on the square flat roof of the main floor.

172. *The foyer of Roy Thomson Hall.*

polished stainless steel for railings, doors, and fixtures. Controlled in both colour and texture, Erickson's concrete is sleek, almost sensuous. In the foyer it is a solid counterpoint to the mirrored surfaces; in the auditorium it is the formal and subdued background for the colourful dress of performers and audience.

The ceiling of the auditorium was intended from the beginning to be a central element in the acoustical character of the space. The concrete shell of the roof is partially concealed by two cat-walk rings of lights, one inside the other, replacing traditional chandeliers. Hanging from the roof are a number of globe fixtures that can be controlled for elaborate lighting effects, as well as ventilation apparatus and microphones and speakers for the sound system. But the design of the ceiling was determined primarily by acoustical requirements. Suspended from it are adjustable plastic clouds and a series of tapestried cylinders five inches in diameter and eleven feet long than can all be raised and lowered to fit specific acoustic needs. The cylinders—or banners as they are frequently called—range in colour from red through deep purple, and were designed by Québec tapestry artist Mariette Rousseau-Vermette. There were originally some 4,000 of these banners, arranged to form a three-dimensional burst of colour above the more muted tones of the seating area. Only a fraction were actually essential to the acoustical system and the majority were removed—over Erickson's protests—when the system seemed not to operate as designed. Unfortunately, in the opinion of many concert-goers and clients, including members of the Toronto Symphony Orchestra, the Hall's acoustical problems have not yet been solved.

Though Thomson Hall has been open for four years, it is still not complete. The acoustics are still being adjusted, and until that work is satisfactorily carried out the new centrepiece designed for the ceiling cannot be installed. More important to the visitor's perception of the building is the uncompleted Marathon Realty development of office towers to the west—a project delayed indefinitely by the glut of rental office space in Toronto. Erickson, who has always stressed the close interrelation of his buildings with their sites, contrived to have the mirrored lobby of Thomson Hall opening out to the surrounding city; and he planned the adjacent project to include an outdoor concert amphitheatre on the shores of the pool that would, in an artfully contrasting manner, extend the facilities of his concert hall. Unfortunately Thomson Hall now appears to float uncomfortably by the shore of a vast sea of parked cars.

Despite these drawbacks, few recent buildings in Toronto

173. *An aerial view of Roy Thomson Hall; to the east are St Andrew's Church (1875) and, across King Street, the Sun Life Centre.*

possess Thomson Hall's architectural self-confidence or display the kind of flair that enabled Erickson, using an entirely different vocabulary, to complement the Edwardian panache of the Royal Alexandra Theatre across the street. Toronto, which is now on the verge of building a grand opera house, will find in Roy Thomson Hall a superb example of the way architectural character can be achieved in a building devoted to the performing arts.

174

THE YORKDALE SUBWAY STATION

THE SPADINA LINE OF THE TORONTO TRANSIT COMMISSION

The William R. Allen Road, south of Highway 401

1977 by Arthur Erickson

No element of Toronto's transit system is more important than the subway; but its first stations possessed none of the dynamic architectural character and presence that could help make the daily grind of commuting a more pleasant experience. The opening of the Spadina Subway line, from the St George Station north to Wilson Avenue along the route of the rejected Spadina Expressway, has provided a welcome change. The TTC has been justifiably proud of its safety record and the quality of service and comfort in its subways. With the building of the Spadina Line it went a step further and created stations that aspired to individualism, style, and, with specially commissioned art works, to genuine civic character. Each of the stations has its own interest, but perhaps the most original is Arthur Erickson's Yorkdale Station, serving Yorkdale Shopping Centre, just south of Highway 401. On a smaller scale than his Thomson Hall (Plate 171), it is just as dramatic in its use of materials and forms, and as finely crafted in its details.

The first proposals for a subway date from 1910 when the city had begun to expand into new suburbs whose distance from downtown made faster public transportation necessary. Unfortunately a referendum on the issue produced a negative vote in 1913, and the disruption of the First World War and the Depression delayed serious public consideration of the question for many years. In 1942, when the city began to consider ways of alleviating the traffic congestion expected in the period of postwar reconstruction, the subway project was again taken up, and in 1945 the TTC authorized the preparation of full plans for construction of a Yonge Street line between Eglinton and Union Station, which opened for service in 1954, with a spur back up to Bloor on University, added in 1963. The first stations were mostly underground structures of strictly functional design and dreary colours and materials. Once the novelty of subway travel wore off, the stations where many Torontonians spend a part of their day were seen to be devoid of interest or stimulation, limbos of watery pastel ceramic tile. It was assumed from the beginning that above-ground facilities would eventually be incorporated into new commercial buildings along the line, and few stations had any architectural identity on the street at all; for most there was only a stairway emerging from the ground. Toronto architects John B. Parkin (a devotee of Modernism), and A.S. Mathers (far more traditional) were engaged to oversee stations with buildings of their own, such as Wellesley and Rosedale. These designs, completed in 1947 but not built

for six years, were simple pavilions of glass, steel, and brick. In spite of changes made in 1984–5, the original buildings—particularly Rosedale and Summerhill—are lasting reminders of the elegant simplicity of 1950s Modernism. Nevertheless the station designs of the system as a whole, repeated on the Bloor line (1966), lacked panache. When Montreal in 1966–7 opened a Metro whose spacious, dramatic, and individualized stations were filled with colour and art, Toronto's safe, efficient subway seemed all the more dowdy and uninviting.

The cancellation of the Spadina Expressway in 1971, the reversal of a TTC decision to phase out its streetcars, experiments with new forms of rapid transit, and a change in popular attitude about the civic benefits and personal convenience of public transportation all contributed to a spirit of high hope and expansive optimism at the TTC; and a public debate took place in 1973 over the route to be used for the next subway line from the northwestern suburbs to the downtown core. Whatever their views on that question, many people believed that the new line should have a more interesting and dramatic character than its predecessors—something perhaps that would compare with Montreal's Métro. The TTC had previously handled most of its architectural work 'in house'; but now, it went out of its way to employ a variety of independent talent. Three major firms, as well as the established TTC team, each designed two stations; and provision was made for major pieces of art to enhance the architectural spaces. These stations were to be more colourful and spacious than any Toronto had seen before, and to enliven as much as possible the act of subway travel. When the line was officially opened in January 1978 it was clear that they had succeeded—and in particular with the two stations designed by Arthur Erickson.

His station at Eglinton West, with its two porcelain enamel murals by Gerald Zeldin depicting Toronto streetcars in various stages of movement, uses concrete and red brick and expansive areas of glass with the open simplicity that is characteristic of much of Erickson's work. The second station, at Yorkdale, serves Toronto's principal suburban bus terminal as well as the gigantic Yorkdale Shopping Centre. The Eglinton West station refines and perfects the standard conventions of subway-station design, but the Yorkdale station is conceived very differently to express the effect of subway travel itself, which is made to seem more dramatic by Erickson's use of metal and glass, and by displaying the most effective piece of art in the entire system.

The Yorkdale station platform, which is the focus of the

design, stands high above its surroundings. Below run the lanes of the Allen Expressway, and a crisscross of service roads, ramps, and parking lots; nearby to the north are more roads to and from the twelve-lane Highway 401. Access to the station is gained from levels below the expressway that are linked by raised walkways to the neighbouring bus terminal, parking lots, office building, and shopping centre. The surrounding network of roadways obliterates all sense of streetscape, and none of the area's buildings attempt to create an alternative. Above this maze shines the station, its glass, steel, and concrete wrapped and shaped into a form that seems—like the subway trains it serves—to have paused there momentarily. The long central platform is roofed with a semi-circular, multi-paned vault of glass that is closed at each end by a curved apse through which escalators and stairs descend to entrances from the surrounding road system. Crossed girders extending from tree-like columns sheathed in brushed stainless steel support the glass roof, through which the light (even on overcast winter days) casts a lattice pattern across the platform and all who walk there. Even without greenery it suggests a greenhouse or a grape arbour. On either side of the platform arriving trains slide into lower curved sheds of concrete, whose groups of seven windows are the shape and size of those in a subway car. Inside and out the smooth concrete sections have an abstract but genuine resemblance to the trains they house. The station's exterior recalls the vaulted form of a nineteenth-century train station. Inside, the platform makes this part of the subway system a distinctive place, where the view of the outside, framed by the car windows and the train-like windows of the shed, acquires an interest hardly to be expected in a landscape of expressways, parking lots, and undeveloped land.

The big forms of the station set its character, but Erickson lavished as much care on the details. Spaced down the platform are shelters with seats. The walls are of steel and glass panels jointed without mullions to form curved enclosures that echo the overall shape of the platform. The use of metal extends to globe lighting fixtures above the stairways, bannisters that are wide but nevertheless fit the palm of the hand in a reassuring way, and large vertical tubes for door handles that make access to this station the easiest on the TTC. The floors are grey terrazzo, laid with circles inside large squares. The triumph of the station, as important at night as the patterns of sunlight through the roof during the day, is Michael Hayden's neon tube sculpture, 'Arc en Ciel'. Along the length

175. *The platform of the Yorkdale Subway Station.*

of the curving vault, braced against every other steel rib, are neon hoops that are invisible during the day but glow at night with all the colours of the rainbow. These hoops pulsate in the direction of travel when a train enters the station—dramatizing the sudden appearance of the train out of the darkness, and converting the possibly frightening experience of its onrushing speed into the pleasurable excitement of light and colour in motion. No matter how often one uses the Yorkdale Station, enjoyment of that lighted vault need never fade: like the glass elevators of the Metro Library (Plate 156) and the Eaton Centre (Plate 158), it appeals to something childlike in the user. Arthur Erickson has a religious respect for Nature and its place in the lives of those who use his buildings. In most of his work the landscape, or cityscape, visible through broad windows provides a benchmark or reference point for the enjoyment of the building. At Yorkdale Station not only the subway passenger but the motorist passing through the mutilated landscape can take delight in Erickson's celebration of the mechanical nature of the subway, the forms and metal of the trains, and their smooth-flowing power and speed.

176. *The east front of the A.E. LePage building, seen across Berczy Park.*

A.E. LEPAGE BUILDING

23 Yonge Street at Front Street East (NE)
1981-2 by Webb Zerafa Menkes & Housden

AND

MARKET SQUARE

Front Street East
Jerome Markson Architects, 1981-3

Toronto's warehouse district and the St Lawrence Market area did not suffer total neglect in the 1960s: two new buildings on Front Street—the O'Keefe Centre (1956-60 by Earle C. Morgan with Page & Steele) and the St Lawrence Centre for the Performing Arts (1967-70 by Gordon S. Adamson Associates)—made architectural statements that were radically out of keeping with the nineteenth-century warehouses. Meanwhile demolition on Front Street robbed the entire north side from Jarvis to Yonge of continuity and streetscape. With everything to the west and almost everything to the east gone, there remained only one forlorn remnant of a bygone era: the Gooderham Building (Plate 66).

The decade from 1975 to 1985 saw a dramatic change, spurred by restoration on the south side of Front (Plates 44-7) and on the north side of Wellington (a row of Greek Revival shops at numbers 36-42 that dates from 1854-5, with an 1898 addition to number 40). New development was encouraged when the city transformed the parking lot west of the Gooderham Building into Berczy Park, in memory of William Von Moll Berczy (1744-1813), the Saxon portrait painter who led a colony of German immigrants to York. Thanks to the city's interest in this area, and to the success of its shops and restaurants, new construction at the end of the 1970s finally began to fill up the obtrusive parking lots. Seventy-one Front

315

Street, begun in 1979-81 by Moriyama & Teshima, is a re-building and extension of a 1950s warehouse that had re-placed earlier buildings, and with its wide arched windows is clearly at home with its Victorian neighbours. Behind, studio and office spaces on several floors overlook a vaulted atrium. (Further back, and invisible from Front Street, is a tall irregu-lar block of condominium apartments). The result is unusually sensitive to the character of Front Street, without sacrificing lake views to the south or the dramatic sense of interior space for which Moriyama is known. Some of the more visible build-ings are less successful: the bay-windowed Gooderham Court (Wellington East at 34 Church, 1981 by E.I. Richmond) is banal; and so are the office and apartment towers of Wel-lington Square (26-30 Wellington East at Scott (NE), 1982 by E.I. Richmond), despite the use of costly black glass and granite and a front plaza ornamented with sculpture. Neither of these recent free-standing buildings answered the prob-lems of scale and design posed by the proximity of the Vic-torian commercial buildings and warehouses—problems aggravated by the Gooderham Building's having been left so exposed by demolition.

There are, however, two very successful additions to the area. Though they are large buildings, they have been de-signed—without recourse to hackneyed neo-Victorianisms and meaningless details—to accord with their older neighbours. The first, the largest, and most conspicuously modern of them is the A.E. LePage Building by Webb Zerafa Menkes & Housden. Built by one of Canada's biggest real-estate sales and rental agencies (now expanded to become the Royal-LePage Real Estate Services), it covers the entire block bounded by Front Street East, Yonge, Wellington Street East, and Scott Street. Clad in silvery-blue mirror glass, it appears to be a single mass from several angles, but actually consists of two low office towers: one running east-west along Wel-lington Street; the other following the diagonal line of Front Street SW-NE from Yonge to Scott. Between the towers rises the most attractive of the many atriums designed by Webb Zerafa Menkes & Housden. Its ground plan is an extended trapezoid, with the space rising past tiers of open balconies and divided into east and west halves by a free-standing bank of elevators from which bridges extend to the office floors. Facing Yonge Street, the vertical rise of the glass façade—stepped forward at the corners and raised on tall concrete columns—reflects the red and yellow brick shops from the 1850s across the street. (This is one of the very few instances in Toronto where mirror glass actually does the reflecting job it is supposed to do. Usually the mirrored surface reveals only clouds and sky or occasional passers-by.) The colon-nade and the shops and restaurants it shelters are continued along the line of Front Street, where set-backs in the build-ing's height prevent it from overwhelming the smaller ele-ments in the streetscape. In this section of the colonnade both the columns and the second-floor walkway, with curving solid stairs leading up to it, show the influence of the Franco-Swiss architect Le Corbusier.

177. *Berczy Park, looking east to the mural by Derek M. Besant on the end wall of the Gooderham Building.*

The designers of the second notable project in the St Law-rence Market area, the Market Square condominium com-plex, had a larger site to work with but a more complicated program to satisfy. Bounded by the Market Lane Park west of St Lawrence Hall, Front Street East, Church Street, and the service lane opposite St James' Cathedral on King, the site is at the very heart of Toronto's history. Though densely covered in the 1960s with the buildings of a prospering com-mercial neighbourhood, the area was included in several plans for wholesale urban renewal. By the end of the sixties demo-lition had destroyed most of the buildings, except for a few along King, and they had been replaced with an expanse of parking spaces. So it remained through the 1970s, with the parking lot ironically serving as a major support facility for the growing use and popularity of the St Lawrence Markets to the east, and for the stores, restaurants, and offices that were installed in the renovated buildings on the south side of Front (Plates 44-7). It was only after much discussion that the site passed to Market Square Associates (a consortium of Olympia & York and Canadian Landmark Developments), who agreed to build a mixed commercial and residential de-velopment on the site that would be in keeping with City Coun-cil's expressed desire for more housing in the downtown core—a desire that was already being pursued in the St Law-rence Neighbourhood (see pages 302-5) to the south and east.

Jerome Markson Architects, who received the commis-sion to build the project after a private competition held by the development company, set out to integrate into the St Lawrence Market area an eight-storey development of 306 condominium apartments (plus related facilities), arranged on seven floors above a ground floor of indoor and outdoor commercial space, with a three-level parking garage as well. The initial studies were directly concerned with preserving the vistas through and past the area and the landmark status of the Gooderham Building. One vista posed both a problem and a tremendous opportunity. In the late 1930s the demolition of a building at 115 King Street East had opened a large gap in the streetscape along the south side of King, directly opposite St James' Cathedral. A plea was made for the preservation of the view by Eric Arthur in *Toronto: No Mean City* (1962), and by the 1970s it was one of the elements that Council accepted as important in the redesign of the Market area. In 1980-1 the city's Urban Design Group, with private funding, was able to turn the King Street parking lot into a landscaped garden. Overlooked by restaurants in the restored shops on either side, there was space for a wall waterfall and changing displays of large-scale sculpture. To preserve and enhance the view north from Front Street the architects arranged the Market Square development in two blocks on either side of a terraced walkway that was aligned with the tower of St James' and connected with the Sculpture Garden. A dramatic view of the cathedral façade and tower now added a new and picturesque element to Toronto's downtown—an area graced by few architectural vistas. The walkway/courtyard creates a sheltered enclave, and the vista north to St James' makes the central landmark of Toronto in the 1870s a focal point for Front Street in the 1980s. Though the Cathedral and its tower have been exploited in the design of the complex, one's appreciation of them has been enhanced. The result clearly reveals the value of old buildings in an urban context as features that can animate and distinguish new construction.

The character of the buildings framing the view of St James', and fronting on the surrounding streets, was obviously of tremendous importance, and to accord with the nineteenth-century buildings in the neighbourhood the designers chose buff brick with red brick trim as the principal materials. But unlike several other designers in the area, Markson avoided a Neo-Georgian or Neo-Victorian style and sought his inspiration in the multi-storey factories and warehouses that lined the south side of Front Street. Appropriately the steel and concrete frame used for Market Square and the large windows called for in contemporary condominium design related closely to the post-and-beam structural system and generous windows of the earlier buildings. The repeated verticals of the new structures—the dominant elements in the façades—form the piers for the ground-floor colonnade that shelters shops and restaurants; the piers also rise between the wide panels of factory-like windows on the front of the eighth-floor penthouse apartments. Between them floor-to-ceiling windows were placed singly, in pairs, or at

178. *Market Square condominiums, showing the vista north to St James' Cathedral.*

the chamfered or angled corners of the blocks in the broad bays of spacious sunrooms.

The Market Square condominiums are perhaps the most attractive and sensitive urban project that the development firm of Olympia & York has been involved with in Canada; and in designing the A.E. LePage Building the Webb Zerafa Menkes & Housden firm employed equal sensitivity and perception. Each approached in different ways the problems of building in an established context. The A.E. LePage Building employs massing and modern materials to complement 1850s shops to the west and to create a sympathetic background for the Gooderham Building to the east, mitigating the orphan-like status in which demolition had left it. The Market Square project, using more traditional materials, enhanced an existing vista to give itself a prime position within the St Lawrence Market area. It is one of the notable achievements of Toronto's recent history that the move towards total demolition and renewal of the St Lawrence Market area was stopped and replaced by a sequence of positive changes: the restoration of buildings, sympathetically designed new developments, and the provision of new park space. Thus was created an environment in which the architecture of the past became a harmonious setting for the works and activities of the present, and the historic core of Old Toronto receives the tribute of enjoyment and use.

179. *A composite of many periods, looking west along Front Street past the Market Square Condominiums (on the right) to the Gooderham Building, the A.E. LePage Building, the towers of the Royal Bank Plaza and of the IBM Building in the T-D Centre, and the CN Tower behind: the landmarks of a rejuvenated downtown.*

GLOSSARY

APSE A semicircular termination to the CHANCEL—the location of the altar—flanked by aisles. (St James' Cathedral)

ARCADE A row of arches, carried on PIERS or columns, sometimes with a covered walkway behind. (The south front of the Library in University College.)

ARCHITRAVE The lowest of the three main parts of an ENTABLATURE.

ATRIUM A high inner courtyard, in Canada usually with a glazed ceiling. (Osgoode Hall, The Royal Bank Plaza)

ATTIC STOREY A storey above the ENTABLATURE of a building, or the space under the sloping roof of a house. (The south front of Osgoode Hall)

BALUSTRADE An ornamental PARAPET around a terrace or skyline of a building, made up of a rail and a row of vase-shaped posts (balusters). (Osgoode Hall)

BARGEBOARDS Boards placed along the edge of a GABLE to protect the beams of a roof—in Ontario often fancifully cut and ornamented. (The gates of the Necropolis.)

BAY The basic division of a façade defined by a door or window: e.g. Campbell House is five bays wide: four windows and one door. A bay window is one that projects from the façade of a house.

BUTTRESS A mass of masonry or brickwork projecting from a wall to give it additional strength. (St James' Cathedral)

CANOPY Roof-like projection over a door, tomb, pulpit, etc.

CANTILEVER A beam that projects from a wall to support a balcony or an upper floor. (The Royal Bank Plaza: the end wall of the atrium)

CASEMENT WINDOW A window with panes of glass mounted in frames that swing out. (Wychwood Park)

CHAMFER A right-angled corner, with the actual corner bevelled off. (St James' Cathedral)

CHANCEL The continuation of the NAVE of a church in which the main altar is placed and the clergy and choir are located. (Timothy Eaton Memorial Church)

CLERESTORY The upper stage of the walls of a church, or any large space, pierced by windows. (St James' Cathedral, New City Hall)

COFFERS Panels recessed into a ceiling. (Osgoode Hall Library)

COLONNADE A row of columns or PIERS supporting an ENTABLATURE or other horizontal element, often with a walkway behind. (Crombie Park in the St Lawrence Neighbourhood.)

COLONNETTES Little columns frequently used as ornamental detailing, especially to frame windows or fireplaces. (Consumers' Gas Building)

CONCOURSE A wide, generous passageway or meeting-place in a building. (Union Station)

CORBEL A projecting block, usually of stone or brick, supporting a beam, an ENTABLATURE, or the eaves of a building. (University College)

COVED CEILING A ceiling that rises in a gentle curve from the sides to a higher flat, frequently ornamented, centre. (Osgoode Hall)

CORNICE Projecting ornamental moulding along the top of a building or around a room.

COURSE Continuous horizontal layer of stone or brick in a building.

CUPOLA A dome on a circular or polygonal base crowning a roof. (St Lawrence Hall)

CUTSTONE Smooth-faced masonry.

DADO Lower part of a room wall when faced or coloured differently from the upper part.

DORMER A window cut through a sloping roof with a roof of its own. The front profile of a bonneted dormer is curved, like a nineteenth-century lady's bonnet.

EMBRASURE The cutaway thickness of a wall that frames a window or door.

ENTABLATURE The upper horizontal parts of a Classical order of architecture resting on the capital of a column; it includes the ARCHITRAVE, FRIEZE, and CORNICE.

FANLIGHT Fan-shaped window over a door.

FENESTRATION The arrangement of windows across a façade.

FLUTING Vertical grooves in a column or PILASTER.

FRENCH DOORS Double doors fitted with glass and used as a window. (Colborne Lodge)

FRIEZE The most ornamental part of the ENTABLATURE, between the ARCHITRAVE and CORNICE; band of decoration around a room near the ceiling.

GABLE Triangular upper part of a wall to carry a pitched roof.

GLAZING BARS The vertical or horizontal wooden bars that support panes in a window.

HAMMERBEAM ROOF   An elaborately beamed roof in which the principal rafters are on a short beam projecting from the wall. (The Great Hall of Hart House)

KEYSTONE   The central stone of an arch.

LANCET WINDOW   Slender, pointed window without TRACERY, often grouped in threes or fives. (St James' Cathedral)

LINTEL   Horizontal beam of stone, wood, or iron supporting the wall above a door or window.

LOCULUS   A deep niche in a mausoleum containing a coffin. (The Massey Tomb)

LOGGIA   An open gallery, sometimes arcaded. ('Donningvale' in Bayview)

LUNETTE   A semicircular section of wall under the curve of a vault, sometimes opened to make a window or sometimes decorated. (St Anne's Church)

MANSARD ROOF   A roof with a double slope, the lower one steeper. (The former Bank of British North America)

MULLION   A vertical post dividing the casements or panels of a window.

NARTHEX   The antechamber to the NAVE in a church.

NAVE   The body of a church from the main entrance to the CHANCEL, where the congregation is seated.

OGEE ARCH   Double-curved Gothic or Moorish arch. (Massey Hall)

ORIEL WINDOW   An overhanging bay window on the upper floor of a building, supported on a bracket or CORBEL. (Hart House)

PALLADIAN   In the Renaissance style of the Italian architect Andrea Palladio (1508-80). A Palladian door or window is divided into three parts: the centre is round-arched, the sides are flat.

PARAPET   Low wall at the edge of a roof, balcony, or terrace.

PEDIMENT   A low-pitched triangular GABLE on the front of a building, especially above a PORTICO. (The Grange, Campbell House, St Lawrence Hall, etc.)

PIER   A vertical masonry support, sometimes free-standing, sometimes built into a wall. Blocked piers are decorated with raised blocks of masonry. (Don Jail)

PILASTER   A column flattened against a wall.

PORTE-COCHÈRE   A porch for wheeled vehicles. (George Gooderham House, Timothy Eaton Memorial Church)

PORTICO   A roofed porch, often with columns and a pediment, usually the centre-piece of an architectural composition. (Osgoode Hall, Bank of Upper Canada [which is without a pediment])

REREDOS   The architectural background for the altar, usually consisting of panelling; it is sometimes fitted with statuary and painting.

RUSTICATION   The finishing of blocks of stone to look rough or rock-like. (Old City Hall)

SILL COURSE   The course or line of brick or stone running under a window. (St James the Less)

SKYLIGHT   A window set in a ceiling.

SPANDRELS   The triangular section of wall framing the curve of an arch.

STRING COURSE   A continuous projecting horizontal band set in a wall; the horizontal course of masonry that marks the floor levels of a building on the exterior.

TERRACOTTA   Glazed or unglazed fired clay used for modelled ornamentation. (Robert Simpson Company, King Edward Hotel, Dominion Bank)

TRACERY   Intersecting lines of stone that ornament a Gothic window and help support the stained glass.

TRANSEPT   The transverse arm of a cruciform church, usually between the NAVE and the CHANCEL.

TRANSOM   Horizontal bar of wood or stone, supported on a MULLION, across a window; a movable panel of glass above a door.

TREFOIL   A window shaped like a three-leaf clover.

TYMPANUM   The semicircular space above a door set within an arch. In churches this space is decorated. (Holy Blossom Synagogue)

VERMICULATION   Decoration of masonry with irregular shallow channels as if the stone had been eaten by worms. (Osgoode Hall, Don Jail)

VOUSSOIRS   Wedge-shaped stones that make up an arch.

WAINSCOTTING   Wooden panelling on the lower part of a wall.

INDEX

NUMBERS IN BOLD FACE REFER TO MAIN ENTRIES; NUMBERS IN ITALICS REFER TO PLATES.

ARCHITECTS, LANDSCAPE ARCHITECTS, AND ARCHITECTURAL FIRMS ARE INDICATED BY AN ASTERISK (*).